Balancing the
Federal Budget

Balancing the Federal Budget

Eating the Seed Corn or Trimming the Herds?

Irene S. Rubin
Northern Illinois University

CHATHAM HOUSE PUBLISHERS
SEVEN BRIDGES PRESS, LLC
NEW YORK · LONDON

Seven Bridges Press, LLC
135 Fifth Avenue, 9th Floor
New York, NY 10010-7101

Publisher: Ted Bolen
Managing Editor: Katharine Miller
Production Supervisor: Linda B. Pawelchak
Composition: Big Sky Composition
Cover design: Stefan Killen Design
Cover art: PhotoDisc, Inc.
Printing and Binding: Phoenix Color Corp.

Library of Congress Cataloging-in-Publication Data

Rubin, Irene S.
  Balancing the federal budget: eating the seed corn or trimming the herds? / Irene
S. Rubin.
    p.   cm.
  Includes bibliographical references and index.
  ISBN 1-889119-62-8
    1. Budget—United States—History—20th century. 2. Administrative agencies—
United States—Finance—History—20th century. 3. Government spending policy—
United States—History—20th century. I. Title.

  HJ2051 .R82 2002
  352.4'0973—dc21   2001055968
                                                                          CIP

Manufactured in the United States of America
10 9 8 7 6 5 4 3 2 1

Contents

Tables

Preface

THIS BOOK BEGAN as an effort to respond to critics of an earlier book, *Shrinking the Federal Government*. In that book, I argued that budget cutbacks under the Reagan administration did not lead to more efficient government but rather threw a number of agencies into chaos, with reductions in force, bumping of personnel into unfamiliar jobs, and widespread loss of morale. It took several years for agencies affected by these cuts to recover their former levels of efficiency. Critics suggested that if I had looked at those agencies over a longer time span, I might have seen adaptations to lower staff levels and improvements in efficiency. The argument caught my attention. I thought they might be right, and if they were, I had to set the record straight as soon as possible. I set out to restudy some of the agencies I had done cases on in the mid-1980s.

By the mid-1990s, when I was doing the field work for this book, many of those same agencies had been cut again, sometimes several times. Rather than a model of one set of cuts and recovery, these agencies were often on a seesaw, sometimes dealing with buildups and sometimes with cutbacks. The concept of the book began to change, to focus on what these agencies learned over time in terms of how to survive cuts, what strategies they used, and what they became—leaner, more efficient, or hollower, providing services of lower quality.

To what extent was the federal government learning how to cut back in a wiser way, prioritizing, cutting waste, and maintaining program quality and to what extent was it cutting across the board or where it was politically easy to do so, hiding the damages along the way? One end of the continuum I called *trimming the herds,* skillfully pruning the size of government until it matched the resource levels available, much as hunters trim the deer herds of the old and sick so the herds will not overgrow their food supplies. The other end of the continuum I called *eating the seed corn,* consuming the basic information, quality staff, knowledge base, and credibility of the agencies, ultimately making any kind of recovery very difficult, if not impossible. If farmers eat their seed corn, they have nothing to plant the following spring.

The scope of the study expanded in several ways. On the one hand, the choice of agencies shifted to include some not in the original study to better focus on the issue of eating seed corn or trimming herds. On the other hand, the topic grew to include how and when government learns.

The effort to balance the federal budget reflected a number of deeply held (and sometimes contradictory) goals. Many actors wanted to claim credit for achieving these goals and were reluctant to take the heat for service or program cuts or tax increases, creating enormous pressure to make the budget look more balanced than it was. The budget and finance offices were under great pressure, as was the Bureau of Labor Statistics with its potent cost of living index, the CPI, to come up with the "right" numbers. How these agencies balanced such pressures against the need to maintain a reputation for impartiality and professionalism became part of the story.

The field work was done in summer and fall of 1996 in Washington, D.C., with the support of a sabbatical from Northern Illinois University and a fellowship from the Woodrow Wilson Center for Scholars in Washington, D.C. At that time, the deficit was still raging, but by 1998, the budget was nearly in balance. The efforts to balance the budget were beginning to look like a success story; how had this been achieved? What had the government learned over this time period, from the tax breaks of the early Reagan era in 1981 to 1998, when the budget achieved balance? It was not only a matter of whether the agencies survived and what they learned and became; it was also a matter of how Congress learned. How did the failures of the Gramm-Rudman-Hollings deficit reduction legislation become the relative successes of the Budget Enforcement Acts of 1990 and 1993? Who, if anyone, learned from the failures, where was that knowledge stored, and how was it called on later? What was the trigger that turned the game playing and obfuscation of Gramm-Rudman-Hollings into the relative discipline and openness of the Budget Enforcement Act?

If the federal government did indeed learn to balance the budget, then perhaps it can learn to solve other policy problems as well. This book suggests, tentatively, that government can and sometimes does learn, but the mechanisms for learning are fragmentary and fragile. One of the more tantalizing findings was the discovery of the existence of a network of budgeters, across agencies and across branches of government, who often switch between agencies and between branches of government during their careers, leaving trusted peers behind who continue to call on them for advice. This network was simultaneously a repository of learning and a means of teaching.

People disagree on the importance of balancing the budget as a policy goal, but it is typical of the kind of policy problems government has to try to solve—messy problems with little consensus on means. To the extent that eliminating the deficit resulted from legislative design and political will, as opposed to a booming economy (both played a role), we should have more confidence in our ability to solve other messy problems, such as Social Security and housing the homeless. In the interim, however, we should pay more attention to the structures through which learning in government takes place and ensure that accumulated knowledge is not allowed to drain away in the name of cost savings. That would truly be eating the seed corn.

The problems addressed in this book are not going away, despite the achievement of budgetary balance after years of massive deficits. Within a couple of years of achieving balance, the outcome is again in question. With increased expenditures for the damage done in the terrorist attack of 11 September and the ensuing military action in Afghanistan, the increased budget for the military in future years, a marked slowdown of the economy (formally designated a recession), and the tax reductions of the George W. Bush administration, deficits seem likely to appear in 2002. Given Bush's determination not to raise taxes—"over my dead body" he is reported to have said—and the increased costs of rescuing the economy, pursuing terrorists abroad, and domestic defense, deficit spending may well return.

The problems of eating the seed corn have intensified. Years of frozen hiring have left some agencies with major skills gaps and an aging workforce. Many senior staff with years of accumulated knowledge of governmental programs and budgeting techniques are planning retirement within the next few years. Emphasis on contracting out rather than hiring in-house means that a change in contractors often results in a loss of experience and institutional memory. Years of reducing the quality of programs to save money have left some agencies frayed, their reputations eroding, and the usefulness of their products declining. Budget strategies designed to get agencies and programs through tough times are not meant to last over decades.

Agencies find that they cannot defend themselves by arguing that budget and staffing reductions have hurt their ability to produce a quality product, lest they be punished or even terminated because they are not doing a good enough job. So they accept cuts and continue to claim that they can do the jobs they have always done. The elected officials in Congress and the White House continue to believe or at least argue that they are eliminating waste and making agencies more efficient, but it is not clear that is always the consequence of cuts. The pressure to measure performance and punish poor performers with budget cuts remains high. For some agencies, the result is likely to be a cycle of cuts, poorer performance, and more cuts. This is not the way it was supposed to be. The relationship between appropriate levels of budget and good-quality services and products has yet to be recognized, and it is not clear how governmental agencies will be able to make that argument. While predictions are always risky, I am willing to predict that there will be continued resistance to detailed performance measurement because of this cycle.

I have tried to pick out a justifiable chunk of the story to tell, from 1981 to 1998, from the buildup of deficits in the early Reagan administration to the balanced budgets of the later 1990s. There was a pause and an outcome of sorts when budgetary balance was achieved. But the story continues, the stakes are enormous, and much remains to be learned.

Acknowledgments

I ACKNOWLEDGE WITH GRATITUDE the help of many people in preparing this book. Roy Meyers, Marvin Phaup, and Phil Joyce helped orient me to the field and the players. I am particularly thankful to my interviewees, who gave me their time and explained to me what budgeting was like during the Reagan and Clinton administrations. Some of them are quoted directly in the chapters in which their agencies are discussed, and others asked not to be identified. I am also indebted to those who read and critiqued chapters for me, including Allen Schick and Robert Reischauer, and a number of agency people who declined to be named. It has been a source of great pride and pleasure for me to work with such people; they have demonstrated the helping and learning networks that are the subject of this book. Through a lifetime of effort, they have raised the level of public discussion.

I would also like to acknowledge the Woodrow Wilson Center in Washington, D.C., for a fellowship in 1996, which gave me a base in Washington, access to the Library of Congress, research assistance, and an identification tag that allowed me to enter federal buildings. Helpful staff and stimulating colleagues made this stay in Washington exciting and productive. During the same time period, Northern Illinois University granted me a sabbatical leave to do the field research.

Balancing the
Federal Budget

CHAPTER 1

1981–98: Balancing the Budget: What Have We Learned?

DEFICITS WERE A CHARACTERISTIC of U.S. budgeting for many years. As long as they were moderate in size, they caused no particular alarm or embarrassment, but major tax breaks, a deep recession, and a defense buildup in the early 1980s contributed to an embarrassing increase in the size of the federal deficit. By 1993 outgoing president George Bush issued a budget projection indicating that there would be a deficit of $327 billion that year, and he predicted that the deficit would be markedly higher near the end of the century. Huge deficits constrained budgeting, locking in old priorities and crowding out genuine choice.[1] By the end of fiscal year 1998 President Clinton announced a budget surplus and it looked as if surpluses would continue for some time.

This book analyzes 17 years of efforts to balance the federal budget, from the early Reagan presidency in 1981 to the surplus budgets beginning in 1998. When appropriate to describe ongoing adaptations, the study is extended to 2000. Was balance achieved as a result of intentional efforts on the part of government officials who learned from trial and error how to regain budget balance? The historical record suggests that learning did take place but provides only hints about what may have been learned by whom. It was not immediately clear whether the federal government learned to set priorities or to make meaningful tradeoffs. The government curtailed growth in spending, but to what extent did it "eat the seed corn," that is, consume its capital, in terms of knowledge, skills, and programs, or "trim the herds," that is, cut back the deer population to what the land would bear, or, less metaphorically, reduce programs to a sustainable level, given the negotiated size of government and level of taxation? Cutback does not necessarily lead to better and more responsive government at lower costs; it may result in worse management and less responsive government at higher costs.

At the macro level, this book examines budget processes, revenue increases and decreases, and summit agreements that contribute to balanced budgets. At the micro level, it looks at the agencies' responses to a continuing level of budget uncertainty; to budget and staffing cuts; to threats of termination or dismemberment; and to pressure to provide better, more responsive services more cheaply. The focus is on what was learned and not learned over 17 or more years.

The analysis takes place in the context of one overarching story. The president and Congress tried a number of times to balance the budget between 1981 and 1998, with some dramatic failures and, finally, with increasing success. Success was due in part to a long-term, booming economy that produced unexpected revenue, but it was also due to tax increases and to staffing and budget reductions. The budget process itself was changed several times in an effort to find a formula that would strengthen discipline. The changes in the budget process helped to bring about balance.

If the federal government did indeed learn to solve the policy problem of huge structural deficits in the budget, even if imperfectly and with the help of an expanding economy, then it may be able to learn to address other serious policy problems. If government has learned, then there must be mechanisms for learning that can be strengthened or weakened. This book addresses the question of learning exclusively in the context of balancing the budget, but the analysis has broader applicability because budget balancing shares features of many other policy problems.

WHY BALANCE THE BUDGET: DEFINING THE PROBLEM

The goal of a balanced budget is fundamentally a political one, not an economic or technical one. Its value was defined and redefined by governmental actors and nongovernmental organizations (NGOs) over the 17 or so years covered by this study. As one interviewee explained, there was no clear economic justification for why the deficit had to be brought down:

> We [at OMB] used to say we had to bring down the deficit because it caused inflation . . . but then there was little inflation and there were still high deficits, so the argument faltered. We don't say that any more. It is all political.[2]

Along similar lines, a former agency budget director argued,

> The economists overemphasize the importance of the deficits. Other countries have much larger deficits with respect to GNP. The elimination of the deficit is more a matter of priorities for programs than economics.[3]

While some economists argued that the deficits did major harm to the economy, others argued that sharp, short-term declines in spending might put the economy into a tailspin. The fear of precipitating a recession by bringing down the deficit gradually dissipated with experience:

> One thing that we have learned is that there is less reason to be concerned about the macro effect of restraints. The effects of deficit reduction are less than the economists thought. We can reduce the deficit by ½ percent or ¼ percent of the GDP without exaggerating cyclical swings. Monetary policy is more important than we thought [and deficit reduction less important].[4]

The economists were not able to provide a standard that said, this much deficit is okay, but that much is too much; nor were they able to say that the deficit could safely be reduced by this much but not that much. In the face of this lack of knowledge, there was not much agreement on how important it was to reduce the deficit or how fast it needed to be done. Many people believed that cutting so much money to balance the budget was wrongheaded and took resources away from more important problems. They recognized that budgetary balance was not just a technical goal, but also a political and symbolic one, laden with values and ideology, fraught with distributional and redistributional consequences.

Robert Eisner, an academic economist who often wrote on the deficit, argued that it was too low. At around 1 percent of GDP, the U.S. deficit was the lowest in the industrial world. He asked why we should not run deficits of 3 percent of GDP like other countries and suggested the range of benefits that would come from the additional spending:

> Imagine what we could do in education, in health care, in infrastructure, in fighting crime, in moving people from welfare to work and bringing our frightening underclass into constructive roles in our society, if we thought not to eliminate that last one percentage point of deficit but to raise the deficit, say to the European target of 3 percent.

Eisner also sketched some potential negative consequences of further deficit reduction, including lower purchasing power, that might slow the economy.[5]

Senator Ted Kennedy, who argued that he favored a balanced budget, commented on the May 1997 presidential-congressional plan to balance the budget in terms of who was being helped and who was being hurt. He noted that cuts up to that point had fallen disproportionately on the poor and that the tax benefits in the new agreement benefited the very rich disproportionately. He also argued that the benefits to the rich would become more costly after the target year of 2002, possibly forcing additional spending cuts later, at the same time that Social Security and Medicare would be demanding more spending to meet the needs of an aging population.

That balancing the budget is a political goal rather than a technical problem best undertaken by economists is underscored by the fact that economists have not agreed on the importance of deficits or on the nature of their impacts on the economy, and they have also changed their arguments over time, as one or another claim has proven incorrect. Aaron Wildavsky, an academic who wrote on both budgeting and the role of policy analysts in influencing government, argued that economists were trying to influence the public policy debate, so that "otherwise trustworthy economists sometimes shade their arguments for effect in order to push the policy they desire. Excessive condemnation of the deficit has proceeded, in part, from such experts putting the matter too strongly for fear of otherwise being ignored by politicians, or in order to counter the minority of economists who dismiss the deficit's importance."[6]

Regardless of the actual economic consequences of a reduction or elimination of the deficit, eliminating the deficit was taken as a governmental goal. In the absence of technical standards, political policy preferences reigned. Different actors had different preferences. One factor that became relevant was the political payoff for deficit reduction:

> If the deficit is too large and you reduce it, you are better off with [a] lower than [with a] higher deficit, moving in the right direction is positive. It is not irrelevant. But to the extent that the popular imagination has been captured by zero as a religious icon, when one is in a situation of a $220 billion deficit and one has to engage in substantial pain to go from $220 to 180 billion in the early 1980s, there is a sense in which policy makers would conclude there is not much gain for all that pain. In contrast, for the last couple of years, at the risk of sounding self serving, because of the 1993 actions of this administration, people could speak realistically about a balanced budget, there has been more in it for policy makers.[7]

Getting to zero became politically feasible after a major tax increase combined with continuing spending discipline. But zero was not everyone's target. It was popular with the public but not with those who had been using the elimination of the deficit as a way of reducing public spending and the scope of governmental activities. For them, zero deficit would be a kind of stopping point when what they wanted was to keep going. They wanted to shift grounds to paying off the debt rather than stopping at zero deficit:

> If zero is taken as bliss, one defines policy to get to zero. You can find yourself where people of extreme political stripe—zero isn't good

enough—doesn't force the kind of change in government that they wanted. That is why the administrative proposal was so dangerous to them. If zero is the target, how can you go beyond zero? Balance cuts out from under you things that you really want to do.[8]

At the Committee for Economic Development, spurring faster economic growth was the target. Zero deficit was not the aim; the goal was a surplus:

> This organization [Committee for Economic Development] supported a surplus, not balance, for macro-economic reasons. Trying to compensate for low savings by reducing the debt. No new debt. It would increase national savings by default. . . . It is important to move in that direction because of our low savings rate. Other countries have 4–5 times the rate of private savings.[9]

In short, the goal of balancing the budget was not a single goal on which all the key actors agreed. Some believed the budget should not be balanced if balance could be obtained only by burdening the poor. Some wished to merely reduce the size of the deficit; others wished to bring it to zero; while others wanted the government to run a surplus in order to pay off the national debt. Some wanted to appeal to citizens who believed that budgets should be balanced (the magic zero); others wished to cut back the size and intrusiveness of government and use the deficit as an excuse to do so; others were more interested in shifting the distributional burden of government so that the rich paid less for and the poor benefited less from governmental services. The technical decisions regarding how to bring about balance were made more complex by lack of agreement on what was to be accomplished, for whose benefit, and what the result of cutting the deficit would actually be:

> The problem of the deficit is the plight of politics and polity. The numbers don't drive this; politics are behind it. Party politics in this case. It is also bound up by interest group politics, unions, corporations, and ads to manipulate public opinion.
> Mostly it is lip service to balance the budget, but there is no agreement on specifics, the numbers are close, but not the content. The Republicans insist on a tax cut, the Democrats won't accept a tax cut.[10]

The subjectivity of the problem and lack of agreement on goals showed up distinctly in the nongovernmental organizations that clustered around the budget balance issue, trying to shape the public's, the press's, and the politicians' views of the problems. These organizations put forward different positions on which taxes to maintain or to cut, which tax breaks to eliminate or maintain, which agencies and programs to eliminate or maintain, and the definition of balance itself. The Concord Coalition and the Committee for a Responsible Budget were deeply involved and primarily focused on budget balancing issues. Organizations such as the Committee for Economic Development and the Center for Budget and Policy Priorities had other goals, such as economic growth or support for the poor, that became entwined with issues of budget balance. Coalitions of community organizations lobbied against the Balanced Budget Amendment, though their real focus was elsewhere, on housing the homeless, creating jobs for the unemployed, and improving the quality of life in the inner cities.

The Concord Coalition was particularly interesting because it was a grass-roots organization trying to create an environment that would facilitate political agreement over the deficit. If it could reach and mobilize the public to make demands on politicians, it might make what was politically difficult less costly. The Committee for a Responsible Budget, though emphasizing legislative proposals to balance and otherwise reform the budget process, also maintained a grass-roots educational campaign to raise the awareness of citizens about the complex choices confronting decision makers.

There were interest groups operating at nearly every level to influence the public directly and the elected officials indirectly and to lobby politicians and shape the understanding of the issues in the press. For nearly every possible major choice, there were interest groups pro and con, making nearly every choice politically risk-laden.

Over time, there was a shift from balancing the budget through a combination of increased taxes and program cuts to cutting programs and not increasing taxes. Then pressure increased to actually cut taxes while trying to balance the budget. With such heavy emphasis on cutbacks, deciding how to allocate remaining resources became crucially important and triggered partisan quarreling. The breadth of effects of potential and actual budget cuts makes budget balancing a messy problem, not easily solved incrementally but almost impossible to deal with more globally.

While there is relatively little technical agreement on how the goal of balancing the budget is to be achieved, there is a widespread public expectation of an idealized solution. It is an example of a highly politicized goal, based on anticipated winners and losers. Because there is little agreement on the means but a general consensus that achieving the goal, variously defined, would be good, politicians sometimes indulge in symbolic politics, such as long-term agreements to balance the budget with the majority of the cuts set for future years or with the establishment of overall targets that would then be evaded by all parties. Such symbolic stances stretched out the time it took to learn how to solve the problem. The failure of such symbolic approaches ultimately made the elected officials look foolish, motivating more serious efforts to address the problem.

LEARNING HOW TO BALANCE THE BUDGET

In the 17-plus years of efforts to balance the budget, many changes occurred in policy and process. Weak laws resulted in embarrassing outcomes that in turn produced tighter and better legislation. The newer legislation was generally effective. One can infer from these developments that discipline was exercised and that learning occurred.

In the 1980s budgeters would probably have come to a different conclusion. Laws to reduce the deficit were routinely ignored, deficits continued to mount, and budget balancing seemed to be more a matter of the manipulation of symbols than an exercise in discipline. Many budgeteers described each major change in the budget process as an independent and somewhat startling event, making it nearly impossible to see if learning had occurred from one change to the next. But looking back from the late 1990s, it was clear that these changes were part of an ongoing effort and that there had been a kind of progression, from symbolic action to real discipline, from unworkable approaches to politically feasible and technically acceptable legislation. It looked as if learning continued from one Congress and one administration to the next.

When participants in the federal budget process were asked to react to the tentative conclusion that government had learned to solve the deficit problem, they expressed considerable skepticism. One reason for skepticism was that there were other ways to explain the outcomes. For example, when asked whether the progression from Gramm-Rudman-Hollings (GRH) to the Budget Enforcement Act of 1990 represented learning, Robert Reischauer, former director of the Congressional Budget Office, argued,

> It wasn't learning so much as being backed into a corner. Lawmakers say, we are going to balance the budget. And then they don't want to take the action that is necessary. But the public said, "you promised to make the cuts. . . . By 1990, lawmakers had backed themselves into a corner. If they implemented Gramm-Rudman, the across-the-board cuts, the sequester would have been over 30 percent of discretionary spending, excluding defense pay. That was irrational, it would have decimated Head Start and other popular programs. . . . The limits, avoided by Congress in one year, only got harder to adhere to in the next year. So lawmakers would redefine the limits. They were up against the wall in 1990. They would have been hooted out of court if they had said they wanted to revise the limits again.
>
> They got themselves into a situation that was difficult to back out of. It was a stupid promise. They said, "I am going to walk on water," and gathered a crowd to watch them. They had no way to avoid stepping into the lake. It was not necessarily learning, it was

painting themselves into a corner. They concluded that for political survival, it was better to bite the bullet than snub their nose yet again at a promise they had made.[11]

Another reason for skepticism was that many budgeteers were located in institutions whose role included monitoring and eliminating budgetary strategies, sometimes called *games*. Some watched the Office of Management and Budget (OMB), the agencies, and legislative committees develop evasive strategies year after year and concluded that this behavior was endemic and would continue to generate deficits in the future.

Barry Anderson, at the time of the interview a high-level civil servant in the OMB, argued that the political tendencies that created the deficits were still in place. Pressures for dynamic scoring and rosy economic scenarios remained high.[12] A few individuals at the OMB and in Congress had learned to make more conservative estimates of the economy, but you could count them on your hands. Moreover, the agencies would eventually evade whatever rules were devised to keep budget requests under control. The longer the rules were out there, the more agencies learned to game them.[13] As Tom Cuny put it, "in my 25½ years at OMB and CBO, I constantly ran across people who tried to have their cake and eat it too."[14]

A third source of skepticism stemmed from watching elected or appointed officials recycle old proposals year after year. Career officials struggle to put together evaluations and figure out how proposals will impact budget processes, accountability, understandability, and outcomes. But their testimony, their reports, and their recommendations often seem to have little effect on proposals that keep coming back, literally and figuratively. One interviewee reported that a briefing manual was thrown against the wall, narrowly missing her. Another argued that you just cannot kill a bad idea; it keeps coming back—it is hydra-headed.

Such episodes breed a deep sense of skepticism about whether politicians can learn and whether career officials can teach them. Tom Cuny described the longevity of supply-side economics, the inability of budget director David Stockman to educate President Reagan, and the willingness of politicians such as Jack Kemp to go into the wilderness for the idea. Cuny concluded that such persistence in the face of experience "represents economic ignorance; we have a lot of economically ignorant leaders. Some people just don't learn."

Old proposals keep coming back in part because of turnover. Newly elected officials come in and bring back old ideas, without any experience of how they work or why they might not work. But even old-timers tend to hang on to ideas, bringing them up over and over. For them, a defeat means only delay and another opportunity to try to pass the same, slightly reworded legislation.

The determination of appointees and elected officials to implement their ideas despite the opposition of the career staff results in part from a lack of enthusiasm for new ideas on the part of the career bureaucrats. Some career officials, congressional staff, and lobbyists for public interest groups see themselves becoming jaded over their careers. They see so many proposals go down in flames, so many ideas they think would or could work, that they learn not to get too excited. In this sense, they understand why enthusiastic appointees intent on making changes need to bypass them and their collective memory of what does not work.

Some of the difficulty that career officials have in communicating their experience to appointed officials occurs because the latter express disdain for careerists and sometimes come into their appointed office with a belief that career officials will thwart their policies. One interviewee, after describing the negative attitude of an appointed official toward staff work, said the appointee thought that bureaucrats were dumb and stubborn. When a staff recommendation was negative, the appointed official assumed that the career official could have made it work but chose not to.

Al Kliman, former budget director at Housing and Urban Development (HUD), added that as soon as you managed to educate some of the appointees, they left, so long-term learning was difficult, if not impossible. He also noted that there were more political appointees at HUD than in the past, a fact that exaggerated the problem:

> One of the reasons why HUD has been unable to learn is that it is one of the more politicized agencies. Over the years the . . . politicization has gone lower and lower. Political appointees were not just at the top; they pervaded the top and middle of the agency. When the administration changes, they all go, you have to start all over. They don't know anything until someone teaches them.[15]

Kliman also mentioned the difficulty of getting a point across to appointed officials of the other political party: "They won't pay any attention to advice from people in the other party, those few of us who lasted from one administration to another. You can't say, 'it's dumb'; you have to lead them to that conclusion on their own, [and] it takes time."

The relationship between legislative staff and members of Congress was equally problematic, but for different reasons. The normal assumption about congressional learning would be that staff would know or find out and teach their bosses what they needed to know to make a contribution in areas of concern. This model breaks down, however, if the staff are not knowledgeable or if they do not stay in place long enough to have any memory of prior legislative efforts on the same subject. Even if staff stay in place, legislators turn over. When new legislators come in thinking they already know everything they need to know, the problem of learning and teaching is exacerbated.

Transition from dominance by one party to dominance by the other adds another layer of difficulty. During the transition to Republican domination after the elections in 1994, many longtime staff members were fired. This was partly an effort to reduce legislative branch costs, but it also reflected both ideology ("I know what I need to know already") and the transition itself:

> There has been huge turnover among staff and downsizing of the entire staff. Some committees, such as Finance, are in the midst of reforming Medicare and Medicaid, yet they have only a handful of staff who know much about either program. Maybe it's a function of the transition. Substantive congressional staff are usually hired by the majority. The minority staff are usually picked more for their political skills; they have to be good at press releases and attacks. When Congress turns over, the people who were knowledgeable about policy leave and earn some money in the private sector; they know they won't be making policy as part of the minority. The new majority elevates the faithful.[16]

The faithful are those with political loyalty and political skills—the attack specialists—not those with technical knowledge of the policy issues or budget process.

The problem is not just lack of expertise but also, in some cases, lack of experience or history. Relatively few staffers remain on Capitol Hill for any length of time. The work is incredibly demanding, and staffers tend to stay a few years and then move on. As one congressional staffer put it,

> We learn temporarily, in that we are temporary. The average tenure on the Hill is 3½ years for a staffer. I have been here 10 years. Some people have institutional memory, but much of the staff is gone more quickly. They represent the institutional memory of the time. I was just talking to a reporter who used to work here. We were talking about the early Reagan period. Very few staff go back that far. Members go back that far, but it is rare in staffers.[17]

Legislators turn over too, with greater frequency in recent years as longtime incumbents have retired. Because the budget process is intricate, complicated, and changing over time, turnover in staff and in membership makes budget learning much more difficult. Learning requires both longevity and interest in the subject: "When staff directors or committee chairmen turn over every two years or if the chairmen are not interested, not much learning goes on."[18]

Turnover makes unavailable much of the teaching and learning that does go on. When Robert Reischauer was director of the Congressional Budget Office, he took it as his responsibility to meet with members of Congress to try to educate them. In the following passage he describes a successful effort to teach them but concludes by saying that even when teaching works, inevitably the person you have taught leaves; furthermore, the teacher may also be replaced:

> RR: I testified on dynamic scoring, which, on the surface, seems to be a sensible approach. Members believe the legislation they are proposing will affect the economy and those effects should be reflected in the bill's cost estimates. I would point out that for most bills, those effects are tiny, uncertain, and unlikely to occur for a number of years. Major legislative changes are incorporated into the budget resolution. Their economic effects are already built into the economic assumptions of the resolution. Since they are built in, you can't count those again later when CBO scores your bill. That would be double counting. Oh, they say, you were not just screwing us. In 1990, Congress passed a big package that would change the course of the economy. CBO built that into its economic assumptions which were used for the budget resolution. They were always surprised to hear this.
>
> IR: You are teaching them.
>
> RR: Yes, but they get defeated, and I don't stay forever. And there are times when you can do it and times when it is not welcome.[19]

Chairs of committees, who are often more knowledgeable, sometimes try to educate the members of their own committees. These efforts may also come up short, because it is so difficult to get the attention of legislators for general background information as opposed to educating them for upcoming legislation.

Rep. John Kasich, chair of the House Budget Committee after the Republican turnover in 1995, was concerned about his committee members' lack of knowledge of the budget process and called a series of hearings that were less oriented to specific legislative proposals than to educating his committee. He publicly expressed his annoyance at the low attendance of committee members.

Hearings in general bred skepticism, because although they were common and many people testified at them, they were not effective tools for teaching and learning. Hearings were often polarized and scripted, dominated by the majority party, usually with an intent to control the information presented by witnesses through careful selection and advance discussions. Staff would normally present members of Congress with questions to ask. The legislators themselves would come in late, read their questions, listen to the answers, and often leave immediately afterward. Some would learn from the questions they were reading. Every once in a while, the witnesses might say something that several members of Congress learned from, but it was reportedly a rare event:

> There is not much learning as a result of testimony. Out of all the times I testified, only a few times was there any back and forth learning that involved more than one member, maybe less than ten times out of more than a hundred occasions. Members come and go during the hearing, they read things. There are little flashes of learning here and there.[20]

The skeptics made a number of good points, but they did not rule out learning completely. They listed many of the obstacles, without indicating how they are overcome or the extent to which they are overcome. Sometimes their judgment was too harsh. When Reischauer claimed that Congress's passing of the Budget Enforcement Act did not represent learning so much as embarrassment at the failure of Gramm-Rudman-Hollings and the publicly apparent gap between political promises and actual behavior, he was describing the motive, not the process. Embarrassment may have been the reason for a display of political backbone, but even so, there had to be learning. If Congress wanted to bring down the deficit, how could it do so? If it wanted to avoid the embarrassing violations that had marked Gramm-Rudman-Hollings, how should it proceed, what loopholes needed to be plugged, and how should that be done? Experience with GRH was fed by staff members into the congressionally approved Budget Enforcement Act of 1990.

While it was true that some agencies had many more political appointees than in the past and that communication between senior staff and appointees was often problematic, some agencies were comprised mainly of longtimers and few political appointees. For example, the Bureau of Labor Statistics (BLS) was able to develop solutions and maintain them over time in part because of the longevity of the staff. The agency had a family-like culture, and staff tended to make their careers there. In addition, unlike HUD, the BLS had only one political appointee, the commissioner:

> Each office in BLS has its own culture and organizational memory, and there are a considerable number of people, from the Senior Executive Service [SES] on down, who have been here for decades. (I'm on my 23d year!) As far as I can tell, we have had no loss of memory. Aside from the commissioner there are no political appointees at BLS—and even she is a nonpartisan academic type. In fact, the commissioner has a fixed four-year term, unlike comparable assistant secretaries of labor who come and go every 16 to 21 months. So the commissioner has a pretty good memory, too. Her predecessor, Janet Norwood, stayed for

three full terms, appointed first by Carter, then reappointed by Reagan. No one at the top or SES level has forgotten Nixon's attempt to politicize BLS, and the editorial pages of the *Washington Post* and *New York Times* once or twice a year denounce any budding attempts to politicize the bureau.[21]

The skeptics pointed out that hearings were often scripted dramas rather than inquiries for purpose of learning. Although many of those who regularly testified on Capitol Hill believed the hearings were not effective, a congressional staffer argued that their expectations were too high, that hearings did help some congressional members learn. Equally important, hearings helped the staff members learn:

> Members don't attend whole hearings. Except chairs and ranking members. But members learn the answers to their one question. If the objective is modest enough, that is significant. In comparison to the totality of information conveyed at a hearing, they don't pick up much, but from the perspective of the congressmen, this is an important source of acquiring information.
>
> I have learned a lot at hearings, but I stay from beginning to end. I suppose it is my job to listen, to look out for an opportunity for members to learn [something they need]. It is an adversarial environment, to present or refute a case. You present your case through selection of witnesses and chronology of questions. Members have to learn questions. There is sometimes learning [from testimony]. That is not its main purpose, but it is a side light.[22]

Dauster also argued that continuing changes in the environment, rather than preventing learning, meant that learning had to be continuous:

> We learn, and then have to relearn. Changes come from the political environment. The answer to your question "What we have learned" would be different if we looked at this in 1990 or 1993 or 1988. Then we had to balance with shared sacrifice, between revenues and outlays; that was the political environment we had to negotiate. Now, you are accused of being a tax-and-spend person if you talk about taxes. So the requirement of balancing tax increases and program cuts has to be unlearned now.[23]

The necessity of relearning occurs not only because the definition of political feasibility changes, but also because of the growing complexity of the budget process. Some key budget actors—for example, Leon Panetta, John Kasich, and

Pete Domenici—have a general idea of the process but do not know the intricacies. As Reischauer put it, "You could spend a whole lifetime learning and relearning" the budget process.

Relearning is partly a function of the changing environment and partly a function of the turnover. For example, budget scholar Allen Schick argued that although many agencies experienced cutbacks in the early 1980s, they were often unable to use that experience in the 1990s when cutbacks recurred, because so few of the staff members who had lived through the early cutbacks were still around for the next wave.[24] With no one around to tell them how it worked the last time, the agency officials sometimes had to learn what their predecessors already knew.

Most of the interviewees, while calling attention to the problems of learning in government, did not categorically say it did not take place. Rather, they argued that it was rare in hearings, that it was made more difficult by suspicious appointees, and that they often had to start again from scratch with new legislators or new appointees. Even the most skeptical indicated that staff members and bureaucrats did not give up trying to educate elected and appointed officials. They continued to testify at hearings; they continued to argue and persuade appointees; they took the time necessary to get their superiors up to speed—they did it over and over. They sometimes despaired of long-term learning, wondering how it could occur, but they had confidence in shorter-term learning.

Institutional arrangements militated against long-term learning. Cutbacks exaggerated the barriers by increasing early retirements and layoffs among longtime professional staff. Shifts in party dominance in Congress made long-term learning even more difficult. Nevertheless, long-term learning did take place. Even some of the skeptics recognized and acknowledged this learning process.

Considerable evidence shows that long-term learning did in fact occur. As many skeptics charged, games were played in the budget process; nevertheless, the spending caps put in place in 1990 held, which, as Robert Reischauer put it, was one of the greatest public policy successes in many years.[25] Agencies did try to game the budget process, find loopholes and crawl through, but CBO and OMB were getting better at finding the tricks and stopping them, sometimes cooperating across branches to block the evasions. Congress passed and the president approved legislation to stop some of the more egregious efforts to get around budget limits. The political environment did keep changing, but staff kept learning, trying to work out new adaptations.

In 1993 President Clinton risked a tremendous amount of political capital to bring down the deficit. After that, the deficit began to fall and kept falling, the result not just of a growing economy but also of spending control. The striking decline and fall of the deficit represented more than chance. It also represented trial-and-error learning:

The evidence, however, shows that the political system is capable of self-correction and fiscal discipline. How else does one explain the reduction in the budget deficit from $290 billion in FY 1992 to $107 billion only four years later? How does one explain the explicit commitment of the President and congressional leaders to adopt budgets that will eliminate the deficit by 2002? How does one explain why the deficit has been reduced from 4.7% of GDP to 1.4%, the lowest rate among major democracies and less than half the deficit permitted by the Maastricht Treaty for countries in the European Monetary Union? Deficit reduction did not happen by itself. True, the task was aided by the end of the Cold War and by robust economic growth, but these conditions would not have sufficed without strong political will. The deficit has been reduced because Congress passed the Budget Enforcement Act of 1990, because it and the President negotiated budget reconciliation bills in 1990 and 1993, because congressional adherence to the discretionary spending caps has driven annual expenditures in this part of the budget almost $100 billion below what it would have been if spending had grown apace with inflation, and because Congress has complied with the PAYGO [pay as you go] rules and has curtailed new entitlement legislation. Budget policy over the last dozen years has been a laboratory for testing which rules work in a political environment and which rules don't work.[26]

Even skeptic Robert Reischauer argued that Congress is capable of learning, if slowly. He observed that Congress sometimes tries the same maneuver several times, though it fails each time. Finally, it learns not to try it again.

Long-term learning did happen, but how? There has to be a way for learning to occur and to be saved or stored, and then passed on at the appropriate time. There has to be a way for Congress to get up to speed on legislative matters, despite short-term staffers on Capitol Hill. One cannot legitimately talk about learning unless a mechanism is postulated, someone or some group monitors experiences and draws lessons from them and is then in position to make suggestions for improvements.

One answer is that although there were many short-timers, there were also a few long-time staff on Capitol Hill, and they in turn relied on an extensive network. Staff members educated themselves, often by creating informal brain trusts:

I would hunt people. For example, on income, I talked to the inventor of the poverty line. I called academics and think tanks, a joy, and got a free lecture. I was close at times to CBO, Rand, the Urban Institute, and Mathematica. I got to know individuals, followed their studies.

Informal brain trusts. I read program summaries from CRS [Congressional Research Service], CBO, Rand, Mathematica, and elsewhere.[27]

Describing his own education, Dauster offered,

BD: I started off by speaking to everyone in the business. What do I have to learn to do? I did reading, although there is not a lot to read on the process. Then I learned by application. People ask you questions, you have to research the answer and respond, and try to keep track of your responses.

IR: You said you talked to everyone in the business. Who does that include?

BD: Mainly on the Hill. Senate committees about institutional issues. CRS and CBO's legal shop, the parliamentarian's office, how things work on the Hill. A number of staffers pointed out as being useful by experience.

IR: Not a network of budgeters specifically?

BD: There are not that many budgeters. I did consult with GAO and OMB. My relationship with OMB was cool in the beginning, [it being controlled by the] opposition party. [I got used to it.] I never adjusted to having an OMB of my own party. I spent a lot of time with people who held my position in the past, that was important. I would talk with a group outside, think tanks, observers: the Center on Budget and Policy Priorities, Brookings, Carol Cox's group, Committee for a Responsible Federal Budget, Martha [Phillips] and the Concord Coalition, that wasn't there when I began, though. Those sort of groups, you would speak to and get to know their perspectives. Maybe depending on their positions, spending more time with one or another.[28]

This list of sources is interesting in part because it mixes indiscriminately Congress's research shops—the Congressional Research Service and the Congressional Budget Office—and private think tanks, such as Rand, the Urban Institute, and Mathematica.

Budget committee staff knew who was knowledgeable on given subjects and were able to invite these experts to talk to the members in their offices as well as at hearings. Experts were also invited to Thursday lunches. Staff and members attended these lunches and reported them very useful for learning.

While congressional members may not have learned much from testimony of witnesses at hearings, they learned from the briefings their staff members gave them:

For [Senator Lawton] Chiles, I developed a format that was a combination of a briefing and a set of questions. In the first paragraph, the member would read, "It is my understanding that a recent study said blankety blank. Given that, what do you say about *x*?" I taught them through the questions they ask. Members love that. They rush here and there without a lot of preparation. Making them look good, staff does the work, they walk in a half hour late, you say, these three questions are still relevant.[29]

This latter technique presumed an informed staff member, however, a condition that has not been as prevalent in recent years. In the earlier years, there was more dependence on senior congressional staff, later, more reliance on CBO or GAO.

Dauster relied on a network that included some budgeters and some budget agencies. An informal network of budgeters, including present and past Capitol Hill staffers, public interest group lobbyists, budgeters in CBO and OMB, and retirees, maintained contacts, shared information, and provided some historical memory. Informal, fragile, dependent on personal ties, and subject to disruption, this budget network facilitated long-term learning and was capable of storing highly detailed histories over time, such as the history of efforts to reform the way credit and borrowing are accounted for in the budget or of legislative efforts to balance the budget.

Most of the information transmitted about the history of decisions was done at the staff level. The new staff coming to the budget committees learn by themselves and from CBO. They also learn from the House Budget Committee majority staff, many of whom used to work at CBO. And staffers from the Hill move to CBO, where they remain a valuable source of information about Capitol Hill. Jim Blum at CBO offered some examples of how this information is transferred:

Gail Delbalzo, general counsel at CBO, has been around a long time. . . . She used to work with the Senate Budget Committee and the parliamentarian's office. And then she came here, before BEA [the Budget Enforcement Act of 1990]. She had such experience, people call on her constantly for information relating to the rules, procedures, and process on Capitol Hill. We are a source of theory and information for the Hill staff. That is even true for the appropriations committee staff, surprisingly. Priscilla Acock, who heads up our scorekeeping unit, was asked to come up and explain scorekeeping and how we do what we do. We do serve as repositories of knowledge. That knowledge is usually transmitted at the staff level. There is very little contact at the member level.[30]

Susan Tanaka, a former OMB staffer who later served as a key staffer for the Committee for a Responsible Federal Budget, added to this picture of a budgeter's network in several ways. She described this network as relatively small and oriented to technical decisions. She said that a high degree of consensus on these technical issues existed among these budgeteers, and they often opposed political positions. She argued, for example, that there was widespread agreement among budgeteers with Robert Reischauer's controversial technical decision as director of CBO to score health care costs imposed on the private sector as if they were a tax. Many politicians opposed that decision.

This network of budgeteers helps educate the staff on Capitol Hill, who in turn help educate the members. The network is broadly defined. Dauster's description of how he learned his position confirmed the existence of this budget network and its educational function and revealed its cross-branch nature. While Dauster primarily relied on congressional branch agencies such as the CRS, GAO, and CBO, he also relied on OMB, even when OMB was controlled by the opposite party. Other interviewees confirmed that in carrying out their work, cross-branch cooperation took place between CBO and OMB.

A former staff member from OMB described a routine work process in which OMB examined legislative proposals coming up from the agencies. Someone in the budget concepts group would examine proposals to see if they disagreed with credit reform or put something off budget, but not every division was able to identify PAYGO implications. A new examiner might not be able to see if an agency's budget proposal was intended to get around the budget law: "The next step is to call CBO and see if Jim Horney has looked at it." CBO and OMB routinely cooperated to see that agencies complied with the requirements of the budget law. They sometimes disagreed on interpretation—one might let something go and the other would not—but what was more important was that they routinely consulted and did so through budgeting networks.

Networks are part of the answer to overcoming the impact of staff turnover, lack of experience, and lack of historical memory among congressional staff. But within these networks are key nodes, particular organizations that have longer-term staff and that make a more explicit effort to provide precedent and history. OMB, the much younger CBO, and to some extent GAO served as repositories of learning for Congress, and congressional staff went into and out of these agencies, enriching the pool and creating sharing mechanisms.

When asked if CBO functioned as the institutional memory for Congress, Deputy Director Jim Blum answered with a grin:

I am laughing because 20 years ago, we were the new kid on the block. We had no idea how long we would survive, now we are the institutional memory. . . . There are only a few that have been here the whole time, but many people go back to the late '70s or early '80s, so it's true, there is institutional memory here.[31]

Part of the reason that CBO was able to play this function is that it was generally considered nonpolitical. There was fear that the agency's top echelons would be removed after the shift to Republican dominance of both houses after the election in 1994, but that fear was generally not realized. The director and one top staff member changed; other than that, there were no major changes. That was the tradition of the agency, and the result was a level of stability that enabled the agency to play the role of institutional memory.

Once one recognizes that CBO and to a lesser extent GAO provide memory to Congress and that OMB provides learning to the executive branch and sometimes to staffers on the Hill and to CBO, it becomes important to know how these organizations and Congress learn and retain what they know.

OMB seems to be the most aware of the need to maintain institutional memory and has a variety of mechanisms, none of them systematic, to provide some continuity beyond the memory of individuals:

> To some extent, there is formal training. To a larger extent, there is a lot of guidance from longer termers [on] how you do this, joint projects between more and less experienced people. And there are some cross-cutting work groups. Credit [reform] is an extreme example of a network. . . . It is a more complicated issue and we get more done through an informal network. Examiners who know will train others, even [outside] their group. [It's] a network of friends, who you can go to and talk to when you are puzzled.[32]

The learning of individual staff members gets formalized into transition papers or summaries that are used to train new directors:

> We do transition papers for every transition. It is a nice historical record; how we educate new folks. Black binders like you wouldn't believe, for the new director. Credit reform, insurance, the troika in economic assumptions, etc. You name it, we do it. The budget process and how it went, what proposals are flowing around the Hill, biennial budgeting or who knows what.[33]

While the senior people tend to have had long-term careers in OMB, younger people tend to turn over quickly. Budget examiners tend to stay only two to three years. When junior people leave, they need a way to leave their work records behind. As one former OMB staffer reported, "They saved all my e-mails on credit reform." OMB tried to preserve the learning of a departing staff member in a way that would be useful to others.

Memory is also formalized into circulars. "If it will recur, it is built into the A-11 that this is how it will be done," a former OMB staffer reported. On most topics, the discussion that preceded the circular would not be available, but "the credit section of the internal home page does have stuff like that pertaining to implementation."

At one point, OMB actually put together a training course, but it was not clear if this course was being used. The main approach seemed to be mentoring. People in OMB described themselves as mentors or as students of other mentors.

The learning process at CBO was a bit different. Like OMB, CBO relied on pairing more senior staff with junior ones as a way of learning and teaching. They also relied on exchanging staff to and from the Hill. Thus Gail Delbalzo, who was parliamentarian on the Hill, was now in legal services at CBO, and a key resource for Capitol Hill staff members. But much of what CBO did was react to and implement new legislation. This work was not easily routinized, so formal training did not make much sense. Instead, when new legislation was passed, CBO set up groups of employees who might know about various aspects of implementation. As Jim Blum notes, these group members raised questions, tested examples, worked out solutions, and then tried to codify for themselves the decisions already made so they could implement them with some consistency:

> IR: What steps do you go through when a new piece of legislation is passed that affects the budget process and CBO?
>
> JB: We react to it, a reaction mode. As a support agency it is difficult for us to make things happen. We have to react to initiatives that are forthcoming, from the president, from Congress. Gramm-Rudman-Hollings was a sort of happening. . . . Here at CBO, it was the first real occasion to work closely with OMB. Before that, we had exchanges of information, but not all that much going on at upper-management levels. That all changed, joint reports. That gave a rationale for lots of meetings with OMB, lots of meetings within CBO, how to apply it. We used to call [it] "sequester court."
>
> We would address issues of how to apply the sequester. That would be $12 billion sequester that first time. We had to interpret the legislation, after we helped write it; how did it apply to individual accounts? During the meetings, in the Budget and Analysis section, how would we apply the law to particular situations?
>
> That tradition of implementing laws applied elsewhere, such as to the current unfunded mandates law; we used the same process, only this law is even more poorly written than GRH. Are these private sector

mandates or state and local mandates? Mandate court meeting. Are these mandates? That is how we manage the process. We get everyone together who has anything to contribute and problem solve. Is this a federal mandate?

Not unlike scorekeeping issues. There are always scorekeeping issues that have an effect on the budget. . . . There have been attempts on the part of committees to evade the consequences of scoring, to find ways around the rules. We have always been in a reactive mode.

Not unlike sequestration and mandates, every year with score-keeping issues, we keep a looseleaf notebook of scorekeeping. We might say, there is a precedent for doing this, our precedents are. . . . That has just evolved. Gail [Delbalzo] is talking about codifying this. Using Internet technology with links, we could figure out how to do this.[34]

Both OMB and CBO were discussing the options of putting the information they use as backup on internal home pages, for their own staff, but not printing the material for public consumption, although circulars and CBO studies and reports have been published at intervals. By contrast, GAO was primarily a research organization, and much of what it researched was published or at least made available to Congress and the public in reports.

While OMB and CBO were deeply involved in working out what each new piece of legislation was about, and hence moved systematically from issue to issue, GAO was called in episodically. When asked a question about the history of the budget process, staff might have to go out and research the answer rather than remember it. But if GAO had studied the issue before, the new report would refer to the earlier one.

GAO was not the only organization doing studies that were then available for reference years later. The Merit Systems Protection Board studies were publicly available, and the National Academy of Public Administration, a congressionally chartered private evaluation group, put out reports on key issues from time to time. Sometimes events were sufficiently traumatic that they left written traces all over Washington.

Another way that learning was carried over from one administration to another occurred when a response to cuts was embodied in routine accounting and budgeting structures. As will be described in chapter 3, the Bureau of Labor Statistics developed a way of accounting for projects that allowed it to cut back product lines rather than draw down the quality of all data collection efforts across the board. This budgeting and accounting structure not only remained in place for later use, it became part of the organizational culture and lore, a point of pride with agency staff. When cuts came, this agency cut by product line rather than across the board. In a second, somewhat different example, the Office of Personnel Management (OPM) covered some operating costs by charging revolving funds for overhead. Once done, this charge remained part of the agency's adaptive repertory, available for use when necessary. The original inventors had long since left the agency, but the choices left not only a record, but a predisposition to do it again. It was easier to keep responding in the same way than to change.

Fragility of Learning Paths

The traditional patterns of learning deteriorated during the mid-1990s. Part of the problem was the increase in the number of ideological members of Congress. While Robert Reischauer attributed the decline in knowledgeable staff to turnover from minority to majority party, former Capitol Hill staffer Ron Boster attributed the decline to more ideological members. Ideologues "don't have policy wonks on their staff; they hire press relations instead. Not people who can help them think analytically."[35] The result of more ideological members was less comity in general and a reduced capacity to learn:

> IR: People told me that there is less learning at hearings because they are so confrontational.
>
> RB: Confrontations at hearings isn't the way it always has been. . . . The level of comity has dropped. The learning process is being short-circuited in some ways. Those people just don't like each other. It is better to learn in a friendly environment. Ways and Means under Rosty [Dan Rostenkowski] brought in a distinguished faculty on a topic and had retreats; they came back smarter. AEI [American Enterprise Institute] used to have new member education at Williamsburg. This time, [the] Heritage [Foundation] held it just for the Republicans in Annapolis. That did violence to the concept. The new member training [in the past] was balanced. . . .
>
> So many things contribute to member learning. It has to take place over time. It is not apparent in a snapshot. Some of this has broken down; there has been a ratcheting up of partisanship of the committees.
>
> They [members] learn from each other, but the breakdown in comity reduces the ease of learning. It is harder to ask questions.[36]

Reducing the policy expertise of staff and making it more difficult for members to learn from one another reduced the overall level of learning in Congress. This trend was exaggerated by decreased reliance on the neutral research agencies that Congress had traditionally called on. Several informants reported that requests to the Congressional Research Service were down. Boster explained, "The people I talk to at CRS say the Republicans don't ask them; they will get the wrong answer." Similarly, some committees stopped using CBO and instead used other agencies that could be depended on to come up with the desired results:

> OTA [Office of Technology Assessment] did the foreign trade study [way out of its area of expertise] because the committee couldn't get the "right" answer from CBO. That brought the OTA down. People are shopping around for analysts. If you want to show the evils of foreign trade, CRS and CBO won't say that.[37]

For the members, learning is nearly always linked either to constituency requests or to legislation being proposed in committee or on the floor. Much of what they want to know about and are exposed to is political feasibility, party position, and impact of particular legislation on their district. Programmatic knowledge tends to be a secondary issue, sometimes ignored, as at Chairman John Kasich's hearings to educate the members of the budget committee about the budget process. Members came to present their own legislative proposals, not to listen to how the law got to be the way it is.

When members stop using the relatively neutral agencies such as CBO and CRS and try to use agencies that will produce a product with a desired conclusion, the amount or possibility of learning deteriorates. What is less visible is the kind of pressure that is put on the more objective providers of information to come up with particular conclusions. These pressures, and agency responses to them, are discussed in later chapters.

In short, while government has learned some things over 17 years of effort to balance the budget, continued learning is not a given. The process by which learning takes place is fragile and unsystematic. It may be destroyed, weakened, or politicized. The agencies whose primary role it is to provide information for decision making may be cut so badly that they provide information that is less accurate than before. Alternatively, they may be pressured to provide only the information that current dominant coalitions wish to hear. Learning may not be the norm. Particular sets of circumstances or mechanisms may have to be in place, and they may occur only from time to time. This study examines not only the circumstances that prompt learning but also how that learning is gathered, stored, and recalled, and under what conditions it deteriorates.

Eating the Seed Corn or Trimming the Herds

What has been learned over roughly 17 years? The goal of balancing the budget should be not only to make revenues cover expenditures but to figure out how to prioritize, to retain the most important and popular programs, to spin off functions that do not need to be performed by the federal government, and to operate more efficiently and effectively. Balance needs to be combined with flexibility, leaving open the possibility of responding to new needs or to downturns in the economy.

The goals of increased efficiency and responsiveness were articulated by the Clinton administration's National Performance Review (NPR). But the diversity of purpose of different actors who supported the drive to balance the budget—some who wanted to reduce the scope of the federal government and reduce taxes, some who were deficit hawks and thought the government should not borrow for operating expenses and that a tax increase was okay, some who wanted to respond to an increasingly popular citizen goal—assured that coming to agreement on priorities would be difficult if not impossible. If there was no consensus on how to reach balance, what actually happened?

Did the government just cut the so-called controllable portion of the budget because it was relatively easier to do, without much prioritizing? If so, what are the likely consequences of such a set of choices? Did budget cuts translate disproportionately into service cuts to the poor? Did the administration and Congress create a government that costs less and works better, or did they yield to pressures to cut across the board, bringing down the quality of management and reducing capacity to solve problems collectively? What does the pattern of cuts that occurred and the manner in which they occurred tell us?

What did the agencies learn while coping with unpredictable budgets and cutbacks? Did they learn to make short-term accommodations that would draw down resources (eating the seed corn) or did they make long-term accommodations, adopting new technology, reorganizing for efficiency and flexibility, reinventing work processes (trimming the herds)? Or did they learn practically nothing at all because they lacked a way of saving their experiences and drawing on them later and because the political environment changed so continuously that prior learning was invalid? It may be that cutbacks introduce a necessary amount of chaos, but that cuts will be followed by learning, experimentation, and improvement in management. A 17-year time span should allow at least a glimpse of answers.

Some learning had to take place to get near zero deficit in FY 1998, but budget actors may have learned some things that others wished they had not learned. Not all learning is good from a public policy perspective. What is learned may be what works for the moment—it may not work for the long run or it may work to the satisfaction of particular interests but not the collectivity. Spending reductions may result in agencies making low visibility cuts that erode quality; winners and losers may be decided not on the basis of efficiency and effectiveness but on the basis of current political coalitions; accretions of temporary solutions may become roadblocks to better solutions.

DESIGN OF THE STUDY

The study is based on a combination of interviews, documentary data, and participant observation. I conducted 82 interviews during 1996 in Washington, where I was based as a research fellow at the Woodrow Wilson International

Center for Scholars. Most of those interviews were face to face, but some were by telephone. The phone interviews were with former congressional staffers and former agency appointees who were no longer living in the Washington area. Key informants were interviewed several times.

The interviewing proceeded in three sometimes overlapping stages. In stage one, I identified and interviewed general informants, many of whom were former employees in the budget agencies, OMB or CBO. Besides getting from them an overview of the issues, I also obtained their recommendations regarding who was knowledgeable on the subject and who might be willing to talk to me. In the second phase of the interviewing, I concentrated on the macro level, exploring the legislative process of moving from one effort at budget balancing to another and the negotiation process between Congress and the president that created specific budget targets. I focused on congressional staff members and officials in OMB. I also examined at this stage the budget information networks, how people learned and stored the knowledge they gained, and the obstacles to that learning. This part of the interviewing focused on the grass-roots lobbyists; the institutional memory of CBO, GAO, and OMB; and the informal network of prior and present budgeteers in a variety of current positions. The third phase of the interviewing was in the departments and agencies. An effort was made, and in most cases was successful, to get up into the subcabinet level of the departments and the upper administrative ranks of the agencies such as GAO and CBO.

Participant observation was opportunistic. I was able to attend some closed meetings of budgeteers at which they shared their views of current budgeting events. I also attended some budgeting hearings. I had lunch with informants in agency cafeterias, observing conversations between my informants and others in their departments.

The documentary sources used were extremely varied. Collection continued well after my return from the field. They included newspaper stories, agency annual reports, notes and procedures posted on agency Web sites, budgets, congressional hearings, committee reports, studies carried out by the National Academy of Public Administration, the General Accounting Office, the Merit Systems Protection Board, the National Performance Review, and the Congressional Budget Office. I was occasionally able to supplement these materials with academic articles in journals. Some former officials shared their files with me, helping me get a longitudinal view.

I was grateful to the Wilson Center not only for the study resources, but also for the federal identification tag, which made access to federal buildings much easier. For many interviewees, I found I needed a Washington identification of some sort; being an academic from Dekalb, Illinois, did not "compute." If the Wilson Center identification was not sufficient, I used identification from the Smithsonian Institution, in which the Wilson Center was at that time housed and whose resources the Wilson Center used.

I employed several processes to assure valid results. First, documentary and interview data were continuously compared throughout the project. Second, efforts were made to find interviewees who were known to be candid. Third, several people were interviewed from each department or agency, insofar as possible. For the departmental cases, drafts of chapters were sometimes submitted for comment to someone in the agency who was not an interviewee. This person's comments pointed out places where I might have misinterpreted the data and suggested new leads. Academics who had been employees in the agency were also pulled in as chapter reviewers. People in the agencies who had been quoted sometimes requested to see not only their own interviews, but also the cases themselves. The resulting versions might not please every actor and might still contain some biases, but every effort was made to get a reasonably balanced picture that was recognized by the participants as descriptive of their world.

The agencies studied were chosen for several reasons. The budgeting agencies were a natural focus of a study on budgeting but were also of relevance because of my interest in pressures on agencies to provide biased information as the level of partisanship increased and norms of agency independence were threatened. Since the budget agreements depended sometimes on projections of the size of the deficit or surplus, and since routine budget implementation required special scoring rules under the budget balancing legislation, budget agencies had a crucial role to play in the story. CBO and GAO faced enormous pressures to come up with the "right" answers. The extent to which these agencies were able to maintain their integrity and independence is one measure of the extent to which the government ate its seed corn, that is, weakened budgeting institutions. OMB and CBO were both important as well in the phase of the study that dealt with institutional memory.

In addition to the budgeting agencies, the study included two statistical agencies that provide information not only for the federal government, but also for the public and businesses. One of those agencies, the Bureau of Labor Statistics, was an important resource for two reasons. First, it routinely calculates the CPI, the consumer price index, which seemed to many politicians to be a possible quick fix for the deficit—if only they could redefine inflation to run at a slower pace, the government could spend less on inflation-indexed benefits, helping to curtail entitlements and balance the budget. But politicians did not want to be seen as cutting back the pensions of the elderly, so they insisted that the bureau do it instead, under the cover of technical expertise and technical corrections. The deficit thus put enormous political pressure on an agency that treasured its reputation for political independence. The Bureau of Labor Statistics was also important to the study because it had worked out a way of preserving quality during cutbacks and set a pattern or standard against which other statistical agencies—or any agencies that sell accuracy and quality—can be measured.

The study compares the Bureau of Labor Statistics with the Bureau of the Census, a related agency. To the extent that cutbacks and political pressures were eroding the quality of information provided to the nation, the government could be said to be eating the seed corn. Pressures against the census included general ideological resentment at the intrusiveness of government combined with partisan concerns about allocation of seats in the House and districting decisions. If the census budget is cut because Republicans fear that a more accurate census will somehow aid the Democrats by counting more of the poor in the inner cities, then one would hardly expect improvement in the quality of management as a result of the cuts. Census is also interesting because it defies annual budgeting, with buildups and wind-downs of several years' duration as the agency prepares for the decennial census.

Two agencies were chosen for the study because I had studied them before, in the early Reagan years,[38] and thus would be able to compare their responses then with their responses when a similar round of cuts visited the agencies a second time. What did they learn from the first go-around that they were able to use the second time? These agencies were the Department of Housing and Urban Development and the Office of Personnel Management.

The Department of Agriculture was included in the study for a similar reason, although I had not studied it earlier. It had been deeply cut back in the 1980s and had been left in a badly adapted position, with curtailed staffing and budgeting but without a commensurate reduction in mission. I wanted to see what the agency had learned from that experience and whether it tried to cut back in a more rational manner in the more recent period and, if so, what degree of success it met with. Similarly, the Department of Commerce was included in the study because it had been cut back in the early 1980s, and some of the same people who were in the agency then were still there in the early 1990s, confronting even more dramatic threats to terminate and scatter the agency. In this case, I could examine not only what might have been learned from prior experiences but also how a department copes with threats of termination. HUD too was struggling with intense pressure to dismantle it, but unlike HUD, Commerce had presidential support at key points.

The agencies studied have some interesting parallels with one another, but also some important differences. Some were large, such as Agriculture, some small, like OPM; some had a marked and dedicated constituency, others had only ambiguous support and little consent on the legitimacy of their domain. They were threatened to various degrees not only with budget cuts, but also with termination and dismemberment. If it is true that nothing concentrates the mind like one's execution in the morning, these agencies should have been profoundly motivated. What did they propose to do, and what did Congress and OMB allow, encourage, or forbid them to do?

ORGANIZATION OF THE BOOK

Chapter 2 describes the macro-level learning that occurred as the deficits grew and efforts to control them succeeded each other. Chapter 3 examines some of the statistical agencies whose job is to provide neutral information for decision making and the effects of budget and political pressures on those agencies. Chapters 4 and 5 describe the effects of cuts and political pressures for "the right answer" on three budgeting and accounting agencies, OMB, CBO, and GAO. Together these three chapters focus tightly on the question of eating the seed corn, the extent to which government is losing the capacity for objective analysis for decision making. Chapters 6 through 9 provide case studies of the Agriculture Department, the Department of Housing and Urban Development, the Commerce Department, and the Office of Personnel Management.

Chapter 10 summarizes what government has and has not learned and the extent to which decision makers have learned to trim the herds (prioritize) or eat the seed corn (make short-term decisions that reduce capacity to solve problems collectively).

CHAPTER 2

What Happened
and What Was Learned

FROM 1979 ONWARD, deficits began to grow, seemingly uncontrollably. Awareness of deficits and various responses to them, both symbolic and real, began in
1981, during the early Reagan administration, although some participants start
the story earlier or later. Major events are listed in table 2.1.

To explain this chronology briefly, during the first year of the Reagan administration, major spending cuts (called Gramm-Latta after their legislative sponsors) and a huge tax reduction (Economic Recovery Tax Act) were passed. The
budget cuts and tax reductions were followed by a deep recession. Supply-side
economists had argued that a tax cut would stimulate the economy and the
resulting growth would enhance revenues and balance the budget. The promised

Table 2.1   A Chronology of Major Events

Year	Event
1981	Gramm-Latta budget cuts
1981	Economic Recovery Tax Act
1982	Tax Equity and Fiscal Responsibility Act
1982	Balanced Budget Amendment passes in the Senate, August; fails in the House
1985	Gramm-Rudman-Hollings, Balanced Budget and Emergency Deficit Control Act
1986	Balanced Budget Amendment narrowly fails in the Senate
1990	Budget Enforcement Act
1992	Balanced Budget Amendment fails in the House
1993	Deficit Reduction Act
1994	Workforce Restructuring Act
1995	Balanced Budget Amendment passes in the House; fails in the Senate by one vote
1996	Balanced Budget Amendment fails in the Senate by two votes
1997	Balanced Budget Amendment fails in the Senate by one vote
1997	Balanced Budget Act and Taxpayers' Relief Act promises a balanced budget by 2002
1998	Budget produces a "surplus"

growth in the economy from the tax cuts did not materialize and deficits soared, from $79 billion in 1981 to $128 billion in 1982 and $207 billion in 1983 (table 2.2). Though the recession clearly contributed to the deficit increase, the lost revenues from the tax reduction would have nearly, if not completely, wiped out the increases in the deficit (table 2.3).

The reactions to the recession and growing deficit included both a substantial tax increase in 1982 and an effort to pass a balanced budget amendment to the Constitution. The latter failed in the House after passing in the Senate.

The deficit jumped from 1981–83, then dipped in 1984, but grew again to new highs in 1985 and 1986. The growing size of the deficit helped precipitate deficit reduction legislation called Gramm-Rudman-Hollings. This was odd legislation, focused on reducing the size of the deficit year by year, according to preset targets. Failure to reach the targets would trigger an automatic across-the-board cut, called a *sequester*, that would presumably reduce the size of the deficit to that required by the law. The idea was that the potential negative consequences of a sequester would be sufficiently threatening to both Democrats and Republicans that they would make the necessary cuts beforehand to meet the targets. However, Gramm-Rudman-Hollings targets were never met, and the legislation was revised to ease up the targets and delay them, while the amount of a necessary sequester grew from year to year. The size of the deficits dropped somewhat, but the failure to meet Gramm-Rudman-Hollings deficit reduction targets and the open evasion of the law were embarrassing to politicians.

Table 2.2 Deficits and Surpluses in Nominal Dollars, 1975–99 (in $ billion)

Year	Deficit	Year	Deficit
1975	−53.2	1989	−152.5
1976	−73.7	1990	−221.2
1977	−53.7	1991	−269.4
1978	−59.2	1992	−290.4
1979	−40.7	1993	−255.1
1980	−73.8	1994	−203.3
1981	−79.0	1995	−164.0
1982	−128.0	1996	−107.5
1983	−207.8	1997	−22.0
1984	−185.4	1998	+69.2
1985	−212.3	1999	+124.4
1986	−221.2	2000 (est.)	+166.7
1987	−149.8	2001 (est.)	+184.0
1988	−155.2		

Source: Historical Tables of the U.S. Budget, FY 2001.

Table 2.3   Estimated Revenue Impacts of Tax Legislation, 1981–97 (in $ billion)

Tax Act/Year	Amount per Year				
	1st	2d	3d	4th	5th
Economic Recovery Tax Act, 1981	−37.7	−92.7	−150.0	−199.2	−267.7
Tax Equity and Fiscal Responsibility Act, 1982	18.0	37.7	42.7	51.8	63.9
Deficit Reduction Act, 1984	1.1	10.6	16.5	22.5	25.2
Consolidated Omnibus Reconciliation, 1985	.8	2.5	2.8	2.9	3.1
Tax Reform Act, 1986	11.5	−16.7	−15.1	8.0	12.0
Omnibus Reconciliation, 1987	9.1	14.1	15.1	not projected	
1990 BEA	Tax increase, five-year estimate: $164.6 billion				
1990 BEA	Tax breaks, five-year estimate: $27.4 billion				
Omnibus Budget Reconciliation Act, 1993	26.4	43.5	51.5	60.7	58.5
Balanced Budget Act, 1997, and Taxpayers' Relief Act, 1997	−9.0	−7.0	−23.0	−27.0	−15.0

Sources: Through 1987, from Schick, *Capacity to Budget* (1990), p. 136, taken from Joint Committee on Taxation; 1990 legislation, from John Yang, "Bush Says He'll Sign Five Year Deficit Plan," *Washington Post,* 28 October 1990; 1993 legislation, from Schick, *The Federal Budget* (1995), p. 5; from CBO, *The Economic and Budget Outlook, An Update, 1993,* table 2.2; 1997 legislation, from CBO, *The Economic and Budget Outlook: An Update, 1997.*

Note: CBO estimates effects at the time of passage; real effects may have differed from projections.

Finally, the size of the needed sequester got so large it became politically impossible to enact. Congress then passed the Budget Enforcement Act (BEA), which used a different approach. Rather than trying to reduce the size of the deficit each year, the BEA tried to control spending and strengthen the norms of balance. Many observers believed that the new approach was weaker than the old, but the new approach worked; its spending caps generally held, at least until balance was reached. When combined with a tax increase in 1993, the BEA helped bring down the deficit.

As part of deficit reduction and efforts to make government more responsive and better managed, the Clinton administration in 1993 announced its National Performance Review (NPR). The review came up with a number of reform proposals, including reducing the number of federal employees by 252,000, or about 12 percent. Many in Congress responded well to this proposal, passing the Workforce Restructuring Act to facilitate reductions by attrition rather than reductions-in-force. Congress added an extra 20,000 to the total of employees to be reduced. The workforce downsizing in the NPR proposals was intended not only to save money, but also to reduce the number of supervisory staff. The supervisors were seen as unnecessary and threatening to the initiative of those on the front lines. Supervisors and controllers, such as budgeters and human resources personnel, were to be reduced by half.

In 1997, after several years of negotiations and the threat of a balanced budget amendment, Congress and the president came to an agreement on a balanced budget act and a tax reduction. The aim was to balance the budget by 2002. Along with a growing economy in 1996 and 1997, unexpected revenue increases brought the deficit down to balance far ahead of schedule.

Virtually throughout the period, those who sought to enforce balance by writing an amendment to the Constitution vied with those who sought legislative and more flexible solutions. Each time the balanced budget amendment came up for a vote, it put pressure on political actors to do something about the deficit to avoid the straitjacket of a constitutional amendment. The amendment came close to passage on several occasions.

Several events and efforts were repeated during the period. There was a round of tax cuts early in the Reagan administration and another round of tax cuts in 1997; there was a period of staffing reductions early in the Reagan administration and another round in the Clinton administration. Throughout the period some political actors tried to lock in a balanced budget requirement through an amendment to the Constitution. The magic asterisk of the Reagan era (balancing the budget with savings to be determined, which never were realized) and the evasions and postponements of the Gramm-Rudman-Hollings period had their echo in the end-loaded proposals for cuts in the 1997 balanced budget agreement and the rising costs of tax cuts after the 2002 deadline. Skeptics argued that little had been learned. But a closer examination of the period suggests that even when the same events seemed to recur, they did so in a slightly different way, suggesting some learning.

As the deficit grew and seemed out of control, the pressure to take symbolic stances against deficit spending also grew. Legislation, such as Gramm-Rudman-Hollings, was passed and evaded. The constitutional amendment to balance the budget was brought to the floor and voted on, but it never quite passed, allowing many legislators to claim credit for having voted for it, without actually having to live under constitutional constraints. But the symbolic stances resulted in escalating deficits that became embarrassing in the context of all the rhetoric of zero deficit. Embarrassment pressed elected officials to do something more effective to keep their promises. The politicians began to seek formulations that would work, that would curtail the evasions they had devised for themselves. On the one hand, politicians were boxed in by their own rhetoric, but on the other, political embarrassment may have led to real learning about how to balance the budget.

As various efforts were made to balance the budget, some symbolic and some more serious, mistakes provided a second trigger for learning. Sometimes the problems and remedies were so traumatic they were remembered collectively and shaped future responses to similar problems.

WHAT HAVE WE LEARNED: THE LESSONS OF THE LATE 1970S AND EARLY 1980S

You Cannot Balance the Budget with Tax Reduction

The prediction in the early Reagan administration that a major tax reduction would have such a beneficial effect on the economy that the tax yield would actually increase was met with widespread skepticism. It appeared to be a convenient rationale for a huge tax cut for traditionally Republican supporters. Efforts were made to convince President Reagan that the plan would increase deficits, but he would not budge.[1] Despite the widespread skepticism about the effects, the tax cuts passed in Congress, in part because many House Democrats wanted to claim credit for tax cuts and so went along with and even expanded the Reagan proposal.

Many observers concluded that the tax cuts were the cause of the major rise in deficits that haunted the whole period. As Richard Darman, former director of OMB, wrote, "In the Reagan years, more federal debt was added than in the entire prior history of the United States. Interest costs alone rose to hundreds of billions of dollars per year. For federal policy-makers, the large deficit became an obsession and an albatross."[2]

Not everyone took the same lesson from the failure of the Reagan years. But regardless of the particular message that policymakers took out of the buildup of deficits during the Reagan administration, the massive budgetary failure of those years was remembered by all. Neither budgeters nor politicians could forget as long as huge deficits remained, choking the capacity for choice in the budget. References to the Reagan tax cuts continued through the 1990s, as elected officials debated whether tax cuts should come before or after balance was achieved, and later as discussion commenced on what to do with a surplus.

At the end of 1997, during the discussion of what to do with a surplus, President Clinton's economic adviser, Gene Sperling, tried to remind the disputing parties of the lessons of 1981:

> "The worst thing that could be done," Mr. Sperling said, "is if—based on a surplus—long-term promises on either tax cuts or spending were made that would prove completely unsustainable if the surplus went away or was less than projected. Repeating the mistakes of 1981 should not be an option."[3]

The message of 1981 was remembered in Congress as well as in the White House. In 1995, for example, Senator Byron Dorgan was discussing the appointment of a new director of CBO and was concerned especially with the new director's attitude toward dynamic scoring. He explained,

> I can remember in 1981, the first year I served in the Congress, in which we had some very dynamic scoring by the Office of Management and Budget. David Stockman, a fresh, new face, was selected to head the Office of Management and Budget. They came up with a strategy that said, "Well, if we do the following things, we will produce enormous new revenue, and we will balance the budget by 1984." He subsequently wrote a book after he left the Government that said none of that was realistic and it was a horrible mistake. . . . The point is we have been through periods where people have developed new scoring approaches, new devices, that have been unrealistic and have caused this country great problems and left us with significant debt and deficits.[4]

Congressman Martin Sabo testified at a joint hearing of the House and Senate Budget Committees on Dynamic Scoring, reminding colleagues that the same type of calculation had led to the huge deficits:

> Policies, similar to the Contract, in the 1980s left us trillions of dollars deeper in debt when wildly optimistic supply-side predictions about the effects of tax cuts proved to be greatly inaccurate. For those who don't remember, we were promised that the 1981 tax cuts would generate extra economic growth that would pay their $750 billion costs and would also balance the budget within three years. Instead we got deficits averaging more than $200 billion a year for the next 12 years. We simply can't afford to make that mistake again.[5]

When presidential candidate Senator Bob Dole in 1996 proposed a major tax reduction, his proposals met with general skepticism and he was not elected. Even the public seemed to have associated massive tax reductions with increased deficits. President Clinton did propose tax reductions, perhaps in competition with Dole, but they were more moderate and partly offset by tax increases. And rather than project a rosy economy into the future and thereby push up the date of proposed balanced budgets, the Clinton administration stuck to the balanced budget agreement worked out with Congress in 1997. The reasoning was explicitly linked to the events of 1981. The "mistakes of 1981" had become a shorthand reference to an overly large tax break with negative consequences for the deficit.

Avoid Reductions in Force (RIF) to Slim the Workforce

The budget cuts of 1981 and 1982 were complicated by requirements that agencies absorb some portion of salary increases, a dollar amount that was usually not known fully in advance. Budget uncertainty combined with actual cuts to create reductions in force in a number of agencies. Some agencies were forced to reduce staffing not because of budget cuts but because of lowered personnel ceilings.[6] Attrition reductions could not operate fast enough to save enough money during the fiscal year and furloughs could not achieve long-term savings, only savings for the year. But there was also a sense at the time that many agencies "RIFed" when they did not need to. Possibly due to lack of communication, many employees were not convinced that a RIF in their agency would be conducted in good faith.[7] In any case, for many agencies, this was the first time ever or at least the first time in memory they conducted RIFs. OPM was busy designing procedures while the agencies were busy implementing them.

The experience in most cases was poor, in the sense of the amount of time required to plan and execute the RIFs, the inability to target with any degree of selectiveness who would be sent out the door, the complexity of managing reorganizations at the same time or in sequence with RIF, and the complex bumping and retreat rights that often affected as many retained employees as involuntarily terminated ones. Senior people would often get bumped down to lower ranks or retreat to former positions, while newer employees were actually fired. RIFs were expensive, due to lump-sum payments due at the time of separation; appeals and court cases, which often dragged on for years; and paying senior people to do junior people's work. The effect on morale was depressive. Moreover, studies showed that the effects of RIFs on women and minorities were disproportional, in part because women often lacked the protection of military service, and in part because both women and minorities tended to be latecomers to the agencies. In some agencies, women and minorities were concentrated at the bottom of the hierarchy where most of the actual forced separations took place.[8] The RIF procedures put heavy emphasis on seniority.

The experiences of RIF in the early 1980s were remembered by agency staff and administrators and were documented by some of the federal government's research agencies.[9] When the new round of cuts was announced as a policy by the Clinton administration, many federal employees went to talk to their members of Congress to remind them of the costs and the effects on morale and on women and minorities.

RIFs were recorded not only in the minds of those who had experienced them and in the reports of those who studied them, but also in legislative records. The legislators who represented many federal employees, and those on authorizing committees who were sympathetic with the goals of programs they supervised, had reacted with frustration to the RIFs of the early Reagan administration, since there had been no time to oppose them. A loose coalition sought to prevent RIFs in the future. In a hearing on 10 June 1982, Congressman Steny Hoyer, representing the many government employees in his district, noted:

> I might say that the budget that passed today included the sense of the Congress that the reductions in force ought to be accomplished through attrition and not through reductions in RIFs. Therefore the budget document just passed some 40 minutes ago specifically has within it a policy statement that RIFs are not consistent with the sense of the Congress in terms of priorities of reducing the numbers of government workers. That is appropriate.[10]

While caught unawares by the Reagan administration, the legislators who opposed RIFs had plenty of time to think about how the reductions would occur during the Clinton administration. Moreover, the administration was clear about preferring attrition reductions to RIFs. The Clinton administration wanted to target supervisory positions and could not do so under RIF regulations that would normally cause lower-level staff to depart. Savings would also be less and greater numbers of reductions would be required if the people fired had lower salaries, as they would under a reduction in force.

In short, much learning resulted from the RIFs in the early Reagan administration, including a heightened sensitivity to tradeoffs between voluntary and involuntary separations to reduce staffing levels. A consensus gradually emerged that attrition and moderate incentives such as buyouts were generally more cost effective and less damaging to management and the diversity of the workforce.[11] While OPM disagreed with some of GAO's figures, it did agree that buyouts were generally more cost effective than RIFs.

The information on dollar savings from buyouts that was gathered by GAO, OPM, and CBO probably contributed to Congress's willingness to allow buyouts rather than encourage RIFs. Congress granted broad buyout authority in 1994 and renewed this authority after it expired. In the second round of buyouts, Congress added requirements that the agencies submit a plan for staffing reductions and that the plan be approved by OMB before the buyouts could be implemented. Most agencies did what they could, in accordance with OPM guidelines, to avoid or reduce the size of RIFs in 1994 and thereafter, in marked contrast to the Reagan years. Some agencies that did employ reductions in force spent time designing them to minimize bumping and retreats, so they would be more targeted. The shift from RIFs to attrition and buyouts, and the improvement of buyout legislation over several iterations, clearly reflected experience, studies, and accumulated knowledge that was widely shared.

Finding a Budget Process That Discourages Deficits

Congress experimented with different budget procedures in an effort to make it easier to balance the budget. The first major change after the 1974 Congressional Budget Act was Gramm-Rudman-Hollings (GRH), passed in 1985. Many who talked about the origins of Gramm-Rudman-Hollings were at a loss to describe where it came from in terms of legislative precedents. The deficit reduction features of the legislation sprang up suddenly. As a result, they had not been tested before and, not surprisingly, did not work exactly as hoped. While GRH may have held down the growth of deficits, the deficit reduction targets were not met, but more important, as it operated, its flaws showed congressional staff members what needed to be changed to create a more flexible law. The result was the Budget Enforcement Act (BEA) of 1990, which worked much better.

Gramm-Rudman-Hollings. The Gramm-Rudman-Hollings legislation had two major portions. One was a deficit reduction mechanism; the other was a change in the budget process. The deficit reduction features of GRH were attached as an amendment to a debt limit increase in the Senate and were not even considered in the House until the conference. But while the deficit reduction portion of the legislation was new, the budget process portion of the legislation emerged from the experience of using reconciliation as a way of cutting the budget in the early 1980s. This second portion of the legislation represented years of careful learning and sifting of proposals. To some extent, the deficit reduction portion of the law and the budget process reform portion were contradictory.

Budget Process. The deficit began to grow rapidly during the late 1970s and early 1980s. The need to trim spending and strengthen the relationship between revenues and expenditures moved up on the list of priorities. Features of the 1974 Congressional Budget Act allowed for something called *reconciliation,* a process that required the budget committees to set goals that the other committees had to stay within, on both the revenue and expenditure sides. The process was first used in 1980.

Staff and budget committee members began to learn what was necessary to make this part of the law work. The way the budget process legislation was written, reconciliation guidelines were issued twice, once at the beginning of deliberations and once toward the end. With experience it became clear that this part of the budget law did not work well. But budgeters learned other things as well during the late 1970s and early 1980s. As one former congressional staffer recalled,

> Most people who were running the show in the 1980s, particularly in the Senate, were active and learned in the 1970s. What parts to go after was learned in the '70s.
>
> The reconciliation process, used in 1981 [in the Reagan administration], was used first in 1980 in the Carter administration. Using the first resolution rather than the second, 1980 was the first time. . . .

In the 1970s, we [learned we] couldn't tackle things on a one-year basis. The big money was in the entitlements. Politically, we couldn't wait until major legislation wended its way through and then tell people at the end to undo their deals. By 1980, a consensus had developed on both sides of the aisle in both houses that we needed a new enforcement strategy.

The money was in the entitlements and we had to do it on a multiyear basis. In 1979 or '80 we experimented with a multiyear approach.

We had tried it year by year, the result was outright fraud. Periodic payment to hospitals from Medicare and Medicaid, monthly advances against billing. The last payment slips across the end of the year line and "saves" ½ of the cost. It was well understood and developed.[12]

In short, by the early 1980s Senate budgeters had learned that a year-by-year approach would be gamed, that expenditures would be delayed to make the budget look more balanced than it was; they had learned that the major spending problems were in the entitlements; and they had learned that whatever spending and tax targets were set had to be deployed at the beginning of the process, not at the end.

While some experimentation began right away, resentment against the reconciliation process simmered, and a task force was appointed to see if the budget process could be improved. Rep. Anthony Beilenson chaired the task force in 1984. He was known as an intellectual who was seriously dedicated to improving the budget process. Insights from the early years of using reconciliation were distilled by the Beilenson task force and put in the form of a legislative proposal. The proposal did not get out of committee, reportedly in part because Beilenson did not drum up support for it with committee chairs.[13] The leadership was also concerned about opening up the budget process beyond the careful deliberation of the Beilenson task force to any legislator who wanted to change it one way or another and hence was reluctant to bring the Beilenson proposals to the floor under an open rule. Instead, the Beilenson proposals were rolled, almost intact, into the deficit reduction and debt limit increase legislation known as Gramm-Rudman-Hollings in 1985.[14]

The Beilenson task force proposals included dropping the second budget resolution, so the committees would not do work under a ceiling and then be told at the end that the ceiling had lowered and they had to undo all their negotiations. The Beilenson proposals also included a multiyear framework and consideration in the budget resolution of expenditures that had been off-budget. The budget resolutions were to include tax expenditures, revenues, and loans and loan guarantees as well as routine appropriations. Targets were to be by committee, and the committees were to allocate targets to the subcommittees.

Before this revision to the budget process, the targets for spending and revenue had been on the aggregate level, not the committee level. Macro targets had been a problem, because committees that produced appropriations legislation later rather than earlier were more likely to breach the total, even if they came in under their own target. Similarly, a committee that was able to get its proposal out earlier could possibly breach its own limits but not the aggregate's. The Beilenson task force proposed that a point of order be made against the committee that exceeded its own target. What had been learned was that committees should be given a single target to shoot at and should be made responsible for staying within that target.

What is especially interesting about the Beilenson task force is that it represented active learning and sharing between members and staff and that its work was eventually embodied in legislation. Longtime budget observer Jim Horney from CBO described the Beilenson task force as highly studious: Their proposals were carefully examined for several years; a lot of exchange took place between staff and members; many people took it seriously. Moreover, as a former staffer described, in the final legislation a whole slew of procedures were included to deal with the games that had emerged over the previous ten years.[15]

Deficit Reduction. The budget process reform part of Gramm-Rudman-Hollings represented a serious effort at problem solving based on experience. The deficit reduction portion of what came to be known as GRH had a far shorter pedigree. The initial idea came from Senator Phil Gramm, but his proposal ended up being thoroughly rewritten before final passage. In comparison to the budget process changes that had been studied by the Beilenson task force, the deficit reduction proposals were hastily put together and were not based on prior experience of what worked and what did not. Much of the negotiation and design phase occurred during the technical drafting period. A staff member in the House described the drafting process in the following terms: "I must have drafted 70 versions of GRH, 100 days of constant work, every day of the week."[16]

The basic idea of the deficit reduction portion of the legislation was to set diminishing targets for the size of the deficit until the deficit was gone. Each year had a fixed maximum for the allowable size of the deficit. In any year in which the deficit reduction target was not met, the number of dollars needed to reach the target would be sequestered, or set aside, to be cut more or less across the board from nonexempted programs. The legislation had been prompted by a combination of the size and persistence of the deficit and gridlock, differences of priorities between the president and Congress about what should be cut and what protected. A provision for across-the-board cuts would offend both sides and presumably would force the president and congressional leaders to negotiate to come up with an acceptable set of cuts so sequester would be unnecessary.

The effectiveness of Gramm-Rudman-Hollings in reducing deficits has been debated. The size of the deficits moderated under Gramm-Rudman-Hollings, but the deficit reduction targets were never met. The legislation was defined by many as a failure because it did not eliminate the deficits and because it caused such publicly visible evasions of the sequester provisions. Forcing the parties to negotiate when they completely disagreed about priorities did not work. Inability to agree to cuts in advance should have led to sequesters, which none of the actors wanted. The result was various kinds of fudging and evasions, including rosy scenarios from OMB and manipulation of expenditures back and forth across fiscal years. It also led to major efforts to exclude a variety of programs from the across-the-board sequesters.

One interviewee described some of the evasions:

> After the target for the sequester date was passed, you could repeal the cuts [never taking them in fact, but avoiding the sequester by saying that you would]. . . . It was too flexible in that sense. At the same time, it reinstitutionalized one-year budgets, which shift spending into the next fiscal year and later put it back in the previous fiscal year.
>
> . . . In 1987, the first full running year, OMB came along with August numbers, it needed $10 billion more than it planned. The question was how. Jim Miller at OMB passed a list, exclusively of timing shifts. A timing shift makes one year look better and future years worse. Those proposals epitomized what was wrong with Jim Miller and GRH1.[17]

The two major portions of Gramm-Rudman-Hollings had opposite thrusts. The budget process reforms embraced the principles of multiyear budgets to help prevent pushing expenditures forward or revenues backward, but the deficit reduction targets were annual and encouraged such manipulations. The budget process reforms supported the idea that each committee needed its own target and the target should be enforced by a point of order, rather than controlling the process through aggregates and blaming the individual committee that breached the aggregate limit. But the deficit reduction targets put into place a sequester if the size of the deficit rose because of a drop in the economy or other unexpected event. A change in the aggregate size of the deficit, regardless of cause, could require a sequester and force cuts; appropriations subcommittees that had been careful in their spending and had not contributed to deficits were required to make cuts.

The Budget Enforcement Act of 1990. The multiple problems with the deficit reduction portion of the legislation ultimately led to the Budget Enforcement Act (BEA) of 1990. The BEA had two major strands. One dealt with efforts to strengthen the norms of budgetary balance, making it harder to unbalance the budget; the other, related effort was called credit reform. The latter was a technical change in the way expenditures associated with loans and loan guarantees were reported in the budget.

Strengthening the Norms of Balance. Gramm-Rudman-Hollings deficit reduction targets had been too inflexible. They did not take into consideration contingencies or emergencies that could increase spending. Such emergencies could cause a sequester or across-the-board cut,[18] even in appropriations subcommittees that had carefully adhered to spending constraints. Discretionary spending[19] was capped but the caps were flexible, allowing for inflation and emergencies such as hurricanes and wars. Committee members were thus not held responsible for changes over which they had little control. Despite some fluctuation from year to year, the overall trajectory of deficits under the BEA was down, especially due to the caps in the discretionary spending accounts. Until the deficits were turned into surpluses, these flexible caps held. Exceptions for emergencies were generally limited and played little role in generating deficits.

Instead of aiming to control the size of the annual deficit, BEA strove to strengthen the norms of balance. First, it set spending caps for the discretionary portion of the budget and, for the first few years, set up barriers between spending categories, so savings in one area could not be spent in another. Second, for entitlement programs, the law emphasized offsets; that is, if spending were to be increased in some places, it had to be decreased elsewhere or revenue had to be increased to compensate. Similarly, if revenue were to be decreased in some area, it had to be increased somewhere else or an expenditure had to be reduced to prevent an increase in the deficit.

This latter principle, that increases in entitlements or decreases in revenues needed to be offset, was called pay as you go, or PAYGO. PAYGO applied only to the so-called mandatory side of the budget, where the entitlements were. This provision of the law required offsets for any new legislation that increased spending, but it did not require offsets if the value of existing tax breaks increased without new legislation or if the cost of entitlements went up because the economy weakened and more people needed benefits. Thus legislators were not responsible for making cuts resulting from increases they had not caused. The law focused attention on not aggravating the deficit by passing new laws or liberalizing old ones to make them more expensive without offsetting those expenditures.

The BEA thus not only strengthened the norms of balance, but also held legislators accountable for only those outcomes that they controlled. A number of interviewees confirmed that this feature was built into the BEA because of negative experiences with Gramm-Rudman-Hollings.

One CBO staff member explained how these provisions evolved out of dissatisfaction with Gramm-Rudman-Hollings. Under GRH, a change in the economy that increased the costs of entitlements could increase the size of the deficit and trigger a sequester. Because many of the entitlement programs were exempted from across-the-board cuts, these sequesters fell on the discretionary appropriations, even though the legislators in charge of those committees had not caused the problem:

> One group hit by GRH was Appropriations. It had its allocations [and stayed within them], but OMB would decide that a sequester was needed. Appropriations would say, "We did everything you told us to do, we stayed within the figures." Yet it was hit with a sequester that hit only the discretionary side. That led to a separate system of mandatory and discretionary [controls]. PAYGO would hit those who caused the problem.[20]

Setting spending ceilings on the discretionary side, instituting offsets (PAYGO) on the mandatory side, and making legislators responsible for outcomes they could control all helped strengthen the norms of budget balance. The rules were enforced less by sequesters after the fact than by scoring rules when a proposal was first made. Every bill was reviewed for PAYGO implications, and if, according to the scoring rules, cost increases were found, Congress had to find offsets. As one longtime Capitol Hill staffer described the process,

> This kind of system works pretty well. PAYGO, except for OMB cheating on the farm bill, works on every bill. The first question is, how will you pay for it? . . . How to pay for it in that bill or point to something else that will pay for it. It has changed the debate. You didn't used to say how you paid for it. It is effective. The fear of sequestration keeps people to the numbers, keeps [proposals] deficit neutral. They will work with us like crazy, to find offsets. When a bill is introduced, we [CBO] estimate the cost as $20 million, they ask, where are the offsets. Finding offsets isn't our job. They scramble off, to find something. [The caps] have worked well on the discretionary side, set limits not to exceed. The emergency provisions haven't been abused as far as I can see.[21]

After a fair amount of experimentation, Congress and staff had indeed developed a process that favored budget balance.

Credit Reform. The Budget Enforcement Act responded to the failures of GRH in another way. GRH had emphasized the annual reduction in the size of the deficit. The question arose as to what would count toward a reduction in the deficit. For example, would temporary revenues from the sale of property or businesses count? Would loan origination fees count even if they increased the overall risk exposure of the federal government and resulted in larger expenditures or an increased deficit later? These issues had not been well thought through at the time and resulted in some perverse incentives. For example, loan guarantee fees and insurance premiums were recorded as income and appeared to reduce the deficit in the short run while increasing government spending in the long run. Loan guarantees actually increased after the passage of Gramm-Rudman-Hollings, despite the fact that GRH had introduced a separate credit ceiling. (The increase was from $410 billion in 1985 to $588 billion in 1989.[22]) As the totals for loan guarantees increased and the costs of insurance failures became increasingly visible, pressure built in Congress to come up with an accounting scheme that would lead to a more realistic costing formula for credit. The result was a major credit reform included in the BEA in 1990.[23] The credit reform made the costs of borrowing clearer at the time when approval for program expansion was being approved.

Credit reform had been on the agenda many times before, but it came to the fore again in the late 1980s as the amount of guaranteed loans increased and began to affect the deficit in ways Congress could easily perceive. There was considerable learning between the first few attempts at credit reform and the adoption of legislation in 1990. One former staffer at OMB described the process as "sifting and iterative." The process of developing ideas and getting support for them was managed primarily by OMB. The attitude was one of trying new things and seeing what would work. There was a lot of back and forth with the agencies.

Credit reform began all the way back in the 1960s, well before the concern about balancing the budget became prominent. These early efforts worked out the concepts but failed in practice:

> Credit reform was proposed in Johnson's administration, in the Commission on Budget Concepts. They wanted a credit subsidy but not the cash flow to show in the cash budget; that is the essence of the current credit reform. Back then, people didn't know how to estimate costs; now we know somewhat better, though problems remain.[24]

Chapter 5 of the *Report of the President's Commission on Budget Concepts,* in October 1967, outlined the basic principles of credit reform. First, loans needed to be separated from other kinds of expenditures. Basic loan activity should not be considered part of the calculation of the deficit when evaluating the impact of the deficit on the economy, but subsidies, which consist of both loans issued below market rate and losses through defaults, should be included in the budget as expenditures.[25]

The commission's recommendations were to be implemented in the 1969 budget, which was to be drawn up only a few months after the commission's recommendations were submitted. No one knew how to estimate the loan subsidies that were supposed to go into the expenditure portion of the budget and there was no time to learn. The commission members had expected that over time, the Bureau of the Budget and the Treasury would learn how to make such estimates, but that expectation proved too optimistic.[26] Loans were recorded at par in the loan accounts, rather than separating out the subsidies and putting them in expenditures. The split between loan activities that should not be recorded as expenditures and a subsidy that should be recorded was rendered meaningless and was dropped in the 1974 budget. In 1972 rough estimates of subsidies were reported in a special analysis on credit, but they were not integrated into the budget.

In the late 1970s and 1980s a different approach was taken to controlling credit, a credit budget. Here, limits were established for the face value of new debt issued. The limits did not apply to all programs, excluding those loans and guarantees deemed to be entitlements, such as guaranteed student loans and veterans' loan guarantees.[27] OMB set up the credit budget and it was adopted as part of the congressional budget process in 1985.

The credit budget was seen as ineffective in part because the caps were often set so high that they had no effect.[28] In addition, they were not really integrated into Congress's financial controls:

> The credit budget was an add-on; it didn't change the rules. It gave an overlay, in which new direct loans and loan guarantees were supposed to be controlled through specific votes. The president recommends a limit of x amount on REA loans, and Congress votes those limits into the budget resolution, so that would have a legal effect. But it didn't work, it was a good effort, but it didn't resolve the problem.
>
> Congress generally was willing to vote the caps, but they were sufficiently large that they didn't bind or they voted a new cap. It didn't control; there was no incentive to keep the cap down, because it didn't count against spending. It was just an add-on thing.
>
> Suppose you were teaching sixth-graders, trying to get kids to learn. One incentive they have is report cards. Parents might be upset if they get Fs. If the teacher says that doesn't count on your report card, their incentives are different. This didn't count toward the deficit, the basic score card. It was too weak to work. That was in effect a number of years, a bona fide effort, but it didn't work.[29]

While the caps were used, the amount of credit outstanding continued to grow and finally to appear both out of control and problematic. Credit appeared to contribute to the deficit and reduce congressional flexibility in budgeting. Budget Director Richard Darman underscored the urgency of doing something when he described in his budget introduction contingent risks of credit and insurance as among the "hidden PACMEN, waiting to spring forward and consume another line of resource dots in the budget maze."[30] As the perceived urgency increased, those who had been pushing for different kinds of approaches to credit control came together to support credit reform and back off from opposition to other approaches.

OMB director Richard Darman had been supporting enforcing the credit caps with sequesters, parallel to the mechanisms in Gramm-Rudman-Hollings. Though many agreed that Gramm-Rudman was ineffective at meeting deficit reduction targets and encouraged gaming, there was room to believe that GRH had kept the deficit lower than it would have been without it. Others disagreed with Darman that ceilings and sequester enforcement were the appropriate routes. By 1990, however, Robert Reischauer from CBO, Charles Bowsher from GAO, and Richard Darman from OMB agreed that something should be done and that it did not matter that much which approach was used. In testimony before Congress all three argued that it was time to adopt credit reform. That hearing proved the turning point. The question became not whether, but how it should be done. The answer drew on years of effort by staff members in both the executive and legislative branches to find a technically effective solution.

To underscore the extent to which different staff agencies cooperated and worked on the problems together, section 212 of the Balanced Budget and Emergency Deficit Control Reaffirmation Act of 1987 required the CBO to prepare a study of credit reform in consultation with the General Accounting Office. In addition, staff of the Office of Management and Budget "contributed valuable reviews."[31] The OMB staff who helped prepare the CBO study included the OMB team that had been working on credit reform.

As early as 1984 OMB issued a revised circular A-70, "Policies and Guidelines for Federal Credit Programs." This circular required agencies to estimate the subsidy costs of loan and loan guarantees. The method specified was to compare the government loans and guarantees to private financing terms. This circular was important in elevating the issue and improved the comparability of direct and guaranteed loans, but it was never made part of the budget and could be enforced more or less rigorously depending on the OMB examiner and the views of the OMB director.[32] One prominent approach to figuring out the subsidy level was to actually sell the loans and reinsure the guaranteed loans. This approach was supported by some economists, some members of Congress, and, for a time, OMB. Another approach supported by the executive branch at one time was a voucher system that turned the subsidy portion of the loans into something more like a grant. The years of effort and learning paid off: "Congress finally adopted credit reform in part because repeated experiments with subsidy estimation provided a minimum of comfort with the quality of estimates."[33]

The proposal that finally passed was complicated and implementation was problematic. Skeptics worried about the quality of the data and the difficulty of implementation and feared that this round of credit reform would meet the same fate as earlier rounds. Yet the general sense of both participants and observers was that credit reform has been a success in part because it did achieve a reorientation of incentives in Congress.

As a former OMB staffer reported,

> The credit reform worked because Congress responds to scoring issues. Scoring is the means that the CBO uses to tell committees the costs of legislation they are proposing. Under the BEA, they have to pay attention to these scoring numbers in order to stay within the caps or fulfill PAYGO requirements. The cost of direct loans had been overestimated and the cost of loan guarantees had been underestimated, leading to overuse of the loan guarantees. More realistic estimates of costs, even when not perfectly accurate, led to reduced reliance on this type of spending.[34]

The face value of outstanding direct loans increased 26 percent from 1980 to 1989; from 1989 to 1996 the face value of outstanding direct loans decreased by 20 percent. The effect on outstanding loan guarantees was parallel. Between 1980 and 1989 the face value of loan guarantees increased by 96 percent; from 1989 to 1996 the face value of guarantees increased by a considerably slower 36 percent. At the same time, the face value of loans issued by Government Sponsored Enterprises, which remained uncontrolled by credit reform, continued to grow at a very rapid rate, increasing more than 100 percent from 1989 to 1996, adding $226 billion in face value of loans from 1995 to 1996 alone (table 2.4). Credit reform may not have been inclusive enough.

From 1996 to 1999 the face value of direct loans grew at a rapid 41 percent, but the growth of guaranteed loans continued to slow down, from 36 percent in the previous period to 21 percent in the most recent period. These figures suggest that Congress had come to understand that loan guarantees did cost something—they were not free.

While the face value of loans is a measure of overall activity, it is not the most relevant figure to measure the effect of credit reform. A more important figure is the estimated cost to the government—including subsidies and defaults—of the loans over their lifetime. These costs are estimated, reflecting

Table 2.4   Federal Credit: Face Value Outstanding (in $ billions)

	1980	1985	1989	1993	1994	1995	1996	1997	1998	1999
Direct loans	164	257	207	151	155	161	165	196	217	234
Loan guarantees	299	410	588	693	699	727	805	822	916	976
GSEs	151	370	763	1,255	1,502	1,514	1,740	1,730	1,997	2,417

Source: U.S. Budget, various years.

Table 2.5   Federal Credit: Present Value Future Costs (in $ billions)

	1995	1996	1997	1998
Direct loans	47–69	37–57	30–51	33–57
Loan guarantees	9–44	26–58	18–46	12–42

Source: U.S. Budget, various years.

guesses about future defaults based on past history. Because of the inexactness of the estimation process, such costs have sometimes been expressed as a range, rather than as an absolute amount. Such estimates suggest the costs to government of direct loans were relatively stable from 1995 through 1998, perhaps falling slightly. After rising in 1996, the guaranteed loans decreased in expected costs for three years, though not sharply (table 2.5). These results suggest that Congress found a way to compare and control the costs of both direct and guaranteed loans.[35]

The face value of the guaranteed loans increased while the estimated costs to government decreased. That observation seems contradictory, but it may reflect guarantees covering a smaller portion of the loan, lower risk loans, and improved collection procedures. Much attention was placed on improving loan collections, and some programs intentionally reduced the proportion of the loan the government would guarantee. The result was more dollars out the door, with less government liability.

Credit reform is one of the clearest examples of learning in the long-term effort to balance the budget. That learning occurred in several locations. OMB learned and taught the agencies ways to figure out the level of subsidies of loans and the costs to the government of loans and guarantees; some agencies took a long time to learn how to do this,[36] and there was some concern that agencies would learn to game rather than follow the accounting rules. Congressional committees learned from the failures of previous credit budgets that credit ceilings, even when enforced by sequester, were unlikely to work. They ended up with an incentive system that allowed control at the point the decisions were being made and that allowed flexibility and tradeoffs.

WHAT WE HAVE NOT LEARNED

In lurches and halts, with occasional reversals and possible backsliding, the federal government did learn to control the deficits. The government learned how to control discretionary spending levels and how to control proposals for new or expanded entitlements. The fact that these procedures were not closely adhered to after the budget began generating surpluses does not detract from the fact that the government did adhere to them when it needed to eliminate deficits. The very success of the government in balancing the budget led some to question

Table 2.6   Growth of Discretionary and Entitlement
Spending, 1990–99 (percentage increase)

Year	Discretionary	Entitlement
1990–91	6.5	12.0
1991–92	0.2	1.9
1992–93	1.1	2.8
1993–94	0.5	6.3
1994–95	0.3	4.3
1995–96	−2.0	4.7
1996–97	2.6	4.5
1997–98	1.0	4.7
1998–99	3.6	4.0

Source: Calculated from the table Outlays by Major
Spending Category, Fiscal Years 1962–1999, CBO,
Historical Budget Data, Appendix E of *The Budget and
Economic Outlook, Fiscal Years 2001–2010*, 26 January
2000. Washington, D.C.: U.S. Government Printing
Office.

whether the difficult problems were tackled or whether the government took
only relatively easy steps, with some apparently irrational results.

Entitlements were controlled only at the margins. The cost of existing entitlements continued to grow, requiring ever deeper cuts in discretionary programs
to balance the budget (table 2.6). Rather than a policy that dictates priorities,
the division of the process into two parts with different kinds of controls resulted
in one part growing and the other shrinking, regardless of priorities.

The Implications of the Division between Discretionary and Mandatory Costs

The Budget Enforcement Act controlled the growth of costs of entitlements by
discouraging legislative changes that would liberalize benefits. Either more
revenue had to be found to fund such increases or cuts had to be made in other
entitlements. The BEA did not address increases in costs of existing entitlements
unless they required legislative changes:

> We have not learned to deal with the existing stock of entitlements, what
> has been called "no-fault budgeting." PAYGO, all it does is not make
> matters worse. The budget process doesn't control growth beyond
> revenues. Social Security, Medicaid, Medicare, 20 to 30 years from now,
> there will be real trouble if we can't find a way to communicate to people
> that they can't have as much from government without paying more.[37]

Entitlement costs have continued to increase, despite the controls of the BEA. These mandatory cost increases put pressure on the discretionary side of the budget, which has had to be cut disproportionately to accommodate entitlement growth. The result may be, as Robert Reischauer argued, that some discretionary programs are being cut too much.[38]

Others agreed that the discretionary portion of the budget was getting hit with a disproportionate amount of the cuts. Longtime budget participant and later budget observer Tom Cuny argued that the budget process had created an imbalance that was structural and destructive of traditional, nondefense, general government in a broad sense:

> The pool, the magnitude of the pool available for retrenchment once we rule out social insurance trust funds and defense, given the size of the problem—and given that we have latched onto revenue levels relative to GDP that are several percentage points below spending levels— we want to pull it [that huge number] out of the compartment in which stuff [nondefense discretionary] is all socked.[39]

Others argued that much of the cuts had been taken out of defense, but as the ability to cut more out of defense reached a point at which no more could realistically be taken, nondefense discretionary would have to bear a deeper and deeper set of cuts.

Discretionary programs were cut disproportionately and possibly too deeply. The logic by which programs were sorted out for deep cuts did not support the "leaner government is better managed government" thesis. The level of cuts in many domestic programs depended not on the level of need, the quality of the program or management, or its relative importance but on increases in uncontrollable costs, such as in health care.

Program supporters in Congress and in the agencies perceived these tradeoffs between domestic discretionary and entitlement programs clearly. For example, as one legislative roundup noted, "Newly confirmed chairman Ted Stevens announced on January 8 that discretionary spending for 1998 will likely remain the same as that for 1997, if entitlement spending continues to rise." On a similar note, Nebraska Senator Bob Kerrey, who was on both the Agriculture and Appropriations committees, told reporters that a $1.6 billion cut in the FY 1998 budget for the Agriculture Department might be needed to help offset a 1.5 percent growth in federally funded entitlement programs.[40]

Tradeoffs within the Discretionary Portion of the Budget

This logic for choosing areas to cut—one group of expenditures goes up so another group has to come down—avoided any real prioritization. Programs were cut because of the category of the budgets they were in, rather than their importance, efficiency, or effectiveness. The structure of appropriations committees and the allocation of spending caps exacerbated this problem. Within the discretionary portion of the budget, each subcommittee had its own caps. Each subcommittee was responsible for several functions, which may have been only loosely or not at all related. If a subcommittee increased the allocation to one of those functions, other, unrelated functions in the subcommittee's jurisdiction had to experience a decrease, without regard to their worth and without comparison to programs in the jurisdiction of other committees. If spending for Veterans Affairs, a perennially popular program, went up, spending for Housing and Urban Development had to come down because HUD and the Veterans Administration are on the same committee. If the Justice Department, because of its crime focus, increased spending, then Department of State and/or Commerce Department spending had to come down, because Justice, State, and Commerce are in the same appropriations bill.

In addition to this competition within appropriations subcommittees, competition intensified among programs within departments. As one former departmental budget officer put it, individual deals at lower levels in the organization no longer worked, because if you succeeded, other programs within the same caps would be affected. Deals had to be negotiated by the secretary, and even then, "If the secretary wants to fight for more, it has to come from somewhere else. OMB cannot hold back as much to create allowance for special purposes."[41] Comparison among programs within a department is not necessarily illogical, if the programs have been grouped into the department because they have something in common, but in some departments, such as Commerce, programs may be extremely different from one another, raising the question of how reasonable it is to intensify the competition among them.

Unintended Consequences

The Budget Enforcement Act's successes created a raft of unintended consequences. One of the most important was the elevation of enforcement of budgetary balance above making good and effective public policy. Enforcement was achieved through "scoring." In scoring, the Congressional Budget Office evaluates legislative proposals in terms of how they would affect the caps and the paygo provisions of the BEA. Legislators and agency policymakers became focused on scoring decisions:

> There is a lot of policy on the hill, draft legislation. They [the drafters] think almost as much about how the Congressional Budget Office will score the bill as is this good policy. He or she is as excited about the scorability as he or she is about whether this is an appropriate activity for the government to perform.

> People have no idea whether an idea is good but will sit down with a CBO person and ask, how would you score this? They are trying to meet their reconciliation targets. They are looking for any way to structure their expenditures so CBO will give them savings to meet their targets.[42]

The budget scorekeeping rules generated some evasive tactics and some new strategies, not all of which made good policy sense. For example, a tax break for businesses engaged in research and development was renewed annually. Discussion revolved around why this tax break was not passed for a multiyear period so businesses could plan on it. One argument for annual renewal was to avoid a new and possibly expensive entitlement, but the more dominant concern was that a more permanent tax break would have to be offset by five years of revenues to cover the costs. Finding that much additional revenue was much more difficult than finding enough revenue to compensate for one year's tax losses. In this case, the budget rules discouraged or at least did not maximize private companies' investments in research and development, which normally return more to the economy and to the government in future growth dividends than they cost.[43]

For some observers, it was not just budget rules and scoring that supplanted policy decisions, but the enhanced focus on budget balance itself. That focus seemed to detract from solving major problems rather than to promote solutions. As one interviewee argued, "The current focus on deficits is silly. If we want to prioritize problems, look at health care and social security. It is good to see CBO moving to that. I don't know how the political system will move toward that."[44] Another interviewee was slightly more optimistic about the long-range potentials while observing the same problem: "We got overly focused on reducing the deficit. We didn't learn how to focus on that and other important things at the same time. We still have too short a time frame, but we are improving."[45] He continued:

> This is all part and parcel of the change in the budget process from priority setting to an enforcement process. From the mid-1980s enforcement has had more influence. Without regard to whether it is good or bad, there have been unanticipated consequences of changes in the budget process. One consequence has been to make enforcement of budget [balance] a stronger activity than priority setting. Priority setting had been the typical way of viewing the budget process, now the primary process is enforcement.
>
> If they started somewhere else, such as, we have these six public policy objectives, how should we get there, they would end up in a different place than [when] they have a $20 billion target and need to write legislation to meet that goal. It is a wildly different orientation.[46]

Another kind of unintended consequence of the BEA was that the division into discretionary and mandatory portions made it more difficult to increase spending on reducing fraud and waste:

> BEA is destroying policy in ways that are not productive. Consider the fraud and abuse issue. It was similar to the IRS when they wanted more staff to collect taxes and claimed the net benefits of doing so. HHS claimed that additional spending for additional people to fight fraud and abuse would produce net savings. But the increased cost would be on the discretionary side and savings would be on the entitlements side, so it couldn't be done because of the fire wall [between discretionary and mandatory].[47]

The options under the Budget Enforcement Act were to increase the discretionary cap to deal with the increased expenditure; not to increase the cap, but to cut something else in the discretionary side to offset the increased expenditure there; or to redefine the increased discretionary spending as mandatory, which would be illogical but would allow the savings to occur:

> CBO said it had calculated the savings and they would be sufficient to offset the costs. So they [Congress] put IG [Inspector General] spending on the entitlement side because of the BEA rules. I found that disheartening.
>
> Any administrative agency can say its administration is involved in avoiding abuse. This could be a precedent. Other agencies could do this too. Some people think that it would be better to keep them in discretionary (and reduce other spending there to compensate) and not move to the entitlement side. One problem with putting it on the entitlement side is there is no mechanism to go back and see if savings occurred. It doesn't come up regularly like an appropriation.
>
> CBO did not say it should be on the entitlement side, just that the numbers worked. The IRS kept its spending in the discretionary side but allowed cap adjustments; that works fine—continuing discretionary status with a cap adjustment rather than [being redefined as an] entitlement.[48]

It was not only very difficult to increase spending for greater enforcement and better collections but also difficult to reduce the cost of staff because there were savings on the discretionary side but increases in pension costs on the entitlement side. As Phil Joyce, former CBO staffer, noted,

> Particular policies that would cause one part of the budget to increase and other parts to decrease, for a net savings, can be difficult to do,

regardless of the net savings. There was the example of the policy to not replace those with high salaries or to replace them with lower salary people. All the savings were in the discretionary portion, but the expenses, for increased pension payments, were in the PAYGO section and had to be separately offset. The discretionary savings could not be used to offset the increases. They had to find other places in mandatory spending to cut. That is the downside.[49]

In addition, as Joyce noted, "It is okay to raise taxes to pay for more entitlements but not okay for discretionary items. That is the effect of the balkanization of the budget. The flip side, if you want to cut taxes, you can pay for them through mandatory spending, but not through cuts in discretionary spending."[50]

A related unintended consequence was an effort on the part of some agencies to move program spending out of the discretionary portion of the budget, where the caps were tight, into the mandatory portion of the budget. As one informant explained,

> What HHS was after was getting those people [the Inspector General's staff] out from under the caps. That was better politically than trying to raise caps. Same as transportation, to get out of the discretionary caps. Some people think caps should not be raised, should take cuts instead, but an explicit cap adjustment is better than redefining discretionary as entitlement. Agencies will learn that this is a new way to argue they should be exempt from the discipline of appropriations caps. They do talk to each other.[51]

Efforts to Curtail Entitlements

The fact that the entitlements remained uncontrolled and that control and balance dominated the discussion, eclipsing many policy concerns, led to a variety of efforts to control the growth of entitlements, with varying levels of success.

One effort, described in detail in chapter 3, was to redo the consumer price index (CPI) to slow down growth in the cost of entitlements. Many major entitlements are linked to the CPI; when the CPI goes up, so do benefits. Hence pressure was enormous to curtail the index, if not inflation itself. Many arguments were put forward to suggest that the index overestimated inflation, so that a technical correction was needed. The effort was to make it look as if prior benefits had been overly generous, and therefore future ones would be not stingier but more accurate. Not all the evidence was convincing, however, especially concerning the amount that the index might have overstated inflation. In any case, a variety of changes were made in the index that all had the effect of reducing estimates of inflation. The impact was necessarily to reduce the level of benefits of those receiving inflation-adjusted entitlement payments. The process has been done slowly and carefully, and since there will still be increases, and recipients will not have a good way of viewing inflation to see if their payments are keeping up with it, this cost control will probably not cause major political upheaval as it is phased in.

A more dramatic and encompassing approach was to turn the entitlement programs into block grants or cap them as entitlements. One such proposal was made in 1997 (called Barton-Minge), but it came from a coalition of legislators who argued, as a condition of their support for the balanced budget agreement, that their proposal would be brought to the floor of the House. It was brought to the floor after bypassing committees of jurisdiction. The committee chairs therefore opposed it, and it did not have the benefit of the kind of improvement and logrolling that occur in committee. In fact, the sponsors were not allowed to make any changes in it before it was voted on, so the agreement to allow the proposal to come to the floor was honored, but in such a way that all the flaws of the proposal were intact and highly visible. The measure granted the president the power to set caps on entitlements, had a sequester provision if entitlements aggregately exceeded the caps, and promised to cancel tax breaks if revenues fell below targets. The proposal was complex and poorly worded, and it did not pass the House.

The plan to turn at least some entitlements into block grants or closed-ended rather than open-ended payments was more successful in agriculture. Major agricultural support programs were redesigned in 1996. On the one hand, subsidies for specific crops, such as sugar, peanuts, and tobacco, were narrowly retained; on the other, the link between government payments to farmers and agricultural prices was eliminated. Farmers who had participated in wheat, feed grain, cotton, and rice programs during any of the previous five years were eligible to enter a transition program under which they would receive a fixed dollar amount each year for seven years. The fixed payments had nothing to do with what was planted or the income from those crops and were conceived as a transition to complete termination of the farm income support program, although Congress had the option of renewing the payments at the end of seven years. What had been an open-ended commitment dependent on the vagaries of the market became closed ended and controllable, even though the dollar cost was actually higher for the transition payments than for the open-ended subsidy. The one sign-up period in 1996 would allow the amount of the financial commitment over the seven years to be known in advance. After seven years, this entitlement was to end completely. This legislation was implemented for several years, until the farm economy fell on hard times and pressure to supplement farm payments accelerated.

The most important entitlements, and the ones that were most responsible for the increases in spending that were pushing out discretionary spending, proved difficult to control. The balanced budget agreement between the president and Congress, finally achieved after years of negotiation in spring 1997, would cut Medicare by $115 billion and Medicaid by $15 billion by 2002. But the cuts to Medicare were primarily reductions to payments for health care providers. These cuts did not reduce eligibility or benefits, nor did they really hold down the growth in health care costs. Though they were targeted to doctors and hospitals that used an unusually large number of tests and procedures, many doctors and hospitals argued that Medicare payments already failed to cover costs. The new provisions may have exacerbated a gap between health care costs and federal payments. If so, the result is likely to be reductions in the quality and quantity of health care provided, not in the cost or the government's obligations. Even more important, the balanced budget agreement did nothing to help anticipate the aging of the population and the necessarily larger medical expenses of a greater number of older people after the baby boomers retire.

Increases in the costs of health care through the entitlement programs of Medicare and Medicaid were undoubtedly drivers of the deficit and pose problems that will get dramatically worse in future years. The BEA controlled them at the margins but left alone the basic structure. Federal agencies that have major budgeting responsibilities and nongovernmental organizations that make reform proposals and/or lobby at the grass roots have made a point of dramatizing the future needs of these programs and the consequences of delaying decisions. They have succeeded in bringing the issue of more fundamental reform onto the policy radar screen, but it is not clear what would be needed to bring about a consensus on some of the more far-reaching proposals.

Efforts to curtail a third group of entitlements, so-called tax expenditures, have also not been particularly effective. Tax expenditures are monies owed to the government under the existing tax structure, which are not collected because a law was passed to exempt particular taxpayers for some policy reason. For example, purchasers of homes are exempt from paying income taxes for money they spend on interest on their home mortgages. The goal of this tax break is to encourage home owning and home building. Under the BEA, tax expenditures are treated similarly to other entitlements or mandatory expenditures. They are controlled at the margins, in that any new tax breaks have to be funded by tax increases or decreases in mandatory spending. But like other entitlements, existing tax expenditures have become more expensive with the passage of time and a changing tax structure. Changes in the tax structure sometimes make existing tax breaks more valuable.

During the years of efforts to control the deficits, there was some discussion of trying to restructure the tax expenditures or eliminate many of them, but in fact, relatively little has been accomplished. A major tax reform was passed in 1986 that eliminated or reduced many tax expenditures, but existing provisions continued to grow in expense after 1986 and a few were expanded legislatively. Line-item veto authority was granted to the president and included an option for the president to veto tax expenditure proposals, but the scope was limited to new proposals that affected 100 or fewer taxpayers. Efforts to examine and systematically recommend elimination of existing tax breaks were limited and generally ineffective. Radical proposals to eliminate the graduated income tax and substitute either a flat tax with no exemptions or a sales or value-added tax have not been accepted. More moderate proposals to evaluate the outcomes and impact of tax expenditures parallel to direct programmatic spending seem to have the best chance of effectiveness but have not yet come on line. In 1997 Senator John McCain tried to introduce legislation to form a commission to recommend the elimination of particular tax expenditures on the model of the commission set up to determine which military bases would be closed. Such a commission would take the heat off Congress for withdrawing benefits popular with particular groups. This proposal was not successful. McCain introduced an identical proposal two years later, a measure of lack of progress in the interim.

Senator Robert Byrd described tax expenditures as being on "automatic pilot." The tax break part of the budget, he argued, did not get the same level of scrutiny as the rest of the budget.[52] This description applied in 1997, after 16 years of efforts to balance the budget. New proposals for tax expenditures were controlled, but existing ones were not.

Short-Term Focus

Some effort to increase the time horizon of budgetary decision making has occurred in recent years. CBO, GAO, and OMB have all lengthened the time span of their studies, to show the impacts of present decisions and of population trends for future years. Nevertheless, the balanced budget agreement had a strange, short-term focus. The budget was to be balanced in 2002, even if it became unbalanced shortly thereafter.

The balanced budget agreement of 1997 was not only charged with making short-term changes that might make matters worse in the long run for Medicaid and Medicare, but also with making matters worse in terms of tax breaks after 2002. In general, the budget deal was end loaded. One of the things that was not learned throughout this period was how to avoid claiming credit now for putting off difficult decisions and painful cuts until later. The focus on balance by 2002 had become so intense that it did not seem to matter initially what would happen after 2002.

After the balanced budget agreement was reached, a *Washington Post* commentator worried about what would happen after 2002:

> Even as budget negotiators slapped one another on the back for finally closing a deal, fiscal experts cautioned that yesterday's agreement would do little to hold the budget in balance beyond 2002 when retiring baby boomers stop paying taxes and begin to claim Medicare, Social Security and other costly federal benefits.
>
> And many experts warned that the tax cuts outlined in yesterday's agreement—a package estimated to lower federal revenue by $250 billion over the next 10 years—could make the long-term deficit outlook considerably worse.
>
> . . . Many of the tax cuts—including capital gains tax rate reduction and provisions for expanding participation in tax-favored individual retirement accounts—are structured in such a way that experts expect them to cost the government far more money beyond 2002 than in their first five years.[53]

Several days later, Senator Edward Kennedy made a statement raising a number of questions about the budget agreement. He was concerned about the distribution of the benefits primarily to the well-to-do and the increasing costs of the tax breaks after 2002. He was especially concerned that under the BEA, those decreases in revenues resulting from the tax breaks either would generate a new round of deficits or would trigger a huge new round of cuts in programmatic spending. Echoing arguments outlined earlier, he warned, "We must do all that we can to ensure that Congress does not repeat the mistake of the excessive 1981 tax cuts that led to the massive Reagan-Bush budget deficits."[54] Kennedy worried that the decrease in revenues would become most severe precisely at the time that the Social Security, Medicare, and Medicaid problems were hitting a peak:

> The great danger is that these pressures on the deficit will explode exactly at the same time that the country faces the severe budget pressures caused by the retirement of the baby boom generation. We already know that we face intense long-run problems with Social Security, Medicare, and Medicaid. The last thing that we should do in the current budget agreement is to make those long-run problems worse.[55]

Kennedy questioned not only the distribution of the cuts and the benefits because the cuts fell disproportionately on the poor and the benefits disproportionately on the well-to-do, but also was concerned about the composition of the cuts because of the BEA's structural bias toward cutting discretionary spending.

He emphasized that many of the programs in this portion of the budget supported a variety of infrastructure investments:

> But the agreement slashes domestic investments by at least $60 billion below the level needed to maintain the current level of services. That is roughly a 10 percent cut in real terms. Discretionary spending has remained relatively flat since 1991 and is already at its lowest level as a share of the economy in 60 years. These dramatic cuts will mean less for vital investments in areas such as research and development funded by the National Institutes of Health and the National Science Foundation, less for crime prevention and police officers on the street, less for repair and upgrading of our nation's highways and bridges, less for education, health and safety, and the environment. Can the country afford to continue to shortchange the key public investments needed to keep our economy strong into the next century? It is only through investment that the nation can sustain needed economic growth. Using the definition of public investment accepted by the General Accounting Office—including education and training, public infrastructure, and civilian research and development—public investment accounted for 2.5 percent of the economy under President Reagan. Today, it has fallen to 1.7 percent of the economy. How much lower is Congress prepared to see it go?[56]

Among the items Kennedy believed may have been underfunded was defense, and he was concerned that any future increases in defense spending should come from a reduction in the tax breaks.

Senator Kennedy thus raised the question of the longer term implications of what spending was being cut. In asking about infrastructure, he posed a question of concern in this book. In balancing the budget, to what extent have we trimmed the herds or eaten the seed corn? Are we systematically underfunding our infrastructure because it is easier to make those kinds of cuts than cuts in entitlements?

While Kennedy provided one side of the argument, Jim Blum from CBO provided the other side. He agreed with the need for infrastructure support but wondered about whether the budget cuts necessary for balance were really eroding useful components of that infrastructure:

> There are a wealth of activities that are needed in any economy to provide public infrastructure, education, research and development. [But] how to distinguish the good from the poor [infrastructure programs] in that case? Highways, you can build highways that don't go anywhere. Maybe we would get more payoff from maintenance and reducing traffic congestion. In the case of education and training, the

federal government, what role does it have? Education is largely state and local. Training programs we have had since the 1960s, the Training and Development Act of 1962, but hard evaluation of how good these training programs are is missing. Over 30 years, we are hard put to come up with solid evidence. It's a hard question to answer, are we eating our seed corn. It is easier to say in theory than in practice, in terms of actual activities we are funding.[57]

The short-term focus of the balanced budget act raised the suspicion that in many cases what would be cut was that which was easy to cut, rather than that which needed to be cut. It was not clear that in general, seed corn, or long-term investment, was being eroded, but there were a number of reasons to suspect that it might be, if those investments were perceived less in terms of highways and hardware and more in terms of people, skills, and program knowledge. Some agencies found their ability to collect quality data for decision making compromised; some agencies had difficulty finding the funds to modernize their information systems; and many agencies found that their staffing levels and their work requirements had gotten out of whack. For some agencies, the way cutback occurred threatened to create a hollow government.

Hollow Government

Hollow government occurs when government promises more than it can deliver in the way of services. For example, Congress and the president may pass legislation to provide clean air, but the regulations to achieve that goal may not be enforced or may be weakened, or the human resources to enforce the law may not be provided. Hollow government is a real risk during a period of cutback, because missions may not be curtailed proportionately with dollar or staffing cutbacks. Cutting back missions, especially popular ones, is politically hard to do; cutting back dollars while leaving missions in place makes it look as if agencies are providing more service for less money. From the agency's point of view, cutting back mission is dangerous, because it may never get the mission back, and it may lose the constituency support that allowed it to survive. Hence cutting back mission and responsibilities proportional to budget cuts is very difficult. In some cases program benefits have been pared, and some programs have actually been terminated, but scaling down mission proportionate with spending cuts has been an elusive goal.

One of the important things that was not learned over 17 years was how to match staffing levels and workloads during a period of cutback. The easiest way to do that is to allow the budget cuts to determine the size of the workforce. A second approach is to develop workforce planning models that move from the mission and the workloads to the staffing requirements needed to accomplish that workload. Neither of these approaches was taken; instead, the emphasis was laid on reinvention and productivity improvements.

Productivity improvements can accomplish a great deal, but it is not clear how far they can go. Surely there are limits to productivity improvements, even with reinvention. If missions are not trimmed proportionately to budget cuts, allowing for modest productivity improvements, the impression is that agencies can do as much or more with fewer resources. They cannot show the effects of cuts (because if they do, they will be seen as inept and their budgets will be cut further), and hence they have to make cuts in those places that are least visible, whether that makes administrative sense or not. Thus agencies have to absorb quality reductions and often obscure them. By doing so, they encourage future cuts, because they seem to have proven that there was slack in the system and that no harm was caused by budget cuts.

The budget cuts in some agencies did determine the size of staffing reductions, but the ability to do this was curtailed by the administration's proposal, supported by Congress, to reduce staffing levels by 250,000 or more federal employees. (The final legislation required the elimination of more than 270,000 positions.) This goal was independent of budget cuts. It was possible to be able to afford and need more staff but be unable to keep them under these personnel reduction targets. Since mission and budget allowed or even required more employees than the staffing ceilings allowed, many agencies increased the amount that they contracted out for services.

The ability to link mission and workload with the number of employees in various categories was limited by this desire to reduce the number of staff regardless of demands on the agency. Workforce planning models were considered ways the agencies could use to get around workforce reductions and hence were discouraged. Former agency budget director Al Kliman described what happened to workforce planning over the years of efforts to balance the budget:

> We used to have a workload measurement back in the 1970s. For example . . . Community Development monitoring, it took x staff years to do a task, what you did expressed in terms of staff resources. We started off calculating the volume of work to be done. You could take economic assumptions, the total number of housing starts, the percent that were HUD related, and the like, to get the HUD workload. Some introduced this administrative argument with OMB on what the level of the workload was to determine the staffing.
>
> Reagan started with a prejudgment that the staff had to be reduced. He claimed that the workload measurement had a bias toward increases and abolished the work measurement system. We will give you the numbers of staff [the administration said]. I fought

back with an intermediate system: it was how the Social Security Administration did it; it was more primitive. It involved actual staff and actual workload. We put that in place a few years later. We stumbled along for a while, until after I left. Now, they don't have interest in it.

. . . The Clinton administration is just as bad in predetermining the results without looking at what you are trying to accomplish. That is what NPR became in the end. [Secretary Henry] Cisneros abandoned a system that comes up with numbers that no one will use.[58]

Kliman concluded that one of the consequences of the drive to reduce federal employment was that government could not manage the programs that it has. He referred to the outcome as hollow government.

The difficulty of linking a work plan with revamped organizational goals was not simply a function of the separation between staffing levels and budget and mission in the aggregate, at the policy level of the president and Congress, but also a function of the inability of agencies to reconsider and redesign their missions. In the State Department, workload was expanding, budgets were stable or declining, and the environment was radically changing, resulting in a major need for redesign that would in turn dictate staffing requirements. But the agency found it impossible to reformulate its mission and goals. Workforce planning had to take place in the absence of such a redefinition, an effort of questionable worth. Former State Department official Richard Morse described the linkage between mission and workforce planning:

We are struggling toward it [workforce planning] still. The idea is to say, how many people would you need at what point with what skills and how do you get from where you are today to there. Then you have to break it down into different components. Ideally, you design it based on vision and mission, thinking about how you are going to do it. That informs who you need with what skills, and when. We need fewer generalist political officials, and more people with eclectic interests from nuclear weapons to drugs; we need more versatile people today than we needed before. You don't need so much data gathering; it's all available. You need advocacy, promotion overseas; you need different kinds of foreign service officers.[59]

In the absence of any agreement about where the State Department was trying to go, the workforce plan stalled.

As staffing reductions bit into agencies' ability to perform their tasks, the amount of outside contracting was increasing all over government. In many cases, the result was clearly beneficial. In other cases, the contracting was controversial. One problem was that it was not clear that there was a net savings in dollars for the government from contracting out. Sometimes it was cheaper to provide services in-house. One adaptation to this problem was for some governmental agencies to provide services for others, on contract, rather than going to the private sector. Some big departments with good computerized data processing began offering services to other, smaller units. The practice was controversial because in some cases it replaced contracts with the private sector. Representatives of those companies and industries believe that there was not a level playing field and that they could not compete because of the way that overhead was calculated on these intragovernmental contracts.

While contracting within government generated only a little controversy, contracting that extended beyond housekeeping tasks such as payroll and cleaning services to core functions was more problematic. OPM contracted with an ESOP [Employee Stock Ownership Plan] created by its own RIFed employees to provide background checks for candidates for federal employment. Such background checks had been a core function for OPM. HUD used contractors for technical assistance to grantees. Employees in agencies doing that kind of contracting, as well as observers, wondered if enough in-house expertise was being maintained to supervise the contractors. Contractors turn over, and when they do, all the experience they have gained may go with them if there is not a sufficient core of contract supervisors in the agency. Informants expressed the following reservations:

> Another part of this emphasis on reduction in staff and increase in contracting out is an increase in unmonitored third-party government. Ron Moe has written on this, in PAR [Public Administration Review], in regard to NPR. Ron points out the situation—the administration is eliminating middle management and emphasizing contracting out, but middle managers were monitoring the contracts; now no one is watching.[60]

> Our response on staffing has been totally irrational. Contracting out has been a reactive response; we have been fortunate to have money for technical assistance, for grantee support functions. A lot of grantees don't have program training from HUD in three years; who knows what they [the contractors] are telling people. I don't have confidence in the quality of what is being told. Do they really understand programs and requirements? The field offices select more of the contractors. Some field officers are good, but there are an equal number of weak offices. To what extent do the contractors selected have a good knowledge base or understand if clients are being correctly informed?[61]

Hollow government results not just from contracting out with inadequate supervision, but also from weakening of the organizational memory and from loss of key staff. Longtime hiring freezes that prevent the hiring of people with key skills in high turnover slots also contribute to less effective government and government that looks like it can do more than it can.

The focus of the administration in the NPR was to reduce the number of government overseers, those in the agencies and in the Inspector Generals' offices whose responsibility it was to check on the work and honesty of the remaining officials. The goal was to reduce staffing at these senior levels dispro-portionately. Part of the effort to avoid RIFs was to prevent the loss of the new hires rather than the old ones. Buyouts were generally more effective than RIFs in controlling who would leave the agency. While it looked to the outsider as if a massive number of highly experienced staff were leaving more or less at once, many agencies did not report problems as a consequence, but for some, the result was serious loss of institutional memory:

Of the SESers in OPM, only about ten or fifteen are left. I just heard about another one who retired. Everyone who can is getting out and the others are in marginal positions where they cannot affect policy. There is no institutional memory left. They used to talk about short-term memory loss, now they are talking about Alzheimer's.[62]

For some agencies, the inability to hire new staff to fill gaps in staffing was more severe than the loss of senior staff. The General Accounting Office, for example, was wrestling with skills gaps years after its major personnel reductions.

CONCLUSION

A great deal was learned in the federal government over 17 years of efforts to balance the budget, especially at the macro level of designing legislation that would encourage balance. But that learning should not be overdrawn; it is important to pay attention as well to the problems that were not solved, the things that were not learned. The continuing erosion of funds in the discretionary portion of the budget and cuts from major entitlements were not planned rationally, in the sense of considering the most important policy issues first or addressing the long-term issues and not making short-term decisions that would exacerbate the long-term problems. Some programs may have been cut more than they should have, considering their impor-tance and effectiveness. But the issue of whether the agencies were manag-ing better with less, as promised by the NPR, really depended on the adaptations and responses of the agencies themselves. When confronted with the question of whether they were eating the seed corn or trimming the herds, most gave a qualified answer of some sort, such as, "There is no clear answer to the question you pose. We do some of each."[63] The following chapters examine what happened to a number of agencies and how they adapted to the kind of pressures they were subjected to over 17 years of efforts to balance the federal budget.

PART ONE

Eating the Seed Corn?

CHAPTER 3

Information Agencies: Bureau of Labor Statistics and Bureau of the Census

ONE LOGICAL PLACE to look to see if the amount of seed corn is being reduced is agencies that supply information to the public to make business decisions and to government to make policy decisions. These agencies provide an information infrastructure, analogous to bridges and roads that are part of the physical infrastructure. But how would one know if these agencies had been damaged sufficiently to argue that the seed corn was being consumed?

Generally speaking, if the quality of information they provide is reduced or if information is delayed and made less timely, it would seem that seed corn is being depleted. If the agency is pressured to distort information or is forced to lower degrees of accuracy because of lack of funding or lack of authorization of research programs to update measures, then one can argue that seed corn is being consumed. If senior, experienced staff are quitting and new hires are not being made, one can argue the agency is drawing down its reserves. However, if the information agencies are cutting back low-priority programs or if important and useful programs are being shifted to the private sector where they are being provided at a reasonable price, these agencies may be trimming herds rather than eating seed corn as they cut back.

The Advisory Commission on Intergovernmental Relations (ACIR) and the Office of Technology Assessment (OTA) were terminated (ACIR in 1996, OTA in 1995); the General Accounting Office staffing was reduced by 25 percent over two years in the mid-1990s; the Bureau of Labor Statistics and the Census were under continual financial pressure. Even the National Science Foundation's social science programs came under attack. Interviewees argued that there was no pattern of intentionally weakening the information provision function of government, but weakening of information-gathering agencies does serve an anti–big government agenda. If data are not collected, then the severity of problems will not be reported and addressing such problems will not become a governmental mission. This argument was made by Senator Daniel Patrick Moynihan when the Advisory Commission on Intergovernmental Relations was terminated:

> Earlier this year, the House Treasury-Postal appropriations bill (H.R. 2020) zeroed out funding for the Commission. The Senate bill provided $334,000 for the Commission, but stipulated that no further Federal funds would be made available. . . . Mr. President, the first principle of public affairs is that you never do anything about a problem until you learn to measure it. I would add a corollary: if your purpose is not to address problems through government, you will put an end to attempts to measure them. I wonder if that is what is at work here. Surely, we are not going to balance the budget by eliminating the ACIR. What is this all about? . . .
>
> Mr. President, the ACIR does important, if largely unheralded, work. And we stand on the brink of terminating it. This is a mistake which we will regret. . . . Mr. President, getting back to my first principle of public affairs, Lord Kelvin stated it best: When you can measure what you are speaking about, and express it in numbers, you know something about it; but when you cannot measure it, when you cannot express it in numbers, your knowledge is of a meager and unsatisfactory kind: it may be the beginning of knowledge, but you have scarcely, in your thoughts, advanced to the stage of science.
>
> Mr. President, without the ACIR, our knowledge of important matters will never be anything more than meager. The action we are about to take will harm our capacity to govern effectively.[1]

Whether or not the weakening of the information-gathering agencies was intentional and policy related or just part of the general downsizing of government, many of the information agencies were cut back in budget and staffing. Two of the information agencies, Census and the Bureau of Labor Statistics (BLS), got caught up in policy and politics, increasing their visibility and making rational cutback more difficult. Information agencies trade on their reputation for professionalism and neutrality; if that reputation is damaged, they become more vulnerable to cuts and manipulation. The Bureau of Labor Statistics was necessarily caught up in the redesign of the main inflation index because of the desire of politicians to help balance the budget by slowing down the growth of outlays pegged to inflation. The Census Bureau tried to redesign the Census to save money and in the process antagonized congressional interests.

The BLS is in the Department of Labor, and the Census Bureau is in the Commerce Department. BLS and Census are similar agencies in function, often contracting work to each other. They each provide information for decision making, inside and outside of government. Erosion of the quality and timeliness of information they provide is likely to affect adversely the quality of public and private decisions.

BUREAU OF LABOR STATISTICS

The Bureau of Labor Statistics was cited in Washington as an illustration of an agency that was able to cut back in a rational manner. The agency had devised an accounting system before the cutbacks began that allowed managers to figure out exactly what each product line cost and to cut by product line rather than across the board. The result was continuing high-quality products. Also helpful, the agency had a history of long-term, professional directors and a reputation for neutrality, staying above the political fray. There were efforts to politicize the agency and to manipulate reports during Richard Nixon's presidency, but those efforts were remembered and still sensitive in the 1990s. Agency staff felt protected and secure, staying in place many years, providing continuity and memory. Though confronted with threats of layoffs and furloughs, the agency staff believed they were part of a family that would cope together.

In some ways, the Bureau of Labor Statistics pointed up what so many other agencies did not have and were unable to put together: a plan, stable apolitical leadership, loyalty, and an ability to drop some product lines rather than cut across the board.

Devising an Accounting System

BLS devised an accounting system in the late 1970s for management purposes and then found in the early 1980s that its accounting system was invaluable in handling cutbacks because it allowed the agency to know the cost of each product line in detail. With the accounting system in place, when cutbacks came the agency had only to determine which were the core functions of the agency and which were peripheral. Former commissioner Janet Norwood recalled:

> Then, in the first Reagan administration, there were large cuts. We had to go to OMB and Congress with a reduced budget; we had decisions. We wouldn't cut across the board. It would have been easier for management, but it is a terrible way to run a government or a company. We decided—I decided—not to do it that way. Define the basic core of data, and then the periphery. That was difficult, everyone thought that theirs was core. We had to have the CPI, unemployment, business survey, wage data, productivity, define the core. Some things outside core were useful, but not core.[2]

Norwood argued that the agency would not have been able to get through the cuts in 1981 without the accounting system.

As the associate commissioner for administration, Dan Lacey, summed it up,

> We do budgeting by program and product line. There are 20 major programs, such as employment and unemployment, the CPI, the international price program, etc. Each component has an individual budget rather than an object class approach that pushes them together. The result, the bureau has the capacity to add and subtract from the budget in clear programmatic terms. When the level of the budget drops, we stop a product line, put a program out of business, rather than pare every program and make them all suffer. We can keep only the organizational core of programs adequately funded.[3]

Neutrality and Technical Expertise

Since the beginning of the BLS, the agency had a reputation for technical skills and political neutrality. The BLS was headed by a commissioner with a four-year appointment that was often renewed from one administration to another. The commissioners carefully nurtured their image as nonpolitical, not involved in policy. The agency in general did not like to be connected with the "politicals" in the Department of Labor. Commissioners were picked who had impeccable professional reputations and who were outstanding leaders in their field of expertise. Their long terms in office enabled them to develop relationships with Congress over the years.[4]

Lacey described the agency's reputation and ethos with a great deal of pride:

> BLS has one of the highest reputations for the quality it produces. We have been heralded for 100 years as the most objective or one of the most objective. We enjoy that reputation. It spills into everything we do. Our technical staff is always concerned with the quality of data, won't produce questionable data. A minimum threshold of quality is ingrained in the institution and in the budget. If you produce schlock— we won't produce schlock. It's the institutional posture. . . . Goes back to the early years, the formative years of the institution.[5]

Norwood confirmed that the agency kept out of policy disputes. She said the agency's role was to formulate the problems, so the political folk would know what to pay attention to, but to stay out of policy issues. She noted that when reappointed by President Clinton, she was confirmed in the Senate by both Democrats and Republicans. "I am proud of that," she said; the agency "is nonpartisan and professional. That has helped." Norwood argued that staying out of policy issues while being useful helped maintain the independence of the bureau.

Norwood was not inventing a strategy of neutral expertise, but carrying on the traditions of the agency:

> The bureau has had that tradition. The first commissioner was commissioner for 20 years. He really established principles. The bureau would be involved in judicious investigation of fact, fearless publication of the results thereof. The bureau has had a long history of independence.[6]

Norwood's long term in office and her reputation for professional integrity allowed her to take an active stance in educating Congress about the technical issues the agency confronted. She prepared assiduously for Capitol Hill hearings and spent a lot of time educating staff who were users of BLS data:

> IR: The essence of your system was the need to maintain quality.
>
> JN: Yes, but it was my judgment; my judgment about quality might be different from someone else's. How to explain that? You have to develop a reputation as a professional. Some people will understand. And we explained everything, we made a real effort to work with staff all over Congress who made legislative use of our data. I wanted to know what they were using it for, so we could tell them how to use the data, so they wouldn't be blindsided.
>
> [I spent] a great deal of time and effort on budget preparation. Very high standards. We had all the answers on the Hill. That was very important, I felt.
>
> They asked about the cost of the program. Why it was important, how it was different from the past, why we needed equipment. Sometimes they thought we were going a bit too far, but they accepted much of what we did.[7]

Despite the agency's best efforts, however, it did get caught up in a very tense policy debate over the recalculation of the Consumer Price Index. In the middle of that debate, Commissioner Katharine Abraham argued at a hearing that if asked for a recommendation by the president, her response would be that it was his policy decision and not her role to make a recommendation. Her responsibility extended only so far as explaining where the bureau figures came from. As Abraham reiterated in her testimony in 1997,

> As you know, the Bureau of Labor Statistics is not an agency with policy responsibilities or, indeed, an agency that appropriately involves itself in any way with policy decisions beyond providing relevant information to policymakers.[8]

This strategy of policy neutrality did not protect the agency from all cuts, nor perhaps was it intended to. The agency took direction from Congress as legitimate and cut accordingly, sometimes with relatively positive results. The agency weeded out less important programs, those that could be provided by the private sector, and weaker programs.

Negative Effects

Positive outcomes were jeopardized in several ways. First, it was difficult to get targeted cuts through the White House and Congress. Second, in a more or less frozen budget, once the agency had successfully trimmed down to basic core programs, it was difficult to cut one program to improve another one. Third, constraints on management, including those on staffing levels, made it more difficult to manage the agency's limited resources wisely. Finally, contracting out created some management problems that made rational cutback techniques harder to implement.

Opposition to Targeted Cuts. Programs proposed for elimination had clienteles that often argued vociferously for continuation. Norwood said she had gotten a lot of criticism for making targeted cuts. "The users can be vocal, they can get to the White House and Congress. We got calls from both of them. Even though the White House was instituting the cuts. People who lost their data were upset."[9]

The associate commissioner for administration, Dan Lacey, indicated that the agency was not always successful in getting its proposals for cuts approved:

> Every program has a broad and influential constituency, states or businesses or academicians. A group of influential and satisfied clients. Eliminating those things [programs] is a problem. . . . We have to discuss the consequences of operating at reduced levels and what will be given up. We are sometimes told that we cannot give up a particular item. Congress has restored funding that we would have eliminated. Congress does not wish to have [some things] eliminated. . . . They can say yay or nay. We proposed some eliminations they did not want and some others they accepted.[10]

Inability to Modernize. A second problem developed; that is, once the core functions were defined, weaker programs weeded out, and programs with narrower constituencies turned over to the private sector, the strategy of targeted cuts was difficult to repeat. As Norwood commented, "We eliminated everything around the core. As time went on, there wasn't much left but the core." It became difficult if not impossible to fund the research necessary to keep up-to-date and get the conceptual issues correct:

> The most serious problem that gets short shrift is research for improvement. That is what you lose, particularly in the future in BLS. Maybe

it is different in different kinds of organizations. Statistical indicators, you have to keep improving them, you can't stand still. There was some damage of that kind.[11]

Lacey explained that new programs had replaced the older ones, but that modernization of existing programs had become impossible. The amount of money spent on programs, adjusting for cost increases, was pretty flat for more than 20 years, but within those numbers there was a lot of churning. Old programs were eliminated in larger numbers during periods of cutback and more newer ones were added during periods of recovery. The number of new programs just about covered the number of older programs eliminated, but these periods of dieback and new growth did not account for the costs of modernizing the continuing programs:

It costs $50 million to revise the consumer price index every 10 years. And modernizing some of the other surveys, the current population survey that we do jointly with Census, that hadn't been modernized in 50 years. That was expensive. All of this is going on in fixed numbers. The state agencies collect a lot of data, their costs make costs increase. These are nonprogrammatic.[12]

Detailed Controls. Detailed budget controls, across-the-board cuts, and especially staffing controls made it more difficult to manage money wisely. The agency was pressured to comply with the Government Performance and Results Act, which emphasized plans and documented outcomes, and the National Performance Review (NPR), which advocated more managerial flexibility to reach those planned goals, but the reality was that the agency was still hemmed in by rules that made good management more difficult. The caps and cutbacks, divorced from programmatic concerns, made it more essential to budget every dollar wisely, but the spending rules made that enterprise more difficult.

Norwood was sensitive to the contradiction between the output measurement focus and the input controls on staffing and other constraints on budgetary implementation. Inability to carry over money from one year to the next for capital purchases was frustrating, and constraints on the numbers and rank of employees reduced the discretion of managers:

All the budget process, it almost seems as if it were developed to make it more difficult to manage. We went through several periods when we had to go through budget on the basis of people, not dollars. Constraints on dollars wasn't as serious as constraints on the number of people who worked for the government. Grade restrictions problem.[13] I am out of sympathy with that. If you want it rationalized you should give money and leave the grade level controls to the managers.

Every administration wants to prove, or alleges that, it reduced the number of people on the government payroll. Reagan, Clinton, Bush, Carter, it goes on and on. The focus was on people and grade levels. I used to get angry. If I can get the job done with 10 grade 15s and lots of machinery, I should be able to do that. But then the grade level of government would go up and that wasn't permissible. There were controls. Maybe some managers needed controls, but maybe all managers feel they don't need controls.[14]

Contracting. A final difficulty mentioned in terms of managing the cutbacks to maintain quality in remaining core programs was created by contracting out. The Bureau of Labor Statistics used to share some programs with the Census. When it came time for cutbacks, BLS did not have the freedom to cut these programs in the same way it did its own. As former commissioner Norwood described,

> We used to contract with the Census Bureau. Census would collect household data and Bureau of Labor Statistics would collect data on establishments. We did contract work. Basic labor force data, the Census Bureau did that. As manager, that was difficult when we were cutting back. It was harder to manage quality because it was in the Census Bureau. They would cut out all training, I would never do that. If my staff came in with something like that, I could say, We can't do that, look at *x* or *y* instead. But when you contract with another agency, it is harder to do; there is a different perspective.
>
> As we move more into public-private partnerships, we need to keep that in mind; we need to keep people in-house to ferret out these differences. You cut your own programs more than something you have contracted out.[15]

Protecting Employees and Employee Morale

Agencies were threatened not only by actual cuts, but by possible cuts. Fear that cuts might occur during the year were particularly problematic, given the dual goals of maintaining the quality of the data and protecting the employees.

Norwood noted that because Labor's budget was considered with Health and Human Service's (HHS), whenever HHS's budget was held up, say, over an abortion issue, Labor's budget was held up as well. This caused enormous stress on management and threatened personnel with furloughs because the agency administrators had to guess at the budget and estimate how much work they could accomplish but were not allowed to overspend. If agency managers overestimated and spent too much on data collection and analysis, the overage would have to come out of staff salaries in terms of a furlough:

> One period we went without a budget for a whole year. We struggled. It's a felony to overspend. But on the other hand, we wanted to protect the quality of the data and the staff. A lot of agencies furloughed. They played it safe. I didn't want to unless it was absolutely necessary. We would do it at the end of the year if necessary.
>
> We had a series of meetings with all the employees. They should know what was going on, even if it wasn't good information, it was all we had. We talked about the need to cut back. We might need furloughs. We asked them to find ways to save money to avoid furloughs. We made them feel a part of the decision making and made them feel that senior people cared about the staff. That is tremendously important.
>
> We got through that year. We did finally get a budget, and no furlough. A furlough at the end of the year would have been worse for the data, but it was worth the risk.[16]

This episode illustrates not only the agency's efforts to protect the employees, but also to keep them informed and to draw them into the decision making, using their ideas and making them less helpless in the face of budget cuts. From 1993 to 1996 the agency managed to avoid reductions in force through buyouts, evenly spread between headquarters and the field, and nonreplacement of staff who left. The buyouts were concentrated in the secretarial and clerical ranks, because more modern technology made many of these positions superfluous. This pattern, of avoiding RIFs and furloughs, of including employees and keeping them informed, was repeated through many episodes of cutback. The result was a loyal and long-term workforce. As one employee put it, "On the whole, BLS, metaphorically, likes to see itself as a 'family,' with a strong paternalistic streak among its senior executives. 'We take care of our own.'"[17]

Political Pressure

Information agencies can become more vulnerable to pressure to distort information during a time of cutback. They may be able to resist such pressures less than in the past for fear that resistance would show up in budget cuts, and elected officials may be more willing to pressure the agency to enhance the appearance of balancing the budget. BLS staff generally believed that pressures on them to distort the budget were far in their past, that they had successfully maintained their independence, and that the newspapers were helpful in alerting the public to any efforts to compromise the agency. If the agency were under political pressure to change data, however, staff might not be willing to talk about it.

Despite assurances from staff that the agency had strictly maintained its professionalism and not been pressured recently to change data, it was clear that the BLS had not escaped completely from pressure to reduce the consumer price index. The CPI became a major policy issue in January 1995, when Alan Greenspan, chair of the Federal Reserve, reported to the budget committees that the CPI was highly biased upward. Subsequently, the Senate Finance Committee held a series of hearings and then appointed an advisory commission on the amount of bias in the CPI. The commission's interim report indicated the CPI was biased upward, that it had been biased as much as a percent and a half in recent years, and would be biased by a percent or so over the next few years.

Responding to Greenspan's insight that it would be easier to balance the budget if the CPI were reduced, Speaker of the House Newt Gingrich tried to force quick changes on the Bureau of Labor Statistics: "This weekend, when asked about [Alan] Greenspan's comments, the Speaker of the House said that he would give the Bureau of Labor Statistics people '30 days to get it right' or he would fire them and give the job to the Fed." Newt Gingrich's position was that if BLS did not revise the index downward quickly—presumably without technical study—it would lose the responsibility for making the changes. Gingrich reportedly threatened to cut the BLS out of the budget if it did not make the changes in 30 days.[18]

Reducing the CPI was expected to help balance the budget by reducing Social Security payments (which are indexed to the CPI) and increasing payments of income taxes (which are adjusted downward for inflation). For political reasons, it would be easier for elected officials if the BLS altered the index to make inflation look lower instead of directly reducing benefits that were linked to the CPI or increasing taxes. If the BLS made the changes, the costs to recipients of the payments would be considerable, but the politicians would not have to take the blame.

There was widespread political support for revising the inflation index so that it reported a slower inflation rate, but it was not clear that a technical reevaluation of inflation would come up with such a conclusion. The Boskin Commission, convened by the Senate Finance Committee, argued that the CPI seriously overestimated inflation. Not everyone, however, accepted the work of the commission as either neutral or research based:

> The Boskin Commission's work is a poor basis for changing the CPI. As the Commission itself acknowledged, it did little original research. The Commission's membership was stacked with economists who believed that the CPI was overstated. According to Dean Baker, an economist at the Economic Policy Institute, "All five members had previously

testified that they believed the CPI was overstated. Economists who gave contrary testimony . . . were excluded." According to Joel Popkin, another expert on the CPI, the Commission comprised five of the six witnesses before the full Finance Committee who gave the highest estimates of bias. As Mr. Popkin also pointed out, the interim report of the Commission falls far short of presenting adequate justification for its conclusions and therefore provides no basis for Congress to change tax policies or entitlement programs such as Social Security.[19]

Present and former officials at the Bureau of Labor Statistics were skeptical about the level and the direction of bias in the measure. They generally agreed that there were a variety of problems with the measure but argued that there were insufficient data on many points to know whether the index seriously overestimated inflation.

Former BLS commissioner Norwood argued that the CPI might actually understate inflation—a technical reevaluation might go in the opposite direction to what the politicians wanted to see. The BLS does a separate study of the purchasing habits of the elderly and found that the CPI may underestimate inflation for this group because of the cost of prescription drugs. Presumably the elderly are an important subgroup when considering inflation adjustments for Social Security recipients. The present commissioner claimed to be agnostic on the subject of whether the CPI was biased substantially upward.[20]

Those pressuring the agency to revise the CPI downward wanted the impression of technical neutrality, but not necessarily the reality. The reality was that much of the research necessary to determine how much and even whether the index overestimated inflation had not been done or was not complete. The precise number that the Boskin Commission came up with was a case of misplaced concreteness—that is, making something look much more exact than it was. To support its conclusions and make it look as if there were widespread consensus among technical experts on the Boskin figure, Michael Boskin took a survey of specialists on the CPI and announced that they all agreed with the Boskin Commission estimate. Boskin sent the survey to 24 people, of whom 18 responded. But despite the intent to show broad support by noncommission economists, Boskin included the four other commission members in the survey (two of whom did not respond); they thus agreed with themselves, a heartening response, but not convincing about the existence of a broad consensus. Moreover, others who were known to oppose the Boskin results because the underlying data were not there were not surveyed.[21] Regardless of the quality of the survey, it represented an effort to muster support for a particular number that the index should be reduced, in the absence of sufficient information.

How did the agency respond to all the pressure, knowing that the technical issues were substantial, that the politicians wanted the index to move downward quickly, and that there was insufficient evidence at hand to warrant specific technical changes of the size the politicians wanted?

The initial response was twofold. One part of the early response was to make some necessary technical adjustments quickly, to provide a reduction in the index smaller than what the Boskin Commission suggested, but that was based on easily justifiable technical grounds. A second part of the agency response was to say, leave the issue with the agency, we understand the sources of bias and are working on reducing them. Do not legislate a solution without adequate technical grounding.

BLS supporters in Congress underscored the plea for patience. They probably thought that waiting for the BLS to document the level of inflation better would slow down the process of cutting the entitlements to the elderly and would result in less dramatic drops in the estimates of inflation:

> The major problem with the [Boskin] Commission's analysis is that the sources of bias it identifies are also identified by the nonpolitical professional economists at the Bureau of Labor Statistics in the Department of Labor. They have the responsibility for setting the CPI each year. They do so fairly and impartially. They make periodic corrections to take account of any biases—up or down—that affect the index. The Bureau already plans to reduce the CPI by about two-tenths of 1 percent in 1997. This reduction is already assumed in the budget projections for the next seven years.
>
> The issue is not whether there should be changes in the CPI, but who should make them and how large they should be.[22]

A second level of response was to demonstrate to Congress that the agency was being responsive to the recommendations in the Boskin report insofar as they were technically sound and to point out the ways in which the Boskin report was not sound. In some cases, the agency had sufficient data from other sources to be able to comply on an experimental basis with the recommendations of the commission. If the experiment did not work out, that component could presumably be modified before including it as a formal part of the CPI. The agency thus bought itself time on the one hand and argued for technical correctness on the other. In other cases, the data did not exist to do what the commission recommended or technical problems remained, and the BLS commissioner carefully pointed out these areas.[23]

A third level of response was to point out the effects of resource constraints on the agency and on the research necessary to make the recommended improvements. President Clinton recommended funding for CPI research in BLS in the 1998 budget proposal, and the BLS commissioner in addressing the Senate Finance Committee referred to requests the agency would be putting in.

In hearings before the House Budget Committee on the CPI, both the chairman of the committee and the ranking minority member repeatedly offered to see that any agency budget requirements necessary to speed up the revisions in the calculation of the CPI would be met.

Did the BLS yield to pressure on this matter? It did lower the CPI, but by nowhere near the amount demanded and made no changes without solid numbers underneath. Some members of Congress, however, were not satisfied with this BLS response and the pressure continued.

One congressional response was to set up a commission outside of the BLS to fix any remaining bias in the index that the bureau was unwilling or unable to fix. The commission would be composed of respected economists. The Clinton administration offered guarded support for the proposal, but some Democrats in Congress, including House minority leader Richard Gephardt, opposed the plan, as did some Republicans, saying that it was sprung on them without gaining much political support in advance. Gephardt argued that the decision should remain with BLS and be made on technical grounds.[24]

Adding to the heat, Senator Trent Lott told President Clinton that he would lose an opportunity to come to agreement on a balanced budget by 2002 if he did not yield on the matter of setting up a commission to change the CPI. But House Republican leaders Newt Gingrich and Dick Armey tried to curtail Lott's enthusiasm, arguing that open Republican pressure to reduce the CPI would be used by Democrats against Republicans in the next elections.[25]

At the end of February 1997, White House Chief of Staff Erskine Bowles began to explore the feasibility of the commission idea. He was reportedly asked in a meeting with Newt Gingrich, Dick Armey, and Senate Democratic Leader Tom Daschle, all of whom opposed setting up a new panel to change the CPI, whether a new commissioner could be chosen who would be willing to change the index more radically, and if so, whether changes could be made fast enough to enter into the current year's budget calculations.[26] They were reportedly told that the commissioner could not be removed before the end of her term in October 1997, except for cause.[27] For precisely the purpose of buffering the agency from political pressure, the BLS commissioners are not appointed at the pleasure of the president. These opponents of a commission were not against changing the CPI but wanted the BLS to do the job and were willing to change the director or threaten to change the director to get the index changed by the BLS.

Greenspan weighed in again on 4 March 1997, on the side of setting up a commission outside the Bureau of Labor Statistics to make changes in the CPI, although he tempered his comments with requests for the Bureau of Labor Statistics to make whatever changes it could make quickly and for Congress to see to it that the BLS had the funds to carry on the research necessary to get better figures. At the same time, however, he argued that enough information currently existed, without additional research, to lower the CPI figure. Greenspan argued,

The essential fact remains that even combinations of very rough approximations can give us a far better judgment of the overall cost of living than would holding to a false precision of accuracy and thereby delimiting the range of goods and services evaluated. We would be far better served following the wise admonition of John Maynard Keynes that "it is better to be roughly right than precisely wrong."[28]

After a week of trying to drum up support on the Hill for the commission approach to adjusting the CPI, President Clinton backed down from supporting the proposal, despite the resulting threat to the balanced budget negotiations. White House officials argued that Clinton had been unable to muster the bipartisan support necessary to back the proposal because of a widespread public perception that an adjustment to the CPI made by an ad hoc commission would not be based on technical changes to the index but would be a quick fix to balance the budget.[29]

In response, BLS updated for the first time in eleven years the market basket of goods purchased. This change resulted in a relatively noncontroversial reduction of about 0.2 percent in the consumer price index. Then the BLS made a change in the formula used to add up prices of different items and in handling hospital charges. The estimated immediate reduction in the index was an additional 0.3 percent.

On 16 April 1998 the Bureau of Labor Statistics reported that it had adopted a new way of calculating the CPI that included a substitution effect—that when the price for one good goes up, consumers often purchase something else, closely related but cheaper, instead. The BLS announcement indicated that the agency had examined purchasing data and looked over the literature and found support for the idea of substitution but was unable to document the extent to which the phenomenon occurred.[30] The Boskin Commission had argued for including substitution effects, and several years after the Boskin recommendation, the bureau adopted this approach, while admitting that it had little data documenting the extent to which substitution occurred. The BLS estimated this change would lower the CPI by about 0.2 percent per year, beginning in January 1999.

This change to include substitutions was controversial, since it is not clear when people do make these substitutions, and whether the substitutions are of comparable goods or services or represent quality declines. Switching from a model that assumes no change from one product to another to one that assumes people always change does not anchor the results in detailed research and suggests that the agency was still trying to demonstrate compliance with the Boskin report.

The first two changes were expected to result in a reduction in the CPI of 0.5 percent; the third change should add an additional 0.2 percent, for a reduction of about 0.7 percent annually in the index, as compared to the 1.1 percent over-estimate reported by the Boskin Commission or 0.5 to 1.5 percent overestimate described by Alan Greenspan.

It appeared as if the bureau was slowly yielding to pressure, but not without some underlying research. While seemingly yielding at this level, the agency was holding out for a selective use of the substitution model. That is, people may switch from Granny Smith to Delicious apples when the price of Granny Smiths increases and Delicious apples are less expensive, but people may not switch between prescription medicines in a similar situation, and the degree to which they would switch was considered a matter for research to determine. Bureau commissioner Abraham continued to resist the external commission idea as a way of adjusting for any additional (upward) bias in the index, and that put her on a collision course with some legislators.

In early January 1997 Commissioner Abraham made a presentation to the American Economics Association in which she argued that her agency would not and should not produce a CPI based partly on subjective judgments. Then she argued with the Finance committee that the BLS's role was to produce "statistics using reproducible methods that yield reproducible results, methods that we can write down and describe. . . . If we get into the business of making judgments about things that are not measurable—guessing, even if it's . . . a best guess—we . . . would be undermining the credibility of all of the data we produce."[31]

The pressure on the BLS was intense. One cannot say that data results have been distorted by the political demands of budget balancing, although research that would lead to an *increase* in the CPI has certainly not received the attention that means of *reducing* it have received. One can say that pressure to report numbers without sufficient research underlying them has been much greater in recent years and that the agency has had to devote much more attention to responding to these pressures.

A lower inflation index would have made it easier to come to an agreement to balance the budget by 2002. If the bureau made the reduction, rather than a commission or Congress through legislation, the bureau would help protect politicians from the fallout of reducing inflation increases to Social Security recipients. In the face of enormous pressure, including the possibility of creating a commission to do what the bureau would not do or would not do fast enough and inquiries about firing the commissioner or at least replacing her after her term was up in October 1997, the agency's response has been measured. For several years, at least, the BLS has taken the high road, educating everyone on the Hill whom they could reach. Whether the results are seen as biased or not depends on whether one agrees that the CPI overestimated inflation in the first place and, if so, by how much. But at least part of the downward shift in the CPI was based on incomplete research, by the BLS's own reckoning.

In general, the Bureau of Labor Statistics is a success story. The agency was able to maintain the integrity of the numbers produced in the face of budget constraints and intense political pressure. Congress did not allow all the agency's candidates for program elimination to be terminated, but the agency was able to sort through core and peripheral programs and cut back to the core, eliminating weaker quality programs and less central programs. The agency avoided RIFs in more recent years and furloughs in the earlier years, through a variety of techniques including buyouts of clerical positions no longer needed because of computerization. Agency morale remained high.

Part of the agency's success may have been due to its scrupulous neutrality, the high esteem of the commissioners, and the continuing efforts of the agency to educate Congress and congressional staff. As Norwood put it, the agency was not involved in policy, but it was useful. However, the agency did eventually get drawn into a policy debate. Its CPI program became increasingly sensitive as a way of cutting entitlements and increasing revenues (just change the indicator of inflation). While the director drew criticism, the agency was not explicitly sorted out for deep cuts. Bouts of cuts were alternated with periods of recovery. The major problem over the long haul was no increase in the budget and the resulting inability to do the research necessary to update data-collection programs. This problem was serious and represented a gradual depletion of seed corn for this agency, despite its policy of targeting budgetary cuts. Ironically, the pressure on the agency to reduce the CPI may result in more adequate funding of research in an effort to speed up the technical work.

CENSUS

The Census Bureau is an executive branch information provider like the Bureau of Labor Statistics. Like the BLS, the Census Bureau emphasizes professionalism and accuracy of information. The Constitution of the United States requires a decennial enumeration of population, counting all residents, as a basis for the apportionment of representatives in Congress. The Census Bureau carries out this census and performs a number of other tasks involving collecting and analyzing survey data.

The Census Bureau is a little more structurally vulnerable than the BLS:

There is a difference between the commissioners of BLS and the Census Bureau. [The] Census [commissioner] is a presidential appointee with Senate confirmation, who serves during the president's term. The maximum is four years, but they never start at the beginning of the new administration, so there is turnover every two to three years. BLS is more fortunate: it has more stable leadership; tenure is five to ten years. The BLS commissioner is still nominated by the president, but the terms don't coincide with the terms of the president. I would like to see us get to that point, all the statistical agencies should have that structure. It gives more independence to the commissioner.[32]

Because the director of the Census does not usually start at the beginning of the president's term but does end with the president's term, the typical director's term is two-and-a-half to three years, compared to five to ten years for the commissioner of the BLS. The former BLS commissioner proudly referred to her tenure through many administrations, Democratic and Republican, but the Census director could not claim such longevity. Holding their office at the pleasure of the president, Census appointees are necessarily closer to the fray than BLS commissioners, who can be removed only for cause.

The Census Bureau also became a bit more vulnerable in the reorganization of congressional committees that occurred in 1994, when the Republicans took over majorities in both houses. The committees that have jurisdiction over the Commerce Department do not have jurisdiction over the Census Bureau. The Census itself has a permanent authorization, and so the oversight committee for the Census has no role in authorization of its budget; the appropriations subcommittee is more important to the decennial census. Moreover, in the 1994 reorganization the committee that did have jurisdiction of oversight for Census was eliminated, and the committee that was given the oversight role had neither knowledge nor much interest in the census, except as the issues affected them more broadly as members of Congress, namely reapportionment of seats and balancing the budget. The support that agencies often get from their authorizing committees was just not there for the Census Bureau.

In general, low priority was placed by a number of members of Congress on data needs; some legislators pressed for the elimination of the long forms that were sent to a sample of households and for simplification of the short form. The goal was not only to increase the mail-in response rate, and thereby lower costs, but also to reduce the level of intrusiveness of government into private lives.

At a session with census advisory groups, Dr. Martha Riche, then the Census Bureau director, reported that Rep. Hal Rogers (who handles oversight of the bureau as well as appropriations) opposed providing funds for the long-form questionnaire regardless of previous legislative requirements and was very critical of the redesigned, user-friendly, short-form questionnaire. Another Census Bureau staff member added that the FY 1996 budget hearings before Congress had a chilling effect on several aspects of the year 2000 census design process, particularly the overall questionnaire design and the prospect for collecting comprehensive data using a long-form questionnaire administered to a sample of the population.[33]

The focus of congressional concern was initially on simplifying the forms, but after the bureau's announcements of its reinvention plans for the year 2000 census, the attention shifted to the bureau's efforts to save money and improve counting of minorities and homeless people through sampling techniques. In particular, many members of Congress were concerned about whether the count would allow for an accurate redistribution of House seats based on population changes.

If the Census Bureau's structure and the division of power among its oversight and appropriation committees exposed it to more pressure and gave it less support than the BLS had in the Department of Labor, the Census Bureau's location inside the Commerce Department exposed it to further problems. Commerce has been a highly politicized agency, working directly with the Democratic president and the Democratic National Committee in the 1990s. When the Republicans took over Congress in 1994, Commerce was a special target for them. Attacks on the Commerce Department in 1995 threatened the Census Bureau with across-the-board cuts.

But Census's main problem in the mid-1990s was how to gear up for the decennial census. The Constitution requires an enumeration, or counting, of every individual. The costs for the decennial census build from year to year until they swell massively during the count itself and then taper off. The pattern of gradual buildup to the census year and tapering off expenditures after the census year did not fit into the glide path of budget balance in 2002; the census's costs were going up just when Congress wanted them to go down. Congress was not being obliging about funding the decennial census, putting enormous pressure on the agency to bring down costs, but at the same time, some in Congress were highly critical of the Census Bureau's plans for cutting costs.

The second major problem was that the Census Bureau was often unable to fully fund surveys other than the main episodic ones. When funding got tight for these other programs, the Census Bureau was often not able to eliminate programs or product lines in the way that BLS did when money got tight. For one thing, until 1996 the Census did not have an accounting system that would allow it to make the kinds of adjustments that the BLS routinely made. Second, the Census Bureau found that it often was not permitted to cut out product lines. The result was a continuing erosion of the existing programs.

These two problems resulted in a number of consequences. The Census Bureau often had to reduce sample size, to the point at which the reliability of the data was beginning to come into question. Even on the decennial census of population, cost-cutting proposals led to reduced quality checks and bureau admissions that the quality of data might be deteriorating.[34] Some products were dropped, at least one was shifted to another agency, and there was enormous pressure to simplify the forms and reduce the amount of information collected.

The Decennial Census of Population and Housing

The Census Bureau began to run into trouble as early as the 1990 census. As the decennial census reports came out, it became clear that many people were not counted; moreover, costs were going up and voluntary response rates were going down. The Census Bureau was advised by the National Academy of Sciences to get costs down and, it was hoped, boost accuracy in counting, by using in a limited way statistical sampling for the households that did not return the survey. The plans for the year 2000 looked reasonable technically, but there was a possibility that they violated the constitutional requirement for an enumeration. (The Supreme Court did later judge that sampling techniques were illegal for the purpose of determining the number of House seats.) Many representatives were upset with the proposals because they appeared to introduce an element of subjectivity into the politically crucial apportionment of House seats by state, a process dependent on the head count of population.

Those who supported the census sampling procedures did so in the hope that the new process would eliminate the undercount of the poor and minorities; those who opposed the new procedures were more interested in accurate counts of population shifts between states and believed that such counts should be the priority of the Census Bureau and that major resources should go into that endeavor, and if necessary, be withdrawn from other programs. Because the allotment of House seats and possibly the boundaries of elections districts depended on the census, the technical issues of how the census was going to count the public took on a partisan tone.

The Census Bureau confronted a seemingly impossible situation. It had to cut back costs and it had to improve quality. The major source of money saving in the year 2000 census proposal was a one-in-ten sampling for the last 10 percent of respondents (after they had failed to return a census form). The reinvented census also included an intensive sample of respondents that could be used as a check on the mailed-in forms and to adjust the numbers where they did not seem reasonable. This proposal to maintain quality with lower budgets was opposed by some key members of Congress. Those members reportedly took out their anger in further reduced budgets. According to House Report 104-821,

> The Census Bureau has proposed a budget of $3.9 billion for the 2000 census, with major savings achieved by accounting for the last 10 percent of the population through a 1 in 10 sample. However, Congress has shown a reluctance to fund the census at this level. Both the FY 1995 and FY 1996 budget resolutions funded below the requested level, and the chairman of the Commerce, State, and Justice Appropriations Subcommittee has indicated that the Census Bureau will not be funded at the requested level for FY 1997. Both the House and Senate Appropriations subcommittees have proposed funding only about two-thirds of the increase requested to fund 2000 census activities in FY 1997.[35]

Funding for the year 2000 census may have been affected by the sampling issue as early as FY 1995, even though the Census Bureau did not announce a formal plan with sampling in it until February 1996. Rep. Charles Taylor from the House Appropriations Committee noted in questions to the Census Bureau that a number of representatives had written to Commerce Secretary Ron Brown in June 1994 arguing that using a sample to determine apportionment in the House was unconstitutional and violated statute.[36] The bureau argued back that as long as it had tried to enumerate everyone and merely finished up with a survey of the nonrespondents, it was within the constitutional requirements and could sample. That response may have seemed willful to those opposed to sampling.

House Appropriations Committee members were certainly aware of the sampling issue, and some were especially concerned about the implications for apportionment. Harold Rogers, the chair of the House Appropriations Subcommittee on Commerce, Justice, and State, a key actor in determining funding for the year 2000 census, explained his, and the subcommittee's, intense interest in sampling issues. After a strong critique of the short form of the census, he concluded,

> So we are going to ride herd on this thing. This is a special interest to everybody on this subcommittee. My state, for example, lost a congressional seat last time because of the ineptitude of the Census Bureau. In fact, it was my seat that I had to scramble around for. That is a personal thing with me, but that is one of the big reasons for the census, is to reinforce the country's democratic process. And it was botched last time, and that gets to the very basic building block of the democracy we live in.[37]

Rep. Thomas Barrett of the oversight committee for Census was blunt in saying that the budget cuts were the result of opposition to sampling. He also pointed out that if Congress wanted to return to the enumeration model, it would have to fund the census to carry out the enumeration:

> Those of us who oppose the Census Bureau's sampling proposal must put the money where our mouths are and adequately fund the Census Bureau and State and local entities involved with census efforts. I am disappointed that the majority of this Congress has expressed their disagreement with the Census Bureau's sampling proposals by slashing the Census budget.[38]

One might argue that the Census Bureau's cost estimates for the census were inflated, and thus Congress's cuts were not threatening to quality or timeliness. However, the GAO argued that if the year 2000 census were conducted the way the 1990 census had been conducted, it would cost $4.8 billion over 10 years. The

Census Bureau's estimates of the 10-year costs for the year 2000 census, including the effects of sampling, had gotten that figure down to $3.9 billion. It was the latter figure that was being cut.[39]

In 1996 Appropriations Subcommittee members asked about the consequences of the delayed or reduced funding over the next few years. Since the overall budget was based on funding particular innovations, if the funding was insufficient in the years leading to the census, they wondered what would happen. The answer was that the improved address lists the Census had acquired would not be sent to the local governments for corrections; the bureau would be unable to experiment with different forms to see how people respond to them; and the agency would be unable to acquire scanning equipment to read citizens's responses directly into the computer.[40]

The issue of prohibiting sampling continued to come up. In November 1997 the White House and congressional Republicans struck a deal in which House Speaker Newt Gingrich was given the authority to use government money to sue the Census Bureau to prevent statistical sampling. An oversight board was set up to monitor the bureau's preparations for the year 2000 census. In return, the White House got approval to finance continued preparations for the census, including a dress rehearsal for the sampling procedures. Just before Christmas in 1997, the Census Bureau director, Martha Riche, resigned. She reportedly found that the continued political pressure interfered with doing a good technical job. Her resignation made it more questionable whether the agency would have the political clout to resist Republican demands.[41] The administration nominated and the Senate approved the choice of Kenneth Prewitt as successor to Riche. He promised to try to smooth over the conflict on sampling but agreed with the bureau that sampling was necessary. Thus the resignation of Riche and the choice of a successor did almost nothing to tone down the level of controversy. Prewitt and the bureau awaited a decision from the courts as to the constitutionality of sampling.

In the meantime, sparring between Democrats and Republicans over sampling and the budget continued. Republicans threatened to budget only through March for the Census Bureau (in the event, they budgeted through June). Democrats countered that the results would be harmful to the bureau and wanted its budget to continue to be linked to the Commerce, State, and Justice appropriations, as that would add a little more pressure to Congress to make a decision and continue the funding:

> At a news conference before the board meeting, Commerce Secretary William Daley said any interruption in funding would require the bureau to lay off workers and delay signing vital contracts, which "could do irreparable damage to Census 2000." He said he would probably recommend that President Clinton veto legislation limiting the bureau's funding.

Within a few hours, Republicans fired back, with Rep. Dan Miller (R-Fla.) saying that the threat to veto the funding bill could "shut down the FBI, close our embassies and hold up U.S. foreign policy over the Census." Miller chairs the Census subcommittee of the House Government Reform and Oversight Committee.[42]

Interestingly, Republicans on the bipartisan oversight committee wanted more access to Census Bureau offices and records—security provisions required them to request permission in advance to visit offices after hours or on weekends.[43] This complaint made it sound as if the Census were doing something sneaky and that Republican investigators could catch them at it if only they did not have to announce their coming in advance.

In January 1999 the Supreme Court ruled that an enumeration, as opposed to sampling, was required for the determination of House seats but did not forbid sampling for other purposes, such as redistricting or allocation of grant money according to formula. The Census Bureau could thus do both, an enumeration and some sampling, but the costs were necessarily going to be higher than with the sampling alone. The administration filed an amended budget request, reflecting an increase of $1.7 billion. Legislators asked the General Accounting Office to determine if all the increased costs in the request resulted from the Court decision forbidding sampling. GAO responded that as the Census Bureau explained it, most of the costs were the result of the Court decision. Republicans who had promised they would fund the Census if it carried out an old-fashioned enumeration were now stuck with that promise, but they had no way of funding the request under the caps. A kind of compromise was reached, in which the Census request would be fully funded but treated as emergency spending, not offset by other cuts. That compromise struck some legislators as budgetary manipulation, but it did handle the issue of increased costs and included requested funding for checking the results.

Pressure from Congress to micromanage the Census Bureau did not go away, however. Although the Court had ruled that apportionment of seats could not be done on the basis of sampling, it did seem to allow redistricting to be based on sampling estimates. Republicans introduced a bill that would allow a post-census review of the results by local communities before they became official.[44] The effect of such a review would be to allow population estimates to be contested or reversed if redistricting resulted from sampling. At the least it would delay the results of the census. This provision passed the House Government Reform Committee. The committee also voted a number of other measures that would affect how the Census carried out its business:

Also along party lines, the committee voted to require the bureau to send out a second mailing and include 33 languages on census forms, provisions the Democrats oppose as micromanagement and that the bureau says it already has considered.

Commerce Secretary William Daley, in a letter Tuesday to Government Reform ranking member Henry Waxman, D-Calif., wrote that he would urge President Clinton to veto the bills. "According to the Director of the Census Bureau, Kenneth Prewitt, and the professionals at the Census Bureau, these three bills would reduce the accuracy and seriously disrupt the schedule of the Census 2000," Daley wrote.

On a voice vote, the panel also approved less controversial bills that would allow recipients of federal benefits to take census jobs without losing their eligibility; require the bureau to promote the census in all schools; provide an additional $300 million to fund a census advertising campaign; and set up a grants program to promote the census.[45]

The disputed provision on postcensus review did not pass Congress because of the determined opposition of Democrats, but pressure to add postcensus review continued. The bipartisan census oversight committee issued a report in September 1999, arguing that according to its analysis, statistically adjusting the census totals would fail, falling far short of the need, because it might improve the totals for the nation but would not correct totals in localities. The report argued that these statistically corrected totals might detract from efforts to get a better count. The committee issued a number of recommendations, including hiring locals from the neighborhoods where undercounts were greatest and also allowing postcensus review.[46]

While postcensus local review was not adopted in fall 1999, another effort at micromanagement was put in place. The House passed a version of the Commerce, State, and Justice appropriation that contained new rigid appropriation constraints that would force the Census Bureau to ask for a reprogramming to meet virtually any contingency that cropped up during the administration of the census. The result would be delays in the field, not only because the Census Bureau would have to get approval of the commerce secretary and OMB, but also because Congress would have to examine and approve the request or at least not deny it.[47]

Prior to fall 1999 Congress had put various constraints into reports accompanying legislation, without actually including the constraints in the legislation itself. The constraints used to consist of fairly conventional limits on transferring money internally among programs or divisions. But the fall 1999 proposals went considerably further in micromanagement, legislating funding "frameworks." The frameworks were the work components of the census, such as checking addresses, hiring staff, collecting data, and automation. The appropriations language forbade movement of money among these work elements without a formal reprogramming request. The director of the bureau complained that the result would seriously hamstring the bureau in carrying out the census.

The measure passed the House and made its way into the House-Senate conference, but the president vetoed the Commerce, State, and Justice appropriations bill. However, Congress repassed the appropriations bill with the reprogramming requirements intact. The appropriation was enacted into law 29 November 1999.[48] Thus the Census not only had a bipartisan congressional panel to watch the implementation of the census, it also had a redefined budget structure that added many constraints to the budget and increased the requirements for requesting reprogramming permission—thus formally getting Congress into the details of administration.

Politicization of year 2000 census procedures and reduced funding curtailed reinvention and made it more difficult to achieve lower costs with improved accuracy. At the same time, the bureau was getting extensive criticism of the complexity of the forms and their length, the argument being that such complexity and length discouraged people from filling out the surveys. A higher initial response rate would reduce costs of the census substantially. On the one hand, this proposal makes eminently good sense, and anyone who has ever had to fill out the census's long form will undoubtedly agree. On the other hand, the effort was to strip away as much information as possible from the census, virtually everything other than the constitutionally mandated head count for the apportionment of Congress. The appropriations subcommittee members showed little understanding of how the census data were used or what they were needed for.

They seemed particularly eager to eliminate the long form, which is a one-in-six sample that is administered alongside the decennial census and provides much of the detail of the census data. The Census Bureau seemed willing to do so in favor of a continuous gathering of data updated each year, but it wanted to do the long form one more time to establish baselines. User groups were concerned that once the long form was detached from the required decennial census, it would be more vulnerable to cuts, reduced sample size, and possible elimination. Since much of the material requested in the long form is required in the statutes, eliminating it entirely would be more difficult than the committee initially may have envisioned. But any questions that do not have legislative underpinning could be eliminated. And the threat of systematic underfunding, smaller samples, and lower reliability remains real even if the census does manage to change from a decennial to an annual or continuous updating.

A third element in the pressure from Congress on the agency was to get costs shared more with users. Since many users of census data are other governmental agencies as opposed to the private sector, this pressure seemed strangely misplaced. At its best it would shift the cost of the census data from one agency to another, with no reduction in costs to the federal government. In response to this pressure, the Census Bureau spun off the census of agriculture to the Agriculture Department, a move supported by both relevant sets of congressional committees. The spinoff of the agriculture census from the Census Bureau to the

Department of Agriculture did not affect outlays, according to the Congressional Budget Office (CBO) analysis of the proposal. It merely shifted a budget item from one agency to another.

From OMB's perspective, since there was no cost savings, allocation of costs from Census to each of the user agencies was not high priority. Census director Riche expressed surprise at the pressure from the appropriations subcommittee to shift more of the costs of the census onto other governmental users, since it seemed less efficient to put money in each unit's budget and let it buy needed services from Census. One reason might have had to do with the budget caps, as shifting an expenditure from one department to another would ease the caps for one subcommittee and make them tighter somewhere else.

The Ongoing Surveys

Census divides its programs into two types. One, part of the regular salaries and expenses budget, funds the ongoing surveys. As costs in this part of the budget do not swell from year to year and then taper off, these surveys have not created headaches to the same extent as the decennial census or the quinquennial studies. Funding for this portion of the budget has been relatively stable. What has been problematic, however, has been the adjustments to base.

Expenditures increase in nearly any budget, without programmatic expansion, because of mandated salary increases and increases in rents, utilities, postage, and the like. In many years the adjustments to base from required salary increases, increases in postage costs, and other routine expenditures run 4 percent, and Congress grants only 3 percent. The result is a little belt tightening that agency officials believed was probably beneficial in preventing or eliminating wasteful practices. But some years the adjustment to base was 4 percent and Congress granted nothing, forcing the agency to cut 4 percent to come up with the mandated increases.

The Census Bureau had three options to handle this sort of cut. First, it could let staff go; second, it could eliminate programs; and third, it could cut the size of the sample for the sample surveys. Deputy Director Bryant Benton argued that the bureau usually needs the staff on a continuing basis, so that letting staff go was not a viable option. Sometimes it eliminated programs but it often lacked the discretion to cut:

> One of the things that is usually unspoken, I hope Janet [Norwood] told you this, it is not always a unilateral decision about what to cut. Sometimes there is some gamesmanship. Sometimes it is not politically acceptable to cut those. Congress may tell you "no" or the parent agency may tell you "no." That takes away options, you have to use the fall back, cutting the sample to save money.[49]

The most frequently used option was cutting the sample size. When the sample size grew smaller, the margin of error grew larger, and the cost per unit increased:

> With some programs we are getting precariously close to the margin. Because as much as we may footnote the data, most users assume a quality level of stats that may no longer exist. That is a problem for users and other federal agencies that use our data to make significant program decisions.
>
> . . . Budget reductions are having an effect: diminishing quality. Since the Census Bureau has a strong desire for high-quality data, that is very painful. That is not just a professional desire [for good quality] but we know what data are used for and want decision makers to have reliable information.[50]

In addition to reducing the sample size, sometimes the Census Bureau delayed products to accommodate to lack of resources. According to Benton, "As a result, less timely information was made available."

Other Impacts

The limits on the Census Bureau budgets have pressured the agency to prioritize and drop some lower-priority programs. It is not clear how long this process can go on without dropping more important items and those that are linked to other crucial indexes:

> In fiscal year 1996, we eliminated several surveys to fund our work on the new North American Industrial Classification System. In fiscal year 1997 we will continue to eliminate or postpone lower priority surveys and reports so we can focus our efforts on our priorities, namely, implementing Census 2000 and the related Continuous Measurement Program, modernizing our measures of the nation's economy, and increasing the reimbursable work that helps support the census infrastructure.[51]

Periodic programs proposed by the Census Bureau for elimination in 1997 included census of Puerto Rico, Survey of Minority-Owned Business Enterprises, the Survey of Women-Owned Business Enterprises, and the Census of Mineral Industries.[52] In April 1997 a congressman asked about dropping the Mineral Industries Survey. He asked then-director Martha Riche to explain how the decision was made. She replied that the decision to drop mineral industries did the least harm to the national economic statistics, the gross domestic product, and related statistics. Mineral industries was the smallest sector and it had the least growth. The congressman was clearly displeased that something so important could be dropped.[53]

Riche reported that staffing levels at the bureau declined from 1986 to 1996 by 15 percent of the full-time equivalent employees.[54] This figure compares two periods before the major increases required by the decennial census. This change may include the spinoff of the Agriculture Survey, but it also reflects post-1990 reductions in force and more recent reductions by attrition. The attrition reductions resulted in increasing the average age of the labor force and reducing the inflow of young people with fresh skills and ideas. The agency was struggling to cut lean operating budgets to create enough resources to hire some young people:

> There has been minimal hiring in most professional fields for eight or nine years. What that does to us—When I address our staff, the average age of the audience is mid-forties, in fact 44 years. I look at those people and wonder about the future of the organization. We need new blood to become the lifeline to the future of the organization. Senior statisticians, demographers, computer scientists, etc., the pipeline isn't there.[55]

With an average age of 44 and an average retirement age of 56 to 57, many of the employees are at or near the end of their careers. The Census Bureau was feeling the need for new recruits so badly that it cut back on travel to spend more time on recruiting and hiring 150 young people and it planned to do that again.

Another impact of budget reductions has been to reduce the number of Census publications available in hard copy and to increase the electronic distribution. Not all potential users of demographic statistics have access to the Internet, creating a potentially skewed distribution of users. The overall impact of this change is hard to measure.

Summary

Census got caught in politics because its decennial census is the basis for apportionment of seats in the House, a very touchy political issue. With the reorganization of committees in the House, the subcommittee that used to oversee the Census Bureau was eliminated and the new one had little experience with and not much interest in Census. Power shifted more to the appropriation committees. Their interests, as well as the oversight committees' interests, focused on general issues affecting Congress—budget cutting, staying within subcommittee allocations, and apportionment. Unfortunately for the Census, it stood out because the decennial census increases costs in a lumpy way the budget balancing process did not foresee and also because it was located in the Commerce Department, a bête noire of many Republicans. The desire to control costs in the decennial census and improve accuracy led to increased use of sampling and more use of computerization; Congress was reluctant to fund Census to try out the new methodology and mistrusted it to do something as delicate as provide the basis for apportionment. Census's cost-cutting reinvention was thus underfunded. The Supreme Court's decision forbidding sampling for apportionment purposes jerked up the Census Bureau's costs. These costs were eventually fully funded, but as emergency spending that did not come under the caps.

Years of underfunding and cost cutting, combined with lack of freedom in cutting out programs, led to smaller samples in some regular surveys, eroding quality. Other effects included pressure to drop items and simplify the forms and cost share with other agencies, and an increasingly older staff. On the plus side, the agency is engaged in modernization of technology, has improved the address list for the decennial census, will be participating in the new financial management system of the Department of Commerce, and has made some internal tradeoffs, cutting lower-priority programs to fund higher-priority ones.

Congress got much more involved in the managerial details and technical decisions of the Census Bureau than it had with the Bureau of Labor Statistics. Congressional opposition to sampling was so strong that it treated the administration's persistence with a sampling plan as willfulness that needed to be closely watched. Committee members requested access to Census offices and files on weekends and at night without prior permission; they formed a special bipartisan committee to oversee the year 2000 census; and committee members recommended and approved detailed legislation mandating the number of languages in which the census should be sent out. Congress as a whole handcuffed the bureau by writing into the appropriation legislation constraints on spending the money, requiring formal reprogramming requests for shifting money from one work element to another according to need. Due to congressional pressure, the short form was changed from twelve to seven questions, and the long form was to be divorced from the census. The bureau had to focus its priorities on reimbursables that helped pay for the agency's overhead, even if those items were not as central to the bureau's mission. Costs for the census were scattered out to other departments that used census data, which had the side effect of obscuring the costs of the census and data collection. Director Riche was forced by the continuing controversy to resign her position.

The Census Bureau was more vulnerable to pressure than the BLS; it was less able to drop product lines; and its funding for nondecennial census work was eroding, forcing smaller sample sizes and erosion of product quality. The Census Bureau was unable to put in place its plan to preserve quality at lower cost; for the decennial census, it eventually got its funding, at great cost, and with luck, it will get more accuracy than it did in 1990. But the other surveys continue to slowly erode in quality. Congress's interest in the Census Bureau should die down after the year 2000 head count and reapportionment, but it is not clear what will happen to funding for the nondecennial surveys after that.

Conclusions

For information-producing agencies, the trick of cutback management is to reduce expenditures while continuing to provide good data. This difficult task requires a politically neutral leadership whose reputation allows the agency to do things in a technically appropriate manner without much political interference. The tasks for both the Bureau of Labor Statistics and the Census Bureau were made more difficult because they got caught in a political cross fire. BLS's problems occurred because it was the keeper of the consumer price index. A downward revision in the index would make the budget much easier to balance, and if the BLS did the work, the politicians could escape political blame for reducing pensions. The Census Bureau got caught because pressure to cut costs and maintain or improve standards led it to propose a reinvention that included sampling on the decennial head count, a proposal that was bitterly opposed by many members of Congress. While Congress tried to dictate what BLS should find in the CPI revision, it allowed the BLS to come up with the figures in any way it saw fit; in the case of the census, Congress, fearful of what the Census Bureau might find, dictated the process itself. It suited Congress's purpose for the BLS to appear to be independent, so it could claim an arm's-length relationship—the technicians revised the CPI downward, using their own (incomprehensible) technology. In the case of the Census Bureau, however, Congress needed the results of the 2000 census to be credible, but they definitely did not want the bureau to use sampling for reapportionment. Hence Congress fully funded the 2000 census, including quality checks, and it oversaw the implementation of the census in what must have seemed to the Census Bureau to be painful detail.

Both agencies suffered some erosion of quality, but Census probably suffered more, because it had more difficulty dropping product lines and had to resort to smaller statistical samples on its surveys and wider margins of error. Census users probably assume the quality of data remains as it always has, but the facts are otherwise. As for the CPI and the BLS, it is very difficult for a layperson to argue about how much the CPI overestimated inflation, but it is reasonably easy to see that the level of research necessary to make some of the assumptions made in the downward revision of the CPI was not carried out.

To some extent, BLS switched to guesswork from what had been rigorously tested indicators. The guess may be on target, but the process is questionable, especially in the face of the incredible pressure the bureau was under to come up with downward revisions. Much research was underway. It will be interesting to see if in later years any of the technical changes revise the index upward or otherwise modify the changes taken during this period.

CHAPTER 4

Budget Offices

THE TWO MAJOR budgeting offices in the federal government are the Office of Management and Budget (OMB) in the Executive Office of the President and the Congressional Budget Office (CBO) on the congressional side. Their functions differ somewhat but also overlap. They are both staff offices subject to contradictory pressures to perform in a neutrally competent way in order to serve elected officials of different parties and to provide policy advice that will be acceptable to the party in power.

The budget offices are different from the statistical agencies described in the previous chapter. The statistical agencies, ever cautious about appearing neutral, have no obvious role in policy analysis and recommendations. Their normal function was to provide basic information for decision making in a raw form. They got caught in policy imbroglios almost by chance rather than by design. By contrast, the budget offices were involved not only in providing raw data, but also in doing policy analysis and making recommendations in favor of one side or another in a controversy. These budget agencies could not duck policy issues. Efforts to balance the budget exaggerated the importance of their policy roles. Both agencies sought to find a balance between neutrality and credibility on the one hand and usefulness and centrality on the other. These budgeting agencies worked out different balances.

The politics of budget balancing made the role of the budget offices more difficult, in part because the numbers produced by these offices determined whether the politicians were in fact balancing the budget. The budgeting agencies faced overwhelming pressure to exaggerate the anticipated growth of the economy or underestimate deficits. The Congressional Budget Office had to deal with pressures for some type of "dynamic scoring," building in feedback effects of legislative changes on the economy, and later had to cope with pressures to make the surplus look larger; OMB had to wrestle with "rosy scenarios" and "magic asterisks," exaggeration of the predicted growth of the economy, and making the budget look more balanced than it was by claiming future savings not yet specified. CBO's role in implementing budget balancing legislation such as Gramm-Rudman-Hollings and the Budget Enforcement Act of 1990 gave it enormous power over legislative budget proposals, but no matter how it scored or evaluated the predicted budgetary impact of major proposals, either Democrats or Republicans would be irritated. CBO was directly in the line of fire.

The budget offices were not just more directly involved in policy decisions than the statistical agencies, they were also considered housekeeping agencies; that is, they served an internal, not an external, governmental clientele. Both the BLS and the Census Bureau had external constituency groups, user groups that wanted their products continued and wanted the government to uphold the quality of the products. In some ways those constituency groups made cutback more difficult and less efficient, because they made it more difficult to drop product lines to protect the quality of the remaining core items, but they also argued for continued funding for the statistical agencies. The Census Bureau was able to shift the census of agriculture to the Agriculture Department because there was a clientele group that wanted the data the Census Bureau had provided. By contrast, the staff agencies had only internal constituents, and when those turned angry or a legislator was unsatisfied, the budget agencies had little recourse.

The openness of the technical decisions made by the statistical agencies gave them some protection from charges of bias. When there was a question about methodology, the BLS posted every step it took on the Internet, maintaining a discussion of methodology with every possible user. Similarly, the Census Bureau tried to engage anyone who would listen in a discussion of the techniques and strengths of sampling, and how they intended to use it. But in agencies such as CBO, which seldom publicize the assumptions they make in their studies, it was easy for members of Congress to argue that CBO was making the wrong assumptions. OMB similarly has always operated out of the limelight. CBO and OMB could claim they were not biased, but no one would know for sure.

The problems confronted by OMB and CBO were both similar and different. OMB was a longstanding agency that had to be able to serve presidents of different parties credibly, over time. It could comply with desires of the current president but had to maintain its reputation for responsiveness and accuracy or it would be unable to serve the next president. OMB had an institutional reputation to maintain, which depended a great deal on who the directors had been and how those directors had seen their role and the role of OMB in the political system. CBO was a considerably younger agency that served Congress, which consists of majority and minority parties in both houses—sometimes a Democratic majority in one house and a Republican majority in the other at the same time. It developed a scrupulously nonpartisan approach to analysis, often presenting reports without conclusions or advice. Generally, Congress valued that nonpartisanship and helped preserve it, but if the majority party was determined to undermine that neutrality, the CBO was in a vulnerable position.

The main danger to CBO was less from budget cuts than from politicization. OMB had to deal with threats to budget and staffing levels as well as threats to its reputation for neutrality. OMB was vulnerable for several reasons. First, it was unpopular among governmental agencies, in part because it seemed to allocate cuts to them. Second, it was difficult or impossible for OMB to resist cuts while it was engaged in recommending downsizing for other agencies. Fighting threatened cuts would appear hypocritical. OMB administrators stated in hearings that they could not in good conscience ask for more money while they were asking other agencies to live within their means.

What has happened to these budgeting agencies over the 17 years of efforts to balance the budget? On the one hand, their responsibilities increased due to budget balancing activities and they became even more central to the policy debates, heating up the pressure to cook the data and bias the results. On the other hand, their impartiality became more important to brokering deals and defining balance. What happened to the quality of information provided to decision makers as they tried to balance the budget? What happened to the agencies themselves?

CONGRESSIONAL BUDGET OFFICE

The Congressional Budget Office is a small congressional agency with 232 authorized positions. It offers advice to the congressional committees that work on the budget, such as the Budget, Appropriations, and Revenue committees, Ways and Means in the House and Finance in the Senate. Created by the Congressional Budget Act in 1974, the CBO was intended to give Congress independent advice on the budget assumptions in the president's proposals and help Congress put together its own budget proposals. Part of the latter responsibility has been fiscal noting, that is, estimating the cost of proposed legislation. As the federal government struggled to rebalance the budget, CBO got an additional responsibility—to see if the new budget rules were being observed. This responsibility has been called "scoring" or "scorekeeping." Legislators often call CBO staff to ask, Can I do this? Will it violate the limits? How will this proposal be scored? CBO's role in monitoring compliance with budget ceilings and requirements for offsetting revenues or spending cuts has been contentious in part because the interpretation of the rules has sometimes been up to CBO. This scorekeeper function catapulted the small agency to a highly visible role[1] and increased the pressure on it to interpret rules one way or another. In addition to its direct and mandated role as scorekeeper, CBO has also had the role of estimating the degree of balance in the president's proposals. This assignment, too, put the agency into the line of political fire.

Neutral Professionalism

Like the Bureau of Labor Statistics, the Congressional Budget Office prided itself on its neutral professionalism. The agency boasts that it is composed primarily of economists and policy analysts with advanced degrees. Many staffers have had long and successful careers on the Hill or at OMB before coming to CBO and hence are known and respected on the Hill. As at the Bureau of Labor Statistics, the directors of the CBO have been economists and analysts of distinction.

One function of the CBO is to outline policy options, but the agency typically does not make policy recommendations, because the budget office for Congress must be strictly bipartisan. The agency's role as arbiter and scorekeeper or, as one congressman put it, referee in the budget process requires neutrality for effectiveness. Over the years, CBO's estimates of the deficit have tended to be slightly more accurate than those of the Office of Management and Budget, aiding the agency's reputation for neutrality.

CBO's directors are not as independent structurally as the commissioners of the BLS. They are appointed for four-year terms and can succeed themselves, but they can be removed by a resolution by either house of Congress. Between 1975 and 2000 CBO has had five directors: Alice Rivlin, Rudy Penner, Bob Reischauer, June O'Neil, and Dan Crippen. Crippen was in his first year in the year 2000; the average term for his predecessors was about six years.

Despite its best efforts to remain neutral, CBO's scorekeeping role has not allowed the agency to stay out of policy disputes. Former director Robert Reischauer had a reputation for offending both sides of policy issues equally, calling the shots as he saw them. This role became especially problematic when Reischauer scored the Clinton administration's health care reform proposals as costing the government money, despite the fact that much of the burden was to be picked up by the private sector. CBO's scoring probably contributed to the failure of the proposal on which the president had staked much of his political capital. In this instance, CBO was not only in the middle of a policy debate, but a key player.

What was worse, from the agency's point of view, was that staff did not and could not come up with firm numbers to support the position they took. Such numbers did not exist. All the agency could do was come up with estimates:

> The health care reform had to be scored by CBO. The agency did the analytical equivalent of picking numbers out of the air, well, that is too extreme, but picking the numbers from a range. The budget cannot use a range, so you pick a number from the range. People were uncomfortable with their role in the health care debate.[2]

Though the CBO is nonpartisan, it is necessarily involved in policy debates on subjects that are continually changing and for which decent methodology may not have been worked out. On the one hand, CBO is a mediator, often telling critical actors that they cannot do something—it violates the rules. On the other hand, CBO staff often do not have the certainty that BLS staff can have at their best. BLS staff are often looking at how people actually behave based on survey data; often CBO is trying prospectively to figure out how a piece of legislation might affect behavior. So CBO is both more vulnerable structurally than BLS and more structurally plunged into political controversy. Given this situation, its appearance of neutrality is crucial for its functioning.

As a result of its highly publicized policy stance in the health care arena, CBO relearned the importance of appearing neutral:

> CBO learned what Alice Rivlin [the agency's first director] knew from the beginning. CBO's credibility is tied to the perception of objectivity of its numbers. CBO calls it as it sees it. That is important. It was in the agency's interest to do that. The people at the top believed that leaning to the Democrats when the Democrats are in charge and to the Republicans when they are in charge is a losing strategy. Lots of staff on Capitol Hill are partisan; their advice has little credibility. Why does CBO have credibility? Because people believed CBO's numbers were not infused with politics. That belief did not apply to anyone else.[3]

When Congress changed hands in 1995, the Republicans, triumphant after many years of being totally excluded from power, were intent on putting their own people in key positions. This political thrust from Congress combined with the increased policy role and visibility of CBO to suggest that there might be major firings at CBO and a general politicization of upper-level staff, many of whom had been with the agency for its entire life or nearly so. In fact, however, major firings did not occur. The director, Robert Reischauer, was not reappointed, but only one other staffer was removed and that was reportedly the result of a personality clash between the new director and the staff member, not part of a Republican purge or agency politicization.

The shift away from threatening to make the agency more political through appointments reflected to some extent the emerging congressional understanding that CBO's reputation for neutrality was useful to the Republicans. They began to demand that the president's proposals for a balanced budget in 2002 had to pass CBO's scoring; CBO had to pronounce the proposal balanced. The president could not use his own estimates, prepared by the OMB.

Holding the president's proposal for balance up to CBO's standards served the Republicans' interests. In this case, the neutrality of CBO was crucial; the Republicans wanted a neutral and technically accurate arbiter, rather than the president's politically biased Office of Management and Budget. At the same time, however, a number of Republicans wanted larger tax breaks than the president was willing to grant as part of the balanced budget agreement. Some of these folks wanted CBO to certify that the Republican proposals for balance, which included large tax breaks, were sound and that the tax breaks were paid for. The result was some pressure on CBO to exaggerate the positive effects of the balanced budget proposals on increasing federal revenues and decreasing federal expenditures. The Joint Committee on Taxation was responsible for estimating the effects of tax cuts on the economy and hence dollar losses (or gains) from tax reductions; it fell to the CBO, however, to come up with dynamic estimates of the impact of budget balance, apart from the effects of tax cuts. A kind of dynamic estimate, involving feedback and secondary effects, this calculation was called the *fiscal dividend* of budget balance.

Dynamic scoring in terms of estimates of the impacts of tax cuts was used to justify major tax cuts during the Reagan administration. The argument was that tax reductions would stimulate the economy to such an extent that revenues would actually increase. Instead, a major recession occurred, reducing revenues and seriously increasing the size of the deficit. This memory was sufficiently vivid that many recalled it on the floor of the House or Senate while considering tax cut proposals in the early and mid-1990s. Senator Bob Dole in his 1994 effort to unseat President Clinton proposed a form of dynamic scoring in his campaign, but his loss to Clinton was interpreted by some as the public's loss of interest in proposals that seem to be too good to be true.

Dynamic scoring and fiscal dividends are both estimates for which there is little underlying data or knowledge. Despite the historical experience, pressure to use dynamic estimates kept recurring. The issue was salient in the selection of a successor to Robert Reischauer as director of CBO and in a proposed amendment to the legislative appropriations bill requiring the Joint Committee on Taxation and the Congressional Budget Office to provide dynamic analysis on request from the House, for informational purposes.[4] Pressure for dynamic estimates picked up again after the balanced budget agreement in 1998, when Republicans wanted to further reduce the capital gains tax. Because they were required by the Budget Enforcement Act (BEA) to find offsetting revenues for this substantial tax break unless they could show that it would not increase the size of the deficit, key Republicans wanted to increase the estimates of revenues and hence of budget surplus, so there would be no need for an offset. Bolstered by CBO's history of underestimating revenues during the latter half of the 1990s, Republicans pressed CBO to use more dynamic scoring:

> Gingrich and other GOP leaders have been hoping for a "July surprise" in the form of revised CBO estimates showing budget surpluses much higher than the $43 billion to $63 billion the CBO is forecasting this year, followed by $39 billion in fiscal 1999 and nearly $80 billion by 2002. Some GOP leaders said if revised surplus figures

were considerably higher—as much as $100 billion to $300 billion a year through the early years of the coming century—Congress could use part of the surplus for tax cuts and the rest to bolster Social Security.[5]

CBO and the Joint Committee on Taxation, which share responsibility for these estimates, responded to this pressure by indicating that future estimates of tax yields were unlikely to be high enough to satisfy the Republican need to show the tax cut as funding itself. Nevertheless, "CBO and Joint Tax Committee officials have agreed to rethink their analysis of the effects of reducing the capital gains tax rate."[6]

When asked how CBO had responded to this sort of pressure, then–Deputy Director Jim Blum denied that the agency was subject to much pressure for dynamic scoring, because most of the estimate of tax effects was done by the Joint Committee on Taxation. What fell to CBO was predicting the future of the economy, including the interest rate. Blum argued that CBO had long since been doing some kind of dynamic estimation of the fiscal dividend, that is, estimating that the economy would grow faster if the budget were balanced. The agency had been doing some form of dynamic feedback and fiscal dividend estimation since 1990. The estimates for the dividend reached a peak in 1995:

> We are responsible for bringing it [these dynamic effects] into use with the fiscal dividend from the balanced budget over six years. You would see higher growth rates if the budget was balanced. It was not really new, but it got big play last year. We did start that in 1990, during the summit negotiations [for the Budget Enforcement Act]. Because the economic situation was changing, we always needed a new forecast for the summits. The fiscal policy assumptions were $500 billion deficit reduction over five years. Developing that forecast, we did lower interest rates more than would otherwise have been the case, but we didn't make a big deal of it. Dynamic feedback effects.
>
> That came into bigger play last year [1995]. Our annual report a year ago, in January, . . . what if there were a balance accord? There would be a positive effect. [We estimated there would be] $140 billion [fiscal dividend] over a period of time. That was in the annual report of January 1995. We kept refining that estimate. [We paid attention to] the interest effect in the beginning, then we used economic models, there could be an economic growth effect, small but significant. We kept getting greater effects. It decreased in size later. Changing with new estimates for the economy. In December, after the president vetoed the reconciliation bill. We got the fiscal dividend way up. That is dynamic scoring. That is more than anyone has talked about since.[7]

By August 1995 the CBO had estimated the fiscal dividend resulting from a balanced budget in 2002 as $50 billion in 2002 and $170 billion from 1996 to 2002.[8]

In 1995 several changes had taken place that had the result of increasing the size of the estimate of the dynamic effect. Former CBO director Robert Reischauer had opposed the pressure for estimating a fiscal dividend, not because he thought there were no effects of balancing the budget, but because those effects were already taken into account in the economic assumptions underlying the budget. Reischauer had worked hard to educate Congress about the implications of dynamic scoring, but he was no longer director of CBO. Reportedly his successor, June O'Neill, was more supportive of dynamic analyses. Second, the Senate Budget Committee requested that CBO provide estimates of the interest costs that would be saved and revenues that would be increased if the budget were balanced in 2002.[9] CBO complied. However, by January 1997, while CBO was still reporting a fiscal dividend, it had gotten the numbers down from $170 billion over six years to $77 billion over five years.

While congressional leaders merely threatened to replace the BLS commissioner, but lacked the power to do so, they were able to replace the director of the CBO because his term was up. Some congresspersons were upset not only with the change but with the increased politicization of what should be neutral analyses. Senator Byron Dorgan was critical of the appointment of June O'Neill to be director of the Congressional Budget Office, in part because she was not of the professional stature of her predecessors and in part because she had said in testimony that she would consider dynamic scoring. Dorgan addressed the issue on the Senate floor, and though his discussion relates to taxes rather than to the fiscal dividend, it suggests the level of controversy around dynamic assumptions as a basis for decision making:

> I want to talk about referees for a second, though. One of the most important appointments that we are going to make in Congress is going to be the appointment of somebody to head the Congressional Budget Office. This person will, in effect, be the referee on budget issues, tax issues, economic issues. . . . We understand that the majority has decided to appoint Prof. June O'Neill to that post. . . . I come to express great concern about this appointment and to say, along with my colleague, Senator [Kent] Conrad, I am sending a letter to the President pro tempore asking that he not effect this appointment of Professor O'Neill to head the CBO. . . . I do not know much more than what I have read, but if what I read is accurate, then I am very concerned with the notion that they are finding someone who believes that when you score issues, they ought to be scored dynamically. What is dynamic scoring? This theory says that if you cut tax rates, economic activity will

increase to such an extent that the Government will actually collect more revenue. If you cut capital gains taxes, for instance, the Federal Government will supposedly collect a lot more money. Well, we have seen that sort of dynamic scoring in the past. This theory held sway in 1980 and 1981, and the result—$3¾ trillion later—was massive hemorrhaging of red ink in our Government. That is the result of dynamic scoring. Well, that is the kind of refereeing I do not want to see happening at CBO. I want scoring to be professional and to be nonpartisan.

There is a question about the Consumer Price Index—do we put somebody at the head of CBO who believes the CPI radically overestimates inflation, as Alan Greenspan said? The consequence would be to reduce the deficit, if you can say the CPI is overstated. And you can cut Social Security payments and increase taxes, as well.[10]

CBO director June O'Neill was reported to feel pressure from Congress to use dynamic estimates. She would certainly have been aware of a House proposal in July 1996 to require CBO and the Joint Committee on Taxation to provide alternative data with dynamic assumptions on request. The amendment was passed by the House, but the Senate budget committee stripped the provision from its version because it violated the Senate rules for considering a budget matter. The matter was resolved in conference when the House acceded to the Senate version and dropped the amendment.

Many relevant points came up during the debate on the amendment. One was that there was no agreed-on level or model that would generate dynamic effects accurately; another was that Congress should not be dictating assumptions for economic analysis to the CBO and the Joint Committee. A third point was that both organizations were already using dynamic scoring in those places where it could be reasonably justified. Fourth, though the amendment was presumably advisory, rather than mandatory to the budget committees, which make the final decisions on the assumptions in the congressional budget, all information from the CBO and the Joint Committee has the same status as recommendations that can be accepted or rejected.

Those who opposed the amendment pointed out that the goal of the amendment seemed to be to pay for the tax reductions that the Republicans wished to include in the balanced budget 2002 proposals, that the Republicans had sought to pay for the tax reductions under budget law in the prior year through cuts to health care and education, and that the public had objected, so that now the Republicans were trying to pay for the tax reductions by changing the assumptions underlying the budget. Republicans pointed out that with static budgeting, revenue tended to be overestimated when tax rates increased; the Democrats countered that Republicans overestimated revenue when tax rates were cut, when they used dynamic scoring. Equally important, opponents of the amendment pointed out that dynamic scoring of taxation was related to the huge overestimates of revenues that occurred in the Reagan administration that led to huge deficits, and that Reagan's budget director, David Stockman, had later repudiated dynamic scoring.

In fall 1996 CBO had its regular meeting with its panel of economic advisers and the topic turned to various kinds of dynamic assumptions. A GAO observer at the meeting noted the economists' discomfort with building dynamic scoring models into projections and Director O'Neill's insistence that something had to be done to comply with congressional pressure for dynamic analyses:

> There was a lot of talk about dynamic scoring, but the bulk of the economists who were there disagreed that the work should go in that direction, because it outstripped the literature, too much was unknown. Reischauer had commented that the direction of the relationships was often unknown; a tax reduction could reduce savings rather than increase them, because people's wealth goals were met. O'Neill said that she was getting requests from Congress on this, that they had to do something, at least a memo. What would be in the memo had not been worked out.[11]

The idea of dynamic scoring, using assumptions about people's behavior after a tax change or a likely interest rate change, to come up with budget numbers, was logical on the face of it, but there was little underlying data, little knowledge of how to do it or how much to assume. Using dynamic scoring was decidedly less fiscally conservative than not using it. Pressure to use dynamic scoring varied over time but kept coming back; at the same time, members of Congress remembered the consequences of dynamic scoring in the past and brought with them charts and graphs to show the history of underestimates of the deficit.

In early May 1997 the president and congressional leaders finally—after several months of negotiations and failed negotiations the previous year—came to an agreement on an outline for achieving budgetary balance in 2002. The agreement was close to reaching closure when it was attacked from the right and the left, and its fate became unclear. Since the agreement had to go through a variety of legislative hurdles before becoming law, widespread opposition to the agreement in Congress could torpedo the deal. At the last minute, CBO came in with revised estimates of revenue, not only for the current fiscal year but also for the next five years, creating a huge windfall that could be allocated to purposes that would mollify the critics and help ensure passage. The economy was growing rapidly so an increase in estimated revenues was expected, but the estimates for the out-years were not expected. CBO had reestimated revenues before other summits, so there was nothing out of line in doing so this time, but the seeming magic of the last-minute found money made some observers skeptical of what underlay the estimates for the out-years.

After the balanced budget agreement had been reached, and it looked as if the budget would indeed balance, many Republicans focused on trying to get bigger tax cuts. Increased estimates of the economy and revenues would produce larger estimates of the surplus and thus enable larger tax cuts without looking as if they were contributing to new deficits. But the Congressional Budget Office would not increase the estimate of the economy to that level, infuriating Speaker of the House Newt Gingrich, who threatened to punish the agency if it did not come around. Rep. Ken Bentsen protested Gingrich's attack on CBO:

> Today that [CBO] independence is threatened by partisan politics. Just last week the gentleman from Georgia, Speaker Gingrich, and the Republican leadership threatened the CBO because their budget forecasts do not square with the irresponsible budget resolution passed by the House. Truth be known, Houdini could not create the magic budget forecast necessary to make this budget resolution work. In his letter to the CBO Speaker Gingrich and the House leadership wrote that "CBO's low estimates have been consistently wrong and wrong by a country mile."
>
> If the estimates were not changed, Congress then must review the structure and funding for the CBO in this appropriations cycle if CBO did not conform its estimates to the majority's budget resolution. The majority is seeking to abandon fiscal discipline by using ever larger surpluses to pay for tax cuts we cannot afford while making draconian cuts in nondefense discretionary spending and allowing the national debt to continue to grow, putting Social Security at peril. In fact, this bullying reminds me of the old adage, that, "if you don't like the message, shoot the messenger." This is typically what dictators and strong men do when they take power. They terrorize those most likely to question their programs: professors, newspapers and religious leaders.[12]

Throughout the summer of 1998 Republicans continued to press CBO, trying to increase oversight of the agency. The aim was to establish a congressional budget board to oversee the agency, as well as a group of economic advisers who would review all the agency research, and to require CBO to disclose the economic, technical, and behavioral assumptions behind its estimates of revenue or expenditure impact. The agency already had an economic advisory board that met regularly.[13] In January 1999 the proposal was formally reintroduced to Congress and referred to committee, but it never got out of committee.

Throughout all this period, there could be little doubt about the extent of pressure on CBO. Congressional leadership was not happy with O'Neill and the

CBO under her leadership. According to the *New York Times,* "Republicans chose the agency's current director, June E. O'Neill, but House Republican leaders harshly criticized her last June. In a letter they said that the budget office had been 'consistently wrong' and had repeatedly understated economic growth and overstated budget deficits."[14] They chose O'Neill's successor, Dan Crippen, with a view to making the CBO more amenable to their views. Crippen had worked for President Reagan and for Howard H. Baker Jr., the Senate majority leader, in the early 1980s and was described as a pragmatic conservative. The *New York Times* reported that Senator Trent Lott explained to Crippen what was expected of him: "In a meeting with Mr. Crippen this week, Senator Lott made clear that he saw plenty of room for improvements. Some conservative Republicans have complained that the agency is dominated by what they see as the old-fashioned liberal views of career civil servants in senior positions."[15]

Given his party background, there was some concern that Crippen would be more political than his predecessors, especially in the face of this mounting pressure to come up with projections that would back up the Republican proposals for huge tax reductions. However, Crippen maintained the independence of the agency. CBO continued to make reasonably conservative estimates of the surplus, often making it difficult for some of the Republican policy preferences to pass:

> As a result, to an unprecedented extent CBO this year was ordered by Congress to change its scoring to match the more optimistic numbers being produced by the Clinton administration. Although CBO complied, it did so grudgingly; Crippen's crew made it clear that the congressionally mandated scoring did not represent their views of the budget future. In its year-end report, for example, CBO stated both what it had been told to do and what it thought would happen if its preferred estimates were used.[16]

CBO had reminded Congress earlier that the budget committees did not need to mandate particular kinds of assumptions in CBO reports, because the budget committees were free to tell CBO to use whatever assumptions it chose. While that stance shifted the burden to the budget committees, it understated the extent to which CBO would disassociate itself from the assumptions Congress insisted on. CBO thus technically complied, doing what it was told, but it also announced to the world that it did not agree with what the budget committees were telling it to do.

Part of the problem from the point of view of CBO was that the prediction of future surpluses depended on whether the caps continued to hold and what assumptions were made about inflation. Republicans insisted on using the caps and a no-inflation baseline to project future surpluses, both of which seemed increasingly unrealistic as Congress began to evade the caps and spend the surplus. CBO thus proposed to change the baseline to a more realistic one that reflected what spending was more likely to be.

CBO's combination of compliance and defiance resulted in Congress's shifting more to OMB's estimates, in a pattern called *directed scoring*. The budget committees scored the budget and estimated the future surpluses using the estimates it liked the best, in this case, mostly OMB's. In a time span of only a few years, the Republicans shifted from insisting that the president's balanced budget proposals be scored by the neutral CBO, and not the partial OMB, to choosing OMB's estimates of future surpluses and ignoring CBO's.

Overall, while CBO was subjected to considerable pressure to come up with larger estimates of the budget surplus and to use dynamic estimates that had no technically acceptable methodology, the pressure did not get completely out of control. Later estimates of the fiscal dividend were more constrained than the 1995 ones, and Director Dan Crippen has been insistent on moderating estimates of future surpluses, even at the risk of angering congressional leadership. As the deputy director of CBO had argued earlier,

> We just manage doing the best we can as we face new situations. I guess we are always in a situation, we are under a lot of pressure on scorekeeping decisions as to whether we stick to principles or make exceptions, give in to proponents. Our experience is it's better to stick to your guns, you get no credit for giving in.
>
> We may have known that instinctively, that is how we do our business. We are trying to do what we think is right, not what is the current policy of leaders of Congress or the administration. It's a fine line, sticking to guns, but not being so intransigent that you look stupid. You have to bend with the wind from time to time. We are better off standing tall.[17]

OFFICE OF MANAGEMENT AND BUDGET

The Office of Management and Budget is located in the Executive Office of the President. Its basic roles include solicitation of budget requests from the agencies, examination of the requests, negotiation with the agencies, and preparation of recommendations for the president's budget request. OMB prepares the underlying economic assumptions behind the budget, estimates the size of the deficit, monitors compliance with budget agreements, and examines and approves agency testimony and legislative proposals. It also examines and monitors regulations. Its role and mission have become more complex and demanding in recent years, including the implementation of the Government Performance and Results Act (GPRA). Generally, its staffing levels have not kept up with this expanded mission, with the frequent result of employee overload.

Founded in 1921 along with the General Accounting Office, OMB has a long tradition of neutral competence, but in more recent years that neutrality has come into question.[18] In part, the question has arisen because of an increasing number of political appointees in the agency, in part because it has under some directors become highly visible in making and enforcing budget and cutback policy. From 1981 on, when enormous tax breaks put the deficit into sharp relief, OMB has taken a more visible stance in cutting back spending. Decision making has became more top down, adding to the impression of politicization. David Stockman and later Richard Darman became highly visible political actors based on their roles as OMB director.

Throughout the Reagan administration there was an ambivalence toward deficits. More of the fervor of the administration was aimed at cutting back the size and scope of government and its regulatory machinery than balancing the budget. Nevertheless, deficits were embarrassing and the administration pledged to make them go away. The tension was resolved initially by a huge tax break, combined with efforts to make it appear that the tax breaks would not increase the deficits. OMB was at the heart of all this policymaking and implementation. As a result, its credibility and appearance of neutrality were damaged. The problem persisted into the Gramm-Rudman-Hollings years and into the Bush administration, when efforts were taken to avoid sequestration or across-the-board cuts without in fact reducing the size of the deficit by the amount of the targets.

In the Clinton years, the efforts to reach a balanced budget agreement with Congress intensified. The president's proposals were back-loaded, and OMB projected a robust economy throughout the period. The combination of projecting a strong economy and putting all the deep cuts at the end made it look as if the administration never planned to make those cuts.

OMB gained a reputation for politicized budget estimates in part through the confessions of former OMB director David Stockman to a journalist, William Grieder. Stockman admitted in print that he had fudged economic estimates while proposing tax cuts in the early Reagan administration. The goal was to make it look as if the deep tax cuts would pay for themselves by stimulating the economy and enhancing revenues. Stockman used the term that later came to refer to any overly favorable budget estimate, "rosy scenario."

Former OMB staffer Tom Cuny described how the rosy scenario was achieved:

> There was a "troika," consisting of OMB, Treasury, and CEA [Council of Economic Advisers]. Since before I started with the Bureau of the Budget, staff, the director, and the assistant director, with the troika, would come up with economic assumptions. Expenditures were estimated by agencies. There was this guy in the early Reagan administration . . . who was hired or recruited to use people from Claremont

graduate school to make revenue estimates, to bypass the troika. That way we could pretend to get oomph we knew we would not be able to get. We were supposed to get economic feedback by cutting taxes. We were not supposed to get big deficits.[19]

Overly favorable economic assumptions from the White House also characterized the Gramm-Rudman-Hollings years, when both the White House and Congress strove to meet deficit reduction targets without in fact making spending cuts. As one political appointee at OMB reported,

> The budget process has evolved, congressional processes especially, but executive processes too. . . . In Gramm-Rudman-Hollings, people thought they had a formula, reduce the deficit by x amount per year; there were rules that would get us there to zero deficit. We had to be able to say that the deficit would hit the target. Congress tried to meet these targets, while, in fact, not reducing the deficit. That took ingenuity. Not just Congress, either, it also affected the White House. One of my fondest memories from Capitol Hill was in the later GRH. The administration put forward a budget that met the target, but had no intention of finding the dollars that would do so, and threw the weight on Congress, through a rosy economic scenario. The midyear review was suddenly realistic. Both sides played games and became proficient at them.[20]

OMB had a key role in estimating the figures that would trigger a sequester or across-the-board cut under the GRH legislation. As one informant who was based on Capitol Hill reported, "OMB arranged the Gramm-Rudman-Hollings estimates so no further deficit reduction was needed. They did it by ignoring the state of the economy and ignoring how much the FSLIC would spend [to save the savings and loans that were in trouble]. By 1988 everyone knew the failed thrifts would be expensive, but OMB estimated zero cost."[21]

OMB not only made rosy assumptions during key policy battles; it was also hampered in its desire for greater credibility by its role in determining baselines. Thrust into the middle of deficit calculations and political credit claiming, OMB, along with CBO, made assumptions about the baselines from which deficit reductions or program cuts or expansions would be calculated. Decision makers can use the prior year's estimated actuals, prior year's requests, or constant services budgets as baselines. The constant service budget asks how much would it cost to deliver these same services next year, with no policy changes. This figure is then compared to the proposed budget. Constant services budgets can make a variety of assumptions about inflation. They can include the rate of increase in demand in entitlement programs. How much would this program cost if we do not take action to curtail benefits?

Elected officials could claim savings or program increases for the same program and same level of budget proposal, depending on the baseline used. It became difficult to tell what programs were being cut and how seriously they were being cut; it also became less obvious how much the deficit was shrinking and who could take credit for what improvements.[22]

Arguments against the use of baselines included that they did not communicate with the public and that they had built-in biases toward increases, because they usually included inflation and sometimes other kinds of increases; a baseline without these increases built in presumably would start with the assumption that programs would be cut by inflation rather than that they would remain constant with respect to inflation. But the idea of budgeting without baselines at all was not seen as reasonable by the technical, as opposed to the political, people in Washington.

As Ron Boster, a former Capitol Hill staffer argued,

> There are technical disagreements on what baseline to use—current policy and current law. It is a technical matter. Neither one does violence to the concept. CBO used current policy, OMB current law, or vice versa. No one argued against baseline budgeting. There was a kind of agreement.
>
> You can't do budgeting without baselines. Congress uses baselines; it is the only way to look at trends. The Republicans wanted to throw out baselines, but now they use them. You can't do it any other way. Whether you want to call it a cut or not is political, but from an analytical point of view, you have to use a baseline. It is the only thing that makes sense.[23]

The problem was thus not in the use of baselines, but in the fact that there was too little understanding of which baselines were being used by whom, too little agreement on definitions, and too much room for choosing which baseline to use over time and between types of program. The result was sometimes misleading, reflecting back on the credibility of OMB.

Although baselines were generally used consistently across programs and across time, some particular programs were treated differently. For example, in the early years of the Reagan administration, real growth was built into the defense baseline (over inflation), but in later years, the baseline included only inflation. Generally real growth was not built into the baselines. With this politically distorted baseline for defense, anything other than substantial increase in defense was considered a cut in the early Reagan years.

Another problem occurred because the idea and functions of baselines are different in mandatory and discretionary programs. In entitlement programs, comparison with the prior year's actual spending is not meaningful to recipients of benefit programs. They need to know what is happening to the program, and to do that, budget technicians have to factor in changes in demands, such as the number of claimants of benefits and the likely expense of their claims under the current laws or policies. If there are no changes in policies, what will the program cost? Baselines can be much simpler in discretionary programs, such as last year's estimated actuals plus inflation. Because of the conceptually different needs and complexity, standards for setting up baselines have differed between mandatory and discretionary programs. The results can sometimes be complex and sound illogical.

For example, costing out a proposal to change a complex housing program involves two components, one a discretionary portion and one a mandatory portion. On the discretionary side, the baseline was assumed to be the current rents, which were generally above market rates. So a shift to market rates, as proposed, would save money, compared to the baseline. But the result would be a large number of defaults on the properties by the owners, and HUD was liable for the defaulted property. The defaults would show up on the mandatory side of the budget. So, on the mandatory side, the baseline assumption was that contracts would be renewed at market rates. The portfolio reengineering that was being proposed would reduce the number of defaults and thus would save money: "The budget implies saving money on both sides. The main reason is two different baselines."[24] On one side of the budget, HUD assumed present rents, on the other, market rents, as baseline.

The lack of consistent and intelligible rules for calculating baselines contributed to OMB's reputation for declining "neutral competence" during these years. OMB has a unit on budget concepts that is supposed to work out what the basic concepts are and how they should be measured in a consistent fashion, but this part of OMB did not seem to receive much emphasis during the study years.

Budget concepts had always, since their inception, been subject to erosion by political officials. For example, the Commission on Budget Concepts had determined that the budget should be comprehensive. Taking programs off budget should therefore not have been an option. But in fact,

We have a permeable border on what is in the budget and what is not. Due primarily to wanting our cake and eating it too. The budget concepts are as clear and consistent as we could make them. But you cannot tell a budget director [of OMB] you cannot do that [take something off budget]. Shortly after the unified budget was put in place a couple of organizations or programs moved off budget by law, as a result of a deal struck by OMB [formerly BoB] on the Hill. There were off-budget and on-budget deals. You can see them in the historical tables. Shenanigans. The rule was, if it is federal, it belongs in the budget.[25]

The budget concept of inclusiveness has been ignored from time to time, including in the most recent period when proposals were actively debated to take transportation spending off budget. If anything, pressure to come up with a balanced budget has intensified political pressure to take programs off budget. Generally, however, this pressure has not been successful. Very few programs have actually been taken off budget.

It is difficult to demonstrate that budget concepts have less clout inside OMB now than in the past, but there does seem to be less emphasis on training new staff members into the budget concepts. As Rusty Moran, a longtime OMB staffer, described it,

> The transmission of knowledge is largely by word of mouth; it is of some concern to us, because there has to be a reason for an examiner to ask a question or we have to have a reason to communicate knowledge. We have some attempts at formal training; there is a new examiner [training] session; we try to pass it on in a structured way. At times, we have had an examiner handbook, with budget concepts in it, but it fell into disuse and was not kept up-to-date. Maybe we will do it again. We are researching that.[26]

OMB's reputation for neutrality and reliable estimates improved somewhat in the Clinton administration in part because of the excellent reputations of directors Leon Panetta and Alice Rivlin. Rivlin, first as the second in command and then as the director of OMB, had a reputation for being deaf as opposed to overly responsive to political implications. Nevertheless, the administration's proposals for a balanced budget in 2002 were back-loaded—with most of the cuts coming at the end—and assumed positive economic growth throughout the period. This high-profile proposal from OMB suggested political coloring.

The *Washington Post* argued that the proposed cuts in some programs were so deep they could not be real:

> Domestic appropriations account for a sixth of the budget. This is the catch-all category that covers everything from Pell grants to college students to the operation of veterans' hospitals, harbor dredging and the cost of the Border Patrol. Because they don't want to cut elsewhere, both parties have fallen into the habit of proposing without

much elaboration to cut this sector of the budget by anywhere from a fifth to a third in real terms by the year 2002. Cuts that deep can't be sustained, nor should they be; as a practical matter, they're fake.[27]

To add to the conviction that the cuts would never occur, several administrators told Congress that they did not believe they would ever have to take the deep cuts embodied in the 2002 agreements:

Veterans Affairs Secretary Jesse Brown and NASA Administrator Dan Goldin told congressional committees that they weren't worried that the Clinton budget proposed sudden, sharp cuts in funding for their agencies in the latter half of the five-year budget window. Both officials said they had received the president's personal assurance that those cuts would never happen.[28]

Although the president's proposals looked somewhat fake to many observers, it is not clear that OMB was the source of these proposals. Franklin Raines, who was director of OMB at the time of the budget negotiations for a balanced budget in 2002, was in the thick of the negotiations and hence was associated to some extent with the proposals, even though he kept urging the president to make more realistic proposals for cutting the discretionary programs. Though he was continuously present, and often negotiating with legislators on the Hill, Raines did not seem to be calling the shots on the negotiations. Erskine Bowles had that role, according to a newspaper account.[29] It was clear from the negotiation process that Raines (and OMB) was only one of the major actors for the president, and that his advice on the discretionary cuts was pretty well ignored.

OMB was an important actor, but only one of several, in the negotiations. In the words of one of the appointed officials at OMB, it was important because it was always at the table and had institutional memory:

We [OMB] are certainly central, in terms of accumulation of institutional knowledge and experience. Or maybe the Council of Economic Advisers [could do it], but they rotate. They bring fresh ideas, deposit them, and leave; there is no accumulation of institutional memory, no experience of how government works. It's valuable, but not the same kind of role as OMB. We are always in the room. We span the operation of government on the activity side; we have enough expertise on the revenue side and have the role of putting them together. We have to be there in the budget context.[30]

OMB was in the room, but like CBO, if what it recommended was not what the elected officials wanted to hear, its advice was ignored.

How Has OMB Changed?

What makes OMB special is its institutional memory, its experience of how government works. But that experience and that institutional memory have to be transmitted from one generation of employees to the next. During the period of the study, the ability to maintain that institutional memory was challenged. Changing roles of budget examiners, top-down management, and rapid turnover among newer recruits threatened the path by which knowledge was accumulated and passed on.

During the 1980s traditional budget examiners were replaced to some extent with policy analysts who "crunched numbers," providing data for the various scenarios the appointed officials were negotiating about. Rather than expert knowledge of the agencies and programs coming up from the examiner level, policy options came down from the top. Upward channels were sometimes blocked. Career staff waited for the right question from appointed officials before giving information. If the political appointees could not figure out the right question to ask, they did not get the information they needed. One former OMB employee noted, "Downward works okay. Upward, the communication is okay, but the listening is not always good. But it depends on who the PAD [program associate director] is. The PAD is really powerful."[31]

During the 1980s OMB, like many other agencies, was cut back in budget and staffing, at the same time that the nature of the work was changing. In order to adapt, instead of hiring budget examiners from other parts of government, OMB had switched more into hiring young policy analysts directly out of graduate school.[32] They were less expensive than mid-career candidates and they turned over quickly, so they never became expensive. They were sophisticated number crunchers but knew much less about the agencies and the historical context of their budget proposals.

Preceding the change in recruitment practices, there was a change in the role of the examiners. They did less traditional analysis of budget requests and more monitoring of the fate of proposals in Congress:

> The consensus among OMB staff is that there was a net increase in the amount of time examiners spent on congressional monitorship. One former political-level policy official estimated that examiners were probably averaging about half legislative and half budgetary activity as compared with 80 percent budgetary activity and 20 percent legislative activity before 1981.[33]

The examiners could answer questions such as what will happen to the budget numbers if we make this assumption rather than that one but were less able to see the big picture and make recommendations based on detailed knowledge of programs and operations. They worked very hard, for long hours. They had more to do as the mission of OMB expanded during the 1980s and 1990s, tracking reconciliation legislation, scoring Gramm-Rudman-Hollings, and implementing the Budget Enforcement Act, as well as dealing with the variety of management improvement legislation turned out by Congress in the 1990s, including the Government Performance and Results Act, the Chief Finance Officers Act, and reforms in purchasing. David Stockman estimated that the average examiner was responsible for $5 billion a year in 1985, while a decade earlier he or she had been responsible for about half that much.[34] The increased responsibilities were not handled through increased budget and staffing, but by stretching the existing staff.

OMB shrank in size throughout the 1980s.[35] Congress was apparently irritated at OMB's determination to eliminate programs that Congress had continually approved and supported and decided that OMB should take its own medicine.[36] Staffing fell from 614 staffers in 1971 to 598 in 1981 to 525 in 1988 and down to 378 in 1989. Staff numbers rose to 507 for fiscal 1990, and to 540 in 1991, and 553 in fiscal 1992. The numbers reached 561 in 1993.[37] Expenditures had dropped from $35.3 million in fiscal 1981 to $32.2 million in fiscal 1988.

Though staffing and budget had recovered somewhat by 1993, the level of overload remained high and resources did not keep up with increased mission and responsibilities. OMB Director Franklin Raines, in his testimony for the 1998 budget request, remarked,

> OMB is operating with fewer people and very constrained budget. At OMB's request, Congress has held the agency's budget essentially flat since fiscal 1993, when it totaled $56,039,000. Also, since 1993, OMB has cut the number of funded full-time equivalent (FTE) positions by 55—from the 573 in 1993 to 518 in 1998—or nearly 10 percent. Over that time, OMB has cut its administrative costs by 1,467,000—from 6,831,000 in 1993 to 5,264,000 in 1998—or 21 percent.[38]

Two years later, the director made an almost identical report: the level of staffing had remained at 518 in 1999, and the agency was requesting only 518 positions for the year 2000. Thus despite a substantial increase in responsibility throughout the 1990s, the agency remained down about 10 percent in staffing levels from 1993.

With the limited number of positions and increasing workload, an agency that had always been demanding experienced rapid turnover in the new recruits.

OMB came to be considered a good place to start a career, get good experience, and then leave for other agencies. A sharp division grew between the old-timers and the young people, with the institutional memory residing with the old-timers. The agency began to be concerned about how it was transmitting the institutional memory, since it did not seem to be passing it on in any systematic way to a new generation.

Training in OMB is done primarily by mentoring, which is highly dependent on the old-timers remaining in place, being willing to take the time to train the newcomers, and the newcomers staying a while after they learn. One problematic aspect was that the newcomers were not staying: "People come in for two to three or four years and go."[39] In addition, some of the older folks with long historical memories were retiring:

> Some folks have been here a long time, younger people do turn over more rapidly. It wears people out; the budget is so tight, so driven by BEA. Some of the historical memory is retiring; it will be of interest how much remains. We are thinking about things like this. We are in a reflective mode. . . . We consider it valuable, the historical memory, and we try to keep it going.[40]

With the budget examiners turning over every two to three years, they had virtually no historical context. As one recent budget analyst described, when a budget proposal comes in from the agencies, the budget examiner might not know that the same proposal was made several years earlier. It will fall to the more experienced supervisor to catch it. Since the senior staff cannot be counted on to stay indefinitely, OMB was struggling to find ways to write down and make available to new staff some of the experience that had been acquired. A second approach was to try to make the organization more family friendly and improve retention of newer recruits.

One interviewee noted that all her e-mails on a particular project had been saved by OMB to provide a record for the future. She also noted that circulars offered at least some permanent record of what OMB had done in the past:

> IR: At OMB is the institutional memory mainly informal?
>
> OMB staffer: Interesting question. A lot of it is built into circulars. If it will recur, it is built into the A-11. That this is how it will be done.
>
> IR: Would an analyst be able to look up the discussion that preceded the circular?
>
> OMB staffer: No, but it would be good to do that on the intranet. The credit section of the home page does have stuff like that pertaining to implementation.[41]

While the intranet and circulars helped, longtime observers of the process argued that training was still largely informal and depended on the new person asking the right questions. A lot of what was done was "established budget practice" that was not in the circulars: "A young person might ask, 'why is this transaction an outlay, there is no check.' The answer is, 'it is established budget practice.' Some might say back, 'where is it in the law or in an OMB circular?' We can't point to it in all cases."[42] The informality of the process had many senior staff thinking about what could be done to formalize the transmission of knowledge.

These concerns were reflected in the OMB strategic plan, required by GPRA, the Government Performance and Results Act. Among other goals, OMB listed improvement of the work environment. One element was diversification of the workforce. Other elements of the plan more clearly addressed the problems of turnover and transmission of accumulated experience and historical context. OMB planned to try to reduce the turnover rate among entry-level staff and increase staff access to mentors. To accomplish these objectives, OMB intended to develop and carry out a plan for improving the effectiveness of on-campus and mid-level recruiting; exploring ways to create a workplace environment that recognizes individual needs within workload and resource constraints; and continuing and enhancing mentorship programs and encouraging highly qualified senior staff to serve as mentors. The plan acknowledged, however, that the technically trained staff comprised a highly marketable commodity and that other agencies and private sector organizations might bid away their junior staff despite efforts to reduce turnover. Mid-level recruiting assumed the availability of additional positions and sufficient budget to pay a more expensive staff.

One of the methods to be used to make the environment more friendly was to encourage a variety of skills-building and knowledge-enhancing programs inside OMB, such as a rotation of assignments, detailing staff to other agencies, and increased training opportunities inside the divisions. OMB encouraged employees to design and fulfill career goal plans.

As many other agencies had done and would do, OMB planned to continue to automate data and communications to help reduce employees' work burden. The plan listed efforts to keep computers up-to-date; to use the internal and external Web sites to facilitate communication; to improve the tracking of controlled correspondence, automate routinely used forms, and make legislation-related information and statistics and status reports on paperwork reviews and regulatory reviews available electronically to OMB staff. It also included using electronic means to deliver to staff current economic data, economic and technical assumptions, analytical databases and models, staff analyses of short- and long-term economic and fiscal conditions, and other cross-cutting analyses; moving budget systems over a few years from an outdated mainframe computer to distributed technology; improving electronic communications among OMB and the agencies; and facilitating "work from home" options via personal computers. The last item is particularly interesting as a matter of policy, suggesting efforts to make the office more family friendly. Many of these items depend on the availability of funding. Given the tight budgets, it is not clear which of these strategies will be pursued or how quickly.

OMB's budget had stabilized by 1993, but by then, a second shock hit OMB in the form of the National Performance Review (NPR). The National Performance Review, led by Vice President Al Gore, was an effort to make government run better at less cost. Officials from all over the federal government were assigned to a task force and study group to come up with recommendations that covered nearly every aspect of management. After more than a decade of what was often perceived as an imperial or imperious OMB, resentment against OMB ran high, among both secretaries and career officials. As Shelley Tomkin, an academic expert on OMB, described, the budget examiners lost clout with the agencies because so many decisions were top-down. Lacking real power, some examiners, in order to get information from the agencies, began to play on their role in budget implementation: "These examiners became more tight-fisted when apportioning appropriated monies (where allowable by law) as a means of pressuring agencies to be more forthcoming with information and of guaranteeing their compliance with OMB directives." Agency budget officials complained of OMB meddling.[43] OMB staff argued back that agency budgeters sometimes blamed OMB for what their own secretaries were doing to them during budget implementation. Initially, the NPR discussed some radical shifts in the budget role of OMB, including drastic reductions in budget and shifting various OMB functions to other agencies.[44] Past evaluations of OMB were dragged out and the criticisms reiterated. Eventually more moderate feelings toward OMB prevailed.

NPR not only criticized OMB with respect to apportionment of funds and wrestled with serious questions about its role in the budget process, but also criticized its ability to improve management in the agencies. OMB tried to deal with much of this criticism through a thorough reorganization that would allow a better integration of management with budget advice and would encourage more longer-term analysis. The reorganization, called OMB 2000, was carried out in 1994. Preliminary evaluations suggested that it was having some success. Either because of the reorganization or in spite of it, OMB was paying more attention to management issues. Given the spate of legislation that OMB was required to implement on management improvements, it seems likely that this management emphasis will last for a number of years.[45]

The merger of the management and budget sides of OMB raised several issues. One was whether or not those who had specialized in particular management issues knew enough about budgeting to function in the new combined setting. Another was what would happen to their expertise when they were no longer specialists concentrating on particular management issues. OMB tackled these issues through intensified training and organizational arrangements.

According to the 1995 GAO study, despite this added training, some staff believed that management issues were not sufficiently understood by the budget examiners. They were concerned that program examiners did not have the expertise to review audited financial statements and GAO did not know how the program examiners could deal with credit reform and cash management questions.

OMB approached the question of maintaining management expertise in some cases by using a matrix structure; that is, staff would be simultaneously assigned to a unit focusing on technical managerial issues and a generalist budget analysis unit. This arrangement had the difficulties one might expect with matrix structures, reporting to two bosses with different expectations about how much time they could legitimately demand for their work assignments.[46] Overall, the OMB 2000 reform was more successful in getting budget examiners to pay attention to management issues than it was in maintaining the expertise of those who had specialized in particular management issues.

Linking management and budget issues provided examiners with more leverage for change in the agencies. One staff member cited financial management restructuring as an area in which agencies took action more quickly when the issue was raised by a Resource Management Office (RMO) composed of both budget and management functions during the budget review process than when this issue was raised outside budget discussions. But in the important area of getting OMB to think more long term, the results were less positive. The program examiners (the combined position of management expert and budget analyst) had more to do as a result of OMB 2000. Their workload increased in response to such initiatives as reinventing government and congressional agency restructuring proposals. Program examiners told GAO investigators they had not been told to eliminate any responsibilities or tasks as a result of OMB 2000. Because they had to balance competing responsibilities, several program examiners said that less emphasis had been placed on certain management issues— those that lacked a clear budgetary impact, did not require an immediate response to a short-term deadline, or did not reflect the administration's priorities. In particular, they said the short-term pressures of the budget process left little time for long-term analysis. Less expertise was available for the program examiners than in the past, and they had less time to look for the expertise that was still there. Consequently, certain management issues received less attention or were not addressed.[47]

In short, OMB 2000 in its first year of operation had mixed effects. It did seem to help increase the attention to management issues and help leverage some responsiveness from the agencies on management issues by linking them to budgetary issues. But the effort to bolster the level of expertise in the agency was only partly successful. The new program examiners were more knowledgeable about management than they had been, but not as knowledgeable as the management experts had been, and the expertise of the management experts was now diminished. OMB had less expertise to count on. Moreover, the new management responsibilities were added on top of older functions, with restrictions on the number of employees. Not only were some management issues not addressed, but attention was narrowly focused on the dominant policy issues and the short-term issues.

To summarize, as a result of the OMB 2000 reorganization, the agency's performance planning, and its updated use of computerization and internal and external Web sites, OMB seems to be running better now than it did before the NPR. The worst of the NPR criticisms were blunted, and the agency is well suited to carry out its new missions in management. But OMB still has a mismatch between mission and staffing, which has hurt the ability to do longer-term studies and probably contributed to turnover problems. Efforts to make OMB a friendlier place are well placed and necessary if the route from new recruit to division director is to remain intact. That pathway is the key to the agency's organizational memory, which differentiates it from many other policy and budgeting offices. But whether OMB can reduce the turnover and maintain the institutional memory as older staff retire depends on budget and staffing levels, which are not rising. Whether they can recruit more new staff from existing agencies and thereby bolster the contextual knowledge of the examiners also depends on budget levels. In the meantime, the perception on the part of the agencies that OMB staff know the details of their operations has declined. What needs to be done is increasingly clear, but the contradictions that require OMB to take whatever it is dishing out hamper the agency on the budgetary side.

The increased turnover of young people, the problematic transmission of institutional memory, and the decreased expertise associated with OMB 2000, especially when combined with substantially increased mission and somewhat decreased staffing, suggest that OMB is eating some of its seed corn. The high visibility directors of the 1980s and the rosy scenarios of the Reagan administration suggest a corrosion of neutral competence, but fortunately one that depends on the nature of the director more than on external institutional pressures. With different directors, OMB regained some of its status.

CONCLUSION

Both CBO and OMB underscore the importance of the directors in taking the high road and not yielding to pressure, and also the consequences of doing so, namely, that their advice is ignored as elected officials look around for a policy shop that will tell them more of what they want to hear. Ironically, the elected officials themselves benefit from the staff offices' appearance of neutrality— legislators weakened their case when they put pressure on staff agencies to come up with particular conclusions or when they visibly shopped around for assumptions and conclusions they liked.

CHAPTER 5

General Accounting Office

THE GENERAL ACCOUNTING OFFICE (GAO), a congressional branch agency, has responsibility for financial, program, and performance auditing in the federal government. Because of its role in identifying and suggesting solutions for costly managerial problems, the GAO should have become more important during a period of cutback, but it was subjected to several rounds of cuts from 1992 on, totaling about 33 percent of the budget by 1997.

The GAO was particularly vulnerable to cuts. As one of the largest of the legislative branch agencies (the Library of Congress, including the Congressional Research Service, was a little larger), it was an inviting target when Congress decided that it had to cut back its own expenditures to set a good example for the executive branch. However, the size and timing of the cuts are suggestive of more than just being in the way when the juggernaut came through.

Since the 1970s the agency had increased its program evaluation and policy analysis orientation. As a result of this change in emphasis, the GAO was less able to avoid policy controversies. Since the agency gave priority to requests for studies from committee chairs (who are of the majority party), a long period of Democratic Party dominance made the GAO look as if it were supporting Democrats at the expense of Republicans. When the Republicans took over Congress in 1995, they believed they had little for which to be grateful to GAO.

A second feature of the case is that GAO agreed to deep cuts with the understanding that these cuts would be made quickly, after which the agency could begin to stabilize. GAO's initial acceptance of the cuts did not prevent additional, deeper cuts later and did not permit the agency to stabilize and recover quickly:

> GAO's budget story begins in 1992. . . . We agreed to reduce from 5,300 to 4,200 over three years. In 1994, the congressional leadership changed, and there was no buyin to our previous agreement to three years and a stable budget. The Republican Congress was going to reduce us 25 percent on top of the 8 percent we had agreed to. From 5,200 to 3,500, basically a one-third reduction in the size of the organization.[1]

By 1998 the budget had finally stabilized and the major animus against the agency had died down. GAO completed its reports more promptly and the new Republican majority learned to use GAO services and realized that the GAO was not partisan, merely responsive to the committee chairs. Table 5.1 shows budget and staffing levels from 1995 to 2000.

The GAO was unable to document reductions in the quality or quantity of its services, because such declines might be used as an excuse for further cuts or even agency termination. The agency was thus in the position of saying that a cut of over a third in the size of its staffing had no noticeable effects on its products.

A third feature of the case was that the publicized congressional cuts understated the severity of the actual cuts. During the period from 1992–97 GAO was given additional responsibilities, including helping agencies audit newly required financial reports. These new responsibilities were not funded. Moreover, the staffing reductions increased the necessity of computerization, putting additional pressure on the agency to find the funds to buy computers, get new software up and running, and train staff to use it. The agency was required to absorb new equipment and training costs without new staff or funding. The comptroller general initially argued that the agency could carry out all its responsibilities with the newly reduced staff but then came back a little later to argue for increased staff with specialized expertise to carry out the new mission of auditing the comprehensive financial reports. The request was ignored.

A fourth feature of the case is that GAO had to invent new ways of doing business while carrying out the cuts. The agency had faced revised missions in earlier years and had some idea of how to go about dealing with major changes. Nevertheless, the agency had to design reduction-in-force procedures in order to carry out the RIF. The agency's emphasis on documenting the fiscal impact of its recommendations was new and required a different way of thinking among the divisions and issue areas. Both the job reinvention process and

Table 5.1   **GAO Appropriations and Staffing Levels, 1995–2000 (in $ millions)**

Fiscal Year	Appropriation	Full-time Equivalent Staffing
1995	441	4,342
1996	373	3,677
1997	333	3,341
1998	341	3,245
1999	356	3,275
2000	378 est.	3,275 est.

Sources: Appendix, Budget of the United States, various fiscal years.

computerization required a great deal of change. The effects of budget cuts and staffing reductions continued long after the budget had more or less stabilized, when the new comptroller general, David Walker, announced a major internal reorganization to take place by the end of 2000. This reorganization affected not only the structure, but also the organization of the work and the degree of specialization of employees.

VULNERABILITY

Some information-providing agencies, such as the Bureau of Labor Statistics and the Census Bureau, were able to protect themselves by doing self-generated or statute-mandated research and maintaining a reputation for high-quality technical work, without directly participating in policy issues. When such agencies got tangled up in policy issues, as when the Census Bureau became enmeshed in the reapportionment issue or when BLS got caught in the controversy surrounding adjustment of the consumer price index, they not only became more visible (came onto the policy radar screen, in Washington parlance), they put themselves in the line of fire. Even the normally scrupulously neutral Congressional Budget Office got caught in the line of fire by scoring (estimating the cost of) President Clinton's health care policy. As much as possible, the information agencies carefully nurtured the image of technical proficiency, often defined as economic or statistical expertise, and stayed out of the policy limelight. The GAO was foursquare in the policy limelight.

Had the General Accounting Office stayed in accounting, it might have been able to maintain a higher level of support. It could have stayed in the background and relied on a reputation for neutrality. Congressional opponents of GAO in 1993 introduced a "reform" bill that would have returned GAO to an accounting body and would have prohibited the agency from generating any of its own studies. Under the proposal, GAO would have to limit itself to studies requested by Congress. The GAO reform bill did not pass, but it indicated the nature of some of the opposition to the agency. It was not merely that GAO had entered the policy arena, but also that it seemed uncontrollable to some members of Congress. If it could be turned back from the policy role or if it could be made more accountable and responsive to congressional demands and needs, it would be less threatening.

Over the years GAO did some statute-required studies and a little self-generated work, but it increasingly relied on requests from the chairs of congressional committees to generate the work that it did. The work was designed and carried out with the requester in mind. GAO got a reputation for providing reports that were not neutral but were slanted to the needs of the requester. GAO accumulated enemies every time it seemed to favor one side of a controversial issue. Moreover, GAO released its results publicly, sometimes blindsiding those who opposed its findings.

As long as one party retained power in Congress, the pattern of the GAO responding to the requests of the committee chairs worked to protect the agency. The agency was cut some from 1992 to 1994, but the Democratic committee chairs actively thwarted the agency's opponents and kept the size of cuts modest. The defenders of GAO not only predicted in detail what Congress would lose with larger cuts to GAO, they actively intervened in committee to keep the deeper cuts from getting to the floor. When the control of Congress shifted in 1994 from Democrat to Republican, those who had been in the minority in prior years and who believed that their needs had gotten short shrift were suddenly in the majority and in position to exact a kind of revenge.

The felt need to reduce spending on congressional agencies and staff and the desire for payback time combined with many longstanding criticisms of the agency's performance to help explain the depth of the cuts to GAO.

CRITICISMS OF THE AGENCY'S PERFORMANCE

Intense criticisms of GAO were circulating from at least 1992 on. Senators on other committees complained to Senate Appropriations Committee members about the GAO. In response, the Senate Appropriations Committee tried to require as a condition of the 1993 appropriation an outside evaluation of GAO. This study would "have addressed issues such as the clarity of organizational structure, policies governing the selection and manner of evaluation and effectiveness of GAO and its resources, the quality of their work product, and the competency and qualification of GAO staff to do the work to which they are assigned."[2] The House blocked this requirement in 1992 but was willing to earmark funds for a study in 1993. The Senate Governmental Affairs Committee in 1993 contracted with the National Academy of Public Administration to do such a study. Since Senator Harry Reid had offered all the opponents of the GAO an opportunity to lodge their critiques in this format, it is not surprising that the Academy study was negative and highly critical of the agency.[3]

Many critics of GAO argued that the quality of GAO reports was highly variable and that it took too long for them to be completed. Agency personnel who were interviewed explained that part of the problem lay in the way projects were negotiated and that changes were often demanded at the end of the process—sometimes because the design was deemed inadequate. The result was long delay while work was redesigned and redone. Part of the delay in reporting out work was also due to an extensive internal review process that was part of the agency's culture. As an accounting agency, GAO was very concerned to get the details correct, which required multiple internal reviews before release. As one observer noted, GAO was a cautious agency: "Reports get reviewed by so many people at GAO and they change so much from the draft submitted, it takes six months."[4] An agency staffer estimated four months and then several months more for printing and distribution.

BUDGET HISTORY

The agency's budget history was bandied about in Congress, in part to demonstrate that it had grown rapidly in recent years and therefore should be cut back disproportionately to other congressional branch agencies (table 5.2).

The figures published in the *Congressional Record,* shown in table 5.2, preceded the major 25 percent cuts for 1996 and 1997:

> We were given $450 million, roughly, for the budget for 1995. Then 15 percent was cut in 1996 off the 1995 numbers, and then an additional 10 percent off 1995 for 1997. How many staff years can that buy you? The cut was 25 percent. From $450 million to $375 million to $332 million.[5]

An examination of the congressional data on appropriations for GAO shows that although the increases before 1995 were portrayed as out of control, they were in fact moderate and were mainly accounted for by mandatory pay and inflation increases. The number of staff never grew dramatically during the period and was cut back beginning in 1992 to well below the 1984 levels.

AGENCY RESPONSES

The agency responded to these deep cuts in a number of ways, including eliminating field offices, reducing staffing levels, increasing use of computers, and reinventing the process of negotiating work agreements or "contracts." GAO

Table 5.2   **GAO's Appropriations and Staffing, 1984–95 (in $ thousands)**

Fiscal Year	Appropriation	Staffing
1984	271,710	5,000
1985	299,704	5,050
1986	288,051	5,042
1987	310,973	5,042
1988	329,847	5,052
1989	347,339	5,062
1990	363,661	5,062
1991	409,242	5,062
1992	442,647	5,062
1993	435,167	4,900
1994	430,165	4,581
1995	439,525	4,581

Source: Congressional Record, Legislative Branch Appropriations Act, 1995, House, 26 May 1994, H3145.

also changed the product mix and had to transfer staff internally in order to help audit agency financial reports. GAO worked hard to document its accomplishments and especially its cost effectiveness. It also tried to prioritize jobs. GAO responses were partly to cope with reduced staffing and partly to respond to criticisms such as that it was too slow, unresponsive to Congress, or more interested in creating headlines than in serving Congress.

Job Reinvention

The heart of the agency response was a revised work process that emphasized negotiating the scope and duration of projects in advance.[6] The job reinvention process also put more focus on design up front, so there would be fewer complaints about quality when the report was initially submitted and less demand to do work over. One function of the job reinvention was to help the agency improve productivity, to enable GAO to keep providing material to Congress at former levels despite the cutbacks. A second function was to respond to the criticism that GAO was too slow to be of use in policy matters. A third effect was to help control the cost of GAO assignments.

The reinvented job process emphasized identifying all the key stakeholders and getting them to buy into the plans in the beginning so they would be less likely to complain and demand changes at the end. The new work design process was combined with an internal evaluation process that emphasized employee compliance with promised delivery dates. As one informant recalled, she had to sign a promise that the report would be delivered on such a date. She thought it did not matter that much to Congress if the product were delivered exactly on time, as long as members got the material before their deadlines, such as the dates of hearings. But the due dates became rigid inside GAO.

The job restructuring began in 1996, but it did not end there. Comptroller General David Walker, who took office in 1999, added to the job process redesign. Walker summarized the additional changes as expanded use of risk-based approaches while reducing administrative burdens and involving all subject and technical experts on the relevant projects. The new part of the process was the creation of two new forums for management to review new requests and to monitor the progress of ongoing jobs. One forum, called the weekly engagement acceptance meeting, was created to review all new congressional requests, legislative mandates, and division proposals for research and development assignments to determine if they should be done, which skills were needed to do them, and, depending on the risk level, the appropriate level of involvement by the Office of the Comptroller General. The second forum Walker set up was a biweekly meeting to discuss progress on the high/medium–risk assignments and upcoming reports from the operating divisions. The aim of both types of meeting was to reduce levels of review for most reports, keeping the higher level of review only for those projects that needed it.[7] The agency defined high risk as those projects that were expensive, complicated, or potentially controversial.

While a little more caution about the way possibly controversial reports were written and released may have been one goal of the changes in job process, the more fundamental goals of job process reform were to prioritize jobs and to shorten the length of the average project (called a job). According to the 1995 annual report, average job time had dropped from 10.4 months to 8.6 months from 1994 to 1995, before the job reinvention was in place. The 1996 GAO annual report gave somewhat different figures for the average job time, reporting the 1994 average duration of jobs at 9.7 months (rather than 10.4) and the 1995 average duration at 7.7 months, rather than 8.6. The figure for 1996 was given as 6.7 months.[8] The 1997 annual report gave the 1997 average job duration as 5.4 months. The overall trend continued downward, toward markedly shorter jobs.

With a drop of only about 6.5 percent in staffing from 1993–95, GAO managed to reduce average job time during that period about 27 percent and cost per job about 29 percent. The number of jobs delivered during this time period actually increased, and productivity in terms of products delivered per 100 staff members increased dramatically. The agency offered no measures of quality across this time period, however; and the apparent intensification of efforts to keep quality up that are referred to in the 1995 annual report suggests that the agency may have run into increasing complaints about uneven quality in the reports.[9] The agency added an external review component in 1995 to its internal quality monitoring function, called the *post-assignment review* system. The external component included a contract with the consulting firm Peat Marwick to review the quality of its financial audits; in the 1995 annual report the comptroller general indicated plans to expand this review function to other kinds of studies GAO performed.

From 1996 to 1998, with a drop of about 25 percent in staffing levels, the number of products produced increased by about 19 percent, and the cost per product dropped accordingly. See table 5.3 and table 5.4 (page 130) for details.

Table 5.3 Number of Jobs Completed

Year	Reports to Congress	Congressional Briefings	Testimonies
1995	910	166	246
1996	908	217	181
1997	1,006	149	182
1998	1,136	181	256
1999	1,095	182	229

Sources: 1995 through 1998 annual reports; 1999 Accountability report.

Table 5.4   Cost per Job at GAO[a]

Year	Cost
1993	$244,000
1994	257,000
1995	224,000
1996	219,000
1997	169,000

[a]GAO did not report the cost per job after 1997.

The agency's main response to complaints of lack of timeliness combined with reduced staffing levels was to reengineer the job process and focus on shorter projects and products. GAO reported dramatically improved on-time results (table 5.5).

A second and related response was to allow and even encourage staff to report to Congress on work in progress before it was complete, when Congress needed or wanted the report. Sometimes, as a result of this reporting on work in progress, GAO gave identical, or nearly identical, testimony to different committees and to the same committee holding hearings several years in a row. Thus some of the testimonies counted as separate products were really repeats, without additional underlying research. An additional step was to emphasize informal reporting to Congress, such as replies to questions in the form of brief letters. This form of reporting complied with what Congress needed and was faster and more responsive. The agency also relied more heavily on formal and informal briefings.[10] By making the work somewhat more private, the agency responded to criticisms that it was grandstanding and grabbing headlines rather than responding to congressional need.

Table 5.5   Percent On-time Delivery

Year	Percentage
1993	40
1994	43
1995	56
1996	67
1997	91
1998	93
1999	96
2000	97

RIFs and Field Office Closings

With such steep cuts in budget over such a short period of time, reductions in force seemed the only possible way to reduce staffing and stay within budget. Substantial effort was made to minimize damage to the agency through a redesigned reduction-in-force procedure. Targeting the field offices for RIFs, GAO also shut down a number of field offices and reorganized some of the functions of the remaining offices.

One staff member described the GAO RIF as "point and shoot." RIFs do not usually allow for that level of pinpoint choice of who will be separated; GAO had to carefully devise a RIF procedure that would minimize impact on the organization. The basic plan was to limit the RIF to specific field sites, and at headquarters to limit the RIF primarily to secretarial and clerical positions. RIFed staff in the field offices were not allowed to transfer elsewhere. Evaluators in Washington were protected from RIF in order to keep the basic work of the agency going and to continue the contacts on the Hill that the Washington staff had developed. The result was minimal bumping but maximal cuts affecting women and minorities because of the focus on secretarial and clerical ranks.

The fine targeting of the GAO RIF required new legislation, enabling the agency to circumscribe retreat rights. With almost nowhere to go, those who were targeted for cuts had to leave the agency. The rationale for such a targeted cut was to maintain the mission of the agency while downsizing:

> The rationale was to make decisions that would impact the least the services to Congress on reports and testimony. Everything was tested against that. If the proposal suggested a disruption of the process, it was not accepted. That was controversial from the regional office perspective. We closed several regional offices. Hundreds of evaluators in the field, but the same positions were not cut in D.C. A RIF of evaluators in D.C. would have disrupted the work for Congress. You could plan around the field offices and avoid disruption.[11]

Congress had asked specifically for the agency to examine its field structure. That request, combined with the agency strategy of maintaining contacts with Congress unchanged, led to a concentration of cuts in the field offices rather than at headquarters. The field offices in Cincinnati, Philadelphia, Oklahoma City, New York, Detroit, Albany, Indianapolis, San Antonio, Albuquerque, and Honolulu were closed in 1994 and 1995, as well as one overseas office, in Frankfurt, Germany.[12]

The consequences of the closing of these field offices were debated internally. From one point of view, the impacts were minimal, because some of these offices were monitoring facilities that had shrunk or could now be monitored through secondary data and trips from other field offices. From another point of view, the uniqueness of GAO among agencies evaluating policy was that it had a firsthand look at the agencies and projects it was investigating, and the field offices were the source of that freshness. As the role of the field offices was reduced, GAO's reliance on secondary data increased. Interviewees generally agreed that this shift was taking place, although they disagreed on its importance. Some staff worried that almost any data analysts, inside or outside government, could carry out secondary data analysis, and GAO could lose its unique niche and the quality of some of its studies would erode.

One informant who had spent a number of years in the field offices described the difference between the primary data he collected when in the field and the secondary data they are now using. In the field he would not accept reports of weapons performance; he would go to the testing sites and read the machines on-site as the tests were occurring. Similarly, officials in the field offices could check the quality of lumber being used by a contractor and compare it against invoices to figure out whether the contractor was getting the quality of lumber he was paying for. After the closing of some of the field offices, GAO used a lot of secondary data, some of which was not very good. The informant was not sure the change was for the worse, but it depended greatly on the quality of the secondary data.

The most direct effect of the cuts occurred in the field offices, not just in the ones that were eliminated, but also in the remaining ones, because staff assignments and the specialization of each of the field offices changed. The organization at GAO had about 35 (later 32) issue areas at headquarters, and these issue areas generally had some staff at each of the regional offices. Projects would be designed and supervised from headquarters and largely carried out in the field. After the RIFs, some of the field offices became more specialized, dropping staff from a variety of areas, leaving the subject areas at headquarters scrambling for staff in the field. With the number of field staff down, the number and scope of projects (as differentiated from the number of products) that could be done at headquarters also dropped.

Headquarters staffing was also affected, but there were no reductions in force among the evaluators. Instead the reductions were taken mostly among the clerical and technical staff, though there were a number of early retirements and voluntary departures of evaluators. Each division took its cuts differently, depending on how the senior management viewed the problems.

The official rationale for the reduction in clerical staff was as follows:

> The overall staffing levels had come down by a third, so we needed fewer secretaries. The last couple of years we have gotten more into technology—we are all networked, you do your own typing, you have voice mail, you don't need receptionists anymore—but we had receptionists and typists. Now you need only one cleanup typist for 20 people

or so, to fix the margins and that sort of thing. Some jobs had become obsolete, and we were reinventing to reduce the need. So we don't anticipate a major problem there. The administrative staff was too large for a shrunken GAO.[13]

The impact on GAO was not quite as nonproblematic as the rationale suggests, although the effects were not severe.

The goal of the field office RIFs was to get down quickly to the staffing levels the agency could afford and then let the agency recover. But staff members continued to feel vulnerable after this RIF, because Congress could cut them again, and because the agency had already shown a willingness and ability to RIF, especially in the field offices. After several years of limping along with skills imbalances due to hard freezes and low and rigid staffing ceilings, GAO did indeed RIF the field offices a second time in the year 2000 and closed five additional field offices: Kansas City, St. Louis, Portland, Raleigh, and Sacramento. The RIF was expected to affect 4 percent of the agency's remaining staff. This time, affected staff were permitted to apply for transfer from offices that were closing, but there were no guarantees that such requests would be honored.

Comptroller General Walker had argued that the field offices needed to return to primary data collection, that such collection was necessary for the agency to maintain its niche as a special congressional agency, without overlapping the mission of other existing research shops. He had also argued that the RIFs would help the field offices achieve critical mass. However, the closing of additional field offices was likely to contribute to these goals only in a marginal way. Some of the employees in the offices that were closing were expected to retire; others were expected to transfer to remaining field offices and headquarters; the remainder were to be let go. Hence the number of staff transferring into other field offices would probably not be great. This small increase might help those offices increase their reliance on primary data, but the overall impact could not be very substantial.

It seems likely that the purpose of the second round of RIFs and the closing of additional field offices was more related to the comptroller general's often-repeated request for more flexibility and the need to fill skills gaps within the current staffing limits. He had promised Congress that he would not ask for additional staffing until he had demonstrated that the agency was as well managed and efficient as possible, but he needed more flexibility to get that efficiency within the present staffing levels.

In line with his testimony to Congress in February 2000, the comptroller general requested that Congress provide more staffing flexibility. He wanted the ability to offer specific individuals buyouts (separation payments) and early retirement options; he wanted to be able to create high-level positions in areas of technical skills or where the agency was experiencing a skills imbalance; and he wanted the ability to hire experts and consultants for longer than the current three-year limit. He also asked for broad powers to devise RIF regulations for RIFs he decided were necessary, including for the realignment of the workforce, skills imbalances, and reducing the number of high-graded managerial positions.

By closing field offices, GAO could give RIF notices to a number of staff (more than 100) and then select from that number the ones to keep and the ones to whom to offer early retirement incentives. If that plan worked, that is, if the comptroller general got the authorization to proceed to offer individuals early retirement options, he might gain a few positions that he could fill with badly needed experts who cost more than the agency was currently able to offer. He could also replace some of the older people nearing retirement with younger ones to bring down the average age of staff and help transition planning in anticipation of massive retirements expected a few years hence.

The second round of cuts was in many ways a lagged effect of the first round. Living within the tight personnel limitations and trying to keep talented staff in key skills areas had proved difficult. Something had to be done to recreate some flexibility.[14]

Reorganization

Although the staff was greatly reduced, initially there was not much reorganization at headquarters. In the continuing reevaluation of the issue areas, several of them were merged, and one, the evaluation methodology unit, was eliminated. The elimination of the evaluation design unit at headquarters may be significant, but it is hard to tell because at least some of the staff were scattered to other units and may continue to provide design advice from that venue. On the other hand, the unit was not well liked, in the sense that its members radiated superiority, claimed to be the only ones who deserved the title evaluator, and hence were not invited into many different shops when they were broken up. They did not deal directly with Congress and so were considered outside the mainstream of the agency's culture. The elimination of this unit would not be noticed by Congress. While many GAO staffers argued that Program Evaluation and Methodology (PEMD) would not be missed, especially because the other units already had methodologists associated with them, without a critical mass and self-reinforcing culture, it was not clear that methodological issues would receive the same level of creative attention after the dispersion of PEMD staff.

The effect of RIFs and voluntary departures was aggravated by internal transfers. The General Accounting Office was required by new legislation to help audit agency financial statements, but GAO was not permitted to hire additional staff to do the work. As a result, people inside the agency had to transfer to the audit unit. People with any background in auditing were pressured to transfer. They may have been housing specialists for years and preferred that line of work, but they were transferred into the auditing unit anyway. While the GAO did not have much choice about this response, it left many employees disaffected. Nearly every unit felt the impact of the "forced march." On one hand, some units lost skilled staff; on the other, the auditing unit received staff who preferred to be elsewhere and whose skills were often rusty.

By FY 2000 Comptroller General Walker announced a reorganization at headquarters of considerably larger impact. Walker described two goals of the headquarters reorganization. One was that GAO was in a highly competitive environment, with other governmental agencies and with nonprofits, and had to regain its niche in order to prevent a rerun of the cuts in the mid-1990s. The other was that the agency had to adapt to having fewer staff while still remaining responsive to Congress. Both these goals required a more efficient and more flexible operation. Toward that end, the traditional structure of many divisions and issue areas with specific field area expertise was collapsed into 11 teams and several overarching units. The 11 teams were to be acquisition and source management, education workforce and income security, finance and assurance, financial markets and community investments, health care, information technology, international affairs and trade, military strategy and readiness, natural resources and environment, physical infrastructure, and tax administration and justice. These teams matched the earlier structure for some issue areas and differed substantially in other areas, creating questions about who belonged where and what kinds of expertise were required.

The new organization was to function as a matrix structure, so that methodology and field expertise could be drawn on as needed for each project. The goal of added flexibility was to be achieved first by having fewer units with broader subject-matter definitions, so that more people could be put on specific projects if needed (Walker described this process as the elimination of glass walls); flexibility was also to be enhanced by the creation of a pool of nonspecialized staff who could be moved to assignments as needed. The new structure was roughly matched to the strategic plan, with top-level officials in charge of areas representing goals in the plan:

> The new cross-agency units include offices devoted to process and product improvement, strategic studies (including budget issues, government performance and accountability, and human capital), and external liaison (including accountability organizations and recruiting). A new technical services unit centralizes certain functionally based economists, statisticians, actuaries, and other technical and methodological specialists. The quality and risk management function is being strengthened with the addition of several senior executives responsible for each of the three mission-oriented strategic goals.[15]

The plan created more flexibility in a downsized organization, more ability to go rapidly where current congressional interest suggested; it also addressed the need to provide technical and methodological interests by the re-creation of a unit that appeared to play the function of the old abolished PEMD, the evaluation methodology unit. The reorganization plan also emphasized performance measurement, but that measurement focused more on employee attitudes and customer evaluations than it did on evaluating quality of reports:

> We are in the process of issuing a contract to develop our new performance management system. This system will consider such factors as attitude (e.g., demonstrated commitment to our core values, professional standards, teaming, matrix management), effort (e.g., whether individuals are doing their fair share), results (e.g., outcomes vs. outputs), client feedback and employee feedback, as appropriate. Our knowledge and skills inventory is being electronically formatted for pretesting.[16]

Prioritization

Changes in work design could produce only so much improvement in productivity. Ultimately, GAO had to prioritize the work. Assistant Comptroller General Joan Dodaro explained how the agency prioritized:

> There are fewer people doing the analytic work. Every job, we decide, is it a job we should be doing? Does it involve major issues? Is it an opportunity for budget savings? You look through that kind of lens. You need to do that increasingly in the job process engineering. The number one step is prioritize. What job should we be doing? Some should go to the inspector generals; others should go on a waiting list.
> . . . If a chair has a huge number of requests in the hopper, we ask them to prioritize. You can only do what you can do. New requests may have to wait. We try not to do that lest we end up in budgetary free fall.[17]

The reorganization in FY 2000 set up a committee to regularly review possible work assignments. The most important assignments would get higher priority and more workers assigned to them. To make sure there was no misunderstanding, Comptroller General Walker issued a protocol explaining to Congress how the assignment of priorities worked. But assigning priorities meant that some jobs might not get done very quickly or might be refused, a difficult message for GAO to get across at a time when it wanted to please Congress.

Revamping the Relationship with Congress

To prevent budgetary free fall and facilitate agency recovery, GAO had to repair its relationship with Congress. This task awaited the new comptroller general, David Walker. Walker announced initiatives in which he would meet at least annually with congressional leadership, and he and staff would meet regularly with committee leadership. In his plan, congressional requesters of GAO research would evaluate the product they received, and GAO would make clearer how its projects were picked and what priorities were used. GAO drew up a protocol for its relationship with Congress that spelled out many of the issues that had caused confusion or resentment, clarified procedures, and made clear when and how its results were publicized.[18]

Issued after extensive consultation with Congress, this protocol explained that while the agency responded to requests from both committee heads and ranking minority members, the bulk of resources would go to the majority party, whichever party that was. While most Republicans had probably discovered that was the way GAO operated after taking over Congress in 1995, the protocol statement was aimed at simultaneously creating an image of nonpartisanship and conveying the message that GAO was primarily a resource for the majority. GAO needed Republicans to see that when they were in the majority, they would get the bulk of GAO's services.

Another item in the protocol listed which reports would be released publicly, rather than to a specific requester, with a possible one-month lag before release. Members who had requested studies could ask for a 30-day delay in releasing the report and possible extensions after that. They could also withdraw their support from a study and their names would not appear on the final study. These passages were aimed at calming criticism that GAO blindsided Congress by publicly releasing studies that disagreed with particular members' policy stances. The document included a section on press relations, detailing when GAO would talk to the press (it would not initiate press contacts), who would talk to the press (only senior staff familiar with the report in question), and what role GAO would play in press conferences called by legislators (on request, if the press conference was held in Washington). The goal of these statements was to make it clear that GAO was not seeking out press contact or leaking material to the press to garner headlines.

In sum, the protocol made clear the implications of the new job design process, with its extensive up-front consultation, described what the priorities were for jobs and why some jobs might not be accepted, and clarified the agency's relationship with the press. To the extent that these protocols were widely disseminated and accepted, GAO addressed many of the sources of congressional ire against it. In addition to the issuance of the protocol for relations with Congress, the comptroller general embarked on a program of continuous feedback from Congress to GAO. The comptroller general emphasized the response of the customer—was Congress satisfied? If not, what was wrong? What did it want done differently?

IMPACTS

The job redesign, reductions in staffing, the elimination of a number of field offices, the elimination of the internal unit specializing in design, and the "forced march" all affected GAO's work, but mostly in ways that were difficult to measure. One measure that is suggestive of consequences, however, is the number of projects planned, which dropped throughout GAO. Given that "products" for Congress increased in number, this change reflects a reduction in ongoing, longer-term studies that were more or less going on in the background when other deadlines did not interfere. For example, one informant recalled that her unit had dropped a set of studies it had always done proactively and now would report on that subject only when it got a congressional request.

One way of measuring the reduction in the number of projects is to compare the work plans of the issue areas inside GAO before and after the beginning of the 25 percent cuts. These work plans list the projects to be undertaken in the upcoming year. Presumably, these plans would have to be scaled back under the impact of a 25 percent staffing cut, even with an increase in productivity.

The measure is less than perfect for several reasons. Not all the 1995 plans were still available, and not all 1996 plans had been issued during the data-collection phase of this research because they come out at different times of the year. Second, some of the change between years is not due to changing staffing levels or efforts to bring projects in on time but to changing congressional priorities. Third, in some cases what may look like an increase in the number of projects may reflect breaking down larger projects into smaller ones, or a decrease in the number of projects may represent consolidation of projects. Fourth, one of the issue areas, special investigations, did not list specific planned projects, only general areas on which to focus. Regardless of the shortcomings of the data analysis, some GAO staff confirmed that their issue areas were initiating fewer projects and suggested that the trend probably held over all the issue areas. Senior officials verified the drop in the number of projects initiated.

As often happens when comparing units over time, the GAO issue areas were not constant over the period. Some of the issue areas were merged between 1995 and 1996. Units were described as having merged if work traditionally done in one unit was dropped from that unit and picked up in another and if staff at the assistant director level and above moved from the first unit to the one that picked up a portion of the mission. Issue areas are listed in table 5.6 when GAO provided data for both 1995 and 1996. Budget Issues was an exception, with data provided for January 1996 and May 1996.

Table 5.6   Planned Project Starts, 1995 and 1996, GAO, Various Issue Areas

Issue Area	Number of Projects Planned in 1995	Number of Projects Planned in 1996
Fed. Management	19	} 41
Fed. Human Resource Management	37	
Govt. Business Operations	12	16
Admin. of Justice	25	16
Food and Agriculture	25	30
Housing and Community Development	20	20
Financial Institutions and Markets	16	14
Natural Resources Management	15	} 31
Energy and Science	33	
Budget Issues	17	16
Environmental Protection	23	15
IRM-RCED (info. management, community and econ. dev.)	15	} 50
IRM-NSIA (info. management National Security and International Affairs)	23	
IRM-GGD (info. management General Government)	8	
Military Operations and Capabilities	13	14
National Security Analysis	10	14
Program Evaluation and Methodology[a]	26	15
Education and Employment	31	31
Transportation	40	22
Income Security	26	42
Acquisition Policy Technology and Competitiveness	15	} 33
Systems Development and Production	22	} 20
Defense Management and NASA	30	
International Affairs	29	} 25
International Trade, Finance and Competitiveness	20	
	550	465

Source: Data compiled from Issue Area plans, covering various years. The plans are listed here by the date of issue, not the years covered by the plan. There were a total of 35 issue areas in 1995 and 32 issue areas in 1996, but both of those include PEMD, which was being phased out.

[a]PEMD was slated for elimination rather than merger but apparently was being phased out slowly and was still a reporting entity during this period.

Granting the crudeness of the number of proposed new projects as an indicator, there was a decrease in the issue areas examined from a total of 550 to a total of 465, a little more than 15 percent from one year to the next. The drop in new projects resulted from a decline in self-generated projects and longer-term studies. The percentage of jobs that were self-generated dropped dramatically over the next few years. In 1996, 22 percent of GAO's work was self-generated; this figure declined to 5 percent by 1999.[19]

The reduction in number of projects was in part a reaction to the reduction in staffing levels and in part a reaction to criticism that the agency was too slow in getting products out. As one informant reported, many more projects would be planned than staff was available for. The projects would be started anyway, with the result that they would often be produced late and run over cost limits. The new job process required more careful estimates of the amount of work that could be done with the staff and within the budget allocated.

The decline in the number of projects was not as severe as the reduction in budget and staffing levels because the typical product was shorter than it had been. As Joan Dodaro put it, "We are trying to do them quicker through reinvention and technology. So the impact is not as great as it otherwise would have been."[20]

In the effort to respond to as many congressional requests as possible despite the reduced level of staffing, particular attention was paid to negotiating the scope of work and substituting shorter and more informal reports and letters for more formal studies and reports. As Dodaro noted, "We try to figure out what they really need within the time frame, not what they ask for. We negotiate down. The object is to give them the information they need. Sometimes they don't need a blue book [i.e., a formal report]. They need a briefing or informal communication. We are making more use of those kinds of things."[21]

GAO was struggling to find the right balance between types of product. Some studies required a larger context to understand the issues and make recommendations; some required only a brief letter or report. The shift toward shorter products was as much a result of congressional demands as it was a response to the reduction in workforce.

The change in product mix nudged the role of GAO a little further from public watchdog and more toward staff of Congress, especially staff for the committee chairs and majority committee staff. It was difficult for GAO to monitor these more informal products for quantity and quality. During 1996 the agency was beginning to employ tracking mechanisms to count these informal projects, but to the extent that reports to Congress were informal and not written, there was no way to develop quality checks other than noting the satisfaction of the requesting legislators.

Some staffers suggested that the shift to shorter-term products was using up long-term resources that could run out if not replenished fairly soon. The agency had accumulated over a long period in-depth knowledge of particular problems, and that long-term knowledge could be used to answer quick questions from Congress about specific issues; but unless longer-term studies were resumed, it would become increasingly difficult to continue to produce the shorter-term products that were up to former standards.

One staffer, when asked in 1996 how GAO was coping with 25 to 33 percent reduction in staff levels and maintaining responsiveness to congressional requests, answered, "shorter projects, less depth." For example, when GAO was brought into the conflict over the consumer price index, the agency was requested to find out what the Boskin Commission thought about the BLS's efforts to reduce the CPI. GAO interviewed staff at the BLS to find out what changes they had brought about. When BLS declined to estimate how much impact the various changes would have on the index, GAO apparently did not do any independent calculations or ask anyone else. Instead, as asked, it spent time getting the opinions of the former Boskin Commission members on the changes wrought by BLS. The result was opinion on top of opinion, with no independent estimate of what had been accomplished. GAO's study fit the work order but added little that was new to the debate.

Congress was more interested in shorter reports and informal responses in a timely fashion than in longer ones, but to be ready to answer quick questions, GAO needed to continue to generate some projects on its own, independent of legislative request. GAO could still take its suggested projects to Congress and get congressional support, but GAO was doing fewer self-generated studies.

The shift toward responding more exclusively to congressional requests and legislative mandates and away from doing self-initiated studies had begun much earlier and was not primarily a function of recent cuts but of agency redefinition of its mission. In the early 1980s more than half of GAO's resources were spent on studies it initiated itself; by 1987 that figure had fallen to 18 percent, but it slowly rose to 27 percent in 1995, only to drop to 22 percent in 1996 and 17 percent in 1997. By 1998 the figure had fallen to 4 percent; in 1999 it had barely changed at 5 percent. Legislatively mandated activities filled the gap.[22] The drop from 1995 to 1998 may have been in part a response to congressional criticism of the agency and legislative pressure to make GAO more controllable; it may also have reflected the cutback in staffing and the lack of time to do anything other than respond to congressional requests for studies.

The problem of reduced staffing levels and increased demand for studies from Congress continued even after GAO had virtually stopped producing self-generated studies. Pressure remained high to produce studies quickly, with less in-depth work to draw on. Comptroller General Walker, after an intense period of listening to his staff, determined that the lack of self-generated studies was a problem, but he did not seem to have a remedy for it. He tried to persuade Congress that self-generated studies were not a threat but a way for GAO to help Congress anticipate problems before they reached the crisis stage. But his efforts to educate congressional committee members were not accompanied by any specific requests for additional personnel or for authorization to initiate broader studies.[23] As of 2000 the agency had drawn down its knowledge reserves for four or more years without letup. In this respect, GAO was eating its seed corn.

The short time frames for studies combined with the reduction in field office staff and increased reliance on secondary data. At the same time, GAO investigators shifted from more in-person interviewing to interviewing by telephone. It was harder to get good data by phone than in person. As one informant related, people seemed less willing to talk at length over the phone than in person. In person, someone will talk for an hour or two, but not over the phone. As a result, at the same time that the agency was struggling to maintain and improve the quality of its products and did in fact improve the design stage, staffing cuts and the elimination of many field offices made quality improvement more difficult. This trend will continue if the balance between longer-term and shorter-term studies is not adequately resolved; but even if that issue is addressed, the elimination of some field offices will have the long-term impact of eliminating much firsthand data and requiring more telephone rather than face-to-face interviews. Technology helps and makes continuation of the work possible, but not always at the same quality level as before.

By the end of 1997 the agency had endured five years of budget reductions and long, hard hiring freezes that prevented new hires and created skills gaps. After 1997 the agency was forced to absorb some price increases and pick up the costs of modernization of the computers, forcing the agency to reduce staffing levels still further. A few of these positions were gained back, but staffing levels remained well under the informal target of a 33 percent reduction; the comptroller general testified in 2000 that between 1992 and 2000, GAO had experienced reductions in staffing of 40 percent. The resulting skills gaps and lack of new energy from young people entering the organization were exacerbated by the forced march.

There was concern throughout GAO that it had been unable to hire for a number of years. Staff members argued "there is no new blood." Promotions were delayed; merit increases for good performance were suspended and when restored were too modest in size to have much effect. Those who had been promoted earlier believed that after promotion they would have staff members to do preliminary work, prepare charts, and do typing, but they found that with the reduction in clerical staff and increased reliance on computers, they had to do all the clerical work themselves. In some units, senior staff were answering telephones late in the day. Some staff members expressed the belief that they were not making their way up the organization.

Years of hard freezes and low salaries created skills imbalances:

The biggest issue is that we are not replenishing the staff. The real cost is in the future. We have not been hiring since 1992. For a knowledge organization that can be problematic. You can ask people to work harder, put in more weekends and evenings, but you can do that only so long. There is not a lot of fresh blood. We hired some short-term consultants with technical expertise. That doesn't show up right away, the gap in the workforce. Eight or nine years from now, a generation will be missing. That does worry us.[24]

The skills gaps were worse in some areas than in others:

We have some holes, we haven't done any hiring since 1992 and there has been attrition; there are skill areas we are thin in—you can only go so long on that. We need to rebalance. People with skills don't leave you evenly. Maybe accountants have a better job market; they are leaving us faster than others and we have requirements to do agency audits. This will imbalance us. And there are new cost accounting areas in defense, and there is information management. Folks with these skills leave you. These areas cannot take a generalist; you have to hire a specialist. We have to be able to do the work; we need to stabilize enough to fill these slots.[25]

The agency used reductions in force to get down quickly to the level of spending determined by Congress, rather than doing it slowly and relying more on attrition, in hopes that once down to the required level, it could stabilize and begin to hire where the skills imbalance was worst. At least in the short run, this strategy did not work:

GAO took 25 percent, even though the cut was 15 percent in one year, we did it in one RIF rather than two. We went to the Hill and said we reduced more than you wanted; we are down to 3,500—we want to hire in certain categories. The Hill said no. We want to keep you at 3,500. So we didn't roll over, but now there is no choice.[26]

The 3,500-position limit turned out not to be a floor, but a ceiling. GAO found that with limited budget and mandated costs, it could not afford 3,500 staff. Staffing was at 3,275 positions in 1999 and stayed there, despite efforts to convince appropriations subcommittee members that they had agreed informally to a level of 3,450. GAO administrators had envisioned a quick recovery from the deep cuts in 1996 and 1997, because they had RIFed very selectively to minimize collateral damage and because they envisioned a stabilization of the budget beginning in 1998, which would allow them to hire selectively to replace key staff who left the agency. But this imagined recovery did not occur because the agency was unable to make the new hires. All the problems pointed out by interviewees in 1996 were pointed out by the comptroller general in testimony four years later. There was a continuing inability to hire new staff, made worse by uncompetitive salaries in technical areas and imbalances in skills; low levels of training funds had made it difficult to retrain remaining staff to pick up the work of those who had left the organization or to train staff to use the new computer technology adequately. In addition, the organization was aging (the median age was 41 in 1992 and 47 in 1999), and many evaluators and a high proportion of the SES managers were within a few years of retirement.

In budget hearings in February 2000 the comptroller general outlined these problems and asked Congress's help to give the agency additional flexibility to deal with the problems. Walker did not ask for more money or more staff, but for authority for selective buyouts, rather than for a whole group of staff. The purpose of buyouts is to reduce staffing without reductions in force, but if they were available to everyone, the best people and the most crucial people might leave the agency first, exacerbating the skills gaps. But GAO needed somehow to make room under its staffing ceiling for new hires, and to do that it had to either use selective incentives to retire early or resort to a reduction in force. The comptroller general asked for permission to make a RIF very selective and targeted, reducing collateral damage to operations. He also asked for some flexibility in salary caps so GAO could compete with the executive branch for crucial skills.

The reductions in force, the ongoing freezes, the stuck promotions and low level of performance bonuses, as well as the continuing concern that cuts could recur had an impact on morale. In contrast to the Bureau of Labor Statistics, where the focus was on protecting staff insofar as possible, GAO administrators worked hard to protect the agency as a whole, sacrificing staff where necessary, but especially in the field offices. Continuing insecurity was a legacy of the rapid cuts. Nearly everyone knew someone who had been RIFed or who had taken early retirement or another job to avoid a RIF. The field offices in particular felt vulnerable, fearing that any future cuts would also fall on them, as they had in the past. Those at headquarters believed that the spotlight would eventually fall on them as the agency shrank and there was less need for supervisors. Having watched other people they knew get fired, some believed the agency was not loyal to employees. This insecurity led some people to say they would put in their required hours, but no more.

One staffer, who had been RIFed earlier in her career at another agency, described the impact of being fired:

> Until then, I had lots of loyalty to the organization, but I realized the RIF had nothing to do with me. It was impersonal; people who ran the RIF had lots of seniority and were protecting themselves, naturally. It had nothing to do with my job performance. Now my first priority is me; I worry about the organization after that. When it gets to the bottom line, I don't matter. I don't bend over backward like I used to do. I also learned that I can survive, that I have marketable skills.[27]

The effect on morale was marked but not extreme, in part because of professionalism, as senior managers such as Dexter Peach suggested. Protecting Washington office evaluators from RIF also had a positive effect on morale:

> DP: I don't want to discount that morale has an effect, but it was counteracted by the professionalism of our people who stayed focused on the work. Their ability to do so was impressive. There was a lot of concern, but productivity held up pretty well.
>
> IR: Longer hours?
>
> DP: Yes, that is going on.[28]

Reorganization happened slowly. A realignment of the field offices and headquarters was scheduled in 2000, despite the fact that field offices had been reduced from 46 in 1986 to 16 in 1996, including the elimination of four major field offices, eight sublocations, and two overseas offices.[29] Responsibility for overseeing the field offices was taken out of the office of the assistant comptroller general for operations and given to a new ACG, with the idea that having their own ACG would strengthen the voice of the field offices at the top levels of the administration. Two other top-level offices were combined, with the resulting office having responsibility for evaluation of the quality of research and for maintaining focus and control over the higher-risk projects.

AGENCY STRATEGIES

The impact of cuts on GAO was mediated by the agency's strategies. One strategy, described earlier, was to continue contacts with Congress uninterrupted and appear to do whatever the agency used to do, albeit with many fewer staff. This strategy resulted in taking most of the cuts in the field (with congressional encouragement to reorganize the field). In a further effort to continue to serve Congress as if nothing had happened, GAO produced shorter studies and more informal products. It was thus able to meet congressional needs with fewer resources.

Agency strategies also included continuing emphasis on computerization and additional efforts to document the impacts of its own work, especially in dollar terms.

Computerization and Communications

Administrators for GAO emphasized the importance of modernization of technology for helping GAO maintain and improve its productivity in the face of cuts, but in fact, the agency had difficulty, as have many federal agencies, in modernizing its technology. Efforts began with the first set of personnel cuts in 1992, then lagged a bit, picking up again when the second major set of personnel reductions was introduced. After years of effort the agency was finally able to create common files to which field and headquarters staff could write. Staff could comment on and revise files without sending them back and forth. By 1996 nearly all the staff had computers, although some were old and slow and would freeze up if too many applications were in use at the same time. Only a few machines had access to the Internet, while the agency wrestled with the possibility that Internet access might be abused by some. The consensus among staff using the new system was that it was an improvement but did not save that much time. The final effort did not have as much effect as the job design reinvention project but probably did contribute to the improved productivity in the agency. As various difficulties were worked out, the system was becoming more useful. However, the costs of computerization and updating were not initially included in the budget; Comptroller General Walker made a special plea for computer funds to update software in his FY 2001 budget request.

Documenting the Impacts of Its Own Work

GAO began to document the impact of the work it was doing with greater intensity. With the help of the budget issues area staff, other issue areas were encouraged to design their work with a view to how much money their recommendations would save if implemented. GAO then tracked the proportion of these proposals that were in fact implemented. The goal was to show that spending on the GAO was cost effective and, by implication, that cuts to GAO would result in net dollar losses, not effective budget reductions:

> Some divisions at GAO have always given advice on savings, but the word savings was not used with a consistent definition. The context was how to manage federal agencies. Now we pay more attention to translating our work into terms of the budget debate. We used to say "Agency X, Progress Made, but Problems Remain." There was no sensitivity to the budget context. How much would it cost to fix? Now we see it in the [GAO] book, *Budget Implications of GAO Work*. I see it in our consulting work for other units in GAO. . . . We are trying to

increase the sensitivity of the other units to scoring issues, what CBO does [estimating the dollar impact of proposals].[30]

GAO began to emphasize the dollar savings associated with implementation of its recommendations. For 1995 GAO estimated savings of $15.8 billion, $35 for every dollar appropriated for GAO. This figure was prominently featured in the 1995 Annual Report.[31] By 1997 GAO claimed $21 billion in fiscal effects, a return of $44 for every dollar appropriated for GAO.[32] GAO claimed $57 of benefits for each dollar appropriated in 1999.[33]

In a related effort, the GAO sought to show that it had the expertise Congress needed to help it achieve a balanced budget. One effort along these lines was the creation of an extensive list of options for Congress to use in making proposals to balance the budget. This list of options was annotated with GAO studies behind each recommendation. The Congressional Budget Office helped GAO to score the recommendations, that is, to figure out how much savings could be achieved from each one of the proffered suggestions. Reportedly, this volume was heavily used by Rep. John Kasich, chair of the House Budget Committee, and helped GAO through some difficult times.

GAO's list of options for reducing the deficit was similar to one put out regularly by the Congressional Budget Office. The difference was that GAO's was backed up with its own studies. Despite the differences, this product stepped on the turf of CBO, another congressional agency. CBO cooperated in scoring the volume in order to prevent GAO from putting out another set of numbers and making all the numbers look less authoritative as a result. CBO was initially not happy about GAO's intrusion, but adapted well.

CONCLUSIONS

Impacts at GAO are difficult to measure, especially because the agency strategy was to appear to continue to do whatever it had been doing for Congress as well as in the past, if not better. Productivity, in terms of the number of products completed per 100 staff members, increased, but quality, which the agency is anxious to maintain, may be dropping to the extent that the shorter reports are not just shorter, but are also more superficial. The reinvented job process helped reduce design problems on each project, and the more selective upper-level review of work in progress should help streamline the work process, resulting in shorter project time without product deterioration. However, the almost exclusive emphasis on work at the request of Congress when combined with the elimination of a number of field offices and the shift to greater dependence on secondary data may result in a lowering of quality in some products. Some of the changes have clearly been cost effective—some field office operations were no longer necessary, some increased reliance on secondary data is appropriate—but some of the changes will result in reliance on relatively poor data where better data could be gathered.

GAO's strategy has been to improve the work design process and improve computerization and communications to increase productivity. But a second, and unstated strategy has been to draw down reserves, of knowledge and staff expertise and energy. If this process goes on too long, product quality will inevitably deteriorate. The strategy was premised on the understanding that the agency would get down to 3,500 quickly and stabilize and then be able to recruit selectively to get in some new blood and repair skills imbalances. So far, this premise has not been realized. As of December 1997 the agency was finally authorized to hire a limited number of new employees, but those numbers are well short of the 3,450 target. Staffing levels remained stable in 1999 and 2000; the request for 2001 was for no increase in staffing. The agency strategy of continuing to provide service at close to former levels, of not letting anyone see any deterioration, worked against a realistic limit to the cuts.

There is a danger that an agency already known for its caution will become more cautious yet and hence be unable to fulfill the role of watchdog for Congress. Interviewees at GAO argued strongly that the agency had not been blunted. Dexter Peach captured the complexity of issues and the GAO response clearly:

IR: Has GAO become more cautious as a result of threats to the organization?

DP: No, I don't buy that. Over the years, some people have thought of GAO as risk averse, but I look at all the reports. I don't see us operating differently than we did before. We take positions that we think are the right positions, not just supportive positions.

You do have to be careful and aware of the environment at all times. The environment has become—there has been an upward trend in partisanship, since the 1980s. The environment is more partisan. Working with Congress, you have to be aware of the environment into which the work is going. As work goes out, it will draw reactions. You have to make sure you have done your homework. Defend the work if it is controversial. It doesn't mean that you don't put out controversial work; it means you have to be aware of the environment.

GAO was on the cutting edge with the S&L crisis. Equally significant, not everyone was happy with our position on derivatives. The organization is still out front. We said the derivatives could cause problems before Orange County proved the truth of that.[34]

Among the more interesting consequences of the reductions and the agency's strategies of response has been a change in the agency's mission. The cuts have propelled the agency further along a track it had started on years earlier, away from the role of independent critic and watchdog for the public and more toward a staff function for Congress. This change, while apparently necessary for survival, was also fraught with risk. It continued to place the agency in the middle of policy debates, requiring especially careful staff work and backup documents to satisfy those who opposed the agency's results and who questioned whether the findings were objective and professional. At precisely the time when the agency was trying to demonstrate the quality of its products, it was producing more products that were difficult if not impossible for the agency to evaluate in terms of quality. The shorter projects that were internally evaluated were sometimes judged as more superficial. GAO began to emphasize the impact of a smaller number of important studies.

A second and related consequence was that the domain, the accepted area of activity of the agency, got shaky. The elimination of a number of field offices hastened the shift to more secondary data; the use of more secondary data made GAO less distinctive as an organization. Many organizations, both inside and outside government, have the capacity to analyze secondary data. Some GAO members reported recently that studies that would have been done by GAO were given to outsiders, such as the National Academy of Public Administration. Without unique sources of inside data and firsthand reports, GAO was somewhat handicapped in responding to these pressures. Unlike the Census Bureau, GAO could not argue that it was written into the Constitution, nor could it argue as the Bureau of Labor Statistics did that its data on business required a level of security that could not be guaranteed by outside organizations. GAO's putting out a product that overlapped an existing one by the Congressional Budget Office highlighted the problem of loss of uniqueness. GAO will probably find a new niche where it is uniquely valuable, but while it is searching and adapting, its staff may experience further demoralization. The elimination of the small Office of Technology Assessment, in part because there were other agencies that could provide the same information, served as a reminder of what could happen.

Increased efficiency can certainly help during a period of cutback, but it is unlikely to create savings in the realm of 40 percent. Some of the gap will be made up by quality losses and some by prioritization. Because GAO is less driven by its own agenda and more by Congress's, prioritization by the agency is especially difficult. The protocol for dealing with Congress makes it as plain as GAO can make it, while still dealing with generalities, what the priorities are and whose requests come first.

GAO had experience with downsizing and changing mission earlier in its history; it had been continually adapting to changing patterns of requests for studies from Congress. In the 1980s it had routinely altered the proportion of self-generated studies to legislatively requested ones as it changed its role. All this experience was relevant; these strategies were available when the agency needed to adapt again to changing demands. At the same time, it had to invent new responses as it went along, including reinventing the work process, short-circuiting the lengthy review process that had slowed down release of its studies, and increasing its accountability and responsiveness to Congress. It had to computerize operations and keep those operations updated, with inadequate budget for software and training, in order to increase productivity as much as possible.

As GAO has shifted its role, it has become more of a straight staff agency for Congress. Rather than increase its independence, in order to survive, GAO has emphasized its responsiveness. Not only is it striving to do whatever Congress asks of it and have study requesters evaluate what GAO gives them, it is trying hard to reply to all the criticisms that have been leveled against it, such as that it took too long to produce reports; that the agency was hungry for headlines and released studies with too much fanfare, sometimes blindsiding members of Congress; and that GAO was partisan, favoring Democrats over Republicans. But the agency's responses left it vulnerable, because it remains a policy adviser, keeping it visible on the political radar and making enemies on each high-profile project that it weighs in on, and because its adaptations make it more like other organizations that serve Congress. Its continuing vulnerability may make it cautious. The internal reorganization in FY 2000 suggests that the comptroller general's office will give more careful scrutiny to any report that may stir up a hornet's nest. To the extent that the GAO has to compete with other agencies and private organizations that are trying to tailor their results to please their customers, GAO may be pressed to do the same.

While many observers have noted the disruptive effect of RIFs on agency productivity and morale, some have argued that the effects are temporary and that reduced staffing levels motivate management improvements and necessary job reinvention, including the application of new technology. While the GAO case supports this thesis to some extent, it also points out the long-term and ongoing effects of such deep cuts on an agency and the difficulty of recovering, in part because the agency has no way of controlling demand when its ability to supply a product shrinks. GAO could ask committee chairs to prioritize their requests, but it was hard to say no to congressional requests at a time when the agency feared antagonizing members.

The GAO was not able to recover quickly. In 2000, four years after the RIFs and staff reductions, many of the problems created by the office closings and RIFs not only remained, they were worse than they had been. The agency was still experiencing difficulties with skills imbalances resulting from the long hiring freeze, low salaries for specialists, and lack of incentive bonuses for good performance. Discouraged employees may have increased turnover in crucial job categories; lack of new blood at the junior levels of the organization prevented the organization from taking full advantage of new technology; and training funds continue to be too low to make up for skills gaps and create some flexibility. A major reorganization in 2000 kept the organization in tumult. These changes may or may not solve some of GAO's problems, but in any case, the plan for a quick, deep cut followed by rapid recovery has not worked out as anticipated.

PART TWO

Trimming the Herds?

CHAPTER 6

Department of Agriculture

THE LINE DEPARTMENTS such as Agriculture, HUD, and Commerce had a different set of problems than the statistical and budgeting agencies as they wrestled with cutbacks over a period of years. Unlike the statistical agencies and to a lesser extent the budget offices, there was no obvious bottom line, no necessary level of excellence below which it was not useful to go. Census data that are full of mistakes are not much use; a consumer price index that is not updated sufficiently often or that does not reflect continuing research is not very accurate and may flummox users. Budget offices that do not provide unbiased information on the economy and its impact on expenditures and the deficit are vulnerable to charges of nonprofessional behavior. The consequences of a poor budget projection are easily seen. But the line departments do not necessarily have measures of quality that are easily visible to outsiders. There may be more temptation to erode quality as budgets decline. The Department of Agriculture (USDA) faced resource declines and staffing erosion over a number of years, making recovery and adaptation to lower resource levels more difficult. According to its own records, USDA experienced staffing declines from 1993 to 1999. Those declines were only partly linked to reinvented work processes and simplified programs.

The line departments had difficulty when trying the BLS approach to cutting product lines to maintain quality, because their product lines were closely tied to constituency groups. If they wanted to simplify their product lines or close offices, they often faced congressional opposition. The Department of Agriculture was able to get a reorganization through Congress that reduced the number of field offices, but the Forest Service, a major component of USDA, was not included.

The staff bureaus like OMB and GAO had to take cuts without a fight and make themselves a model of how to deal with reduced resources, in part out of pride, in part out of fear of appearing hypocritical if they refused to do to themselves that which they asked other agencies to do. These staff agencies also lacked an external constituency willing to fight for programs and funding levels. Theoretically, the line agencies did not have to take such a role; they could fight back and resist cuts in a variety of ways. Agriculture did not seem to resist cuts but instead sought to comply with the National Performance Review (NPR) by directing and shaping its recommendations. GAO wanted to be left alone to take the cuts in whatever way it thought best; by contrast, Agriculture wanted to be told by Congress and the White House to do that which it had already decided to do. USDA wanted buy-in on its cuts, because it feared that Congress would block its plans if those plans had not been negotiated in detail.

What did the USDA learn over these seventeen years of efforts to balance the budget? To what extent did it learn to manage better, creating a government that works better and costs less? To what extent did it eat its seed corn, absorbing cuts, allowing infrastructure to deteriorate, losing those with special skills, making few fundamental changes in the hope that things would get better? The department did seem to learn some things from past experience, but the department was so decentralized there was very little superstructure to plan and evaluate past actions and cumulate them. Moreover, the environment and the department's mission were changing so quickly that prior learning was soon outdated.

THE USDA

The U.S. Department of Agriculture experienced cutbacks twice during the period from 1981 to 1998, once in the mid-1980s and again after 1993. The department found that there was a kind of bottom line. The quality of management deteriorated when staffing levels got too far out of line with programmatic complexity. The result was terrible publicity and enormous pressure to improve program quality, reduce fraud, and improve its customer relations.

Bad press and serious critiques from GAO accompanied pressure from Congress to improve service and reduce costs. Democratic majorities in 1994 helped pass reorganization legislation; Republican majorities in 1996 helped pass new farm legislation that was more free-market oriented and simpler to administer. Within USDA, continuity of some key staff members helped the agency formulate plans. But the agency's aim to match program simplification with budget and staffing reductions was overwhelmed initially by failure to plan sufficiently for computer modernization and then by having personnel reductions outstrip the program simplifications that Congress had passed. Farm aid programs were simplified, but forestry programs remained a source of contention in Congress and were excluded from reorganization, as staffing continued downward. By the year 2000 major problems with the simplified farm legislation were creating pressure to restore countercyclical aid to farmers, suggesting renewed program complexity and needs for additional staffing in the future.

Background and Overview

Despite its reputation for being an unchanging and unchangeable bureaucracy, USDA underwent major shifts during the period of this study. The shifts included budget cuts, dramatic program changes, reorganizations in the field and at headquarters, staffing cuts, and computerization and telecommunications projects. The changes also included a shift in emphasis from traditional service programs to environmental protection and food safety, after a major shift toward nutrition entitlement programs.

From the Great Depression onward, USDA services were provided to farmers. The agency had about 3,700 county offices, including many in counties that were not rural. As the number of farmers and especially the number of family farms decreased, support for traditional farm-support programs gradually declined. In the early 1980s fights broke out over price supports for crops such as sugar and peanuts. Some specific crop subsidies narrowly held on, but the fights were indications of a heretofore unknown erosion of spending support.

The USDA's mission gradually changed. A substantial majority of USDA spending is not for discretionary programs but for entitlements, such as food stamps. The Agriculture Department also provides surplus food for poverty programs. The department's constituencies have accordingly broadened out to include urban areas. The department acquired new issues as it broadened its focus. The food stamp program was widely considered to be subject to fraud, imposing new managerial challenges. A series of contaminated food episodes put the focus on USDA's food inspection and food safety programs, further broadening its constituencies. None of the department's newer functions have the same local support linkages that agricultural research and pest eradication programs have had.

The USDA grew from 1960 to 1980, at least in part due to President Lyndon Johnson's War on Poverty and the food programs USDA had come to provide. Staffing grew from 81,600 to more than 125,000 staff years.[1] But with the efforts to balance the budget and cut programs, USDA suffered continual staffing declines from 1981–86. OMB reported 117,000 full-time equivalent employees in 1981 and only 103,000 by 1986, a drop of about 12 percent.[2]

The major problem with these staff reductions was that they were not tied to program simplification or elimination of offices. The work remained, the level of overhead was constant, but there were fewer people to manage and do the work. The radical disconnection between the complexity of programs and the staffing levels contributed to major management problems. Criticisms of the department and its programs mounted, and staff were gradually reintroduced, until 1994 when a major reorganization took place and the staffing reductions and budget savings of the congressionally approved NPR proposals went into effect. By 1994 federal staffing levels had recovered from their low of 103,000 to about 110,000.[3]

From 1995 through 1999 the USDA experienced a second round of staffing reductions. From the peak in 1994 of 110,000, staffing was reduced to 95,000 in 1999.[4] Initially scheduled for additional reductions, preliminary estimates suggest that by 2000, staffing levels had stabilized and begun to turn around. OMB estimated 98,000 full-time equivalents for the year 2000 and 101,000 in 2001. Though recovering somewhat, staffing levels remained well below 1994 levels.

The first deep round of personnel cuts was not matched by program simplification; the smaller staff could not run the programs as well as the larger staff had done. The result was complaints against the agency's performance, which contributed to the second round of cuts. During the second round of cuts in the mid-1990s, much more effort was made to simplify programs and reorganize to match reduced staffing levels.

Participants described this effort to match programmatic requirements to reduced staffing levels as only partly successful because the balanced budget requirements were so strict and so independent of programmatic changes. The staffing reductions of the 1990s were framed by stringent budget limitations. Moreover, the agency achieved only a part of the program simplification it hoped for, and virtually none in the Forest Service.

The history of budget growth and cuts is reflected in table 6.1, which lists budget authority for the USDA from 1976 to 2002.

The USDA FY 1999 budget request summarized the budget reductions from 1993 on. The budget request discusses outlays, rather than budget authority, so the numbers are a little different from the figures in table 6.1. The references to the workforce are to total staffing, which combines federal staffing and some

Table 6.1 Budget Authority for USDA, 1976–2002 (in $ millions)

Year	Amount	Year	Amount
1976	20,755	1989	55,733
TQ (transitional quarter)	4,245	1990	55,327
1977	21,897	1991	60,075
1978	26,719	1992	66,288
1979	37,314	1993	67,857
1980	39,628	1994	65,585
1981	47,496	1995	58,571
1982	57,481	1996	58,734
1983	69,921	1997	60,876
1984	46,824	1998	58,300
1985	61,916	1999	67,729
1986	59,249	2000 est.	72,311
1987	52,518	2001 est.	66,362
1988	55,236	2002 est.	64,955

Source: The U.S. Budget, Historical Tables, FY 2001, Table 5.2 Budget Authority by Agency, 1976–2000.

county-level officials, and hence differ somewhat from the figures for federal full-time equivalent staffing levels:

> USDA outlays have declined from $63.1 billion in 1993 to an estimated $54.3 billion in 1999—a 14 percent reduction. These savings have been possible due to the strengthening economy, program reforms enacted by the Congress, and USDA's aggressive streamlining effort, which reduced the size of its workforce by almost 20,000 staff years through 1997 and will result in a further cut of about 2,000 by 1999. For 1999, USDA expects outlays to decrease to $54.3 billion from $55 billion in 1998, due to favorable economic conditions, higher levels of prior year loan repayments, savings through further reductions in employment, implementation of welfare reform legislation, selected program reductions and the shift of certain programs from Federal funding to user fees.[5]

The budget cuts of the 1990s were accompanied by sharp drops in staffing levels, as shown in table 6.2.

The reported staffing level for the federal portion of USDA for 1999 was 95,491, a decrease from 1993 of 16.6 percent. Total staffing for the department was reported at 106,998 for 1999, a drop of 17.3 percent from 1993. The biggest declines were in the Forest Service, which lost about 17 percent of its labor force; National Resources Conservation, also about 17 percent reduction; Rural Housing, which lost about 26 percent of its staffing; and the Farm Service Agency, which lost about 26 percent of its employees.

The 1981–87 Period. The USDA experienced round one of the cuts in the early and mid-1980s. The discretionary programs were cut in 1983 and then again in 1986. Staffing levels decreased throughout the early and mid-1980s. The problem of mismatch between staffing levels and program responsibilities was intense in 1986 when Gramm-Rudman-Hollings sequestration cut dollars during the year. GRH cuts were not related to programmatic revisions; they cut eligible or "sequestratable" dollars during the year across the board, program by program, and nearly line item by line item.

Table 6.2   USDA Staffing Declines, 1993–2002

	1993	1994	1995	1996	1997	1998	1999	2000 (est.)
USDA-Fed	114,542	110,055	103,955	100,710	101,656	99,866	95,491	98,155
Nonfed	14,953	14,176	13,432	12,738	11,729	9,879	11,507	11,388
USDA-Total	129,495	124,241	117,387	113,448	113,385	109,745	106,998	109,543

Source: USDA budget requests, various years.

The agricultural programs of the USDA were deeply cut in comparison to many other federal expenditures: the budget for USDA was only 3 percent of the total budget for the U.S. government, but the Agriculture Department took about 28 percent of the cuts. The reason is that Gramm-Rudman-Hollings exempted many programs from cuts, particularly entitlement programs. The amount of money available for sequester in nondefense programs across the government was only $105 billion. Of that, the Department of Agriculture had $29 billion. The amount of the cut due to the 1986 sequester (across-the-board cut to get down to a fixed level of deficit) for the Agriculture Department was $1.3 billion.[6]

One result of the sequester was a cut in staff of about 6,000 during the year. Many programs were thrown into disarray. Program managers froze staffing levels, planned furloughs, requested permission for early retirements, and began to think about requests to Congress to simplify programs or make them less demanding of staff time. Budget Director Stephen Dewhurst argued that some of the adaptations taken at that time created management problems that lingered in the mid-1990s: "Even today, we continue to receive reports by the General Accounting Office and other oversight authorities that relate largely to program integrity problems that originated in the mid-to-late 1980s when staffing was out of line with programs."[7]

Interestingly, the agency did not plan reductions in force as a result of the 1986 sequestration but instead sought to rely on freezes and attrition, furloughs, and buyouts, because RIFs were perceived as too expensive to save much money during the budget year. As noted earlier, information about the costs of RIFs was widely available by 1984, based on agency experiences in the 1982–83 period. This knowledge about how to reduce staffing came into play again in the 1990s, when the agency asked for and received permission to engage in buyouts.

What made the problem of mismatch between staffing and programmatic requirements especially acute was a farm crisis. In the middle and late 1980s the farm economy was in a shambles, farm prices were dropping, commodity prices were low, and agricultural programs had to bail out farmers. The result was increases in spending and responsibilities. Proposals to seriously revamp agricultural programs to make them more flexible and less costly were not considered during this period of acute farm crisis.

An additional complexity for some programs was the renewed public emphasis on environmental protection. The 1985 Farm Act, which authorized the farm programs of the USDA, made some major changes in the Soil Conservation Service (SCS), which hit the agency about the same time as Gramm-Rudman-Hollings. The SCS experienced some management and morale problems as a result.

The Soil Conservation Service had experienced only a 2 percent increase in its budget in 1982 and drops of 10 and 8 percent in 1983 and 1984, respectively. Personnel levels declined from 14,156 in 1983 to 13,290 in 1985 or by about 6 percent. Staffing levels dropped further in 1986 and 1987, as Gramm-Rudman-Hollings kicked in, to 12,895 in 1986 and 12,393 in 1987, about a 12 percent decline from 1983 to 1987. Program responsibilities increased during this period; the 1985 farm bill, the Food Security Act, revamped the soil conservation program completely, changing it from a voluntary program to a regulatory one in which farmers had to participate if they wanted agricultural program benefits. The new legislation put enormous new burdens on agency staff, to measure and log erodable lands and wetlands and to examine farmers' plans to combat erosion. In an effort to cope, in 1988 the agency had added 1,352 employees, to a level of 13,745, which it maintained more or less until 1993.[8] The legislative redesign of the Soil Conservation Service changed the relationship of the agency with its clientele, the farmers. The SCS had been a resource to answer questions and to help farmers, but after the 1985 legislation, the agency's role had shifted more to a regulatory one, where there were possible clashes with farmers. The support base for the program was thus weakened.

The programmatic chaos in a time of farm crisis resulted in add-backs not just in the Soil Conservation Service, but across the department. According to the CBO data shown in table 6.3, total staffing (that is, federal plus county employees) grew from 111,000 in 1987 to a peak of 122,300 in 1992, at least in part in an attempt to make programs run better.

The staffing cuts in the mid-1980s were problematic not only because they were sharp and occurred during the budget year, but also because programmatic changes and reorganization were blocked: "Enthusiasm for reducing administrative resources was far greater than enthusiasm for reducing programs."[9] Consolidation of programs, field offices, or central administrative staff offices was perceived as impossible in the face of numerous riders on appropriations and other legislation forbidding it. Reorganization proposals were formulated inside the department but never put forward because the environment suggested they would not succeed.

Adding back staff did not resolve administrative problems. The highly decentralized structure of departmental programs made it nearly impossible for the USDA to monitor the farm crisis and explain what was going on, exposing management weaknesses. A series of newspaper stories and GAO reports[10] called attention to specific administrative and organizational problems.

Table 6.3   Staffing Levels, USDA, 1985–92, CBO Data (in thousands)

1985	1986	1987	1988	1989	1990	1991	1992
115.4	111.2	111.0	115.2	117.8	118.9	118.4	122.3

Source: CBO, "Changes in Federal Civilian Employment: An Update," April 1998.

Note: Figures represent an annual average of monthly counts.

The 1988–92 Period. This period was one of add-backs in staffing each year and also one of growth in outlays for the department as a whole. Outlays for USDA for 1988 were $44 billion; by 1992 they had increased to $56.4 billion, an increase of about 27 percent. Part of this increase reflected payouts for food stamps during the recession of the early 1990s and increases in payouts to farmers from 1990 to 1992.

The increase in spending did not reflect increased confidence in USDA management. Complaints against the agriculture department's operations continued to mount. Some of these complaints were aimed at the agricultural support programs. In 1990, in a dramatic confrontation, a task force of the House Budget Committee met with a number of members of Congress from the Agriculture Committee to look for ways to reduce spending on agricultural programs. The Agriculture Committee representatives were defensive, noting that they had already taken major cuts. Congressman Jerry Huckaby, in a statement to the Budget Committee Task Force on Urgent Fiscal Issues, argued against gutting programs because of perceived abuses. He argued that the Agriculture Committee was willing to work with the Budget Committee to eliminate abuses.[11]

Charles Schumer, chair of the Budget Committee task force, was concerned not only about abuses, but also about the distribution of the benefits from farm programs. Part of the concern was that in the restructuring of farm programs after 1985, farmers were paid to do some things or not do other things, getting away from the idea of price supports: "That has ended up meaning that a high percentage of the dollars go to the top end, to the most wealthy people in the agriculture business."[12] Schumer noted that the top 3.6 percent of farms received 42 percent of payments.[13] A major source of political support for farm programs, public attachment to the idea of family farms, had been weakened by the changing program structure. As the program goals changed to prevention of erosion (and reduced acreage being planted, in order to hold down production and keep prices up), participation of large and more successful landholders became more important and more funding went to them.

Rep. Richard Armey agreed with some of Schumer's concerns but also noted that the Agriculture Committee bills routinely vastly underestimated farm program costs: "In 1981, the committee predicted that their farm bill would cost $12 billion, and it actually cost $55 billion. In 1985, they predicted it would cost $52 billion. It ultimately cost $88 billion. If past performance is any indicator, the new bill will likely bust the budget by tens of billions of dollars."[14] Such underestimates had major impacts on the size of the deficit. In addition, Armey was disturbed by the contradictory thrusts of the agricultural programs, limiting acreage on the one hand and encouraging maximum production on the other.

The GAO had been criticizing agency management in a series of reports. One came out in 1989.[15] Another came out in 1991.[16] In critiquing some of the department's programs to enhance agricultural exports, the GAO found major administrative weaknesses in tracking proposals, verifying information used in bid processes, and in documenting price- and bonus-setting activities. The GAO also found some overpayments. GAO spokesperson Allan Mendelowitz noted that the program was complex and that progress had been made in improving program administration between 1988 when the first GAO report of administrative weaknesses came out and 1990 when a follow-up report was done.[17] He noted with satisfaction that the department had assigned more staff to the regulations, procedures, and reports branch of the Commodity Credit Corporation's operations division, to improve the branch's operations, including export enhancement program activities such as bid receipt and program activity reporting. In addition, a planning and evaluation staff was added. By implication, before these staff additions, the department had too few staff to run such a complex program efficiently.[18] In September 1991 the General Accounting Office issued a summary report of its three-year review of USDA's management and structure, which stated in part that USDA's organizational structure was not responsive to the new challenges facing the department. Congress responded to the criticisms with hearings and legislative proposals, ultimately focusing on consolidating and integrating organizational functions.

The agency presented a formal proposal to Congress in fall 1993, but it was 1994 before it passed. The secretary had argued in the interim that reorganization at headquarters should logically precede reorganization in the field, and key members of Congress accepted this addition. By 1993 Rep. Dan Glickman was arguing that reorganization would not only produce better service and save money by reducing staffing levels, but that reorganization should be accompanied by an explicit effort to simplify programs.

Glickman described the response not only of the USDA, but also of OMB to the hearings:

> As a result of the hearings, the Department, for the first time in over a decade, made reorganizing a high priority. Secretary Madigan reinstituted the State Food and Agriculture Councils, first organized in 1982 by then-Secretary John Block, as the major vehicle for looking at overall USDA field structure and recommending improvements. The Department held a series of town meetings around the country and discussed with farmers, county employees, and others their ideas on reorganization and began upgrading and integrating its computer networks. It initiated eight pilot projects aimed at making programs easier for farmers to use and county employees to administer.
>
> The Secretary and the Director of the Office of Management and Budget, Richard Darman, formed a team to review USDA field structure. The team consisted of 30 staff which collected and manipulated useful data on field agencies. It gave this information to USDA, which

in turn, used it to make field office closing determinations leading to Secretary Madigan's decision to close 1,242 field offices.[19]

1993–94 Reorganization and the NPR Recommendations, Savings and Staff Reductions

Agriculture Secretary Edward R. Madigan bequeathed his plan to Secretary Mike Espy, who succeeded him when President Clinton was elected. Espy reformulated the plan to include administration priorities. The internal planning process fed into the NPR study of the USDA, so that the NPR report on agriculture asked for the same changes the department was generally pushing for, and both reflected the criticisms that GAO had been leveling against the department and some of its programs. The NPR report in 1993 recommended a reorganization of the Department of Agriculture to better accomplish its mission, streamline its field structure, and improve service to customers. The NPR report argued that at the field level, the USDA's county structure was symptomatic of its organizational problems and was in need of major overhaul.

The NPR recommended not only a consolidation of programs and of field structure and a clarification and simplification of mission, it also required improved customer services and secondarily, budget savings. These savings would result in part from consolidation and elimination of field offices and reduction in staffing levels. That meant that the reorganization had to get more efficiency out of a reduced number of staff. Normally, reorganizations follow staff reductions and do not produce additional savings, so this one had to be put together very carefully.

The National Performance Review issued a number of reports, some specific to agencies, some more general. Of the more general issues, reducing staffing levels was important and, in particular, reducing the number of what were perceived as controllers, in personnel, budget, and accounting offices, and supervisors of all sorts. The idea was that bureaucrats were limited in their ability to adopt new ideas for greater efficiency by all the rules and rulers. Rules would be simplified or discarded, and the number of supervisors would be drastically reduced. The NPR recommended a series of reforms in budgeting, purchasing, and personnel that would allow such a reduction in staffing. In fact, many of the purchasing reforms took place, but budgeting did not get simplified; if anything, it became more complex as requirements for audited statements were added to performance plans and evaluations. NPR suggestions for using computerization more extensively to replace staff and improve services proved burdensome for many of the agencies, USDA included. Targets were set for personnel reductions that had nothing to do with management improvements, budget levels, or process simplifications. The NPR's staffing reduction targets were increased by Congress. Thus while there was considerable overlap in the specifics of agency reform between the NPR and USDA, on the more general issues there were inevitable difficulties.

THE REORGANIZATION PLAN

At headquarters, in response to the advice to tighten the focus of the department, six mission areas were proposed (seven were later approved) and 43 agencies were combined into 29 along mission lines. Support agencies at the state level were to be combined and reduced—overhead functions were to be centralized, rather than reproduced in each agency. The number of field offices was to be reduced and the Farm Service Administration, NRCS, and the Rural Development Program were to be colocated for one-stop service.

The number of field office locations was to be reduced from 3,700 to 2,500. The goal was a team approach to service delivery. The reorganization was designed explicitly to save money, working from financial targets to reorganization decisions. The goal was to reduce staffing by 16,400 by 2002 and save a cumulative total of $8 billion. The department was ahead of schedule in staffing reductions by 1998. Between 1994, when the reorganization was passed, and 14 May 1997, through closings and relocations, the USDA had reduced the number of county offices from about 3,700 to about 2,650, with the remaining targeted 150 scheduled for merger or closing by the end of the fiscal year.[20]

Congress paid attention to the office closings. Sen. John McCain pointed out in 1997 that there were many constraints in report language and in the agriculture appropriations bill. He noted that there were not only prohibitions on closing particular sites, but also language specifying the level of staffing at particular geographic sites:

> This is the eighth appropriations bill to come before the Senate in these two weeks. And I must say that this bill and report, so far, take the cake for earmarks and set-asides for Members' special interests.
>
> I have several pages listing the earmarks and set-asides for funding in this bill. Most of these earmarks are in the report language and do not, therefore, have the full force of law. But I have no doubt that the Department of Agriculture will feel compelled to spend the funds appropriated to them in accordance with these earmarks.
>
> These earmarks are the usual collection of add-ons for universities and laboratories, prohibitions on closing facilities or cutting personnel levels, special exemptions for certain areas, and the like. There is little on this list that would surprise any of my colleagues.
>
> There is, however, a new type of earmark that I do not recall seeing in other appropriations bills. I am referring to the practice of earmarking funds to provide additional personnel at specific locations.[21]

Despite some interest in some particular locations and localized programs and staffing levels, Congress generally approved the agriculture reorganization with the understanding that if any closures caused undue hardship to farmers, the secretary would use discretion granted in the reorganization legislation to take that office off the list of mergers or eliminations:

> We were going to close a lot of offices. They [Congress] wanted to know which offices. Our administrators said they didn't know yet; they forestalled public disclosure of closure sites until after the reorganization passed. Then they sent a list to Congress with the offer to make changes if absolutely necessary. There were few changes in the plan. A hairy element in reorganization was people's fears about which offices; 1,200 offices were closed, and lots of people affected.
>
> It's now the in thing to close offices. They [legislators] don't get as upset as they used to. It is incredible to watch. In the late 1980s Madigan was secretary; he was tootling through a hearing when a senator from New Jersey, who was not on the subcommittee, but who was permitted to come in and ask questions, began to berate the secretary because we were prepared to close an office in Bayonne. We had a nine-person office. The secretary of agriculture spent an hour with those folks. In the '80s there were conversations like that. Now we can't close offices fast enough. They have to be in favor of cutting federal offices. [He implies here that even if you aren't in favor, you would be embarrassed to say so.][22]

As noted earlier, the Forest Service was not included in the reorganization. Senators saw the need to save money by closing offices but knew that doing so was politically difficult and sought some cover for themselves. Sen. Patrick Leahy argued that he wanted a politically viable way to close regional offices of the Forest Service:

> In order to make office closure recommendations politically viable, we could consider an approach similar to the Commission on Agricultural Research Facilities authorized in the 1990 farm bill. This process was set up to take no more than 240 days from the date of authorization. Alternatively, we could consider a more comprehensive strategy similar to the military base closing scheme. I am most interested in something that is responsible and realistic.[23]

Sen. Robert Byrd described the problem confronting the subcommittee—under the budget balancing pressure, the subcommittee was getting smaller allocations while service demands increased. Greater efficiency seemed to be the only possible answer:

> As we have seen in the Department of Interior's effort to close some Bureau of Mines offices, and in the Department of Agriculture's effort to close some agricultural research facilities, office closures cannot be done in a piecemeal fashion. A politically viable plan must be a comprehensive plan that justifies to Senators the decisions made. It must also take into consideration the changing roles of some of the other players in the Federal family when it comes to natural resource issues.[24]

Sen. Don Nickles explained why it was so politically difficult to close regional offices:

> The subcommittee currently has four members who have regional Forest Service offices in their States. The full committee has six members with regional offices in their State. Several other Senators share a strong interest in this issue, particularly because the regional offices are an important source of jobs and revenue for their constituents. A strategy must account for political realities of the task before us.
>
> We will not be able to achieve the savings that this subcommittee needs to find if we continue with the existing Forest Service structure. Furthermore, we may not serve the Forest Service well if office closures are based on politics alone.[25]

According to this account in the *Congressional Record,* in 1994 senators requested an administratively sound plan for downsizing, restructuring, or reorganizing the Forest Service. The problem, however, was not the absence of a plan but the absence of implementation. As Sen. Richard Lugar pointed out in 1994:

> I requested that the Forest Service examine this issue three years ago. A report was produced describing a variety of different proposals which have not been implemented to date. The Agriculture Committee spared mandatory direction for the Forest Service in S. 1970 because the President had designated the Forest Service to be a laboratory for reinvention. It is critical that this effort produce concrete results that the administration and Congress can implement collectively and effectively.[26]

The budget director of the USDA saw the lack of reorganization in the Forest Service a little differently: "The Forest Service has been hamstrung. They experienced budget cuts. There were some things they could do to save money, but the Forest Service structural changes have been defeated on the Hill; we don't know what to do. We can't get consensus. The Interior committees' oversight is so intense that we don't know quite what to do."[27]

The Forest Service is under the jurisdiction of the appropriations subcommittees that oversee the Department of the Interior. Members on this subcommittee asked questions about each project and program, tracking the amount of lumber logged and issues of forest health in intense detail. While the agriculture committees were interested in good management to save money and provide services, the Interior appropriations subcommittee in the House was concerned with issues of policy and priorities, wanting more logging and more logging roads and less emphasis on endangered species and protecting the environment.

Another factor that may have affected the Forest Service is the change from Democratic to Republican majorities in 1995. The reorganization that passed in 1994 was passed with Democratic but not Republican support; that reorganization excluded the Forest Service. After the Republican majorities took over in 1995, the possibility of passing a reorganization for the Forest Service diminished, because the Republicans had never supported reorganization and because of the increased lack of trust between Republicans on the committees and the (Democratic) USDA.

Regardless of the causes, not much managerial improvement occurred in the Forest Service, which was relentlessly hammered by critics over the next few years. Rep. Bob Goodlatte, chair of the House Agriculture Subcommittee on Department Operations, Oversight, Nutrition, and Forestry, summarized these criticisms in a hearing in 1999:

> In 1996, the USDA Office of Inspector General issued the first in a series of adverse opinions on the financial statements of the Forest Service. What has followed since has been a steady stream of reports by Congress, by the IG and the General Accounting Office with titles like "Lack of Financial and Performance Accountability Has Resulted in Inefficiency and Waste," "Unauthorized Use of the National Forest Fund," "Better Procedures and Oversight Needed to Address Indirect Expenditures," "Weak Contracting Practices Increase Vulnerability to Waste, Fraud and Abuse," and "Barriers to Financial Accountability Remain."
>
> Then in January of this year, the General Accounting Office issued a report identifying the Forest Service as an agency at high risk because of its vulnerability to waste, fraud, and abuse and mismanagement. Let me quote briefly from that GAO report:
>
> > "Inefficiency and waste throughout USDA's Forest Service operations and organizations have cost taxpayers hundreds of millions of dollars. While the Forest Service has made progress in recent years, it is still far from achieving financial

accountability and possibly a decade or more away from being
fully accountable for its performance."

So now the question, should the Congress increase funding for an
agency that has cost the taxpayer hundreds of millions of dollars
through inefficiency and waste, continues to lack basic financial and
performance accountability, and may be a decade or more away from
fixing its problems?[28]

Rep. Goodlatte and the oversight committee used those negative reports on
financial management as a lever to hold down appropriations and threaten the
agency if it did not comply with subcommittee priorities.

1996 SIMPLIFICATION OF AUTHORIZING LEGISLATION

When the reorganization legislation was passed in 1994, congresspersons insisted
that program simplification be part of the downsizing. Applications processes
and forms were to be simplified, record keeping was to be reinvented, and all
the farm service programs were to be made more user-friendly. The department
began a new computerization program, which was supposed to focus on reengineering administrative processes. In addition, various experiments were begun to
improve and simplify services. For its part, after a long struggle, Congress passed
a new farm bill that greatly simplified one part of the USDA's work by substituting substantial but declining annual payments and allowing farmers to plant
what they wanted. The simplification legislation covered only grains and cotton,
however. By 2000, with the agricultural economy again in shambles, the fate of
the Freedom to Farm legislation was in doubt, and new proposals to strengthen
the agricultural safety net were circulating.

Evaluation

How did all this work? Did the agency come up with ways to be smaller and
more efficient, giving better service to customers? Was it able to match staffing
levels to responsibility levels and program simplification? The answer, phrased as
GAO would have put it, is somewhat, but many problems remain. The results
are mixed, getting better in some areas but still problematic in others.

After 1994 the USDA consolidated two of its former county-based agencies—
the Agricultural Stabilization and Conservation Service and the Farmers Home
Administration—into the Farm Service Agency (FSA). The USDA colocated these
FSA offices with the Natural Resources Conservation Service (NRCS) and the
Rural Development mission area into one-stop-shopping centers for farmers. The
goal was for farmers to be able to get farm program information and complete
necessary paperwork requirements at one location. A second goal was to reduce
the paperwork burden on farmers. The GAO confirmed in 1998 that farmers

were spending less time on administrative requirements than they did before the 1996 act.[29] However, GAO was more skeptical about the Agriculture Department's ability to design and implement an information technology program that would make the one-stop-shopping concept work better and less expensively than before.[30]

In 1999 the administrator of the Farm Service Administration (FSA) testified that the agency had made major strides in simplifying forms and regulations but noted that a number of difficulties remained. Some of the lending programs required a certain amount of financial information from applicants, just as banks in the private sector required information; there was a lot of money at risk and care was still required. Other programs required data to work. So there was an irreducible minimum of data the agency had to collect. Second, in order to make sure that information was provided only once by the farmers, the FSA had to cooperate not only with other USDA agencies, but also with state and local government agencies. Major efforts had to be made to make the data compatible across agencies, as well as available across agencies. Finally, the administrator gently reminded the congressional committee that further efforts would require continuing funding, to pay for staff to monitor the paperwork reduction and facilitate merging of data across agencies.[31]

Funding computer modernization and creating a common platform for three colocated agencies to create one-stop shopping remained a problem for the USDA. When legacy computer programs were unable to create records after 1 January 2000, the agency ordered new computers and software but was unable to purchase enough computers to provide one for each staff member. Staff members shared laptops until the budget problem could be solved. The Y2K problem called attention to the fact that creating a common computer environment was not an officially funded program and depended on whatever funding each of the participating agencies chose to give it each year.[32]

The problem was not only that the computer modernization and data compatibility project was not an officially funded program, but also that the USDA had failed in its efforts to reclaim some savings from staffing reductions and reorganization for computerization. Deputy Secretary Richard Rominger explained in his testimony on 29 July 1998 what had been happening and the likely consequences. On the one hand, the department had been pushed too hard too fast to cut back staffing and resources, and on the other, it had not been funded to modernize the technology that would allow this reduction to proceed with the minimum of disruption:

> The streamlining plan was based on the premise that significant savings could be achieved through reorganization and part of those savings could be reinvested in modernizing delivery systems and modes of operation. The response to our requests for additional funds to make

information technology investments has been meager at best. Limitations, which have been recently made even more restrictive, also will hamper the use of Commodity Credit Corporation funding for IT investments in Service Centers. In fact, the proposed limitation of CCC funds in 1999 will not cover more than base maintenance costs, without funds for the Service Center investment. Investments needed to address Year 2000 (Y2K) problems will also constrain our ability to invest in other areas. These constraints will affect the ability of the Department to make progress in completing our reorganization in a way that does not jeopardize our Strategic Plan.[33]

Deputy Secretary Rominger's prediction was valid. The USDA was unable to keep up with new programs passed by Congress when the farm economy began to deteriorate. It was unable to get the new funding to the farmers quickly, provoking criticism from congressional supporters of farm programs. The department was forced to hire temporary employees.[34]

Hiring temporary employees was premised on the idea that the department still had some flexibility and could continue to become more efficient by closing more small offices and reducing the need of farmers to visit those offices and get personal attention. Congress pressed the department to make all funding applications available on-line and allow farmers to submit their applications on-line; it also required the department to post a variety of agricultural information on-line so that farmers would not need to go to local service centers to get information or apply for funding.[35] Part of this additional pressure was based on a continuing desire to reduce the paperwork burden on the farmer, but part was an effort to keep the level of staffing down and the level of responsiveness up, in terms of speed of getting the money to farmers.

While the mismatch in timing among staffing cuts, computerization, and new program responsibilities all contributed to problems implementing one-stop shopping, getting employees to work together from different programs also turned out to be difficult. Part of the problem stemmed from the structure of the farm service programs, which at the local level were staffed with county employees and governed by local boards rather than federal employees. When these programs were mixed with other USDA farm programs staffed with federal employees, a variety of problems emerged. One was that when county employees were terminated, they had no rights to other federal jobs, as federal employees did. Also, the fear of getting fired was sufficiently strong that employees were reluctant to teach someone else to handle their work, lest they no longer be needed. A third problem was that federal employees were prohibited from taking orders from nonfederal employees, which caused tension in individual offices with combined programs. Another problem was that programs with different focuses and different histories sometimes did not get along.[36]

While Congress had mandated one-stop shopping, it was not clear how committed members were to the idea. Some of the steps they took seemed to contradict the principle. For example, crop insurance to deal with agricultural disasters was largely privatized. Legislation in 1994 required landowners and producers to buy federal crop insurance. Landowners did not like the idea of compulsory insurance and commercial crop insurers were afraid they were losing business, so by 1996 Congress made crop insurance voluntary and private: "The decision was a blow to the concept of one-stop shopping, since farmers were forced to go to private insurance agencies to get policies."[37] Congress took the federal crop insurance function out of the Farm Services Agency and put it in a separate agency, weakening the idea of one-stop shopping.[38]

Employees got mixed messages from policymakers on one-stop shopping and service improvement. One employee of the FSA described the one-stop shopping concept from the field workers' point of view: "Early on, we learned that policymakers were not really serious about improving service delivery because they excepted Forest Service offices from service centers, refused to merge FSA and NRCS administratively, [and] would not authorize toll-free telephone access for abandoned communities and clients."[39]

While touted as a money saver, the closing of offices and colocation with others turned out to be more expensive than planned: "We were shocked by the costs. In many instances, we closed offices with free rent and moved into high cost service centers. As a case in point, three nearby FSA offices had free office space in their respective county seats. These offices were closed and moved to a new service center which rents for $75,000 a year."[40] The USDA estimated the costs of colocation at $58 million through 1999.[41] The result in some cases was less accessible service at a higher cost.

An unintended consequence of the merger and reduction in field offices was that services became less accessible to poorer farmers and to those with less knowledge of farm programs. While wealthier agribusinesses could easily take advantage of Internet application processes and posted information on agricultural conditions, poorer farmers without computers and those more dependent on Agriculture Department outreach were disproportionately hurt by the changes.

MATCHING WORKLOAD, PROGRAM COMPLEXITY, AND STAFFING LEVELS

Program simplification was real, if limited. Stephen Dewhurst commented, when asked in 1996 if USDA got the simplification it wanted from the farm bill (called Freedom to Farm), "We had more than 700 pages of legislation; ten would be better. What we got was 350 pages; so as in many areas of government, the difference was split."[42] On the farm payment side of the legislation, there were transition payments that were disconnected from crop conditions. The payments were to last seven years and then stop, but the Democrats did not go along with that; they still wanted income support for weather-related disasters. The Farm Service Administration work is still more complicated than legislators think, compared to the new reduced base. But as Dewhurst added, "the Farm Bill is a net plus" on the side of simplification.

Even though there was some program simplification to go along with the downsizing of staff, there was still a disconnect between staffing reductions and program simplifications. The National Performance Review mandated that staffing reductions take place disproportionately among budgeters, accountants, purchasing agents, human resource personnel, and other supervisors, but there was little simplification of administrative tasks so that the system could be run with fewer people. Some changes envisioned by the NPR occurred in procurement, but not proportionately in personnel or budgeting or accounting or information management. With reduced staff in these overhead offices, the work was simply shipped out to the programs, which were already hard-pressed by cuts.

In budgeting, the CFO act added about 400 requirements to departmental workloads. Budget processes overall did not get simpler either. In personnel, in a big ceremony, OPM threw out its regulations; the government-wide form for personnel recruitment was eliminated. As a result, each department or program had to design its own application form, not much if any improvement in terms of workload. In purchasing, the forms were greatly simplified, but the work involved was not reduced proportionately:

> It is stupid to fill out 400 forms to buy a light bulb. It makes sense to go out and buy it at the market. That has been done. But before, someone else got the light bulb. Now my people have to go out and get the light bulb—a $40,000 a year budget analyst is out shopping for bulbs to get his work done. This may not have been thought through. It is self-defeating.[43]

The mismatch between downsizing and workload was particularly noticeable in the technology modernization and work process reinvention processes, which were both necessary to maintain the quality of customer services with decreased staffing; but the decreased staffing made it difficult to acquire the technology, redesign work processes, and train staff to use the new computers and work processes. The same limited staff needed to handle the emergency payments to farmers when the farm economy fell into crisis in the late 1990s had to do the work process redesign; they were pulled off work process redesign to get the money out to the farmers. Work process redesign continually fell behind schedule.[44] Agency employees at the local service offices thus had the same or increasing workloads to handle with much reduced staff, contributing to a reluctance to learn the programs of other colocated agencies, a necessary step in seamless service delivery and one-stop shopping.

The mismatch was also noticeable in the Inspector General's Office. The NPR was insistent that there were too many regulators and overseers and that as a result managers were afraid of rules and had become timid, reluctant to try new ways of doing business. IG's offices were considered part of this overlayer of controllers, holding back managers. Not surprisingly, then, the IG's office at the USDA was cut back with other headquarters personnel, despite the fact that its work had not been simplified and much of the recent legislative changes had fallen on it. In an unusual plea for more resources, Roger Viadero, the USDA IG, explained the increased burdens, decreased staffing, and the resulting reduction in what the office was able to accomplish. The testimony was rare for its candor, as most agencies were unwilling to admit that cuts resulted in any diminution of their ability to carry on their functions:

> The numbers of special agents and auditors, and the resources available to them, were severely limited when I arrived 5½ years ago, and while our responsibilities have increased since then, our staff and resources have continually diminished. In January 1993, we had 875 employees on board. Now we have only 665—210 less, a 24 percent loss. Yet, the decrease to 665 people means little until one considers that the Department's budget, including loan authority, currently is $177 billion; with a personnel staff of approximately 110,000 for FY 2000. Not included in this dollar amount are the operations and actions of millions of companies, plants, and individuals regulated by USDA. As you know, investigating criminal activity by any of them is the responsibility of OIG agents. Ensuring the integrity of all of these programs is the responsibility of OIG auditors. To put it in perspective, when we compare OIG staffing to the Department's programs and personnel, we find that each auditor must ensure the integrity of approximately $635 million in program activity. Each special agent is responsible for investigating all crimes involving nearly $840 million of USDA funds, and any crimes committed by the Department's approximately 110,000 employees, such as embezzlements, thefts, bribes, or extortions. This lone agent is also responsible for investigating criminal activity committed by immense numbers of companies, plants, and individuals whose actions are regulated by the Department through its animal and plant, meat, poultry, grain, fruit, and vegetable inspection and grading programs. Then, there are USDA's forests. It's like having one police officer and one auditor to handle all crime and corruption in New York City.
>
> As our funding shortages have grown more severe, we have been forced to change our standards for determining which criminal activities we investigate. For years we have declined to investigate large

numbers of prosecutable cases, focusing instead on those with higher dollar amounts or those that would have a significant impact on a USDA program. In recent years, as our resources have diminished, we have had to elevate the standard further, leaving thousands of prosecutable criminal cases in the files. . . . Proactive investigations have been, by necessity, severely curtailed. . . . You must know that there are now huge gaps in that "thin blue line" that is OIG.

. . . In addition to fewer staff, we received no additional resources for such mandated activities as auditing the Department's financial statements, yet this activity consumes about 20 percent of our audit resources. Under these conditions something has to give, and it is reduced coverage of the Department's increasing activities and expenditures. To illustrate this, in fiscal years 1997 through 2000, we determined that on average a little over 100,000 workdays were needed in each of those fiscal years to provide audit coverage. Yet with available audit resources, we could staff only an average of 67,000 workdays, a shortage of 33,000 workdays. In fact, in fiscal year 2000 only 61,400 workdays are available. By way of example, because of these shortages, we have not been able to provide in-depth audit coverage to issues such as the Department's efforts to increase collection of debts owed to it, and the Department's new computer system for tracking the Rural Housing Loan Program. We need to perform more security audits on USDA information systems which involve health and safety, economic matters, and research since these vital systems are increasingly at risk of unauthorized access and possible irreparable damage. At our current staffing level, we are simply not able to deal with crisis issues needing immediate audit and investigative attention without neglecting important work elsewhere. OIG is often required to pull its special agents from assigned investigations of large frauds in USDA's benefits and loan programs to investigate criminal activity that threatens the health and safety of the public.[45]

USDA created a plan for its downsizing, with detailed financial implications, and used the credibility and focus of the plan with OMB when proposals were made to do something "arbitrary." Several years after the plan was put in place, USDA found it increasingly difficult to match cuts to programmatic revisions. The budget cuts and staffing reductions proceeded on a separate track from any planned changes or program simplification: "The budget appropriation is so bad, they cut no matter [what]."[46] The General Accounting Office agreed that there had been some simplification, but that many elements of programs had not been simplified and that the continuing cuts would necessarily affect the way service was being delivered. GAO found that it was unable to separate out the reorganization in the field in 1994 from the legislative simplification of 1996 in terms of effects on workload. Because workload statistics were collated annually at the end of the year, the researchers did not have hard data to work with. With those caveats, however, they reported that workloads overall had probably increased since 1994. The GAO report came up with estimates for the personnel reduction planned for 1998, in terms of what proportion could be attributed to simplification or reduction in workload and what proportion was necessitated by budget cuts independent of workload reductions:

> USDA's budget submission for fiscal year 1998 proposes a reduction of 1,850 former ASCS employees from 1997 levels. This proposed reduction is made up of two components. First, FSA concluded that 850 fewer employees were needed to handle its projected workload. Second, USDA agreed to reduce FSA's staffing by an additional 1,000 employees to meet the budget reduction targets set forth in the President's 1998 budget proposal. Beyond 1998, the Office of Management and Budget has proposed cutting former ASCS employees, now at FSA, by an additional 5,000, down to 4,879 employees by fiscal year 2002.[47]

CONCLUSIONS

Management Improvement

Management improvement did come to USDA as a result of relentless pressure from Congress and the GAO. After slow starts and false beginnings, USDA finally seemed on track. It had downsized staff, reduced the number of offices, done some centralization of overhead functions, merged some services, colocated others, and made a good start at one-stop shopping. But the largest unit in the USDA in terms of staffing levels, the Forest Service, largely escaped reorganization and management improvements, despite the downsizing. For it, legislation was not simplified; its mission remained complex and contradictory. Its decision making remained slow, and its financial management continued to need improvement.

According to Stephen Dewhurst, the budget director for the USDA, getting improvements for the Forest Service was difficult because major changes were blocked by the Interior committees. There was no consensus on what the Forest Service should be doing. The GAO was critical of the lack of effort on the part of the Forest Service to improve its accountability and its decision-making processes but readily admitted that the agency was caught between definitions of its role and that many members of Congress did not agree to the shift of emphasis from producer of lumber to preserver of species. This disagreement over what the agency should be doing made planning and performance measurement difficult and the implementation of plans unpredictable.[48]

Agency costs continued to go up and the number of board feet produced went down. Staffing decreased, but the administrative problems were not solved nor was the basic disagreement as to what the agency should be doing.

Learning

Agency officials reported they learned some things over the time period of the study. First, they learned the necessity of linking program simplification and work process reinvention to downsizing of staff. They learned the value of taking the initiative and having a detailed plan to propose that links cost reductions to reorganization and mission clarification. Having such a plan made it more difficult for outsiders to suggest random changes. They also learned that huge projects such as updating communications and computers needed to be integrated with work process engineering and that overall plans needed to be broken up into much smaller projects.

USDA's first effort to modernize its computers and work processes, called InfoShare, failed despite the dollars and time that went into it. When Rep. Nick Smith asked the chief information officer (CIO), Anne Reed, in 1997, "Did we learn something from the [failure of the] InfoShare experience?" she replied, "No question about it, we learned quite a lot." She detailed what she thought the department had learned: to spend more time and effort in up-front planning, and engage more directly with the people who are responsible for delivering the service. In the days of InfoShare, the problem was just given to the information technology people. Besides planning, Reed argued that the department had learned not to treat information technology as one big project, but to break it up into manageable parts, achieve a set of goals, and then look up to see if it were still going in the right direction. The resulting process is planning, investing, planning, investing, and then planning and investing, in stages. She concluded that that kind of process enables adaptation to changing programs and policy.[49]

In 1997 the FSA engaged in buyouts and RIFs as a result of the 1996 farm bill that simplified agricultural programs. Generally, the buyouts and RIFs were well done, but planning was inadequate. In some cases when buyouts occurred, RIFs would have been more cost-effective. More important, with the buyouts it was not possible to target terribly well who would leave the agency, and some expertise was lost, especially in management and computerization. Agency officials agreed in retrospect that they needed to do more planning for the buyouts and RIFs and especially needed to take more action to prevent the loss of additional expertise. As additional buyouts and RIFs were planned, some staff expressed fears that the next round would impair the ability to deliver services well. The 1997 round had resulted in especially heavy workloads for remaining staff, and it simply was not clear that this particular strategy could be continued.[50]

Contradictions

USDA's downsizing efforts were fraught with contradictions. For example, the department's greatest strength in the past was its extreme decentralization, which had allowed an intense responsiveness to congressional demands. But that very decentralization became problematic when it came time to reorganize and save money, because there was no "architecture" for interagency communication, no commonly agreed-on data elements for shared databases, many different and incompatible accounting systems, and virtually no knowledge of staffing levels and locations in the field. Some centralization was needed to plan and downsize in a rational way. As one official put it, the decentralization meant that no one had ever thought about the cost savings from joint overhead management.

At the same time that Congress was pushing for greater efficiency and some centralization, it also continued to support stovepipe organization (dividing an agency into parallel vertical hierarchies without many interconnections) and tight linkages between committees and agencies, on a program-by-program and location-by-location basis. The Forest Service was whipsawed, with criticisms of its management on one hand and lack of permission to reorganize on the other.

The most intense contradiction, however, remained the disconnect between staffing levels and workload. USDA tried hard, as did Congress, to simplify programs to make them more manageable with fewer staff, but declines in budgets for personnel were more rapid than the rate of simplification of the work. Staffing levels and workload may match up again when the newly reengineered work processes are put in place, but the staffing declines assumed computerization and reinvention that were not there at the time.

Unless the staffing cuts precipitate major changes in the way services are delivered, there will be an increasing mismatch between workload and staffing levels. The NPR emphasized service to customers but also emphasized staff reductions, cost reductions, and reinvention. Different ways of delivering services are not what the customer prefers, according to a USDA study. In the administrative area, the contradictions were even clearer, with the NPR demanding severe cuts in budget, accounting, personnel, and purchasing staff, without achieving the simplification in these areas that could possibly justify the reduction in staffing.

New legislation added to the burdens of these offices at precisely the time the administration was demanding and expecting managerial improvements. The pace of change was frenetic, especially as the farm economy deteriorated in the years following the landmark Freedom to Farm legislation in 1996. The legislation was supposed to last through 2002, but by 1999 pressure was building to halt the stopgap funding and restructure the agricultural insurance programs again to provide a better safety net. Proposals for change appeared in the executive budget proposal for 2000.[51]

Another serious contradiction occurred between fixing the programs to run better with fewer staff and eliminating the programs completely. Throughout the period, discussion continued to buzz around the possibility of eliminating the FSA completely in 2002 when the farm program reauthorization would expire. With continuing downsizing, office mergers, program mergers, retraining, conflicts among federal and nonfederal employees, and the overarching threat of program termination within a few years, chaos, rather than management improvement, may be the result. Congress and the GAO criticized the USDA for its slowness in making the desired changes, but agency officials responded that much of their effort was taken up just trying to implement new legislation.

The USDA tried to take control of the cuts and manage them, hoping for stability, but events outstripped the plan; budget reductions for staffing were continuous and ultimately not tightly tied to simplification. In this sense, USDA's strategy was not successful. But in a broader sense, the agency changed its mission from farm-based services to food and nutrition programs, food safety, and protection of the environment. The Clinton administration fought off an effort to cap food stamp entitlements. In this regard, the department was eminently successful. The secretary of the department was a former Agriculture Committee representative, giving him excellent rapport with congressional committees, facilitating the work of getting congressional approval. This, too, can be considered a successful strategy. But the reengineering of the work processes will ultimately require less direct service to the farmer and a changed relationship between staff and farmers. The colocated services and combined programs required changes in culture as well as work processes.[52] The Forest Service is more environmentally sensitive than it used to be, offending some and threatening forest-products companies, creating ongoing tension between the department and some of its oversight committees. Cutback and reinvention have altered the political support structure for the USDA, and the political environment has not always been sympathetic to the needs of a downsizing agency.

CHAPTER 7

Department of Commerce

THE COMMERCE DEPARTMENT experienced episodes of fiscal stress, cutbacks, and threats of termination alternating with periods of growth during the 1980s and 1990s. When the Commerce Department was attacked, it fought back, engaging in triage in the face of massive opposition. It did not fight to the death and beyond; it gave up what seemed necessary and inevitable but fought to maintain what could possibly be saved. The department's policy of resistance was tempered with an effort to comply with legitimate criticism insofar as possible. This strategy was moderately successful. The department fended off multiple attempts at dismemberment; the Weather Service modernization did take place; the National Oceanic and Atmospheric Agency (NOAA) corps ultimately was preserved and its ship-modernization program continued. The Census, as recounted in chapter 3, was fully funded, after a suspenseful and difficult couple of years. Overall, the department seemed somewhat better managed by the late 1990s, having made major strides in appearing less political and more neutral.

The Department of Commerce is a small department. Its staffing levels were 35,000 in 1995, and its budget has been around $4 billion total. Most of the staffing is in the Census Bureau and in NOAA. But Commerce also is home to a variety of other agencies, including trade assistance, minority business development and economic development, and scientific offices. It houses a telecommunications office, statistical agencies, the Weather Service, travel and tourism offices (until 1998), and patents and trademarks. While the underlying theme of providing infrastructure and common services necessary for business growth ties these agencies together, they lack interdependence. Many could stand on their own or could be grouped with other agencies elsewhere.

Opponents of the Commerce Department have episodically tried to cut it back and dismember it, in part because the agency was viewed as partisan and political; and so its fate has gone up and down with different administrations. The political nature of the department has a number of components, including programs that provide traditional distributional benefits to congressional districts, sometimes defined as pork; a high level of political appointees; programs endorsed by particular presidents or opposed by particular presidents; and a reputation for allocating relief and recovery grants on other than a needs basis. In recent years the charges have included hiring political party fund-raisers and selecting representatives of trade missions from party financial donors.

Efforts to dismember the Commerce Department have been encouraged by the loose grouping of agencies inside it, without clear institutional focus or interdependence. Commerce has been described as a holding company for the almost completely independent agencies inside it, subject to almost continuous organizational change: "Because of the wide diversity of its functions, Commerce historically has not been managed on the basis of a unifying mission or shared goals."[1]

GAO described the relative independence of each bureau and suggested that the loose structure was an adaptation to the cuts in the early 1980s:

> Commerce has decentralized its key administrative functions. Major Commerce components, including the National Oceanic and Atmospheric Administration, the Patent and Trademark Office, and the Economics and Statistics Administration which comprises both Census and BEA, have been granted the authority and responsibility by Commerce for meeting most of their own administrative needs. Thus, Commerce headquarters provides some services but primarily sets policy and provides overall direction and oversight. In some cases, the major components pay for the services provided by headquarters through a working capital fund. Census and BEA receive their legal services this way, for instance. In addition, BEA purchases most of its administrative services from other components of Commerce through a series of cross-servicing arrangements. Commerce's decentralized approach to providing administrative services is a result of its response to significant budget reductions that occurred in the early 1980s. The relative independence of the major components minimizes the disruption that would occur if one or more were broken away in a reorganization.[2]

Because of the loose structure of the department, the arrival or departure of an agency did minimal harm to the remaining operations, but overlap with other agencies outside the department and lack of interdependence made the agencies inside Commerce vulnerable to further efforts to remove them. Moreover, because of the holding-company nature of the departmental administration, the complaint was made that there was no one in the department to hold accountable for management and financial reforms, especially in the area of purchasing.

Calls for dismemberment became particularly strident after the influx of congressional Republicans in 1995. Commerce appeared highly partisan and therefore vulnerable to partisan attacks. The proposals for dismemberment were partisan, but they overlapped with a bipartisan pressure to reduce spending in order to balance the budget. Attacks on the Commerce Department thus gained considerable support as long as they appeared to save money.

Some of the proposals offered in the 1980s and 1990s were just to dismember the department and send all its functions elsewhere; other proposals dealt with one or another function performed by the department. One proposal was to create a statistical agency combining all the major statistical agencies presently in different departments, such as the Bureau of the Census in Commerce and the Bureau of Labor Statistics in the Department of Labor. Another proposal was to take the Patent and Trademark Office out of Commerce and make it independent. At the same time, there was continuing pressure on NOAA to privatize its fleet, to civilianize its corps, and to privatize whatever weather functions it could. Even after the main push to dismember Commerce was defeated, pressures to take one or another bureau out and locate it in a different department persisted.

The budget process added to the vulnerability of the Commerce Department. The Commerce Department's budget was primarily in the discretionary side of the budget where there were reasonably tight caps. Failure to control the growth of entitlement spending meant that major efforts to balance the budget put disproportionate pressure on discretionary programs. These caps on discretionary spending forced tradeoffs in the budget. When there were tradeoffs, Commerce often lost out.

The caps were implemented by assigning to each appropriations subcommittee a total that it could spend. Commerce fell into the jurisdiction of the Commerce, State, and Justice appropriations subcommittee, meaning that it was competing directly with the departments of State and Justice. Because Census had a permanent authorization, and many of Commerce's other programs were often unable to reauthorize programs successfully, the authorizing committees that would normally argue for maintaining programs and funding levels were not major budgetary players. As a consequence, the appropriations subcommittee had more than the normal amount of budgetary power over the Commerce agencies.

Increases in the budgets of Commerce, State, or Justice (especially after the 1990 Budget Enforcement Act) typically had to come from one of the other departments. An examination of the budgets of the Departments of Commerce, Justice, and State shows this relationship over time. Starting with outlays of about the same size, between 1980 and 2000, Commerce grew 158 percent; the Department of State, 333 percent; and the Department of Justice, 630 percent. These figures include the census for the Commerce Department.[3] Administrators in programs located in the Department of Commerce reported that they believed they were competing with Department of Justice programs.

Not all tradeoffs occurred among Commerce, Justice, and State. Before Gramm-Rudman-Hollings and serious attention to deficit reduction during the first half of the 1980s, tradeoffs were broader. Officials in the Commerce Department believed that they were competing against the Defense Department; until the Defense Department buildup eased off, there was no money for growth in many domestic programs.

As the Commerce Department budget director explained,

> Reagan's big defense buildup stopped in 1985. Defense was flat after that. [Commerce] Secretary Baldridge worked hard to influence [Defense Secretary] Cap Weinberger and others to come up with more domestic spending, but not until Congress said no to the defense buildup could we consider replacing weather radar and weather satellites, things that you would assume would be easy to get.[4]

The Commerce Department's failure to compete successfully with these other powerful interests meant that its budget could not grow to accommodate lumpy spending requirements. Increases in one Commerce Department program had to be accommodated by cutting some other Commerce Department programs.

Another major factor in the Commerce case was that it was opposed by some presidents and actively supported by others. Sometimes the department offered programs that were political banners for the president and grew rapidly; sometimes the agency got caught in the split between the president and a Congress led by the opposite party. For the Reagan years, the president opposed the agency, but Congress supported it; President Clinton supported the agency, but the Republican Congress opposed it. Its budget was sharply cut, then grew, then was cut again.

The Commerce Department was more political and partisan than many other departments. The department's accommodation of loyal partisans occurred in both Democratic and Republican administrations:

> Their [Brown's and Kanter's, Clinton's first two secretaries of commerce] willingness to reward loyal partisans has been no greater than previous secretaries such as Robert A. Mosbacher, who served as President George Bush's chief fund-raiser, according to many longtime employees. "These guys were no worse than Mr. Mosbacher, let me assure you," said a veteran career bureaucrat. Nevertheless, this official acknowledged: "This is a very politicized place. And that's why we're in such trouble."[5]

Part of the reason that Commerce was considered so political was that some of its programs were old-fashioned pork programs. Given the overall decrease in the amount of pork as the government wrestled with deficits and the increase in the number of dollars distributed by formula, the dollars that could be allocated as pork took on additional value. At the same time, such allocations created controversy. Some members of Congress believed that the dollars were distributed by politics rather than by need; others were offended that the pork seemed to be distributed on partisan lines, leaving them out. Thus Commerce was both supported and attacked by Congress for its distributional programs.

BUDGET CUTS, THREATS OF TERMINATION, AND RESPONSE

The Commerce Department experienced a roller-coaster budget. The bumpiness was related to the Census's periodic buildup and ease-offs, storm and flood relief in the Economic Development Administration (EDA), and the expensive modernization program in the Weather Service. Also contributing to the roller-coaster effect were varying levels of executive support and congressional opposition.

Commerce's budget was cut by the Reagan administration in the early 1980s but then began to recover slowly. The department's budgets did not actually reach the level of 1981 until about 1988. The budget increased in the Clinton administration in the early 1990s. This presidentially supported increase then ran head-on into the Republican congressional majorities elected in 1994, creating a second major attack on the department during the period of the study. This Republican congressional budgetary attack was accompanied by efforts to dismantle Commerce as a cabinet-level agency. Table 7.1 shows the ups and downs of the Commerce Department budget between 1980 and 2000.

The sharp decline in the Commerce Department budget during the early Reagan administration resulted in part from the wind-down from the 1980

Table 7.1   Outlays, Department of Commerce, 1980–2000
(in $ millions)

Year	Amount	Year	Amount
1980	3,129	1991	2,585
1981	2,296	1992	2,567
1982	2,054	1993	2,798
1983	1,925	1994	2,915
1984	1,895	1995	3,401
1985	2,140	1996	3,702
1986	2,083	1997	3,783
1987	2,127	1998	4,046
1988	2,279	1999	5,036
1989	2,571	2000 (est.)	8,134
1990	3,734		

Source: Historical Tables of the U.S. Budget, 2001.

census, with Census staffing declining from 13,105 in 1981 to 6,345 in 1984, a decrease of more than 50 percent. But from 1991 to 1994 the staffing level in the Census Bureau declined only 40 percent, suggesting that some of Census's decrease after 1981 was not just coming off the national census but was also net, long-term reduction in staffing. In 1981 the staffing for Census was 13,105; 10 years later, at the same point in the Census Department's 10-year cycle, Census's staffing level was only 12,520, a reduction of about 4½ percent.

The Census was not the only unit to experience cuts in the early 1980s. Overall, Commerce staffing dropped from 40,776 in 1981 to 32,636 in 1982. In addition to Census's reductions, Science and Technical Research was terminated and replaced by the National Bureau of Standards and the National Institute of Standards and Technology, with about 800 fewer positions; NOAA lost about 1,000 positions. EDA was sharply reduced, from 746 staff in 1981 to 480 in 1982. From 1981 to 1984 Commerce Department outlays were reduced 17 percent.

In 1986 GRH kicked in, affecting many agencies' discretionary outlays. From 1985 to 1986 outlays in Commerce dropped $57 million, from $2.140 billion to $2.083 billion, a shade over 2½ percent.

In 1990 the Budget Enforcement Act was passed, setting spending caps for discretionary spending. However, after an initial steep decline in Commerce's budget due to coming off the decennial census of 1990, outlays increased: from 1992 to 1997, Commerce's outlays grew by 47 percent. This was the result of the election of a Democratic president, Bill Clinton, who supported the trade mission and industrial policy of the agency; the increase also reflected a massive Midwest flood that boosted emergency spending for the Economic Development Administration. Emergency spending did not come under the discretionary spending caps.

Despite improved presidential support and improved spending levels, the Commerce Department faced major threats when Congress changed hands as a result of the 1994 congressional elections. Many of the newly elected Republicans were strongly opposed to the Commerce Department and energetically sought to dismember it, putting numerous proposals for program termination and departmental dismemberment before Congress. At the same time, the Commerce Department had to comply with government-wide staffing reductions that were to take a disproportionate toll on the supervisors, the budgeters, accountants, and personnelists who were reportedly overregulating and taking the excitement and flexibility out of management. Commerce cut back more staffing more deeply than the average for all departments.

DEPARTMENT-WIDE RESPONSES

The Department of Commerce's overall response could be described as triage, supplemented with coping strategies. The department resisted cuts and dismemberment insofar as it reasonably could but let go that which it could no longer defend or that seemed more minor. At the same time, the department tried to maintain congressional and presidential support, even when simultaneous compliance with both was difficult or impossible. The department complied with most of the criticisms against it:

> Secretary [William] Daley has emphasized that we have to deal swiftly and effectively with any credible criticism that is leveled at us. Right now, he thinks we can do a better job. If criticism is accurate—from whatever source—we need to say so and fix it. Where we may disagree, we need to present our reasons cogently.[6]

General Coping Strategies

Because most of the Commerce Department's budget was in personnel rather than in grants or insurance, budget cuts translated fairly directly into personnel cuts and vice versa. Personnel cuts in some agencies were especially steep. As a result, there was a premium on adaptations to reduced staffing and a major effort to minimize the need for reductions in force. RIFs were minimized through buyouts, through the creation of internal service accounts, and, in the Census Bureau, through the creation of more temporary positions. Fee revenue was levied where possible and appropriate, such as in the National Technical Information Service and the Patent and Trademark Office. Budgeters used the strategy of "nickel and diming," that is, scraping together small savings in the salaries and expenses budgets. For example, the EDA used frequent-flier miles for travel and cut out the employee subsidy for using mass transit.

As in other departments, and in compliance with pressures from the NPR, the Commerce Department emphasized computerization and simplification of regulations and grant application procedures as ways of dealing with reduced staffing. As in many other departments experiencing budget reductions, Commerce had to purchase new computer equipment and get new financial systems in place without additional money appropriated for the purpose. The department asked the agencies to help pay for computerization and other capital items.

Rep. Dick Chrysler had proposed, in addition to dismemberment, 25 percent cuts in programs that were not terminated, including "overhead." Secretary Ron Brown explained in hearings that the department did not charge the programs for overhead but had set up a working capital fund:

> The basis for the Chrysler 25 percent cut below FY 1994 funding totals is not stated in the legislation or the press release. Representative Chrysler indicated on July 24 that the cut was related, at least in the case of PTO [Patent and Trademark Office], to an overhead rate Commerce now charges bureaus. Commerce does not charge its

bureaus any overhead rate. While Commerce sells services through the Working Capital Fund, bureaus purchase an average of 1.4 percent of their available funding in services. All Commerce oversight is funded through the general administration account, $36 million in FY 1995 or about .7 percent of the Commerce total appropriation.[7]

Rather than an overhead tax, to cover administrative expenses, the department set up a more market-like arrangement. On the one hand, congressional committees and the IG's office were demanding that the department beef up its management oversight function, but on the other, there were no funds and no staffing made available to do it. In spring 1996 the central administration faced reductions in force. The only way to continue to provide services to the agencies in light of budget and staffing constraints was to charge agencies for services they requested. As one official described it, in an effort to minimize RIFs, one central administrative office began to operate like a consulting firm for agencies inside the department, providing information functions by contract:

> We turned into internal consultants. We did business plans, and marketing studies, reorganization studies, long-range plans. All of which we do. Before we used to do it out of the goodness of my heart. Now I have to ask them if they can pay for it.[8]

Resistance and Triage

The Commerce Department adapted to personnel cuts as best as it could, while resisting the worst onslaughts against the department. Right from the beginning of the Reagan administration, and despite the fact that the Reagan administration opposed Commerce, the department fought back, giving up only when further fighting would be counterproductive. According to Budget Director Mark Brown:

> The spring of 1981—Secretary [Malcolm] Baldridge was appointed January 29, just after Reagan took office. [OMB Director David] Stockman already had plans in place. On the first day, Baldridge called together the budget staff. He had a list of Heritage [Foundation recommended] cuts, including the EDA, parts of NOAA, etc. We gave up on EDA, but defended other programs, and got thrown out of the office as having the wrong frame of mind.[9]

Later, the department resisted the dismemberment proposals of 1995. Secretary of Commerce Ron Brown argued in 1995: "On the underlying question of whether the United States of America needs a Commerce Department—on this issue I cannot yield."[10]

Brown made a number of arguments in favor of retaining the department as a whole, including that it was effective in maintaining and adding jobs; that there were very few savings to be achieved from dismantling, because most of the functions performed by Commerce would still have to be performed and would cost as much elsewhere as in Commerce; and that there was more synergy among the agencies in Commerce than the committee seemed to credit. Brown argued that the savings to be gained from dismemberment were often wildly exaggerated, for example, omitting the Census ramp up to the decennial count. Brown also argued that the dismemberment would weaken business's voice on trade issues.

In addition, according to Balutis, the secretary focused on assessment, proving the worth of trade programs in particular:

> We also gathered information on effectiveness. Trade missions bring in jobs. And businesses that export pay more wages than average in business. . . . We did a lot of work in response to individual requests for information. The secretary mobilized a fair number of businesses to press their [congressional] members about the effectiveness of the department's programs. The secretary briefed congressional staff, and he met with people in the minority and majority, with the Democratic and Republican leadership.[11]

Secretary Ron Brown's vigorous defense of the department helped defeat the dismantlement legislation, perhaps because by demonstrating that few savings could be realized this way, he separated those who were trying to balance the budget from those who just wanted to terminate the Commerce Department. The department lost only the Travel and Tourism Administration, a small unit budgeted at about $13 million.

Individual agencies, such as NOAA, also fought against cuts and minimized them, especially later when the agency had presidential support. In the Reagan administration, during the early 1980s, the resistance consisted of rounding up constituents, but there was no plan, only a fragmented set of constituency-driven programs. Later, in the 1990s, there was a plan. A NOAA official described how the agency's plan was used to defend the budget:

> Here was NOAA, a Democratic program in a Democratic administration, waltzing up the Hill with our 1996 budget. [Their response was to] dismantle the department and cut 25 percent [across the board]. The cut was familiar; it felt like the Reagan administration up to that point. But the difference was that NOAA had its act together; it acted cohesively. [Undersecretary D. James] Baker wanted to protect programs. Given that, we told people the consequences. If you cut 25

percent, we won't have *x* radars and people will die. Fisheries will collapse if you do this. Ships will have less cargo, because they won't know what the bottom looks like, and they will lose money. Maybe we will have only one satellite; maybe we won't have coverage of Hawaii.

People were infuriated in Congress, especially the Republicans. We kept it up. If you do that, these are the consequences. We didn't do that in the 1980s. This was an agency responding. The agency was cut 5 percent in 1996. That was a tremendous victory.[12]

In short, for both the department as a whole and for the individual programs that were most severely threatened, the response was to fight back and to minimize losses.

Focus

Part of the department's response was to demonstrate that there were good reasons to keep Commerce together. Secretary Brown emphasized the degree of integration and common themes among agencies within the Commerce Department, as a way of fending off the dismantlement threat. Other secretaries followed up on this strategy. The department continued to work at creating goals that crosscut bureaus and programs, making the synergy that Brown talked about more tangible. If programs and bureaus were interdependent, it would be harder to take out particular pieces without hurting those programs and the remaining ones:

> Secretary Daley is facilitating the integration of programs where cross-cutting efforts are appropriate. He recently asked senior executive managers throughout the Department to join together in developing strategies for cross-cutting approaches to half a dozen of our major issues affecting our program direction and internal operations. In each of these areas, he is bringing together intra-departmental teams to lay out strategic objectives and implement actions that will allow the Department to act more cohesively and to bring greater impact to overall federal efforts.[13]

Because of the Commerce Department's history of gaining and losing functions, it had been difficult over the years for the department to maintain a focus and earn legitimacy for what it did. For a period in the 1940s and 1950s, the department focused on transportation, but that dominance ended with the creation of the Transportation Department. In the mid-1960s and 1970s, Commerce had one of the preeminent economic development programs (EDA), but with the creation of HUD and the proliferation of economic development programs in other departments, Commerce could not define itself in this area either. Beginning in the 1970s, however, the emphasis on trade increased, and Commerce tried more successfully to define itself as preeminent in this area.[14]

In 1978 commercial attachés were returned from the State Department to the Commerce Department and supervision of the trigger pricing mechanism and unfair trade practices was moved from the Treasury Department to Commerce. In 1980 the Trade Reorganization Act was passed by Congress, establishing a new export policy. Promotion of trade and policing of exports were then in one Commerce Department agency, the International Trade Administration. In 1982 Secretary Baldridge led the administration's effort to pass new legislation, the Export Trading Company Act, to get smaller and medium-sized companies into international trade.[15]

In Secretary Baldridge's effort to emphasize trade during the 1980s, he exchanged functions with other departments to get rid of programs less central to the mission and gain new ones that were more closely trade related. The transfer of the Maritime Administration to the Department of Transportation in 1981 was reportedly part of the effort to focus the mission of the Commerce Department on trade issues. When Secretary Brown took over the department, he kept up this emphasis on trade.

Winning Support

Commerce had enjoyed considerable congressional support during the Reagan administration when OMB continued to send Congress proposals to terminate the EDA and NOAA. These proposals accounted for more than half the department's budget. Congress did not go along with administratively proposed agency terminations and generally raised the appropriations levels from those recommended by the administration. Later, after the Republicans took a majority of both houses in 1994, Congress was more opposed to the department but even so voted down proposals to dismember it and terminate specific programs.

Officials at the Commerce Department assumed that part of the reason for continued congressional support was that some of the Commerce Department programs offered pork-type distributional programs. In the EDA program, elected officials could claim credit for helping their districts:

> EDA is used like disaster assistance, to create job opportunities, clean up after floods. It is grouped with emergency money with FEMA and SBA. It's been convenient, because it is one of the few agencies left as grant programs change; it is still an old-time political pork program. It provides money to local areas, federal largesse. The rest of the grant programs are peer reviewed and merit based these days.[16]

The EDA, in a continuing effort to gain more legislative support, expanded its mission to include helping communities experiencing military base closures.

This spending was geographically based and would enable members of Congress to take credit for getting money to rebuild local economies.

While pork implies waste, many of the projects and programs were not wasteful, but they were earmarked for particular places in congressional districts. This earmarking extended far beyond the EDA. As Senator McCain's anti-pork campaign indicated, for the fiscal year 1998, many earmarks appeared in the Commerce Department's appropriations subcommittee committee report. These earmarks are suggestive of the range of agencies and programs involved. The following list is from Senator McCain's introductory comments on the appropriations bill on the Senate floor:

- Language urging the Economic Development Administration to consider applications for grants for:
  —Defense conversion project at University of Colorado Health Sciences Center in Aurora, Colorado
  —Passenger terminal and control tower at Bowling Green/Warren County, Kentucky, regional airport
  —Jackson Falls Heritage Riverpark in Nashua, New Hampshire
  —Bristol Bay Native Association
  —Redevelopment of abandoned property in Newark, New Jersey
  —Pacific Science Center in Seattle, Washington
  —Rodale Center at Cedar Crest College in Lehigh Valley, Pennsylvania
  —Minority labor force initiative in South Carolina
  —Cumbres and Toltec Scenic Railroad Commission in Arriba County, New Mexico, and Conejos County, Colorado
  —Fore River Shipyard in Quincy, Massachusetts
  —Native American manufacturer's network in Montana
  —National Canal Museum in Easton, Pennsylvania
  —Cranston Street Armory in Providence, Rhode Island
- Recommendation that Little Rock, Arkansas, Minority Business Development Center remain in operation
- Recommendation that Jonesboro-Paraground, Arkansas, Metropolitan Statistical Area be designated to include both Craighead and Greene Counties
- Language urging the NTIA to consider grants to University of Montana and Marshall University, West Virginia
- Language directing NTIA to fund telecommunications support for the Olympic Committee Organization in Utah to ensure that similar telecommunications facilities as were available at the Atlanta Olympics
- $500,000 earmarked for South Carolina geodetic survey
- $300,000 earmarked for Galveston-Houston operation of physical oceanographic real time system

- $1.9 million earmarked for south Florida ecosystem restoration, including $1 million for Nova Southeastern University for establishment of a National Coral Reef Institute to conduct research on coral reefs, and $1 million for the University of Hawaii for similar coral reef studies
- $450,000 for a cooperative agreement with the State of South Carolina Department of Health and Environmental Control to work on the Charleston Harbor project
- Increase of $6.6 million above the request for the National Estuarine Research Reserve System, which serves 22 sites in 18 states and Puerto Rico
- $4.7 million for the Pacific fishery information network, including $1.7 million for the Alaska network
- Not less than $850,000 for the marine resources monitoring assessment and prediction program of the South Carolina Division of Marine Resources
- $390,000 for the Chesapeake Bay resource collection program
- $50,000 for Hawaiian monk seals
- $500,000 for the Hawaii stock management plan
- $300,000 for Alaska groundfish surveys and $5.5 million for Alaska groundfish monitoring
- $410,000 for the Alaska Eskimo Whaling Commission and $200,000 for the Beluga Whale Committee
- $1 million for research on Steller seals at the Alaska SeaLife Center, $325,000 for similar work by the state of Alaska, and $330,000 for work by the North Pacific Universities Marine Mammal Consortium
- $400,000 for the NMFS in Honolulu for Pacific swordfish research
- $250,000 to implementation of the state of Maine's recovery plan for Atlantic salmon
- $150,000 to the Alaska Fisheries Development Foundation
- $200,000 for the Island Institute to develop multispecies shellfish hatchery and nursery facility to benefit Gulf of Maine communities
- $3.8 million to develop a national resources center at Mount Washington, New Hampshire, to demonstrate innovative approaches using weather as the education link among sciences, math, geography, and history
- $500,000 for the ballast water demonstration in the Chesapeake Bay
- $2.3 million to reduce tsunami risks to residents and visitors in Oregon, Washington, California, Hawaii, and Alaska
- $3 million increase, with total earmark of $15 million, for the National Undersea Research Program, equally divided between East and West Coast research centers, with the West Coast funds equally divided between the Hawaii and Pacific center and the West Coast and Polar Regions center
- $1.7 million for the New England open ocean aquaculture program
- $1 million for the Susquehanna River basin flood system

- $97,000 for the NOAA Cooperative Institute for Regional Prediction at the University of Utah
- $150,000 to maintain staff at Fort Smith, Arkansas, to improve the ability of southern Indiana to receive weather warnings
- Earmarks of $88 million in NOAA construction funds for specific locations in Alaska, Hawaii, South Carolina, Mississippi, and others

Most of these are not large amounts of money, though some are substantial, but many are of intense concern to legislators, who fought to defend them on the floor of Congress. It is not clear the extent to which these earmarks represent a legislative strategy on the part of the department and the extent to which they represent congressional demands to which the department acquiesced. The department was certainly not in a position to resist these earmarks, especially because any defiance was immediately noted in committee hearings and provoked threats of further budget cuts. In other respects, however, it is clear that the department actively tried to win legislative support and deflect the legislative opponents of the department.

Part of the department's strategy was to respond to critics by resisting the more extreme demands but acquiescing to reasonable ones. One strong attack on the department was that it was too politicized, too partisan, too Democratic. One specific criticism was that the department had a disproportionate number of political appointees. These appointees would be Clinton supporters. The department agreed to reduce the number of these positions and did so. A second charge was that trade missions were filled by businesses whose owners were major contributors to the Democratic Party and that party officials would call the department and send over recommendations. In response to the charge, without ever admitting that this had been the practice, the department extensively revamped the process of selecting companies for trade missions. Undersecretary Stuart Eizenstat described in a hearing the nature of the new rules:

> We wanted to deal with the perception which I believe to be a complete misperception. Somehow these missions were seen as something less than completely objective in the way they were selected. So, we worked for about six weeks to develop what is for the first time a fully transparent process. For each trade mission, for example, Mr. Chairman, there will be a written statement in advance that will give the reason for the mission, the market sectors that are to be emphasized, and why the countries were selected for those market sectors.
>
> In addition, we will have a very real outreach to companies through Internet, through flash fax, through newsletters, and the Federal Register for the first time. Federal Register notices will be issued telling

companies that a mission is going, when it's going, and soliciting their company participation.

So, we want companies to come to us. Any factor taken into account in the selection of a company will be put into a record and made available, without a Freedom of Information Act request to the public, to journalists, and to the Congress.

If there is any political request from any political committee, it will be sent back immediately. We will have, for secretarial missions, a career group of people who will make the final selections for the companies with no political input whatsoever.

There will have to be a post-mission report, also publicly available, to describe what success was achieved in meeting the goals of the mission. All of this will be in writing. The policy is in writing. And we did this because we wanted to make sure . . . this was done in a fair way. The reason Secretary Daley took this extraordinary action is because of a perception, not, I hope, the reality, that there was any wrongdoing. We hope, again, that this will still any concerns.[17]

The argument that the department was politically neutral was made again by Assistant Secretary Phillip Singerman, in his testimony on the EDA for the 1998 appropriations. He described the congressional request and the agency's response:

Last year at this hearing, Chairman Rogers asked if EDA would follow the criteria that focus funding on distressed communities that were outlined in legislation that was then being considered by the House. These criteria, in particular, are for communities of high unemployment in which the unemployment rate is at least one percent above the national average, or low income whose per capita income is 20 percent below the national average.

Chairman Rogers asked me if we would follow those criteria in the allocation of funds in our Public Works Program. I said to him at that time that we would. And the answer is demonstrated on the following page in the bar chart. This is a chart that represents each of the 158 public works projects that were funded in fiscal year 1996.

Fully 50 percent of the projects . . . were in communities which had both high unemployment and low per capita income. Approximately 30 percent of the projects were in communities which had high unemployment. Approximately 14 percent of the projects were in communities which had low per capita income. Approximately 6 percent were in communities of mild distress.

Those represent eleven projects. Each of those eleven projects were in communities in which the per capita income was below the national average; primarily in communities in which there were pockets of poverty inside growth centers, or communities that demonstrated distress through other quantitative measures such as population out-migration.[18]

Criticisms of the Department of Commerce went beyond the degree of politicization. The department's inspector general reported to Congress that the highly decentralized structure of the department had left too little oversight capacity at the center. One effect was a huge number of violations of procurement rules. Procurement oversight was essentially distributed out to the programs, so that department administrative staff would be located in the agencies where the decisions were being made. While nominally still central officials, these observers had their performance reports filled in by their supervisors in the agencies, not by the central administration, compromising their independence. In addition, when problems were called to the attention of the central administration, central officials were reluctant to discipline, calling instead for more training. According to the IG, more training was not called for, since those supervisors were already supposed to have been trained and should have known what to do. The IG also reported that lack of planning made costs of procurement unstable. Many observers noted the long time it took for procurement to occur.

The department responded to at least some of these criticisms by revamping the procurement system. Like many other agencies, Commerce issued credit cards for small purchases, to speed up and deregulate the purchasing process. For big items and major purchases, such as ships or laptops for the census takers, Commerce reinvented the process, removing many of the rules and changing the whole RFP (request for proposal) process into a more collaborative one:

> We have been reengineering acquisitions. I worked on this because it was systems acquisition. [For] purchasing items like ships, we have a team. We reengineered the process. We had focus groups with customers and came up with a revised concept of operations. A number of other agencies do this now.
>
> You try to go out as a team, legal, IRM [information resources management], program offices, and ask, what do you need? You don't want a specific detailed list, but what is it you want to do? How would you meet that need?
>
> We didn't use an RFP; we posted on the Internet. On the home page, people can pose questions electronically. We post the answers on the net too, so everyone can read them. The proposals that come in are shorter, but more meaningful; they are not just replying to a voluminous RFP. Then the team meets and does a "down selection." This part is controversial. Maybe 20 firms responded, and of those, 10 firms you know can't make it, and you knock them out at that point. They won't

win in the end. You narrow down the number of firms. Then there is a bid and selection process.

We had six pilots. We have done two, one was an acquisition at the Census Bureau of 21,000 laptops to test for the 2000 census, for the census takers [for direct entry.] The total purchase was about $30 million. The second was in Patent and Trademark, Scientific Dissemination; it is about $20 million. It used to take us about 60 weeks, over a year, to do a procurement of that size; these two took 18 and 19 weeks, respectively.

Have we gotten the right things for the agency? We have to evaluate. It used to be, they said, "I followed all the rules." It is very promising.[19]

The reforms might not have solved all the problems that the IG was worrying about, but it did shift the questions from "did I follow the rules" to "did I get what the agency needed." One consequence was a shorter time period for procurement. The shift away from rule-bound procurement complied with the spirit of the NPR and reinvention—Alan Balutis called it reengineering the process. But the elimination of so many of the rules made an end run around the IG's concerns, which were for compliance with that whole set of procurement rules. The IG suggested more central supervision and more punishment of violators; instead, the department reengineered its procurement process, eliminating a lot of the rules.

In what had the makings of a second clash between the IG's traditional control orientation and the more entrepreneurial approaches of the NPR, the IG also criticized the agency for engaging in franchise activities. These franchises, which were encouraged by OMB, represented the introduction of businesslike competitive principles in government, especially for the business-type activities that government agencies engage in. Under the franchise agreements, some departments would offer administrative services, including computer services, to other agencies for a fee. Under a competitive model, if the departments offering services were not efficient or able to offer low enough prices, other agencies would take their business elsewhere. The result was supposed to be an incentive for more efficient housekeeping functions, combined with some economies of scale because each department and agency would not have to set up its own services.

That Commerce jumped in line to try to offer such services seems like a survival strategy. If the department succeeded, it would get some help paying for its own overhead costs. Also, the franchises represent competitiveness, one of the values the Commerce Department was trying to foster in business. Moreover, the administration was supporting this effort. The department sought to respond to such administrative initiatives quickly, probably with the idea of maintaining the administration's support. However, the IG opposed this initiative on the part of the Commerce Department. He argued that such efforts distract from basic management issues, such as improving the financial management and data systems, and without those basic systems in place, the department would not be able to provide services to other agencies government-wide. He asked that the decision to franchise be deferred until it could be shown to be a sound business decision for Commerce.

The Department of Commerce was as responsive to the administration as it was to Congress, not only in the effort to reform purchasing and set up more entrepreneurial systems, but also in the effort to establish performance-based organizations (PBOs). The NPR initiative to suspend purchasing and hiring rules government-wide did not have much support, so the administration tried to implement its ideas of more freedom to manage by establishing individual performance-based organizations. The goal was to reduce administrative regulations in the chosen agency and make the agency more independent and businesslike; accountability would be achieved through performance contracts. Agencies were selected for possible PBO status if they had their own fee revenue and could operate like a business and had clearly defined outcomes. The Patent and Trademark Office (PTO), which had been considered for government-sponsored enterprise (GSE) status, was the furthest along and so was presented by Commerce as a possible candidate. The department also offered other programs as possible candidates.

For the department, proposing PBO status for the PTO might satisfy those who wanted more independence for this office, without making the PTO a government-sponsored enterprise. The department opposed GSE status for the PTO because it looked like the first slice of dismemberment. Under the PBO proposal, Commerce would retain policy control, but not administrative or financial control, over the Patent and Trademark Office. This policy became law in November 1999.

The Commerce Department tried to respond to major criticisms that were leveled at it directly from Congress and indirectly from the Office of the Inspector General and the General Accounting Office, as those two offices reported to Congress. Sometimes, however, it was difficult or impossible to satisfy Congress in this way, and sometimes individual agencies resisted these external pressures, especially when compliance would make the agencies more vulnerable to future budget cuts or privatization. The result was a mixture of compliance and resistance.

The Census Bureau persisted for years in trying to add sampling to the decennial census to increase accuracy, despite considerable opposition in Congress. Critics of NOAA, one of the major components of the Commerce Department, repeatedly argued that the agency should not maintain its own fleet of ships and its own uniformed services (the NOAA Corps) to run the fleet.

They advocated contracting out for these services. NOAA, however, had begun to modernize its fleet in 1992 and was apparently determined to buy new ships. The inspector general for Commerce, Frank DeGeorge, argued that the reason that NOAA did not comply was that

> NOAA program officials also have an incentive to own a ship rather than contract for better ships at lower cost, since they believe it is more difficult for the Congress to eliminate a newly bought ship than to eliminate the recurrent funding of a program that relies on contracted ships.[20]

If DeGeorge's reasoning was correct, then NOAA was unwilling to comply with criticisms if that compliance would make the agency more vulnerable to future budget cuts. Another possible explanation is that NOAA was just following the administration's policy, which called for a redesign of the fleet, mixing some contractual work and some work by NOAA in some of its own vessels.

To summarize, the Commerce Department fought back hard against the threat of termination and deep cuts. It engaged in triage, giving up what it had to. Generally, Commerce tried to comply with criticism from Congress and from the administration but was sometimes caught between them when they disagreed. The agencies thus sometimes resisted congressional pressures. Commerce tried hard to reposition itself into a more defensible posture, which entailed concentrating on trade, documenting successes, and demonstrating "synergy," showing that agencies in the department benefited from being together in the department. The department tried to establish a new neutrality to cope with the image of rampant partisanship. Many of these same themes were reflected in individual agencies: focus, demonstration of accomplishments, relationship among programs, and neutrality.

Within those overarching themes, the major agencies inside Commerce differed in their structure and their problems and responses. The Census story is related in chapter 3—the Census Bureau had a difficult time dropping programs and focusing more narrowly and could not make itself look less political, because of the sampling issue, even though the agency was politically neutral. The EDA tried to focus with limited resources and adapt by adding a new mission related to existing ones but drawing on a new source of funds and bringing in new stakeholders. The Patent and Trademark Office demonstrates the issues of raising fee revenue to reduce tax-based outlays. And NOAA reflects the theme of performance measurement, goals, and especially the limits and consequences of cuts.

While complying with criticism, Commerce resisted the dismemberment and cuts. Other departments would have considered such a strategy risky, because if they riled Congress, they could have been cut more severely than the initial threat; but when the initial proposal is for termination, not fighting seems to have little payoff. The goal is to minimize the cuts and damage, and failure leaves you no worse off than not fighting.

EDA: CUTS, THREATS OF TERMINATION, AND ADAPTATION

The Economic Development Administration is responsible for helping economically distressed areas. Its basic programs fund local public works projects to help attract industries. The EDA also helps communities recover from disasters, such as storms or floods, and more recently has helped communities deal with military base closings.

In the Commerce Department, the EDA was especially hard hit, with cuts and threats of termination throughout the Reagan years and with staffing reductions and budget cuts during the 1990s. As described by the National Performance Review in September 1993, "Funding rose until the early 1980s, when the Reagan and Bush administrations tried to eliminate the program. The program's current budget is $254 million for fiscal 1994, down from $830 million in 1980 (in 1992 dollars)."[21]

The early days of the Reagan administration were particularly traumatic for the agency, because the department as a whole was unable to resist the onslaught against the EDA. The fact that the EDA was primarily involved in efforts to rebuild economies in central cities and poor rural areas helped to classify it as a Democratic program. Some attacked the EDA because they did not want to support the urban poor; others attacked the program because they believed the government had no legitimate role in economic development or because they found the agency's efforts to demonstrate effectiveness in creating jobs unconvincing. The agency was sometimes described as slow and ineffective. Staffing reductions slowed it even further.

Funding declined for the EDA from 1980 to 1991. It rose from 1991 to 1994, with a peak in 1994 due to the Midwest flooding that increased funding nearly $200 million, from about $340 million to about $540 million. Then the budget tumbled again, with projections for steep cuts in the outyears. The EDA's budget was likely to keep fluctuating because of its function of helping to restore economies after some kind of disaster.

In the 1990s, in line with the NPR and congressionally mandated cuts of staffing, EDA reduced its staffing levels: "We laid off 40-plus employees. We achieved staff reduction, losing 100 FTEs through layoffs, attrition, and buyouts."[22] The agency defined the remaining staff as core. When emergencies occurred, the agency did not add staff; it set up cooperative arrangements with state and local governments. Deputy Assistant Secretary for Economic Development Wilbur Hawkins argued that after the cuts he would say, if you want it, this is how much it will cost, otherwise we cannot do it.[23]

Defining and maintaining the core staff proved difficult. Salaries were too low, some positions were difficult to recruit for, and the demands of legislation such as the Chief Financial Officers Act had to be complied with. The resulting tension between getting the agency's mission accomplished and responding to legal requirements for improved efficiency put the agency in a bind:

> We haven't given performance bonuses in the last two years. It is increasingly difficult to recruit and retain competent people. We have vacant CFO positions with low salary. We are looking for a programmer. Where are we competing? We had to comply with the CFO act. [We try to] minimize the findings of the inspector general, almost annually. We need a professional core. How do you balance service to people and deficit reduction? We have a fiduciary responsibility. We need to get grant dollars out there. Our communities are distressed, in economic transition.[24]

The EDA also had to answer charges that its allocations were politically motivated, not based on need. Hawkins argued directly: "Allocations are based on employment data and per capita income."[25] He continued, "We don't ask the political party when disaster hits. We move quickly and expeditiously to meet grantee distress. Quick performance, and we hope recognition." Getting to an emergency quickly should help the agency reap good public relations and help stabilize the agency. The EDA was dependent on getting good publicity to show Congress how effective its disaster relief program was, because the agency no longer had the staff to bring the message directly to Congress. The reduced staffing in legislative liaison activities created the danger of falling off the radar screen. If the EDA became invisible, it could be cut or eliminated without protest or consequence, so the agency needed to stay visible to Congress and the public. Besides disaster relief, the solution was to rely more heavily on the Internet to communicate with the Hill and the public.

In addition to defining the core staff and the increased use of the Internet for basic visibility, the EDA tried to reposition itself and get some funding from other sources by emphasizing efforts to rebuild economies after the closing of military bases. Initially, the EDA contracted with the Defense Department to help communities hurt by base closings; but after several years, the EDA was able to get a line in its budget from the Defense Department appropriation for this program. On the one hand, this strategy can be thought of as partnering; on the other, it represented an effort to widen the agency's constituency from the urban and rural poor (and often black) communities to a range of cities and towns in need.

The agency adapted by maintaining focus, not branching out to do things the agency did not have resources to do, and by using its existing skills to reach out to new partners and new support bases:

> Focus. There are things we might have had the luxury of doing, but we can't do them now. . . . We are more discreet in the types of partnerships: we maintain the existing ones, attract new ones, without alienating the traditional base of support. It is a delicate balance, bringing in new partners without a new set of skills.[26]

Whether the cuts in the 1980s were based on the ineffectiveness of programs or something else, they did not improve management at the agency. Administrative Data Processing was gutted and, along with it, the capacity to modernize and speed up agency responsiveness. After the Clinton transition, Wilbur Hawkins was called in to manage EDA. He argued that the agency was worth saving, but it "would be a lot of work. The EDA had a 12-year history to overcome. The agency was out of sync with the times. People do a good job, but the processes are slow as molasses." In 1993 the NPR description of the EDA included the following:

> Finally, EDA's uncertain political support has contributed to a variety of problems, including reduced morale, lower staff quality, poor operation and administration of programs, lengthy and complicated grant approval procedures, and the pursuit of low-risk policies.[27]

When Clinton was elected,

> Customer satisfaction was less than 60 percent. Grant processing time was well over 36 to 48 months to get an application through our system. There was a backlog of projects that were never funded. There was no balance or differentiation between the role of headquarters and the role of the field. There were redundant processes.[28]

The effect of the earlier deep cuts in the 1980s had not been to reinvigorate the agency but to leave it maladapted to its changing environment, poorly managed, and risk averse.

Hawkins worked on getting all the staff updated computers, networking between the field and the home office, and getting response time down, in part by computerizing the application submission and review process. Lines of responsibility between the field and headquarters were clarified and made more logical. Agency regulations were simplified and many eliminated in an effort to speed up grant awards and decision making. Hawkins argued that the NPR was the more important driving force behind these changes, but the deficit reductions also had an impact:

> In the long term, deficit reduction puts the mind-set in place; you will always have to deal with this. . . . The personnel reductions encouraged technology improvements. Equipment, and system design and upgrading people's skills on the computer. Windows and WordPerfect are mandated. Every employee will have to manage information systems.
>
> We had 50 representatives in the field, we now have 25, many people cover two states. We had to invest in laptops and communications to interface with potential applicants. Customer satisfaction on a departmental survey has increased to 95 percent. That was good.[29]

EDA was paying much more attention to critics and to customer satisfaction and trying to respond to demands for service more quickly and efficiently. It was also working at demonstrating the resulting increase in satisfaction. Along the same lines, the agency strove to demonstrate that it was effective in creating jobs and leveraging capital. The agency commissioned a number of evaluation studies to document the effects of its grants. Some agency observers remained unconvinced about these claims, in part because of the difficulty of demonstrating that economic development that followed grants was in fact due to the grants.

Part of the agency's strategy was to improve efficiency by reducing the ratio of overhead to program funding, cutting all kinds of expenses from the salaries and expenses budgets in addition to reducing staffing levels. The agency increased its "partnering," not only with the Defense Department, but also with the IGs, who took on more of the routine responsibilities for financial oversight and cooperated with the agency to help clean up problems the IGs discovered. Management improved over this period. Struggling to recover from years of underfunding of computers, the agency improved its efficiency with lower staffing levels and improved customer satisfaction. Doubts remained as to whether EDA was able to accomplish its basic mission of restarting dying economies. There was no sign that funding of the agency had stabilized, but the attacks on it received diminishing support. Finally, as a major step in improved support levels, the agency was reauthorized by Congress in 1998 for the first time since 1982.

The reauthorization reflected improvements in the agency's management and EDA's efforts to document its effectiveness in creating jobs relatively inexpensively. It also reflected congressional effort to focus the program on economic development of hard-pressed economies, curtailing the agency's function as a general public works "pork" program:

> In recent years, in response to congressional concerns, EDA officials have undertaken significant reforms of EDA procedures and programs.

Through administrative actions, the agency itself has been streamlined, undergoing an agency-wide reorganization process that has resulted in the development of a comprehensive Strategic Plan, the implementation of program performance measures in accordance with the 1993 Government Performance and Results Act (GPRA), accelerated resolution of outstanding Inspector General audit issues, and the hiring of a Chief Financial Officer. The number of agency staff was reduced over the two-year period between 1995 and 1997 by nearly 30 percent (from 355 to 255), with the number of political appointees dropping by more than 60 percent (from 14 to 5). With regard to delivery of services, EDA has reduced its regulations by more than 60 percent, simplified the grant application process and begun moving toward an on-line applications process, implemented a team-based approach in delivery of services, and increased delegation of grant approval authority to regional offices. Finally, and importantly, EDA officials have worked to tighten current selection criteria to help ensure that assistance is directed to economically distressed areas.

. . . As reported, S. 2364 reauthorizes EDA for 5 years, with declining authorization levels that are consistent with the Administration's budget request; better targets EDA assistance to communities suffering high economic distress by eliminating or tightening the criteria for eligibility; requires 50/50 Federal/local cost-sharing, with limited exceptions, for all EDA grant programs; provides for increased evaluation of EDA programs and operations; locks in administrative reforms recently undertaken by the agency; and deletes virtually all of three titles of PWEDA (Title II, regarding loans and loan guarantees; Title VIII, regarding disaster assistance and Recovery Planning Councils; Title X, regarding short-term job opportunities project).[30]

The EDA did get some program simplification, especially in its regulations. It was thus able to do more with fewer staff. Between the tightening of standards for grant eligibility and the reduction in the number of political appointees, the agency became less political. Getting out of the political target zone may have helped the agency get out from under efforts to terminate it. By the year 2000 its continued existence, at least through 2003, was more assured: it was managed better, its funds were targeted more selectively, and its impacts measured, but its funding levels were still declining.

PTO: USER FEES AND DEFICIT REDUCTION

In 1982 the Patent and Trademark Office (PTO) began to collect fees and reduce its dependence on appropriations. In 1990, in the Omnibus Budget Reconciliation Act (OBRA), a surcharge was placed on the fees for patent applicants. The surcharge was a temporary fee increase, and the revenue from the surcharge was placed in a separate account. The amount of the surcharge that was agreed to in the summit with the president preceding the OBRA 1990 was 45 percent of the existing fee. The House raised this amount to 56 percent and the conference committee raised the amount to 69 percent. The money was intended to offset appropriations. What had been paid for with tax money would be paid for by fees instead, thus helping to reduce the deficit. Provision was made for the fees to be treated as revenue and appropriated. In 1991, $18.8 million was to go directly to PTO, and $91 million would be subject to appropriations; from 1992 to 1995 all of the surcharge would be appropriated.

Supporters of the PTO presumed that the agency would make a budget request from this fund and the appropriated fees would be allocated to the PTO, since the fees were charges on users. But beginning in 1992 parts of the surcharge were diverted for other purposes. The amount of the diversion increased from year to year. Sen. Dennis DeConcini, a supporter of the PTO, argued in 1993 that he would continue to oppose this diversion of funds; in 1994 the authorizing committee made an unsuccessful bid to forbid this practice and also to forbid reductions in staffing due to across-the-board cuts (staffing reductions would have to come from legislation specifically designed for PTO).

Members of the House Appropriations Subcommittee on Commerce, State, and Justice tried to explain their decision to divert the surcharge. In their committee report for FY 1998 appropriations, they indicated that they had yet again diverted some of the patent fee surcharge funds for other purposes. They attributed the practice to the 1990 OBRA, claiming it was this legislation that increased the fees to offset the federal deficit and diverted the fees from the PTO. In fact, however, the 1990 law did not require a diversion; it merely set up incentives that made it difficult for committee members to resist diverting the fees. Supporters of the PTO argued that the intent of the surcharge was to reduce the deficit by making the PTO fully self-supporting, not by diverting funds from the fee account to other unrelated spending. But the size of the surcharge was such that once a reasonable budget request for PTO was satisfied with fee income, there would be fee income left over. And if the budget of PTO was held down, there would be even more left over. If the "surplus" thus created went to PTO, the appropriations subcommittee would gain no further deficit reduction. If, on the other hand, the fees could be diverted to replace appropriations in other programs, further deficit reduction could be achieved. The subcommittee hinted that other programs had a higher priority than adding money to the PTO. As long as PTO was in their jurisdiction and money taken from it could be spent on other higher-priority items, it was their responsibility to do so. The only solution for PTO was to get out of the jurisdiction of the committee.

From 1992 on the size of the fee diversion kept growing. As Congressman Howard Coble charged, "Beginning with a diversion of $8 million in 1992,

Congress increasingly redirected a larger share of the surcharge revenue, reaching a record level of $54 million in FY 1997. In total, over the past seven fiscal years, over $142 million has been diverted from the PTO to other agencies and programs."[31]

The diversion, especially as it escalated, had an impact on the PTO office operations. The Patent and Trademark Office listed the anticipated effects for FY 1996:

> Although plans for reductions in spending have not been finalized, cuts may have to come from the suspension or delay in capital improvements for information technology such as the suspension of major software development to allow for electronic filing or to allow PTO examiners to have desktop access to a database of prior art. These information technology improvements are designed to lower long-term costs and to improve customer service by facilitating quicker examination, reduced pendency, and the provision of higher quality patents. Additionally, other programs may be hurt. Under consideration are slowing down the hiring of new examiners, postponing efforts to improve the quality of work life, reducing training opportunities for examiners, and letting pendency rates rise.[32]

The predicted diversion did take place in 1996, and the pendency rates (the number of patents pending but not granted) did increase. From 1991 to 1997 pendency rates went up 22 percent. Commissioner Bruce Lehman attributed the increased patents pending primarily to the diversion of the surcharge funds.

Congressman Coble listed some of the consequences of the diversion for FY 1997 and anticipated consequences for FY 1998 and beyond:

> This [diversion], of course, has had a debilitating impact on the Patent and Trademark Office. The effort to reclassify the patent search file to keep it current with developing technologies had to be eliminated. The efforts to provide technological training for patent examiners and to expose them to the latest developments in their fields have been reduced. The support of legal training for patent examiners has been cut 50 percent. One of the most promising cost-saving steps contemplated by the PTO, allowing applicants to file their applications electronically, has been postponed indefinitely. Since the diversion of $54 million this year, the Office has been forced to reduce the hiring of patent examiners 50 percent at a time when patent application filings are increasing by nearly 10 percent annually.
>
> In the budget delivered to this body by the administration last Thursday, the President is proposing that we continue to increase these diversions in the amount of $92 million in fiscal year 1998 and $119 million, the amount of the entire surcharge, in each of the succeeding

years through fiscal year 2002. In anticipation of this denial of user fees, the PTO has canceled totally all plans for hiring patent examiners this year because it would not have sufficient funds to pay for them next year. We cannot afford to allow this dismantling of our patent system to occur.[33]

Given the administration's plan to completely divert the surcharge, supporters of the PTO worked to defeat the renewal of the surcharge and succeeded. They prevented the diversion of the funds but left the agency at least temporarily without this funding source. Some proposed a more modest, permanent fee that would cover the PTO costs and nothing more, a reduction in the size of the user fee. The administration proposed an expanded base fee, as opposed to the surcharge, that would produce more revenue than the request for the PTO required. For the longer term, the only solution seemed to be to make the PTO more independent.

Serious proposals were made to make the PTO a government-sponsored enterprise at least since the early 1980s, but these calls became more serious and more frequent in the 1990s as mandated across-the-board personnel cuts affected the PTO and as some of its revenue was diverted for deficit reduction. A more independent PTO would not be subject to these problems. The Department of Commerce objected to setting the PTO up as an independent agency but was willing to support the administration's efforts to designate the PTO a performance-based organization. Its businesslike operations and fee-based income made the PTO a logical candidate, and the designation would create a lot of the freedom the agency and its supporters craved. From the secretary's perspective, it was important that the PTO still report to the secretary and that the department still had policy responsibility and oversight, even though PTO would have independence in hiring, purchasing, and budget. Proposals and counterproposals flew at a hectic pace in the late 1990s.

In fall 1998 PTO supporters finally passed a reform bill that made the PTO a performance-based organization. The law was to take effect early in 1999 and required the new organization to do a fee study and present it to Congress. In the meantime, it appeared that the surcharge issue was dead and the agency would get all its fees. The fact that the budget was balanced by this time may have helped the agency reclaim its fees and saved them from being used as a way of balancing the budget of other agencies.

The PTO budget was increased under the new regime, and many of the prior management issues that were hanging fire because of reduced spending were immediately addressed:

The PTO is fully funded by fees paid by users of the patent and trademark systems. The President's budget seeks no rescissions, resulting in fees collected from PTO's users remaining with the agency.

The PTO's FY 2000 corporate plan is ambitious and will achieve an average cycle time of 10.2 months for all patent applications and allow examining attorneys to turn around trademark applications in 13.8 months. The budget is geared toward performance-based activities related to the agency's designation by the Clinton Administration as a High Impact Agency.

The majority of the $126 million increase over FY 1999 will go to improve customer service by funding initiatives that reduce pendency and ensure quality of patents and trademarks, including automation expansion.

The following are some of the PTO's FY 2000 budget initiatives that combined will reduce pendency while ensuring quality. The agency will hire 700 new patent examiners, bringing the total number to 3,300. All incoming U.S. patent applications will be converted to digital format. Patent classification and pre-searching will be performed electronically. All patents for biotechnology inventions with gene sequences and all Patent Cooperation Treaty applications will be filed electronically. Trademark examining attorneys will increase to 375, and the agency's 282,000 trademark customers can continue to use the Internet to submit applications, and will be able to send in follow-up material electronically. Customers will also be able to obtain status information about pending patent and trademark applications, and order and receive information products on the Internet. PTO's Web site (www.uspto.gov) will offer free access to one of the largest, if not the largest, federal government databases, hosted in-house. The Web site will provide free Internet access to fully-searchable text and images of over 2 million U.S. patents and over 1 million pending and registered trademarks. This electronic library represents over 20 million document pages of invention and discovery in science and technology, and more than 120 years of marketing creativity.[34]

PTO was able to recover budgetarily and improve management, but it did so by taking its fee revenues and opting out, more or less, from the Department of Commerce. To the extent that PTO had been contributing to a department-wide fund to pay for computer equipment, other programs' management improvements were delayed or derailed by PTO's success, an odd and unmonitored consequence. Even more striking, PTO's situation did not improve until the budget was balanced and the agency was able to restore its funding levels and add staffing and computerization to handle backlogs. Performance-based organizations with their increased freedom to operate and tight accountability for results may well improve public management, but this is an option only in the handful of agencies that produce their own revenues.

NOAA

NOAA is the largest agency in Commerce, operating a number of disparate programs, including nautical charting of ocean bottoms, seafood inspection and fisheries management, the National Weather Service, and protection of endangered species. To some, its role in protecting endangered species made it anathema; to others, its regulatory role in minimizing overfishing made it a target. Opponents of NOAA argued that many of its functions could be performed better and more cheaply by the private sector through contracting out.

Part of the background of NOAA during the period of the study was its expensive and extensive capital needs for Weather Service modernization and fleet renewal. The National Weather Service was engaged in a major modernization effort, estimated to cost more than $4 billion. That money was not available during the Reagan-era buildup in military spending. After the military buildup ended, money was spent on Weather Service modernization, with the idea that there would be major savings to the public and insurers from earlier warnings of major storms and that the agency itself would be able to reduce costs as new equipment was phased in. In addition, many of NOAA's functions depended on monitoring fish and animal species, counting populations, learning about migrations, and the impact of environmental changes. All these functions involved scientific ships. NOAA also used ships to chart ocean bottoms. The agency maintained its own fleet for this purpose and had its own uniformed NOAA corps to run the fleet. It was a small corps, but it was available for long trips in difficult circumstances. Most of the ships were 30 years old and had had minimal updating and repairs during that period. Fleet updating plans, announced in 1992, provoked major opposition.

The federal deficit control process made no distinction between capital and operating expenditures: budget caps did not allow for lumpy capital programs. Contracting smoothes out the bumps, whether or not it in fact reduces expenditures. It reduces the need to cut other programs to fund capital needs. The budget process thus contributed to pressure on NOAA to contract out for services rather than provide them itself with a newly purchased or rehabilitated fleet.

NOAA's major response to cuts and threats of termination was to fight them as best as possible, losing some budget and staffing, but much less than contemplated by its opponents. At the same time, NOAA yielded on many areas other than budget, while holding out on ones it considered inappropriate or more important.

During the Reagan administration, NOAA was grouped with the EDA as an agency slated for termination. It was cut back, but not terminated, despite repeated termination proposals. According to a GAO study, from 1981 to 1989 staffing levels dropped in NOAA from 15,199 to 12,515, a decline of more than 17 percent. From 1990 to 1994, however, staffing rose from 12,918 to 14,591, an increase of almost 13 percent. With the NPR and congressionally mandated staffing reductions and the election of the Republican majorities in both houses of Congress in 1994, staffing began to fall again. The agency's 2001 budget request listed actual staffing levels for 1999 as 12,307, of which 1,009 were reimbursable positions, so there were 11,298 positions that the agency had to budget for. Between 1981 and 1999 staffing levels had dropped about 19 percent; between 1994 and 1999 the decline was 14.6 percent.

Part of these reductions was to be achieved by transferring programs elsewhere, out of NOAA and out of the department. Such transfers help an agency achieve a lowered staffing level and may help rationalize the grouping of services within an agency, but there is no reason to expect them to save money. They do, however, shift some programs out of one appropriation subcommittee into another. Aeronautical charting was to be transferred to the Transportation Department and seafood inspection was to be transferred to the Food and Drug Administration (FDA). The transfer of aeronautical mapping to the Federal Aviation Administration (FAA) was planned for October 2000. The transfer of the seafood inspection program had still not been approved by Congress in the spring of 2000. Because these transfers had not yet taken place, the reduction in staffing was accomplished by RIFs, freezes and attrition, and buyouts.

The impact on some programs was greater than the aggregate figures suggest. First, because the Weather Service increased its staffing as part of its modernization program, other programs took larger cuts to compensate. Second, the cuts made recruitment more difficult, resulting in shortages of quantitatively skilled staff at the entry level. According to the chief administrative officer, Andy Moxam, reductions in force "have a chilling effect on recruitment and also make young people feel insecure, so they find secure employment in the private sector. . . . These young people have good quantitative skills" and they were leaving the agency.[35]

From 1980 to 1990 the budget barely kept even with inflation; from 1990 to 1994 the budget generally increased and then leveled off, actually decreasing some when inflation is taken into account. Budget authority increased from 1998 to 2000, swelled by capital projects including the weather modernization and authorization to proceed with NOAA's fleet modernization.

Moxam argued that the Reagan administration made cuts on ideological grounds: "We were environmentally oriented—that looks liberal: fish lovers, tree huggers. We gave lots of grants external to the federal government, to universities. It was considered discretionary in two senses, one the budgetary sense, and two the common usage of dispensable. They treated it as discretionary. The choice was to cut domestic to build defense and to pay for cuts in taxes."[36] Moxam argued that it took the agency a long time to recover from cuts that paid no attention to impacts.

According to Moxam, in the early 1980s NOAA operated like a holding company. There was no plan. The agency included a number of different programs, with different and seemingly unrelated goals. All NOAA could do was try to get supporters to argue for its programs. As Moxam described it, "whatever constituencies you can work up" you tried to motivate to argue in your behalf:

> We entered a 10-year tug of war between the administration and Congress. The administration would propose cuts off a budget of $1.2 billion; [it] proposed cuts of $200 to $300 million a year. . . . Congress would put them back in. [This was going on] back and forth: [Searching through documents to find actual numbers] in 1982, $41 million reduced, for coastal zone management, grants to states, proposed for cuts. NOAA was $780 million back then. The total was $892 million in 1983; the president proposed a cut of $93 million and $799 million [for 1984]. [He] proposed to cut out specific programs. Fisheries were to be cut $54 million out of a total $146 million. By 1987 [again it was] "Round up the usual suspects"—zero out the sea grant, cut fisheries. This was not taxing decision making; it was just accounting. They argued about the proper role of the federal government: should it be a state or private sector role? There was warfare at this small program level.[37]

Because Congress added back the money the administration proposed to cut, NOAA got the reputation of making end runs to Congress. The strategy was moderately successful, in that the agency was not severely cut in dollars. When inflation is taken into account, the agency was funded at the same level in 1990 as it was in 1980. However, staffing levels, which were controlled by the administration, were sharply cut. NOAA developed a tradition of fighting back, whether or not it had the support of the administration, and developed an expectation of success in doing so. By 1990 the opposition to the agency had softened and the budget began to grow.

With the incoming Clinton administration in 1992, the future looked brighter for NOAA because of the administration's interest in science and in stewardship of natural resources. But the agency found the new administration very policy oriented, and the agency was used to thinking of itself in terms of scattered constituencies, with different goals. The agency was required to produce a plan. Just as the USDA had to prepare a plan and found that plan in place when they needed to cut back, which helped them resist random cuts, NOAA found having a plan in place extremely helpful. According to Moxam:

> You have got to have a plan. In the early 1980s NOAA didn't have a plan. But at the beginning of the Clinton administration, we did strategic

planning stuff. It was a new way of looking at NOAA. We had been defined by constituent subgroups, but what is the point here? One of the big points is advance short-term warnings and forecasts. That didn't involve the Weather Service alone, but also satellites and research. It still came down to programs in Congress, but it helped us internally. Warning time [for tornadoes] is a measure. Do you know what it was in the mid-1980s? Tornado warning time was minus two minutes. We couldn't tell if there was a tornado until two minutes after it hit. Now it is plus 15. That is the metric. What do we need to do to accomplish that? Obviously, radars, satellite data, and researchers, to develop the algorithms to interpret the data. Thinking more strategically, it saves people's lives; [it also] helped us to better defend our programs.[38]

Andy Moxam was grateful for the Clinton administration's focus on strategic planning and the GPRA. The agency responded well to these initiatives:

NOAA was smarter and luckier [than many other agencies]: lucky with the quality of its appointees, smart to do the strategic plan. We are concentrating on what we are supposed to be accomplishing: predicting tornadoes, long-term climate change, fisheries, etc. The programmatic focus has been great.[39]

NOAA's budget had been growing through the early 1990s, but in 1995, with the new Republican majority in Congress, NOAA was again under attack. As in the early 1980s ideology was the criterion for cuts, according to Moxam. The agency fought the cuts and held them to a moderate 5 percent.

Reducing a proposed cut of 25 percent to 5 was a victory for the agency. The strategy was simple: to argue that the proposed cuts have consequences that can be demonstrated. NOAA had one especially strong and popular program, the Weather Service. NOAA made the point that cutting the Weather Service risked lives by jeopardizing early warnings. NOAA also documented the consequences of programmatic cuts for each congressional district:

We fought off the 104th Congress the first year. The second year, we took cuts, but they were limited; we had our act together. We laid out the consequences by district if the Chrysler bill [to dismember Commerce] passed.[40]

But while NOAA beat back the most severe threats to funding at least in the short run (proposals to dismember Commerce and NOAA were still circulating in Congress in late 1998), NOAA still had to deal with a variety of pressures from the administration and Congress and mandated staffing reductions:

There is an undercurrent in the administration, cut, streamline. We are to go from 14,309 in 1993 to 11,998 by 1999—16 percent. We are ahead of plan on that. Things are not so bad. Some of it required a RIF, there was a RIF in NOAA, four to five RIFs in different areas: NOAA Corps, National Fishery Service, National Oceanic Service, Office of Administration, and Comptrollers. We targeted administrative positions and supervisors.[41]

NOAA beat back the most severe of the funding threats. For example, the Weather Service was targeted for major cuts in 1997 in budget and staffing. The Weather Service modernization was supposed to result in reduced costs after it was fully in place, but the budget cuts required pushing up the timing of the cost reductions planned for after full implementation. In testimony, Undersecretary James Baker described the extent of the cuts on the National Weather Service:

The FY 1997 appropriation for NWS base operations is $27.5 million less than the amount appropriated in FY 1996. Of this amount, $17 million in reductions was requested by the Administration in the President's FY 1997 budget, and $10.5 million was identified by the Congress for permanent streamlining of operations and staffing levels at NWS central headquarters in the National Capital Area. In addition to the $27.5 million reduction, the NWS, like all other parts of NOAA, has had to absorb approximately $9.7 million in pay-related inflation and other mandatory pay-related costs, and estimates that up to $5 million will be needed for personnel separations. This totals to a $42.2 million base operations budget shortfall for FY 1997. This figure recently has been revised downward to $41.5 million through a $0.7 million reprogramming request. . . . In addition to the $41.5 million, the NWS contribution to NOAA-wide support and centralized services, such as security, common services, and the Central Administrative Management System (CAMS), increased by $5.9 million in FY 1997. The agency has proposed a broad range of personnel and program actions to address the combined level of reductions and support essential operating requirements.[42]

Undersecretary Baker outlined the cuts required in agency operations to meet the reduced 1997 budget, but he argued that some of them were temporary and could not be sustained without affecting lives and warning times. The argument was that the Weather Service had taken all the cuts it could; future cuts would affect performance. Note the careful avoidance of the argument that prior cuts have affected performance. Agency administrators, including Baker, acted as if they could not say they had been hurt; they had to say they were performing well, at the same time that they argued against future cuts. This can be a difficult line to argue convincingly. To this common theme, however, Baker added the idea that some of the cuts were temporary, and had to be made up the following year:

> To accommodate the overall shortfall, the NWS will implement a number of personnel streamlining and program re-engineering actions. Some of these actions are permanent adjustments to base operations, such as accelerations of planned staffing reductions in programs supporting meteorological and hydrological services. Several of the actions are temporary, and funding has been requested for FY 1998 in the President's budget request to restore these temporary actions. The NWS cannot sustain these temporary reductions in FY 1998 without affecting the provision of warnings and services to the public. For example, the NWS is deferring equipment maintenance and reducing operational stock supplies and training in FY 1997, and intends to restore these activities in FY 1998. Overall, the FY 1997 proposed actions will result in the abolishment of about 185 encumbered and vacant positions in the NWS, including about 113 in the National Capital Area.[43]

Despite the care taken to argue that current services would not be hurt by the cuts, several congresspersons panicked, sure that services to their states would be reduced. The secretary was forced to do some reprogramming to add back selected funds, at least on a temporary basis:

> On April 17, 1997, Secretary Daley provided notification to both the House and Senate Committees on Appropriations of his decision to reprogram $715,000 to restore proposed cuts to the NWS' National Centers for Environmental Prediction (NCEP). The Secretary stated in his letter, "While I believe that the streamlining that we are implementing is prudent, in consideration of the concerns raised by communities, Congressional delegations, and a governor, I have decided to maintain last year's level of effort and funded positions at NOAA's national centers including the National Hurricane Center. At the conclusion of the 1997 hurricane season, we will carefully evaluate the performance of the NHC and the other national centers to determine the optimal staffing level for the future." This restoration will help offset the total FY 1997 shortfall.[44]

Cuts in budget and staffing levels were not the only problems that NOAA faced. The National Performance Review had raised the issue of NOAA's aging fleet of ships and endorsed earlier GAO reports questioning the particular choices of ships that NOAA wanted for replacements and asking for some outside opinion of what NOAA actually needed. The NPR came down on the side of NOAA maintaining some of its own fleet but argued that some contracting out for charting might be beneficial. The report suggested some competition between NOAA and some private companies to determine how much contracting out should go on. The NPR argued for better fisheries management paid for by fee, but industry representatives and Congress opposed fees for this purpose. The third recommendation of the NPR with respect to NOAA was to combine the separate efforts of different agencies in the polar satellite program. Later, these criticisms and others were picked up by GAO and Congress and became demands to privatize all of NOAA's ships and charting functions and to disband the NOAA uniformed corps. Some in Congress refused to fund new ship purchases or major rehabilitation of existing vehicles to force the agency to contract out for these services.

Raymond Kammer, Commerce's chief financial officer and assistant secretary for administration, responded:

> We all recognize that NOAA must have access to seagoing capabilities to meet its mission requirements. The National Oceanic and Atmospheric Administration's fleet replacement and modernization plan calls for the construction of six new fishery research vessels. The Inspector General's report of March 1996 indicates that the National Marine Fisheries Service's data needs can be met by the private sector. The Department's FY 1998 budget request includes funds for architectural and engineering design studies for fisheries vessels. No funds have been appropriated, nor have any been requested to support construction of these vessels.
>
> NOAA's advice to Secretary Daley on the fleet issue is:
>
> - The vessels currently in the NOAA fleet are paid for and the cheapest option for the U.S. Government is to operate them through their useful lives.
> - Conducting oceanic and climate research in conjunction with UNOLS works quite well.
> - NOAA is very interested in accomplishing the major portion of its mapping and charting mission through leasing but suspects that there will be no services available in the Northern Pacific and probably not for parts of the North Atlantic. NOAA has contracted for some hydrographic data and is committed to doing more.
> - NOAA believes that certain of its fishery research vessels must meet some very specific design tests requirements to meet the fish population estimation needs of NMFS [National Marine Fisheries Service]

but is completely open as to whether the fishery needs are met through NOAA or contractor ownership and/or operation of the vessels.

- We expect to address the fleet issue as part of the FY 1999 budget process.
- We are proceeding with disestablishing the NOAA Corps. Draft legislation and the implementing plan were forwarded to OMB in early March. The legislation converts the Corps to civilian status and reduces the number of positions for NOAA. We will be converting those with less than 15 years service and offering retirement to the remainder of the Corps. The Corps has been reduced from 415 in FY 1994 to 299 positions in FY 1997, resulting in savings that will continue to yield $6 million annually.

Disestablishment by the end of FY 1997 will reduce the Corps to about 170 positions.[45]

While offering a tone of compliance, Kammer gently suggested that full compliance with the whole set of recommendations might not be possible or wise. He argued that some of the fleet was younger than 30 years and had some useful life left and cost less to operate than commercial or contract vessels. Kammer also described some of the agency's experiences with contracting out, which were less than satisfactory. In some cases, there were few if any private sector bidders. The IG responded that the agency just did not advertise long enough.

Roughly a year later, James Baker, the undersecretary for oceans, described what NOAA was doing with its ships and with contracting for services. This plan of action conformed more closely to the administration's view than Congress's, although there were some members of Congress who agreed with NOAA's position. On this issue, NOAA continued to resist congressional and other critics' pressure to completely privatize the fleet and contract for services, while yielding on a number of other issues, including initially the dismantling of the NOAA corps:

NOAA is presently using several approaches to collect marine data with ships. For oceanographic and atmospheric data, NOAA is using three agency ships and outsourcing arrangements with UNOLS. For nautical charting data, NOAA is using three agency ships and contracts with private industry. For fisheries stock assessment and research and marine mammal research, NOAA is using nine agency ships and outsourcing arrangements with private industry. NOAA expects to continue this approach for the next several years while expanding the amount of charting data collected by private industry.[46]

The GAO in congressional testimony summarized the status of the fleet modernization effort:

> NOAA now says that it has taken steps to improve the cost efficiency of its fleet and significantly increased its outsourcing for these services from about 15 percent in 1990 to over 40 percent today. According to NOAA, for example, it has removed seven ships from service and brought one new and two converted Navy ships into service since 1990, now outsources for about 46 percent of its research and survey needs, and expects to further increase its use of outsourcing to about 50 percent over the next 10 years.

> Although NOAA apparently has made progress in reducing the costs of its fleet and outsourcing for more of its research and data needs, NOAA continues to rely heavily on its in-house fleet and still plans to replace or upgrade some of these ships. In this regard, the President's budget for fiscal year 2000 proposes $52 million for construction of a new fisheries research ship and indicates that NOAA plans to spend a total of $185 million for four new replacement ships over the five-year period ending in fiscal year 2004—$52 million in 2000, $51 million in 2001, $40 million in 2002, $40 million in 2003, and $2 million in 2004. . . .

> In addition to its proposed acquisitions, NOAA also continues to repair and upgrade its aging fleet of existing ships. Since 1990, it has repaired and upgraded seven of its existing ships and plans to repair and upgrade two more in 1999. According to the President's recent budget requests, NOAA spent $12 million in 1996 and $13 million in 1997 to modernize, convert, and replace its existing ships. Also, it spent $21 million on fleet maintenance and planning in 1998 and expects to spend $13 million in 1999 and $9 million in 2000.

> The question of the viability of the NOAA fleet is entwined with the issue of the NOAA Corps, which operates the fleet. In 1995, NPR, noting that the NOAA Corps was the smallest uniformed service and that the fleet it commanded was obsolete, recommended that the NOAA Corps be gradually reduced in numbers and eventually eliminated. We reported in October 1996 that the NOAA Corps generally does not meet the criteria and principles cited by the Department of Defense for a military compensation system. We also noted that other agencies, such as the Navy, the Environmental Protection Agency (EPA), and the Federal Emergency Management Agency (FEMA), use federal civilian employees or contractors to carry out duties similar to the functions that NOAA assigns to the Corps. Commerce developed a plan and legislative proposal to "disestablish" or civilianize the NOAA Corps in 1997, but the Congress did not adopt this proposal.

According to NOAA and to the Department of Commerce's annual performance plans for fiscal years 1999 and 2000 under the Results Act, the NOAA Corps has been downsized from over 400 officers in fiscal year 1994 to about 240 at the beginning of fiscal year 1999, achieving gross annual cost savings of at least $6 million. In June 1998, NOAA announced a new restructuring plan for the NOAA Corps. NOAA's plan focused on the need for a NOAA Commissioned Corps of about 240 officers. NOAA's June 1998 restructuring plan also called for a new civilian director of the NOAA Corps and a new recruiting program.

However, Congress had other ideas. The Omnibus Appropriations Act for fiscal year 1999 set the number of NOAA Corps officers at 250. Subsequently, the Governing International Fishery Agreement Act (Public Law 105-384, approved November 13, 1998) made other changes in NOAA's proposed restructuring plan. This act authorized a NOAA Corps of at least 264 but not more than 299 commissioned officers for fiscal years 1999 through 2003, requires that a uniformed flag officer be the NOAA Corps' operational chief, and directed the Secretary of Commerce to lift the then-existing recruiting freeze on NOAA Corps officers. According to the NOAA Corps, it expects to have about 250 commissioned officers by the end of fiscal year 1999.[47]

The focus on contracting out for fleet and mapping services was based partly on the costliness of the capital outlays, but also on a general ideology that argued that privatization and contracting were better than governmental services that were provided with governmental employees. In actual situations, contracting might or might not save money, but privatization, eliminating some federal services and giving them to the private sector, would save money. Hence, for ideological and financial reasons, pressures to privatize—to give up some functions completely to the private sector as opposed to contracting for services—persisted. In NOAA, however, privatization had not really gone very far. The claim of privatization was

Sales over substance. Most of what we have of value [are] data. We sit on data. The biggest funder [and purchaser] of federal research is the federal government. [If we contracted for this information instead of providing it ourselves,] we would charge ourselves. Income transfer. It would make costs of research real, but we are working toward more open data internationally [and contracting would make data less available]. Ask people to pay for the weather reports? If we charge, what is it worth? But we privatize at the margins; we give it lip service. Only a little. We stopped doing fruit frost predictions. Is it low lying or not, cloudy or not? Is it valuable to the public? It does keep the juice prices down. It helps the orange growers. [But] we can do privatization there.[48]

Undersecretary Baker described the privatization the Weather Service engaged in:

> In contributing to a balanced Federal budget, NOAA, like all Federal agencies, is utilizing resources more effectively, discontinuing doing things which are not a federal role, identifying and realizing opportunities for savings, and focusing the efforts of government on what matters to people. For example, and in addition to the benefits of modernization, the NWS has privatized specialized weather services including agriculture, fruit frost, fire weather for non-Federal non-wildfire land management, and specialized event forecasts.[49]

The idea that privatization could be more extensive was to some extent based on misconception, according to Andy Moxan.

> AM: Chrysler said of the National Weather Service, he said he could privatize it by using the Doppler Radar Service. But there is no private company like that. We invented the Doppler radar; it has directionality. . . . We invented the methodology. Facts are the enemy of truth. [The truth was] you need to cut to balance the budget. That was the track [everyone] had to follow.
>
> IR: And the consequences didn't matter.
>
> AM: The consequences were not relevant to the debate.[50]

In addition to pressures for privatization, there were also pressures to eliminate overlap and duplication. The idea was to identify programs provided in several different agencies that seriously overlapped and either eliminate one of them or merge the two programs for the savings in overhead.

One area of overlap occurred in NOAA's polar satellite program. NOAA took seriously the NPR recommendation to merge its polar satellite program with those of two other agencies. NOAA and NASA had a cooperative agreement in which NASA did the purchasing and launched the satellites that NOAA used. NOAA worked out an agreement with the Defense Department to merge its weather satellite with NOAA's operations.[51]

A second area of potential overlap occurred in the Fisheries' Service Seafood Inspection Program. An administrative proposal to shift NOAA's seafood inspection program to the FDA had not passed as of spring 2000, but it represented the continuing desire to reduce overlapping programs. Since the inspection program is fee based, there would be minimal impact on the deficit, but such a transfer made sense in terms of focusing on a related set of activities and also in terms of reducing the number of employees in the Commerce Department.

There were also proposals originating in Congress to transfer the Endangered Species Act (ESA) responsibilities of the Commerce Department, including the National Marine Fisheries Service, to the Department of Interior's Fish and Wildlife Service. The overlap in this case was real but relatively minor. The National Marine Fisheries concentrates on ocean fish except where salmon swim from the open ocean up rivers, while the Fish and Wildlife Service specializes in preserving freshwater and land animals.

The intent of this proposed transfer to the Department of Interior was not entirely clear since there was not in fact much overlap. Some opposition to the continued responsibilities of National Marine Fisheries Service in the Endangered Species Act came from each side of the political divide. On the one hand, there was considerable resentment in some states about constraints on the use of water in order to protect fish, and some of this resentment affected the political support for NMFS. But the agency had a dual function, to help maximize commercial yields of fish and also to protect the fish themselves to assure abundance. When overfishing created a situation that required the agency to tilt toward protecting the fish to maintain future yields, it entered a somewhat regulatory area, assigning maximum catches. That role may have created some resentment against NMFS management. As William Stelle Jr., a regional administrator, argued in a hearing, "Some will argue that the main problem is that NMFS is too protective of species in its application of the ESA, and the best solution is eliminating us from the program. Others would argue that we are not protective enough."[52]

Efforts to move responsibility for the Endangered Species Act exclusively to the Interior Department may have represented an exploration of potentially overlapping functions, in which the actual overlap turned out to be minor. But it was probably seen by the Commerce Department and NOAA as part of the continuing effort to dismantle the Commerce Department.

In summary, NOAA fought off the most severe of the cuts and threats of termination but did take some serious hits in budget and staffing. As Andy Moxam put it, "We can run a great NOAA with fewer employees. It will be different, but we will run the joint, count fish, and do it right. We will deal with it. When it is raining, we all get wet."

While NOAA's reactions to cuts and threats of termination shared much with other agencies, it also had its distinctive elements. As a scientific agency, it responded well to the planning efforts involved in GPRA. Agency managers liked having a bottom-line performance level, and especially liked being able to demonstrate the relationship between service quality and impact on the one hand and budget input on the other. Similarly, there was a puzzle-solving element of the staffing reductions that the administration enjoyed. Where before there had been an equation with too many unknowns, now they had a key variable in place—the staffing level—and could work around that. With this number of staff and that performance goal, the work would have to take particular shapes. The cuts in the 1990s seemed more rational because more focused on outcomes, and there was less uncertainty in staffing constraints than in the multiple budgets of the Reagan era.

But perhaps NOAA best illustrates the skillful negotiations between the administration and Congress when their requirements of the agency were contradictory. NOAA answered its critics with mostly yesses, and some laters or in progresses, but also with some nos or maybes.

CONCLUSIONS

The Commerce Department fought back against dismemberment and deep cuts. Resistance when faced with termination as a department seems less risky than total compliance. Commerce was willing to accept its share of cuts, and even more, but set a bottom line that said, after this amount, further cuts will eat into maintenance and service levels. NOAA and EDA both argued that they could live with their cuts and do a good job, but after this, additional cuts would erode service levels. In line with GPRA requirements, NOAA developed a performance bottom line: how far in advance warnings could be issued before a snowstorm, hurricane, tornado, or flood. Increased warning time would allow people to secure property and get to safety. NOAA discussed proposed budget cuts with respect to their impact on warning time. From a budgetary standpoint, this strategy was successful, though it is not clear that it would work in any agency less popular than the National Weather Service.

Part of NOAA's strategy in taking cuts was to divide them between permanent cuts and temporary ones. The temporary cuts would have to be restored in the following fiscal year. They included items such as eliminating maintenance on some equipment. This strategy enabled the agency to simultaneously argue that the cuts had not done any harm to services and that the cuts would do damage and had to be reversed.

Commerce was fighting not just for its budget, but also for its life. In doing so, it needed to establish its legitimacy. It did this by sharpening its focus on trade, emphasizing the synergy of existing agencies located in the department, and reducing the appearance of political partisanship. The process for designing trade missions was altered and made more open; the number of political appointees was reduced; and individual agencies charged with political distribution of project funding went out of their way to demonstrate the objective criteria of need used for allocating resources.

Commerce had historically given up and received new functions, so the idea of trading off functions to get a more defensible core was in place before the major cuts came. Thus the department proposed to make the seafood inspection program a performance-based organization and transfer it to the Food and Drug Administration and gave up aeronautical mapping to the Department of Transportation, but it fought to retain its responsibilities under the Endangered Species Act to protect salmon in the Northwest rather than to give it to the Department of Interior. The latter was much more integrated with research programs and mission than either of the former two.

While toning down its partisanship, Commerce still needed to curry support in Congress, and hence it received and accepted a variety of earmarks in committee reports. These were often for small, geographically important research programs, such as monk seals in Hawaii or brown tide somewhere else. Congresspersons believed very strongly in these small programs and this earmarking was sometimes designated as pork.

Earmarking of expenditures was less important in some ways than earmarking of revenues. As in Agriculture, the fee strategy was very important at the Commerce Department. But in the PTO, it got out of hand, collecting more revenue from fees than the program costs, using the surplus to spend on other programs, and finally, holding down the program's budget in order to capitalize on the excess. Initially a congressional idea, this strategy was eventually adopted by the administration. The treatment of patent fees as general revenue rather than earmarked user fees caused a rebellion among PTO supporters, but as long as it went on, it had the bizarre consequence of taxing inventors to help balance the budget.

One important conclusion from the Commerce case is that it was impossible to come up with a plan in the middle of cuts, as occurred in the Reagan administration. The only strategies that could be used in a hurry were to try to demonstrate effectiveness and round up program beneficiaries and encourage them to argue for the programs with their legislators. But the cuts that occurred in 1995 and thereafter occurred after GPRA was passed and during a policy-oriented administration that demanded plans from departments and agencies. Thus Commerce Department agencies were ready in some sense not only to report their achievements more coherently, but also to cut back if necessary, and to fight off random shots that would do a lot of damage, while accepting those criticisms that made sense. The Weather Service, for example, had a plan in place, and when the cuts came in the mid-1990s, it was able to move up plans in time.

What was also interesting and useful about the Commerce case were the number of major ways in which the agency did respond to a variety of critics, even if not at the pace that some members in Congress would have wished. The department was especially responsive to the administration, even in areas such as eliminating the NOAA corps, which it was clearly reluctant to do. The agency quickly accepted overwhelming criticism of its appearance of politicization and responded with an effort to win back public trust, reducing the number of appointees and redesigning its trade mission process. Commerce began implementation of a new financial management system, reinvented its purchasing procedures for large purchases, and increased the amount of contracting out for services.

The Commerce Department's budget seesawed dramatically, but the first round of cuts was nothing like the second round in terms of agency response and damage done.

CHAPTER 8

Department of Housing and Urban Development

THE DEPARTMENT OF Housing and Urban Development (HUD) was cut in the 1980s and again in the 1990s, with dramatic personnel reductions in the later 1990s. For an agency that had been barely able to do its routine jobs because of a mismatch between program complexity and staffing skills, the management challenges of the later 1990s seemed overwhelming. Congress was reluctant to pass any program simplification legislation, exacerbating the department's problems. HUD had the dubious distinction of being the only department on the GAO list of agencies at high risk of major financial problems.

The department struggled to improve its financial management, while continuing to create "boutique programs," small special-purpose grant programs that came and went from year to year, requiring considerable staff time to draw up regulations, advertise, and launch. The strategy of accepting these boutique programs was made necessary by threats against the agency's existence and the urgency of getting and keeping every possible vote for support. HUD focused on ways of gaming the budget process, legally using its complex programs and its budget reserves to achieve savings under the scorekeeping rules. Since program complexity was increasing as staffing levels declined, HUD had to rely extensively on contracting out for basic services.

After years of severe declines, staffing levels finally stabilized well above the targeted 7,500 level and program levels began to recover (tables 8.1 and 8.2). As HUD Secretary Andrew Cuomo told his managers, the rumors of HUD's death were premature.

HUD experienced budget cuts and personnel cuts in several waves from 1981 on. From 1981 to 1986 there was a decline of full-time-equivalent (FTE) staffing of approximately 21 percent, then, as at USDA, there was some increase in staffing until 1992, when the numbers started down again.

According to CBO figures, from 1985 to 1997 the staffing levels in HUD dropped 9.8 percent. Considering the rounding to the hundreds in CBO data,

Table 8.1   HUD FTE Staffing, 1981–95

Year	Staffing	Year	Staffing
1981	16,094	1989	13,221
1982	14,609	1990	13,440
1983	13,812	1991	13,839
1984	12,462	1992	14,100
1985	12,095	1993	13,300
1986	11,720	1994	13,071
1987	12,282	1995	12,110
1988	12,971		

Source: GAO data provided to the author in 1996.

Table 8.2   HUD Federal Civilian Workers, 1985–97

Year	Staffing	Year	Staffing
1985	12,300	1992	14,100
1986	11,900	1993	13,300
1987	12,500	1994	13,100
1988	13,200	1995	12,300
1989	13,400	1996	11,600
1990	13,500	1997	11,100
1991	13,800		

Source: Congressional Budget Office, *Changes in Federal Civilian Employment: An Update,* April 1998.

the figure is nearly identical with that in GAO data in the 1990s, which allows a merger of the time series and a rough estimate of staffing declines from 1981 to 1997, of about 31 percent. The staffing levels were still headed down, with an initial target of 7,500 by the year 2000. Later this target was moved to the year 2002, to allow for more retirements. Ultimately, the target of 7,500 was abandoned as unachievable without legislative program simplification.

According to HUD data, staffing stabilized at a little more than 9,000 positions. In 1999 HUD reported total staffing at 9,963, and staffing from the salaries and expenditures portion of the budget at 8,957; the estimate for the year 2000 was a little higher at 10,417 total, and 9,200 full-time equivalent positions funded from the salaries and expenses budget.

The size of the workforce did not echo very closely the aggregate budget for the agency, either in terms of budget authority or outlays (table 8.3).

Table 8.3   HUD Outlays and Budget Authority,
1977–2002 (in $ millions)

Year	Outlays	Budget Authority
1977	5,808	33,818
1978	7,650	37,994
1979	9,220	31,142
1980	12,735	35,852
1981	14,880	34,220
1982	15,232	20,911
1983	15,814	16,561
1984	16,663	18,148
1985	28,720	31,398
1986	14,139	15,928
1987	15,484	14,657
1988	18,938	14,949
1989	19,680	14,347
1990	20,167	17,315
1991	22,751	27,634
1992	24,470	24,966
1993	25,181	26,648
1994	25,845	26,322
1995	29,044	19,800
1996	25,236	20,821
1997	27,527	16,091
1998	30,227	21,022
1999	32,794	26,344
2000 est.	30,076	16,290[a]
2001 est.	32,077	34,249
2002 est.	30,416	28,592

Source: U.S. Budget, 2001, Historical Tables, Table 4.1: Outlays by Agency, 1962–2005, and Table 5.2: Budget Authority by Agency, 1976–2005.

[a]The figures for budget authority for the year 2000 are misleading, as they contain huge offsets: $4.2 billion is an advance funding for Section 8, which should show up in the 2001 budget but may be committed in 2000. There are other offsets in the 2000 budget authority as well. The effort to make the budget look smaller than it was reflected the desire to appear to stay under the caps at a time when there were budget surpluses and urgent need for housing. Large offsets mean that spending remains high or is cut slightly while budget authority drops. This did occur in fiscal year 2000.

OMB figures show decreases of more than 50 percent in the budget authority for the agency from 1980 to 1983. Budget authority had not quite recovered to the 1980 level two years later, when it was dramatically cut again in 1986, with the initial Gramm-Rudman-Hollings round of cuts. This time the level of budget authority stayed low, not even beginning to recover until the early 1990s, then dropping again from 1995 to 1997. From 1985 to 1989 budget authority fell by more than 50 percent. From 1991 to 1997 the budget authority declined by about 40 percent. Actual outlays did not drop proportionately, which was a crucial part of the HUD budget strategy, but outlays did jump around in some years. Outlays rose from 1980 to 1985 but plummeted in 1986. The outlays dropped again from 1995 to 1996, by almost $4 billion, and again in FY 2000.

The disconnect between budget authority and outlays represented a strategy on HUD's part to keep up spending levels, pushing obligations off into the future in hopes that the overall budget situation would be better and the need so acute that Congress and the president would come through later with more funds. In the earlier years the primary technique was to change the length of contracts for housing—fewer years meant lower costs, but more frequent renewals—until the agency was renewing contracts each year and the total costs began to rise again. Later, HUD began borrowing from the future through advance funding, using some of the next year's budget in the present year.

The lack of direct correlation between staffing levels and spending was due to a number of factors. During the Reagan administration, determination to reduce the size of the bureaucracy resulted in arbitrary personnel targets. Dollars and positions were budgeted separately. Agency efforts to match the workload with staffing were systematically discouraged. Later, the National Performance Review (NPR) also slated a reduction in the size of the bureaucracy, divorced from program size or complexity. The numbers of staff were not directly related to aggregate agency spending. The NPR recommended that HUD cut 1,500 positions, or about 11 percent. With staffing levels of about 13,000 in 1993, the NPR recommendations would have brought HUD down to about 11,500. Thus the NPR recommendations did not justify the 7,500 figure that emerged shortly thereafter (9 December 1994) and got reified as the number of staff HUD would aim for.

The 7,500 figure was never explained publicly. The HUD inspector general's office complained it was never shown any justification of the 7,500 figure and considered it "somewhat arbitrary."[1] By 1996 HUD's administration conceded in the appropriations hearings that 7,500 staff would not be adequate to run HUD's programs and would make it nearly impossible for the agency to respond to new initiatives or staff-proposed changes. One informant guessed that the figure resulted from a deal struck with the president to provide some additional dollars for other purposes and that because of Congress's reluctance to cut programs, the funds could only come from staff reductions.

When HUD tried to simplify programs to match available staffing, Congress did not pass the necessary legislation. Tight budgets, requirements to pay separation costs and mandated salary increases, and the need for additional training to enable remaining staff to cover for their lost colleagues all ate into limited personnel dollars, exacerbating the disconnect between program complexity and staffing.

The two main responses of HUD, to reduce the budget authorization while continuing to maintain or increase outlays and the dramatic downsizing divorced from programmatic justifications and reorganizations, raise the questions of how long particular strategies can go on and what the natural or unnatural limits are of continuing to engage in strategies that are initially successful. HUD's strategic responses also call attention to the need to respond to threats of termination, often taking actions, such as allowing the proliferation of boutique programs, that work in the short run, even if they cause problems later.

THE REAGAN YEARS

During the Reagan-era budget cuts, HUD devised a strategy that would create the appearance of budget cuts while continuing to support programs. One of HUD's major housing programs, called Section 8, was funded by long-term contracts. These contracts were reflected in the budget authority. In order to cut back the budget while continuing to provide services, HUD shortened the duration of the contracts, reducing the amount of budget authority required without affecting the outlays in the short run. This strategy was reused later, whenever fiscal stress hit the agency, reducing the terms of the contracts progressively, until they were only annual.

A second strategy of the Reagan period to save money and continue to provide services was to downplay construction of housing and instead play up vouchers, which were cheaper. This shift of focus had already taken place by the time of the Clinton administration and could not be taken further.

Although there were some reductions in outlays, the major cuts were in budget authority. The outlays continued to grow, if moderately, in most programs. One informant suggested that conservatives were distracted by the market-like reforms of switching to vouchers and hence did not focus on reducing housing services to poor people. While housing programs survived pretty much intact, community development programs such as the Urban Development Action Grant (UDAG) and Community Development Block Grants (CDBG) were threatened with termination. Administrators of these programs gained the support of the secretary and were able to mobilize program constituents to argue that it was politically unwise to eliminate these programs. Secretary Samuel Pierce called for an evaluation study for the UDAG program and found that it was working reasonably well; program administrators had involved the secretary in making grant decisions, so he was able to argue that the grants were necessary and appropriate, because he knew the circumstances of the awards. The secretary then appealed OMB's decision and overturned Budget Director David Stockman in a cabinet meeting.[2]

Both UDAG and CDBG were cut slightly in program dollars in the Omnibus Reconciliation of 1981. President Reagan called for an additional 12 percent cut for 1982, but UDAG escaped new cuts and, while CDBG was cut further, the cut was held to about 6 percent instead of 12 percent.

HUD initially chose to take the cuts, which were not extreme, disproportionately in programs rather than in the salaries and expenses budgets. For 1982 the salaries and expenses budgets were reduced only 1.28 percent. For 1983 the Reagan administration tried again to terminate both UDAG and CDBG, but the department and interest groups fought off the threat, stabilizing funding.

Despite the reasonably stable funding, HUD experienced reductions in force during the Reagan administration. There was some program simplification and decentralization to the states of the Small Cities program, which could have resulted in downsizing, but RIFs were mandated before the effects of this decentralization were clear. The justification for RIFs was that some units in HUD were going to be above personnel ceilings for 1982, and so a RIF would be necessary, in part to increase the amount of attrition and in part to get down to ceiling levels. Since the department overall was under ceiling and it is within the discretion of the secretary to assign ceilings within the department, all that was required was for the secretary to change the allocation of ceilings. This was not done, giving employees the feeling that the decision to RIF was a political one.

The level of staffing continued to erode throughout the Reagan administration. The salaries and expenses budgets were cut. To slow the staffing losses and help plan for them, HUD initially cut other items in the salaries and expenses lines, rather than personnel services. Former budget director Al Kliman described the process:

> I developed a thesis: no cut is too small to take. Sometimes you hear, especially on Capitol Hill, that is too small to bother with, but I found that sometimes a really big reduction could be accomplished with a roomful of nickels, especially on administrative expenses. There were so many little things you could do. It added up. If you could not avoid what was coming, you could at least delay it in order to manage it [personnel cuts]. Maybe it would be postage: your friends in the research department were sending out all these big books, first class, when they could have sent them book rate. The savings aren't in billions or millions, only in thousands. You can look at telephones. Outside lines with unlimited access, multiply the savings by the number of telephones and the number of people doing it. So you go after peanuts, to postpone or avoid the fateful day, so you can plan more carefully for reductions.[3]

The staffing reductions of the Reagan administration exacerbated already existing management problems, but, in Kliman's view, the problem was less the number of staff than the unhitching of the workload and the staffing levels.

The downsizing of the staff was not systematically linked to program simplification. There was some program simplification, but its goal was probably more closely related to loosening of regulations requiring program money to benefit low- and middle-income families, so that wealthier people could benefit. Applications for CDBG were eliminated, with legislative approval, so HUD could not make awards based on eligibility or compliance with regulations. The most radical of the proposed regulation changes (removing requirements for benefits to go to low- and moderate-income recipients) were beaten back. In one case, however, the administration of a grant program was taken out of HUD's hands and given over to the states (the Small Cities program). The more successful of these efforts had the secondary impact of reducing the need for staff at HUD.

During all the initial cuts and the downsizing, HUD engaged in reorganizing the field staff offices. The reorganization was supposed to save money, eliminating some of the field offices and merging them with the regional offices. The estimates of savings were judged inflated, however, and the real purposes of the reorganization were questioned. Congressional committees intervened, treating the office closings as if they were economically significant to their districts. Some committee members suspected that the real purpose of the reorganization was to shift more power to political appointees, who were in the regional offices.[4]

Many of the strategies established during the Reagan period continued in the Clinton administration or were played out to their logical end. The consequences of many of the earlier actions were also felt during the Bush and Clinton administrations. The department was later criticized for lacking a staffing justification system and for having a field structure that seemed to make no sense administratively. Questions were later asked about whether HUD had sufficient trained and knowledgeable staff to run the agency's programs.

THE SCANDALS

In 1988 and 1989 HUD experienced several highly publicized and highly damaging scandals that provoked a number of congressional committee hearings and studies by GAO and the National Academy of Public Administration (NAPA), as well as the inspector general of HUD. These hearings and studies documented the scandals in detail and came up with causes and recommendations for improvements. The scandals were so serious and the studies so far-reaching in their recommendations that HUD had to respond to the criticisms.

While some of the causes of the scandals predated the Reagan administration, the scandals were worsened by Reagan administration policies. The administration was not very interested in housing, and oversight tended to be lax. Charges were made later that there were insufficient numbers of skilled staff to run the programs properly.

One of the scandals occurred in the moderate rehabilitation program, a small program for minor repairs to existing housing stock. When several other major programs for contractors were curtailed, moderate rehabilitation was one of the few left and demand for it increased. Presumably because there were so few dollars involved, impartial procedures for evaluating proposals were dropped and an ad hoc procedure put in place. This procedure became very political, with approval required by high-level appointees who looked for political sponsorship of requests. These high-level appointees in the second Reagan term were young and ambitious and reportedly had been "dumped" on HUD by the White House. They were interested in enriching themselves at public expense. HUD's secretary took no steps to stop their activities.[5]

The agency suffered from politicization combined with not particularly benign neglect. One congressional committee exploring the scandals at HUD was critical of this politicization:

> Just as it was wrong for HUD to dole out housing units . . . just as it was not right for President Reagan in 1982 to give units to New Jersey to influence a Senate race, so too should Congress not earmark funds for housing projects in appropriations bills. Last year's Supplemental Appropriations bill for HUD earmarked nearly $30 million for 40 housing grants.[6]

While the self-enrichment of builders and appointees and former appointees at HUD got a great deal of attention, it was less important than other scandals at HUD that resulted from a lack of consensus about whom HUD was supposed to serve and from programs that were designed in such a way that they had to fail financially. Moreover, programs designed in one period paid attention to the scandals of a previous period, often jumping out of the frying pan into the fire. When private-sector builders proved too greedy, HUD redesigned some rental housing programs to depend on not-for-profits instead, many of whom were themselves inexperienced and had too few staff.

Another factor leading to scandals was the tension between getting housing produced as quickly as possible and building housing that was financially sound and followed the regulations:

> If there had been realistic processing [in the early 1970s] few projects would have been built. Had the projects been processed using the likely income of the residents (rather than the maximum income limits) and had realistic estimates of expenses been made, the later problems would have been avoided because very few projects would have been built.[7]

Earlier periods of emphasis on getting housing built contributed to a culture in which oversight was minimal, leaving the agency vulnerable to financial scandals.

Many of the rental projects run by nonprofits, many of which were church groups, were in deep financial trouble in the early and mid-1970s. Since they were FHA insured, if HUD foreclosed on the mortgage, the insurance fund, already in the red, would be embarrassingly strapped. Moreover, the housing residents would probably lose their apartments as private buyers converted the housing to more profitable uses. To keep the projects going, HUD increased its subsidies to the projects. But by the time that solution kicked in, many of the projects were seriously deteriorated.

The solution at this point was to enable the nonprofits to sell the physical assets to private investors, who were paid in tax breaks; the money realized from the sale would be used to maintain the properties. The physical assets could be transferred to a limited distribution entity, which would nominally own the property but would resell the tax advantages to private investors. The tax breaks were only marginally legal, the financing complex, and the projects themselves often could not cover their mortgage payments. The money was being made on the tax breaks, not on running the properties well or fixing them up. Many were in poor condition when purchased and some were poorly managed. In 1989 then-Secretary Jack Kemp was horrified by the physical condition of some of these rental units and put the brakes on the program.[8]

HUD had been unable to face the failure of a program that had as renters people too poor to pay the costs for projects that were fully insured by the FHA; instead, it turned to financial entrepreneurs who did not have housing as a primary goal. They were buying property and selling tax breaks for a profit. The schemes by which they accomplished this goal were so complex that the inspector general's office of HUD was unable to penetrate them and GAO did not find them.

One of the most comprehensive and important of the studies documenting the scandals was done by the National Academy of Public Administration.[9] The NAPA study emphasized the combination of long-term staffing reductions and the proliferation of programs that resulted in what the study team called "program overload." The report noted massive staffing reductions of 2,596 full-time equivalents between 1980 and 1992, at the same time that there was a threefold increase in the number of mandated programs and activities, from 54 to more than 200 programs.[10] The proliferation of programs was seen in part as resulting from the tension between a Republican administration and a Democratic Congress, in which the administration wanted to minimize the role of the department and Congress wanted to energize it. The NAPA report documented the mismatch between increasing program responsibilities and decreasing staffing. In housing between 1985 and 1992, seventeen programs were added, some of which were very small (five under $1 million) while staffing decreased 4 percent.[11] Work burdens increased in Community Planning and Development as well as in housing, since each small program required start-up time and supervision.

The reduced staffing and continuing program complexity resulted in slow responses to applications and underwriting submissions and in increased contracting out. HUD's core program knowledge was being depleted in some areas.[12] One problem interviewees identified for the near future was that few experienced HUD staff would be available to educate the contractors after contracts turned over.

NAPA endorsed what HUD called "right-side-up programming," in which the local communities were on the top and HUD headquarters on the bottom. This was to be achieved in part by waiving regulations to allow local experimentation and maximum delegation to the lowest accountable state or local level. The NAPA study argued that HUD had responded to the scandals by reducing agency discretion over grants and contracts, which probably had a positive effect, but which also generated an enforcement or oversight emphasis rather than a partnership with local entities. Consequently, the critics emphasized "right-siding" the relationship.

In 1993 HUD's inspector general reported a variety of problems, including inadequate staff to carry out current programs, inadequate data systems, and inadequate attention to financial control issues. The 1993 report also called attention to some problems specific to individual HUD programs, including continuing vulnerability of multifamily housing loan programs, poor asset management and property disposition, and lack of means for assuring that CDBG grantees were in fact eligible for their grants. Several of these problems were created by or exacerbated by decisions during the Reagan administration to reduce staffing severely and to eliminate the applications and review of CDBG grant requests. Other criticisms of the agency by Congress included that its staffing requests did not seem based on reliable workload data. That criticism resulted directly from the separation of staffing from workload that had occurred initially in the Reagan period.

What HUD had been unable to do over this period of understaffing, scandals, and managerial inattention was to oversee programs effectively, improve data management, and train and redeploy existing staff.

THE CLINTON ADMINISTRATION

During the Clinton transition, the new administration determined that HUD needed to address the management problems highlighted by postscandal studies and to redefine its mission. HUD's programs lacked a unifying theme. The transition team insisted that the changes be made without additional funding. In response, the secretary of HUD, Henry Cisneros, pulled together a planning team and came up with reinvention plans, later called "blueprint one." Input was broadly solicited to redefine HUD's mission and improve services, though most of the advice was not acted on.[13] The NPR, which was running at the same time, instructed the agency to reorganize its field structure by eliminating the regional offices and to reduce staffing by 1,500 positions. In September 1993 the Senate Appropriations Committee instructed HUD to focus attention on consolidating and simplifying programs. At the end of 1994 HUD came up with its reinvention blueprint. This proposal had behind it real concerns that the agency might be terminated. The NAPA study had recommended that if HUD could not get its house in order, the agency should be eliminated.

Secretary Cisneros argued that eliminating HUD would not solve the program or management difficulties that would remain if its functions were scattered to other agencies and that reinvention was needed to solve HUD's problems. The proposed program simplification grouped hundreds of programs into three areas, reducing the number of applications necessary for funding and making it easier for local governments to apply and for the agency to administer. The goal was increased flexibility, but without entirely giving up oversight and rules for compliance in spending the money.

Housing programs would be rolled up into one fund and administered by the states and local governments. Elimination of the constraint that new housing must be substituted for torn-down units would make it simpler to tear down projects. A special feature of the legislation would reward good performance with additional funding. The reform blueprint made housing programs more like markets, substituting housing certificates for rent subsidies, and saved money by continuing to reduce the time period of the Section 8 renewals and by "mark to market" plans that would reduce the overly high rental subsidies HUD had gotten locked into in order to save some overly expensive projects.

The plan was dramatic, with considerable political appeal, but some of its elements were highly controversial, including raising the income levels for eligibility in public housing. Such action would make the housing projects more economically viable and would help stabilize communities by mixing up the income groups rather than concentrating the poor but would reduce the number of units available for the poor.[14]

The entire reinvention plan required legislative approval, which it did not get. While the consolidation and reinvention plan did not work, the field structure reorganization mandated by the NPR did take place. HUD eliminated its regional offices. Under the new system, the assistant secretaries would have more direct control and accountability over field offices, which in turn were supposed to have more discretion. The result was still "cylinder," or program, based, rather than integrated across functional lines. NAPA and several informants expressed puzzlement as to how the reorganization would help solve HUD's problems. This reorganization in the field seemed more like an effort to comply with a specific NPR directive than a well-thought-out reorganization to solve problems.

HUD offered a second blueprint for program simplification in January 1996. This revised plan gave up on a total vouchering of public housing in favor of improving existing housing and tenant-based assistance programs through program consolidations and streamlining. There was also additional emphasis on reducing crime and mismanagement in public housing and on tearing down the worst developments. The emphasis on housing was on self-sufficiency and responsibility. HUD announced a new place-based service delivery concept and plans to close up to ten field offices and create service center operations. Despite the efforts to increase the political appeal of the legislative portion of the package, Congress did not approve it. Many of the ideas in it, however, were inherited by Secretary Cisneros's successor, Andrew Cuomo, and implementation occurred where the agency could act without congressional approval.

Andrew Cuomo became secretary of HUD at the end of 1996. Cuomo's reform proposals continued some of Cisneros's ideas but took a somewhat different tack. The legislative strategy persisted, including continued efforts to eliminate some programs and simplify others. A major legislative victory was achieved in the mark-to-market portfolio reengineering, but other reform proposals requiring legislative approval languished. Cuomo therefore tried to concentrate on improving financial management and reorganizing the agency for more effective operations with fewer staff members.

Cuomo called on famous business-sector gurus for advice and ongoing evaluation to increase the credibility of the businesslike reforms. Agency staff were formed into teams to make recommendations for changes; the proposals were much less top-down than prior recommendations had been.

Management improvements included a new accounting system to replace the 80-odd noncommunicating ones in the department; hiring a new chief financial officer who was able to go over the finances carefully, find unspent funds, and increase the credibility of the agency in financial matters; the creation of a property assessment center to evaluate the condition and value of HUD holdings and investments; and an enforcement office to deal with recalcitrant landlords and illegal gambits. Service delivery was separated into direct contact and back-room operations, using banking and financial houses as the organizational model. Service delivery, to be offered in storefronts with one-stop service, was separated from enforcement. The bottom-up community-empowerment philosophy was implemented by the creation of a new position, a kind of community organizer, who would be trained in a Harvard program specifically designed for this program, would work in local HUD storefronts for two years and then return to the community. These changes were to be implemented in a relatively short period of time, and a year after their announcement many of them were well under way. Interim reports on the nature of the reforms, on their appropriateness to the problems, and on implementation were positive. Secretary Cuomo reported at HUD's 1999 budget hearings that substantial progress had been made in implementation:

> I am happy to report significant progress has already been achieved. To date, HUD has posted and filled 1,100 positions and hired 90 percent of new managers for the new organizational structure, while executing 1,000 buyouts to downsize the agency. The Department also negotiated an historic agreement with the employee unions to staff the new stream-lined HUD with no layoffs before 2002.
>
> Four FHA Single Family Homeownership Centers are already oper-ational. By April 1, all 18 FHA Multifamily Program Hub offices will be operational.
>
> Public and Indian Housing already has 27 Program Hubs and 16 Program Centers operational. By August 1998, the Public Housing Grants Management Center and Troubled Agency Recovery Centers will also be operational.
>
> The Assessment Center is currently using its new physical inspec-tion protocols and handheld computers to inspect a sample of public housing and multifamily properties.
>
> The Section 8 Financial Management Center will be fully opera-tional and handling 100 percent of the Section 8 financial processing by October 1998.
>
> The Enforcement Center has already begun working on cases. Four Assistant U.S. Attorneys have been detailed to the Center.
>
> More than 300 Community Builders from existing HUD staff have already been selected. Their training has just begun and the first train-ing sessions at Harvard University's Kennedy School of Government will take place in August 1998. Outside hires of 230 Community Builders will also be completed by August.[15]

Cuomo argued that the successes of his reforms had helped persuade the Clin-ton administration to propose a higher budget for the agency in 1999.

For the budget year 1999 HUD continued its strategy of trying to main-tain and expand programs without increasing present or visible costs. This strat-egy reflected commitment to its services and clientele on the one hand and the necessity of playing to the budget rules on the other. One example was described by Secretary Cuomo for the 1999 budget request:

> HUD has worked hard to find ways to expand our programs without increasing our bottom line—reforming programs within HUD to accomplish more while costing less. We have identified several such reforms in our budget. For example, our proposal to increase FHA loan

limits would increase homeownership opportunities for thousands of Americans each year and would bring in more than $225 million per year into FHA. Similarly, our proposal to reform our system for disposing of FHA single-family properties would streamline and accelerate processing of defaulted mortgages and save $525 million in FY 1998.[16]

An increased limit for FHA loans would have multiple effects. It would simplify administration by substituting one limit for the many limits then in place; it would allow lower down payments, increasing affordability; and it would allow mortgages for many who want to move to the suburbs but cannot get big enough mortgages. Besides those programmatic reasons, HUD may have been trying to expand the number of middle-class beneficiaries of the program in an effort to increase political support. In addition, the expansion had a kind of budgetary payoff because of the way savings were scored. Similarly, the expedited sale of defaulted property that the agency was asking from Congress would save money.

Cuomo sounded a new note when he described a budget strategy of not adopting new programs, but only working with existing programs that were working well:

> The budget increase will not, however, support new programs. It will not support new bureaucracies. It will not be wasted on programs that are fundamentally flawed or blatantly abused. This new funding will support only those programs that have proven successful and those programs that have been improved or enhanced by design changes. In other words, HUD will put the new funding only where it works best to fulfill our mission.[17]

While HUD continued to earmark CDBG grant funds for special purposes, for 1999 at least, the total requested was higher, rather than dividing the same total into more small earmarked pieces. Efforts were taken to prevent increased administrative burdens each time a new competitive grant was announced. It was not clear how successful this strategy would be, but it showed an awareness of the problem:

> A new challenge facing communities is to make welfare reform work in the context of new regional economies. This initiative is a $100 million set-aside within the CDBG program. It will make funds available by competition to states and localities to cooperate regionally to develop strategic plans that address key regional issues facing the nation's metropolitan areas and rural communities. The initiative will help communities adjust to the significant demographic and economic shifts that are

taking place in metropolitan regions. It will encourage regional strategies that emphasize coordinated metropolitan economic growth and regional solutions to a range of environmental and social equity issues.

HUD will establish an Advisory Board of city and county officials, distinguished urban planners, economists, and regional experts to develop the competition, and expects to contract with a qualified national organization to assist in managing the funding awards process. This will limit the administrative burden on HUD.[18]

HUD continued its strategy of using attractive key words to gain legislative support. It argued that one of its main functions was the creation of jobs and that its funding would be highly leveraged. It also argued that there would be no overlap or competition with other agencies because their programs would be coordinated. This strategy was apparent in the proposal to expand "brownfield" redevelopment, cleaning up of polluted or vacant industrial sites so they could be made commercially viable and reused:

> Each Brownfields dollar is highly leveraged. The $50 million being proposed for 1999 will leverage $200 million in loans and loan guarantees and the clean-up effort will generate 28,000 construction and related jobs precisely where employment opportunities are most needed.
>
> The Administration has established a Brownfields National Partnership among 15 agencies to turn contaminated Brownfields into greenfields of economic opportunity.[19]

Key to understanding what HUD did during the Clinton administration, as opposed to what it proposed, was the portfolio restructuring, which represented an effort to solve some of the agency's financial problems. In the end, because of budget scoring, the program was not as efficient as it could have been in solving those problems.

The Section 8 program is a rent subsidy program. Generally, individuals are given certificates that let them rent almost anywhere. They pay up to a given portion of their incomes, and HUD pays the rest, up to a given percentage of the median rents in the area. When one of HUD's rehab programs experienced problems, to save projects from default, HUD ended up assigning a number of Section 8 subsidies to the properties, rather than to individuals, and these subsidies were often above market rents to cover the large costs of the properties. As Section 8 contract renewal costs began to increase because of the shorter and shorter terms of the contracts (more of them come due each year), ratcheting down the costs of the Section 8 program took on added importance (table 8.4). These over-market rental subsidies became the target for a HUD proposal, initially called mark to market, and later called portfolio restructuring.

Table 8.4   Budget Authority Needed for Contract Renewals (in $ billions)

	1997	1998	1999	2000	2001	2002
Total Budget Authority Needed	2.6	10.5	10.9	12.8	14.2	15.5
New Budget Authority Needed						
(Net of Reserves)	1.5	8.6	7.2	12.8	14.2	15.5

Source: National Low Income Housing Coalition, www.nlhic.org/marktomarket/chart.htm. Copyright © 1998, used with permission.

The mark-to-market proposal addressed the problem that many of these projects were not financially viable without overly generous, above-market rent subsidies. Many projects could not compete in a free market without subsidies; owners would not be able to pay off their mortgages if the rent subsidies were brought down to market rates. Since the mortgages were FHA insured, if HUD saved money on Section 8 by lowering project-specific rent subsidies, or by withdrawing them completely, the FHA (also a HUD agency) would have to pay for the defaults on the mortgages. Mark to market was HUD's effort to get out of this bind by lowering rents and simultaneously restructuring the mortgages to avoid massive defaults.

HUD's initial restructuring proposal terminated the property-specific Section 8 subsidies, giving individual renters Section 8 subsidies at market rates, so they could leave the property and rent elsewhere if they wished. The proposal eliminated the FHA insurance so HUD would not get stuck with increased costs if the market-level rents resulted in loan defaults. The market would thus address the worst problems, and the costs for Section 8 rental subsidies would be reduced. This proposal was not well received by property owners, and the renters feared the properties would default and they would be evicted with nowhere to go. HUD renamed the proposal "portfolio restructuring" and changed some of the features of the proposal, for example, allowing the Section 8 subsidies to remain with the property, rather than going with the individual.

In addition to opposition by stakeholders, HUD's mark-to-market proposal ran into some budget scoring problems. The initial proposal from HUD included properties where the rental was below market, as well as properties that were above-market rental. By raising below-market rentals to market rentals, the costs would go up for Section 8 assistance, but there would be enough money to maintain the properties and there would be more housing for the poor than if these properties were allowed to deteriorate. Dropping the above-market rentals to market level would save money. Unfortunately, the older properties that came due first for renewal were more likely to be the ones with below-market rentals. The savings from market restructuring would not kick in until a number of years later. To handle this problem, HUD had to back off the proposal to raise the rents on the older properties and focus on the savings that would occur from lowering the above-market rentals.[20] Budget scoring thus overwhelmed a portion of the housing policy, undermining to some extent the goals of the program: to keep the multifamily housing units intact and safe.

On another issue, though, HUD found a way around the scoring to facilitate the portfolio restructuring. The restructuring program as it was carried out would cause some troubled projects to default, pushing up costs on the mandatory side of the budget while the rent reductions pulled down costs on the discretionary side. Savings would be scored from a baseline, but the costs and savings depended on the choice of baseline. On the discretionary side, HUD was locked in; the baseline was specified in the Budget Enforcement Act of 1990 at the actual rentals, which were above market. Thus bringing the rentals down to market levels would be scored as savings because the cost of rent subsidies would be less. But on the mandatory side, there was more flexibility in picking the baseline. If the scoring rules gave HUD increased costs on the mandatory side, the BEA would require compensatory reductions somewhere else in the mandatory budget. Such scoring could kill the proposal. So HUD argued that the costs of the defaults that would be caused under their proposed policy was the baseline. HUD claimed that work they did with owners to reduce mortgage costs and thereby reduce the number of defaults was reducing costs and could be scored as savings. As a result, HUD could score savings on both sides of the budget and make the restructuring feasible under the budget rules. The Congressional Budget Office let this proposal pass.[21]

The mark-to-market/portfolio reengineering legislation was enacted in Title V of the fiscal year 1998 Appropriations Act as "Multifamily Assisted Housing Reform and Affordability Act," on 27 October 1997. It was aimed at reducing costs of Section 8 rent subsidies and thus help with the passage of the refunding of Section 8 contracts. In this it succeeded, as the Section 8 rollovers were funded in 1998 without cuts in the rest of the HUD budget.

CONSEQUENCES

By spring of 1998, there was considerable consensus that HUD was making progress in dealing with its managerial problems. Major problems remained, but others had been tackled and were getting fixed. HUD had changed, but maybe not always in directions that were anticipated or would be welcomed by an objective observer who wanted more effective government at less cost.

Scoring

One problem was the overwhelming influence of budget scoring rules that sometimes overcame policy judgments and built in odd or even counterproductive incentives. HUD's overall drive to maintain services to constituents insofar as possible while satisfying the budget cutters led to budget strategies that would make the programs look less expensive by bringing in more revenue. Generalizing from his own experiences as budget director at HUD, Al Kliman argued that the budget rules and scoring took precedence over policy:

> Balancing the budget today means living with strange scoring, designing programs to fit within the new scoring rules, to hell with the best policy or program. You design programs to fit within the budget rules.[22]

For example, HUD changed the timing and the way of paying for FHA insurance premiums:

> During the Reagan administration, we used to do an exercise: what could be done to reduce expenditures? That was the genesis of the front-end premium at the FHA, changes from a monthly premium to paying the whole premium up front on a discounted basis. That has major policy implications, but it was done as a way of bringing in receipts and reducing outlays, without a lot of thought about the implications for the program. The policy was driven by what would impact the budget rather than the best overall policy for the program.[23]

Property sales was another area in which scoring rules rather than policy decisions sometimes determined what would be done. There was always a tension between preserving housing on the one hand and getting rid of problem properties on the other. But to the extent that sale of property was scored as income, there was a temptation to get rid of property quickly to offset other expenditures. Former budget director Kliman explained, "Because the budget process is essentially short range, even now when it is five years, decisions are taken to reduce outlays within the budget period that would cause outlays to grow in the later years. The decision made at that time was to sell assets at whatever price you could get."[24]

Selling assets was not rational, because it gave up a stream of future revenues. The budgetary scoring incentives to sell property ended with credit reform in 1990. The rate of sales of property that HUD had to take over because of defaults had been too high, but after 1990 it fell too low. By 1994 a new law was passed easing the difficulty of selling property. The new law was open to manipulation:

> Property disposition was passed in 1994. It was a budget issue. HUD was building up a lot of property. HUD insures and when it defaults, it [the property] is assigned to HUD, which holds the mortgages. If it [the property] goes into foreclosure, HUD owns the property. . . . HUD didn't want to own. . . . There had always been tension when to preserve property by Section 8 and when to get rid of property. The

requirement at that time [making sales difficult] was in reaction to the time when HUD was doing it fast; now it was too slow.

In 1994 legislation passed to give HUD greater flexibility. . . . They have been doing a pretty good job since then. . . . And reduced HUD-held inventory to—these are rough numbers—2,500 properties, down quite a bit, maybe got rid of 1,000 through loan sales—maybe 1,600. [The dollar value] is about $5.4 billion; it was over $7 billion in HUD-held inventory. People [were freed up] to work on and manage the insured portfolio. The House has raised some questions about how the loan sales have worked.

The process of [estimating the] credit subsidy [under credit reform] is an art, not science, [especially] given the quality of HUD data. HUD could work the loan sale to generate negative subsidies and use them to fund other things; it is a potential gimmick. Congress has been reluctant to give it authority to do that.[25]

While HUD did not appear to be abusing loan sales, it did try to restructure programs in order to score savings. The following excerpt from a National Low Income Housing Coalition Newsletter explains what this advocacy group believed was a serious problem:

Several times in the past several years HUD and/or the Congress have suggested "reforms" to FHA. . . . These include changes in the Assignment Program, Property Disposition Program, Mortgage Sales Program, timing for premium payments and scoring of several mortgage products. These changes were worth billions in budget scoring—the majority of which has gone to initiatives other than housing and community development. Now, first the Administration and then the Senate have proposed more changes which will result in savings in the Budget. The most recent proposals are controversial in themselves and merit discussion but the most critical issue is that every time HUD and FHA act responsibly and figure out how to save costs in these and other programs, the Congress moves the money from housing.[26]

HUD was supposed to keep more of its "savings" than it in fact got. Pressed by Congress, in 1996 HUD began to seriously work on estimating the amount of reserves available in Section 8. The department also took a new look at how much of these reserves it was necessary to maintain. The shorter contract renewal period for Section 8 contracts meant less uncertainty and implied a lesser need for large contingency accounts. By estimating the size of reserves more carefully and reducing the requirement for large reserves, HUD was able to score some additional savings.

Some of the money thus saved was reprogrammed in the 1999 budget, but the savings from the Section 8 reserves did not end up staying at HUD. In 1997 HUD initially estimated $5.8 billion in reserves, later modified to $9.9 billion. HUD and Congress agreed to keeping $2.2 billion in reserves for contingencies. Congress then rescinded $4.2 billion of the $7.7 billion excess, spending the money instead on nonhousing programs. The balance, $3.5 billion, was to be placed in a reserve fund to help finance 1999 Section 8 renewals. The administration budget request reflected this expected funding source for Section 8 renewals in 1999. But Congress passed and the president signed other uses for the Section 8 reserve fund, including paying for disaster relief and peacekeeping.[27]

As these failures to keep these savings suggest, not everything HUD did from the perspective of scoring and savings worked, but HUD kept trying. HUD's budget overseers at GAO agreed that over the years, HUD had become a more sophisticated budget actor, especially on scoring issues: "HUD came across as naive for years, it rested on its huge social responsibilities, it had some degree of protection but helping people isn't the same priority [now], they had to be smarter about how to defend themselves."[28]

Contracting

One of the consequences of the divorce between workload and staffing was increased contracting out. The work was not simplified or eliminated, but the personnel ceilings did not permit the department to do the work with its own staff: "Their management got the right foothold, but their resources are getting cut; they are likely to increase their dependence on contracting for main functions of the department, which will make it more difficult."[29]

To make contracting work, the agency needed to maintain a minimum number of knowledgeable staff to give contractors instructions, to monitor their performance, and to learn from experience as one approach or another was tried and as contractors changed, taking their experience with them.

Some informants worried about whether HUD retained sufficient skilled staff to oversee contractors. One informant, who chose not to be identified, argued that there were advantages and disadvantages to the contracting:

> There is more contracting out than ever before. It is a life saver; it allows us to perform vital functions. The portfolio was a disaster when HUD tried to service it. We spent more time answering complaints than doing the work. It was a wonderful solution, a smart decision to contract out; the private sector can do it better. But other things worry me, in terms of government knowledge. There is so much knowledge in the contractors, no one else knows, when the contract ends.[30]

This informant described particular contracts in which the contractor was maintaining a database, not only recording the original transaction, but also dealing with complaints that funding never arrived. The contractor, using his or her own data, traced the problem and resolved it. Then if a different contractor was selected, who had none of that history, no one at HUD could fill in.

Normally, several HUD staff members went to work for the contractor, providing some continuity. In one case, an informant reported,

> There were two to three key HUD staff; had they not gone with the new contractor, the operation would have been a disaster. There was no one on staff who had knowledge to keep it running. That is fairly common practice; old staff move over to a new contractor, but government is vulnerable. No one on the staff can tell you how this thing works.
>
> There is a buildup of knowledge here too. You gain when these folks aren't on payroll, but you lose the knowledge that people have of these systems. If that contractor doesn't get the contract, you start again. Career people spend a lot of time training contractors.
>
> On the plus side, we get better help on technology. They keep up with the industry better than we do. It is a mixed bag. There should be a middle ground; there should be some people on staff with technical knowledge. We don't have it.[31]

The National Academy of Public Administration in its 1994 report *Renewing HUD* argued that too large a proportion of some functions was being contracted out, that not enough expertise remained in-house. The report singled out information systems as an area where HUD was too dependent on outsiders. In 1994 about 80 percent of information systems were contracted out; NAPA believed that 50 percent might be more suitable.

NAPA also argued in *Renewing HUD* that as of June 1993 HUD reported 3,455 service contracts that cost $483.5 million in 1992. The work performed by contractors would have taken about 5,000 HUD employees, more than a third of the actual workforce. Based on the judgment of managers, the equivalent of about 1,100 full-time workers would have been more efficient inside HUD than provided by contractors.[32] The amount of contracting increased after 1980 not because it was determined that it was more cost-effective to contract, but because staffing ceilings made it impossible to hire in-house staff. HUD promised later to examine the contracts more carefully and only contract in those areas that made financial sense; but since it continued to be constrained by staffing limits, it did not have the autonomy to decide how much to contract out.

To obtain the advantages of contracting, the contracts had to be well done, the contractors well briefed and supervised, and their performance evaluated.

That performance evaluation would presumably influence the choice and training of the next contractor. Not only did this process assume an in-house staff with knowledge of the contracts and work to be done, it also assumed a functioning oversight process.

As Judy England-Joseph, a GAO witness at a congressional hearing, described, HUD's 2020 reform plan depended heavily on contracting:

> HUD awards millions of dollars in contracts each year. The 2020 Management Reform Plan calls for HUD to contract with private firms for a number of functions, including physical building inspections of public housing and multifamily insured projects; legal, investigative, audit, and engineering services for the Enforcement Center; and activities to clean up the backlog of troubled assisted multifamily properties. The plan also encompasses the potential use of contractors to help dispose of single-family properties and to manage construction in the HOPE VI program.[33]

England-Joseph argued that this increased contracting made HUD more vulnerable to mismanagement:

> The Department—with fewer staff—will be responsible for ensuring that agency needs are accurately reflected in contract specifications and that contracts are fairly awarded and properly administered. Inadequate contracting practices leave HUD vulnerable to waste and abuse.[34]

GAO and the inspector general's office had identified the contracting process at HUD as terribly flawed:

> We and the Inspector General have identified weaknesses in HUD's procurement systems, needs assessment and planning functions, and oversight of contractor performance. For example:
>
> > HUD's ability to manage contracts has been limited because its procurement systems did not always contain accurate critical information regarding contract awards and modifications and their associated costs. Although HUD recently combined several of its procurement systems, the new system is not integrated with HUD's financial systems, limiting the data available to manage the Department's contracts.
> >
> > Inadequate oversight of contractor performance has resulted in HUD's paying millions of dollars for services without determining the adequacy of the services provided.

> HUD staff have often not been trained or evaluated on their ability to manage the contracts for which they have oversight responsibility and have not always maintained adequate documentation of their reviews of contractors. This situation limits assurance that adequate monitoring has occurred.

For example, we recently reported that HUD did not have an adequate system in place to assess its field offices' oversight of real estate asset management contractors, who are responsible for safeguarding foreclosed FHA properties. The three HUD field offices we visited varied greatly in their efforts to monitor the performance of these real estate asset management contractors, and none of the offices adequately performed all of the functions needed to ensure that the contractors meet their contractual obligations to maintain and protect HUD-owned properties.[35]

HUD offered to improve the contracting and monitoring process and set federal standards for excellence in contracting and procurement. The secretary commissioned the National Academy of Public Administration to make recommendations for how to fix the process and make it more user-friendly and flexible. HUD's proposals for fixing the contracting process included more training for staff in contract oversight and inclusion of contract supervision in managers' performance evaluations. Supervisory structures, including a chief procurement officer and a contract review board, were set up as well.

Staffing reductions made contracting necessary, but HUD lacked the structure, the culture, and the staffing to properly oversee the contracting process. HUD is engaged in creating such units and in training staff to monitor contracts, but it is not clear if there is enough program knowledge left in some units to do the training or enough staff time to devote to contract monitoring. Moreover, the money for both training and contracting had to come from the highly constrained salaries and expenses budgets.[36] Because the salaries and expenses budgets were nearly flat, an increase in training and contracting had to be paid for by more personnel cuts.

By FY 1999 that bind had become obvious, and HUD was budgeting for additional staff to run the newly reorganized structure. The increases, however, were modest, on the order of 200 staff from 1999 to 2000, with a request for an additional 100 in 2001, for a total of 9,300 full-time equivalents.

EARMARKING AND BOUTIQUE PROGRAMS

One effect of the constrained budgets was a strategy by HUD and Congress to earmark small parts of programs, called "boutique programs." The department had accumulated many of these small programs.

The increase in boutique programs was to some extent a function of the budget cuts and Congress's continuing need to claim credit. The department also established a special projects fund to help satisfy demands from Congress:

> Because of diminishing resources, there has been an increasing inclination on the part of Congress to deal with earmarking of even small amounts. The history of earmarking is known. As the total pot became smaller—no UDAG anymore, CDBG dried up—there was less big money for Congress to get projects they could bring home; there was less opportunity. They found they could get the same amount of credit for any project, which increased the temptation to have smaller amounts earmarked for their favorite proposals. There was a special projects account for a while, when I was there. That is the type of perverse policy result that occurred.[37]

In addition to special projects accounts, earmarking occurred inside the major block grants. One official explained how this earmarking was done:

> HUD official: "They" are adding new programs as if there were no tomorrow. I don't know who "they" are, some combination of interests in the department and on the Hill. The formula programs, HOME and CDBG, have discretionary programs underneath with a set-aside. Housing counseling, $15 million, used to be freestanding; now it comes out of HOME as a set-aside.
>
> IR: What is the purpose?
>
> HUD official: That $1.4 billion in HOME, they take off the top $15 million for housing counseling, to fund it.
>
> IR: They are taking from one program to fund another?
>
> HUD official: They are squeezing HOME and CDBG to fund it; CDBG has been hit harder than HOME in 1995, in 1996, and in 1997. You will see an increasing trend to put smaller programs under block grants without increasing the [total] formula funding.
>
> We have normal set-asides—Indians, insular areas, technical assistance—now we also have housing counseling. CDBG has set-asides; it is a way of tucking favored programs into the budget without exceeding the budgetary ceiling.[38]

At the same time that the department was cutting back staffing and trying to pass legislation simplifying programs, combining some into a more manageable number and eliminating others, the process of earmarking CDBG money for special programs continued. From 1995 to 1997 the total for CDBG did not change, remaining at $4.6 billion. But this apparent stability is misleading because the entitlement portion of CDBG dropped from $3.1 billion in 1995 to $3 billion at the conference for the 1997 appropriation, a drop of $100 million, and the nonentitlement funding dropped from $1.345 billion to $1.293 billion, a drop of $53 million. The difference of about $150 million was in additional small earmarked programs. There were six (or four depending on how two were counted, either separately or as parts of another program) in 1995, nine in 1996, and eight in 1997. Each year some were unfunded and new ones were funded. The result was a continuing requirement for start-up administration, applications, regulations, selection processes, and oversight, at a time of continuing decreases in staffing:

> HUD kept creating boutique programs, unable to tell Congress it could not manage them. A real difficulty with HUD is that their externally imposed agenda drives them, at the political and congressional level. That is why HUD is a conglomeration of 240 programs. They put in more effort on creating than on managing them. They put more emphasis on getting money out [than in overseeing the grants]. They still continue to say to Congress, we can do this.[39]

Earmarking is associated in some people's minds with pork, because pork can be earmarked, but the two concepts are distinguishable. Earmarking means setting aside money for a specific program or project. Such earmarks can be for very worthwhile programs that benefit citizens in any area of the country. Pork, by contrast, is usually for a specific project located in a sponsoring member of Congress's district. Pork was a problem for HUD. The allocation of pork became bolder as budget constraints tightened. Sen. John McCain, who made a personal campaign to reduce the amount of pork in legislation, commented on the HUD VA appropriation for 1998:

> What concerns me most is the growing practice of earmarking funds for a myriad of projects in the report language, but then incorporating that report language by reference in the bill itself. For example, on page 32 and 33, the bill language states:
>
>> Of the amounts made available under this heading, $40,000,000 for the Economic Development Initiative (EDI) to finance a variety of efforts, including those identified in the Senate committee report, that promote economic revitalization that links people to jobs and supportive services.
>
> The report identifies 17 separate projects, in specific amounts and at specific locations, totaling nearly $30 million. The effect of this bill language is to require HUD to spend ¾ of this economic development

money for these particular projects, without any assessment of the relative needs of the communities which would benefit from these projects compared with many other American communities. This is one of the worst forms of pork barrel spending that I have seen in a long time.[40]

HUD, which was being threatened with termination, probably put up less resistance than normal to such proposals and may even have sought out opportunities to please Congress.

One result of boutique programs and pork-based projects was to increase congressional resistance to program simplification: HUD was caught with more programs to administer and a smaller staff to administer them with.

MONITORING AND EVALUATION

Part of HUD's problem in terms of the loss of confidence by the public and Congress was due to its inattention to data systems and its inability to show what was being done for whom with what effects. In the face of continual criticism and threats of termination of programs and the department, HUD struggled to improve its data and evaluation processes. By the end of 1998 HUD had made considerable progress, though it still had some way to go. As mentioned earlier, there was very little in-house capacity for information systems—nearly all of it was contracted out—but it was much better than it had been.

In the early 1980s HUD adopted a strategy of evaluating threatened programs to document their success. That strategy was successful in the 1980s. In the 1990s agency officials also used evaluation and reporting as a defense strategy, but in addition to discreet outsider evaluations, HUD added an ongoing monitoring of program activities and accomplishments. The following is an excerpt from an interview with Mark Gordon, a political appointee under Secretary Andrew Cuomo, in the Community Planning and Development (CPD) section of HUD. He spoke about the evaluations ongoing in that unit:

IR: Where did these evaluations come from?

MG: The one on the homeless was done by an outside university. The economic development study is in a report being published by an outside consultant. How many EDI jobs were created? Something like a quarter of a million jobs more than the prior four years.

IR: Were they commissioned by CPD to show what you were doing and that it was working?

MG: Yes. It is also possible to show [graphically] this is what the program does. If you question what CDBG does, look at the map. You can see it. [This map is available on the Internet, to Congress and to the public.][41]

In the 1990s the secretary watched the budgetary experiences of HUD programs that had better data about the impact of what they were doing. He deduced that self-monitoring and reporting could be useful in fending off cuts and tried to spread the model from the programs that had good data to those that did not. Implementation turned out to be more difficult than expected.

The idea that Congress was cutting agencies more deeply if they could not document their successes was supported by an observer at GAO:

> There aren't data available to assess programs at HUD. Congress is left with lots of information needs. They are saying that is an indication of dysfunction and lack of need. That is why there is so much debate. Lack of documentation of success is being taken as lack of success, like the rest of the federal government. Congress is starting to ask these [outcome] questions. They are being forced by constituents to ask, "What have I gotten for the money?" They are frustrated that they can't get the information.[42]

The HOME program was one of the HUD programs that had better data, but getting it was not easy:

> In the HOME program, we have a state-of-the-art computer system, and a cash and management information system. In order to get their money, grantees have to give information; we don't wait until the end. This is the concept of collecting data as events are occurring, good information; the data has to pass certain edits before the system will accept it. We have the ability to have up-to-date reporting.
>
> Every month, we do a national summary. It is a very powerful tool to show what the program is doing. It got off to a rocky start. People had to figure out what it was about. There were statutory and regulatory obstacles that were corrected early, but it became a political whipping boy. It was passed in 1990 under the National Affordable Housing Act. The first year's appropriation was in 1992. There was a lot of mistrust by a Democratic Congress of the Republican leadership of HUD. When the administration changed, the new secretary wanted to fix the HOME program. The mayors had complained. It got a lot of attention early. We got a lot of statutory changes made. The information system was instituted at the beginning of the program. We have had good data on this program from day one; it was a powerful tool to prevent budget cuts, except for little nibbles, because we are able to show who is benefiting (the poor), the costs per unit, and production. We are the only large program that can do that.[43]

By contrast to the HOME program, Community Development Block Grants (CDBG) had little data, and what they had was old and impossible to disaggregate to the individual projects:

> One of the things that is being introduced is a new information system to help defend programs by demonstrating what they are accomplishing. In this year's House subcommittee report, the subcommittee approved $1.4 billion [for HOME], the same as the administration's request. [By contrast] CDBG was cut $400 million from the president's request.
>
> The report said that HOME was well monitored and they knew what was happening with the program. Of CDBG they said, these are tight times, and everyone will have to share the burden. The implication was they would go for full funding [for HOME] because they understood what was being delivered.[44]

CDBG was restored at the full committee level because of its major political support, but the history at the subcommittee level was suggestive that good monitoring was helpful in retaining funding. Spreading the data-collection process to other agencies proved more difficult than imagined.

HUD not only had difficulty demonstrating the accomplishments of its programs, it had difficulty coming up with consistent budget numbers. HUD's inability to report accurately on future budget requirements for the Section 8 program made the agency look inept. Estimates for the cost of Section 8 renewals kept jumping around, in part because the agency did not know when all the various contracts would expire. The GAO was highly critical of HUD's overestimates of Section 8 renewal needs. But the estimates of needs for new budget authority depended on knowing how much surplus money was being retained by housing authorities in the Section 8 program and how much they needed to keep in reserve, as well as how much of the surplus HUD would be allowed to apply to the refunding of Section 8. The more of its own surpluses it could apply to Section 8 renewals, the less new authority HUD needed. Pinning down the size of the surplus was difficult, and there was little predictability in political agreements to let the agency use the surplus to refund Section 8 contracts. With the portfolio restructuring (formerly called mark to market), a new wrinkle was put in place, as it was difficult to predict what property owners would do when the contract came up for renewal and what the cost consequences would be. In spite of all this uncertainty, however, HUD did get much better at estimating the size of the surpluses and identifying which contracts were coming up for renewal. The National Low Income Housing Coalition reported in 1998 that "HUD's data on renewal needs is steadily improving" and "HUD's data on existing funds available to meet these needs is also steadily improving."[45]

CONSTITUENCIES AND ADVOCACY

As the fate of CDBG, which was cut in subcommittee but restored in full committee, suggests, and as the strategy of earmarking reinforces, HUD has survived in part because it has generated a series of powerful constituencies. Many of these were not the poor and homeless, but building contractors and businesses. From time to time, HUD has had to call out these constituents to save programs. The strategy has to be played carefully, as this evocation of constituents to lobby Congress is constrained by law. Nevertheless, this strategy was visible during the Reagan administration and was reevoked in later years. Because of the law, interviewees were reluctant to talk much about what they saw, but they agreed that it was still going on:

> Developers, lenders, financial people, the marketplace, oh yeah. The secretary has been accused of lobbying constituents to lobby the Hill. The secretary has a legal right to do that, but below that level, no, not directly. Indirect is hard to pin down. But it has become more overt. . . .
>
> The law, dating from 1917, was very general. It hasn't become much clearer since then. Much is allowable even if it is more blatant and more like lobbying than before. . . . HUD has a lot of constituencies. FHA helped 10 million Americans, or maybe more, buy their first home. The FHA single-family program is not targeted to the poor, but to middle America and the finance institutions; they [the properties] had 100 percent backing, assets that cannot fail. The owners of property had tax subsidies to build and rent subsidies. They can put in a little bit of their own money. Tax credits can become a major investment benefit to middle- and upper-income people. The subsidies in rental housing benefit poor people but they had to sweeten the pot and benefit financial structures and middle Americans. . . .
>
> HUD is a significant financial institution. Pull out HUD and it will affect the bond market, the state bond ratings. (Eliminating or enlarging programs has an impact on the economy.) We don't know how much. Depends on the proposal. They [these varied constituents] come out of the woodwork to say, you can't do this. That causes people to think.[46]

One example of how the advocacy process worked in the mid-1990s occurred with the HUD passback from OMB for the 1998 budget request. HUD was protesting nearly all the passback.[47] What is especially interesting about this episode is not only HUD's fighting spirit, but also that OMB was lobbied by hundreds of housing advocacy and urban groups before the final decisions were made:

> Advocates around the country called OMB and the White House this week in protest of the cuts. Two hundred and fifty organizations and

individuals called OMB; no count is available from the White House. Cisneros and [Franklin] Raines were reportedly still having budget meetings late this week, suggesting that the final decisions have not yet been made by the President.[48]

Advocates would not normally know the detailed contents of a passback unless they were informed by the agency. Moreover, the timing of the protest by advocates before the final decision had been made by Franklin Raines at OMB and in concert with HUD is suggestive that the effort was orchestrated. HUD's supporters need little encouragement to lobby for housing for the poor—they monitor HUD's budget closely—but now and then they may need information that is not public in order to act in a timely way.

One observer noted that in 1995 and 1996 HUD was successful in getting its needs into the administration's budget and "the interest groups were concerned about fighting on the Hill to make sure the administrative proposals were successful."[49] This type of activity required no coordination or orchestration from HUD, as it was all public.

Conclusions

HUD went through and is continuing to go through some difficult years. Some interviewees described HUD as an agency that could not learn. There has been too much mistrust between appointed and career officials for much learning to take place, and there was too much turnover for much of the institutional memory to be in place. Nevertheless, there was some continuity of effort and technique—what worked in the early 1980s was tried again and played out, ultimately, as far as it would go.

HUD's success in continuing to provide services while reducing its budget authority by shortening the terms of Section 8 contracts may have suggested the broader strategy of playing budgetary and scoring games; of finding savings, real and imaginary; of defining baselines to prevent negative outcomes on the savings scorecard. HUD tried to create some flexibility within extremely constrained budgets; politicians welcomed the flexibility but did not give all the money "saved" back to HUD. Larger administration budget requests may have been to some extent out of gratitude for HUD's contributions.

The Section 8 contract renewal gambit ultimately ran its course, necessitating increasing costs to maintain the same number of units. This Section 8 funding crisis set off a round of other activities, including the mark-to-market (portfolio restructuring) reforms to lower the costs of renewing the contracts. The need to estimate the costs of the expiring Section 8s called attention to HUD's woefully inadequate information systems, including poor knowledge of the size of existing reserves in the public housing authorities. HUD improved its in-house financial capacity and contracted out for information systems improvement.

HUD was forced to reduce staff independent of program simplification or prioritization of functions. Congress still has not approved the program simplifications proposed by HUD. Therefore, HUD has been forced to increase its contracting, improve its contracting procedures and oversight, and increase training to enable wise contracting and knowledgeable oversight. But the costs of contracting and training have had to come out of the same constrained budget, forcing additional reductions in staffing, making the oversight role more difficult, if not impossible. The continued separation between workload and staffing levels makes it unlikely that the agency will be able to restrict contracting out to only those projects for which it makes sense and saves money.

At every step, the continued downsizing without commensurate reduction in workloads made good management more difficult. The constrained funding made additional training harder, yet the downsized staff made additional training essential. What seems to have motivated HUD to serious reform was the threat of termination and the continuous criticism from the Office of the Inspector General and GAO. The downsizing itself was a less important trigger for improvements.

The overall government budget constraints squeezed much of the pork out of the federal budget for years, making prime targets of those departments that could accommodate some pork. Because of its extreme need for political support, HUD was not able to resist efforts to provide some pork in its budget. Nor was HUD in a position to refuse members of Congress who supported good programs and wanted to earmark funds for them. The result was an acceleration of the creation of boutique programs at the same time the agency was submitting legislative proposals to combine programs and simplify administration. When Congress refused to simplify programs or eliminate many of the boutique programs, management responsibilities were increasingly at odds with staffing levels. As a result, HUD was increasingly dependent on contracting out.

The complexity of HUD's programs, which was creating so much difficulty during a time of downsizing, reflected the multiple constituencies served. From 1995 on these constituencies seemed to become more active in support of the agency. HUD was more successful in the Clinton administration's proposals, possibly because it was improving its management, and with more favorable executive proposals, interest groups were more motivated to act.

Against this background HUD struggled to improve its management, develop a more logical and accountable administrative structure, better data management and accounting systems, and a clearer mission. Without an agreed-on mission, HUD was being whipsawed, told to drop application procedures to simplify work and reduce requirements, and then told that it was not ensuring compliance with the program goals. Amazingly, under the circumstances, HUD was making progress but ran into the limits of its strategies. Trading staffing cuts for additional political support from the administration exacerbated the agency's management problems and devastated morale. Without additional legislative simplification, the target of 7,500 staff was not feasible. The strategy of reducing the length of contract renewals to reduce budget authority also ran to its logical conclusion when all contracts had to be renewed each year. Prior years' strategies had begun to make future years' budgets problematic, as the need for increased budget authority rapidly accelerated. Each year was a cliffhanger, in terms of whether funding for Section 8 would be forthcoming, and if so, where it would come from.

Downsizing of HUD did not bring about efficiencies, though it may have encouraged automation, which was controversial in itself, and it certainly encouraged contracting, which made the agency more vulnerable to mismanagement. Neither the downsizing nor the threat of termination resulted in program simplification or in dropping product lines for a clearer mission. The pressure for survival made the agency more vulnerable to a variety of interest groups, further fragmenting the mission and program structure of the agency.

CHAPTER 9

Office of Personnel Management

THE OFFICE OF Personnel Management (OPM) is a small agency, restructured in 1978 under the Civil Service Reform Act (CSRA). OPM is the personnel office for the federal labor force. Before the CSRA, the personnel office had responsibility for recruitment and testing and for ensuring compliance with personnel laws and regulations. The CSRA envisioned a more decentralized personnel function, with delegation of the older personnel functions to the agencies and a new set of functions for OPM, including oversight of the agencies to assure merit-based hiring and research and policy leadership on personnel issues. The new role was a cultural shock for an agency that had been in the regulatory business. OPM found it difficult to carry out its new mission.

Though small, OPM is significant in a study of agency adjustments to budget and staffing reductions for several reasons. One is that OPM had been cut severely in the early 1980s and again in the 1990s, offering the possibility of seeing whether the earlier cuts helped the agency become more efficient and effective and whether the later cuts were informed by lessons learned in the earlier period. A second reason is that, as a primarily regulatory agency operating inside the bureaucracy, it had virtually no support inside or outside the Beltway. Threats to terminate it were therefore credible and the agency's ability to fight back was minimal. In an effort to win support, it may have been overly enthusiastic in its cutback efforts. Third, major efforts to cut back staff and privatize absorbed agency attention and reduced the number of staff who could pay attention to reinvention efforts. After years of cuts, political rather than technical leadership, and reorganizations, OPM initially had neither the credibility nor the energy and staff to mount a creative effort to be a leader in policy proposals for a reinvented civil service. The OPM case thus reflects the tensions within the NPR between reducing staff and becoming more efficient and creative.

Key to understanding what happened in OPM is that it was threatened with termination. One informant described the sense of threat that OPM lived under because Vice President Al Gore and the National Performance

Review (NPR) believed that OPM was not doing a good job in personnel management:

> Gore was convinced that OPM was a problem, that we didn't need a central personnel office. [OPM director Jim] King gave us the impression that Gore wanted to shut down OPM and they were fighting to keep it open, but one function after another would fall.[1]

Possibly as a consequence of being threatened with termination, OPM tried to make an example of itself by complying with the demands and philosophy of the National Performance Review in a dramatic way. It reduced its staffing by more than any other agency and privatized two of its major functions. So far, OPM has survived. As one informant reported in 1996, the cuts were over. OPM was no longer on the policy radar screen:

> The cuts are huge, but we are not taking them again. We took them all at one time. OMB and the committees on the Hill have answered their questions about OPM for now. I would be surprised to see any other dramatic changes. . . . I anticipate stability for the next several years, until something happens. The 1994 election of a Republican Congress— there are no consequences left from that event for OPM. Clinton and Gore are sated about OPM; there is no reason to go after it again.[2]

Part of the reason that the cuts were over by 1996 was that they were designed to reflect the decentralization of personnel functions to the agencies. Much of the required decentralization had been accomplished by 1993, but the staffing levels for the agency had not yet been drawn down to reflect the change. For example, to a much greater degree than in the past, testing and recruiting were left to the agencies, who could ask OPM for help. By 1991 and 1992 delegated examining authority accounted for about 44 percent of total hiring selections.[3] By contrast, in 1981 only 26 percent of hires that year were done by delegated testing authority in the agencies, and the number of delegations dropped sharply after that.[4] By 1997 OPM had delegated sufficient authority for personnel matters to the agencies that its concern turned to whether and to what extent the agencies were delegating that new authority to the lowest practical level, the frontline supervisor.[5]

It made little sense for each agency to manage its own benefits package, so that function remained a government-wide program located at OPM. Training for the Senior Executive Service (SES) was conceived as the executive office's way of informing senior staff about executive policies; it was a policy implementation tool that could neither be dispensed with nor privatized. OPM was down to rock-bottom functions, managing benefits, training the senior executives, and overseeing the decentralized personnel functions of the agencies to assure that merit principles were being observed. The agency was down to what it considered a defensible core. However, there was no evaluation of whether the remaining functions were adequately funded and staffed.

Rep. Steny Hoyer, who was sympathetic to government employees, asked Director Janice R. LaChance at a hearing whether the agency's staffing downsizing had been accompanied by sufficient reduction in mission, or whether the remaining staff were simply going to be required to do more in an effort to keep the agency accomplishing its multiple missions. LaChance responded:

> The Office of Personnel Management (OPM) has been a leader in downsizing, both by example (reducing its Fiscal Year 1999 Full-Time Equivalent employment level 52 percent below that of Fiscal Year 1993) and by providing guidance and assistance to other agencies in their downsizing efforts. There has not been, however, a commensurate reduction in OPM's duties.[6]

Not every function was cut, and the ones into which resources were added were doing better. After a major reorganization in 1995, OPM improved in visiting the agencies and assuring that merit principles were being upheld. But OPM had a difficult time taking the lead in formulating and selling personnel policy proposals, partly due to lack of staff, partly due to lack of credibility.

OPM has always taken on itself the role of being the model for the federal government, but this responsibility, being the leader in complying with whatever political policy the administration had for the bureaucracy, has not always led to its being a model employer. This was more so under some OPM directors than others, but the agency did not establish a culture and role independent of the directors, making it vulnerable to the more extreme views of several directors. While some of OPM's directors have done a good job, OPM's successes during their terms were attributed to the directors rather than to the agency.

In 1993 the National Performance Review summarized the history of OPM, noting its overreliance on political appointees for policy direction. This reliance on political appointees grew in the Reagan years:

> Former OPM director Don Devine sought to replace OPM's traditional management orientation with an unswerving emphasis on responsiveness of the public service solely to the political direction from within the executive branch. Devine sought to have OPM assert ideological leadership and to establish a system of political administration throughout the federal sector. This approach placed OPM in a bitter adversarial relationship with Congress, labor unions, and other representatives of public service interests.[7]

For the decade beginning in 1981 OPM's budget for direct personnel management activities decreased 45 percent in constant dollars, while the number of political appointees almost doubled.[8] In addition,

> Directors succeeding Devine tried to reverse some of the politicization, but Jim King, OPM director under Clinton and assigned the role of implementing much of the NPR ideology, still looked to the administration for policy guidance. When appointed, King had a long resume of politically appointed positions, was strong in democratic politics, but had no background in professional human resources management.[9]

OPM was political in the sense that its directors often sought and followed direction from the White House, seemingly against the interests of the agency itself. Enthusiastic cooperation with the White House may have bought some support from the executive office when OPM was threatened with termination, giving the agency some time to demonstrate its effectiveness in adapting to the new decentralized environment. Because the policy emphasis of the White House and the NPR was on downsizing and privatization, the cost to OPM was enormous, absorbing its creative efforts in reductions in force, contested privatizations, congressional hearings, and reorganizations when it needed to be rebuilding its research capacity and stabilizing its new role. Moreover, OPM's history of political leadership meant it did not have a track record for neutral research and the credibility to put forth its own policy proposals for an improved public service.

During both the Reagan and Clinton administrations, OPM's efforts to implement executive branch policy led the agency to cut itself more than other agencies were cut. This self-cutting had a devastating effect on morale. For example, during the Reagan administration, when Donald Devine was director of OPM, some employees had T-shirts printed saying "Devine's Guinea Pigs," with the clear implication that he was trying out on them what he sought to do elsewhere in the government and that the experiment was not pleasant.

OPM has been more extreme in its cutback efforts than other agencies. It has reduced staffing and budget more dramatically, has privatized more extensively, and has RIFed more often and more deeply than other agencies, accepting budget reductions that it probably could have resisted effectively. OPM used RIFs while advising other agencies to avoid this expensive and disruptive technique.

OPM's decision to privatize training and investigations was primarily a political act, not a financial one, though it was later justified financially. Jim King, the director of OPM in 1996, described this time sequence in detail in oversight hearings. The steps he outlined began with the investigations program's financial problems and OPM's efforts to curtail them by reducing staffing. OPM separated 443 employees in a RIF to reduce costs. Then, in December 1994 President Clinton announced plans for the second phase of reinventing government, which included privatization of the investigations unit. The feasibility study for the ESOP (the employee-owned company that would carry out the investigations) was done in 1995, and the cost benefit analysis was commissioned in November 1995 and reported in March 1996.[10] The decision to privatize thus preceded the evaluation of options and costs and benefits.

As one informant confirmed, Jim King agreed to the cuts "politically first":

> He [Jim King] wanted to take the lead in being downsized. I heard King say that many times in public settings. He began with that premise; the justification based on efficiency came later. This was political. The president wants us to do this and we will; it was not, we can see, a way to make this work better. That came later. I don't think you will find many people who would disagree with that.[11]

OPM was subjected to two rounds of deep cuts over the seventeen years of the study, only partly recovering from the first round, which occurred during the Reagan administration, before the second round began in 1993. The second round, based on the National Performance Review, was even more severe than the first. The NPR team was composed of staff members seconded from the agencies; they brought with them tremendous resentment of the seemingly endless rules for hiring, promotions, and firing and of OPM's role in enforcing those rules.

The NPR attack on OPM was not just the result of disgruntled victims of OPM's regulations, however. One underlying principle of the NPR was that administrators were hampered by excessive rules and were unable to manage. To get a government that worked better and cost less, the rules and the rule overseers had to be reduced in number. In the agencies, the inspectors general were supposed to develop a more cooperative working relationship with managers, and the numbers of auditors, budgeters, and human resource personnel were to be reduced by 50 percent. At OPM, the regulations manual was thrown out in a dramatic ceremony, and personnel functions such as testing and recruitment were left much more to the agencies, despite their reduced staffing precisely in the areas of new responsibilities. OPM was supposed to help them learn how to cope, acting as contract agency if necessary or desired. Thus a changing role and set of functions for OPM was core to the achievement of NPR goals. With OPM's severely depleted budget and staffing levels, this transition was slow and difficult.

THE REAGAN YEARS

The Reagan years were particularly difficult for OPM. Staffing was dramatically reduced. Total staffing for OPM in 1980 was 8,213 and only 5,929 in 1986, a reduction of 27 percent.[12] To get down to this level, OPM ran a substantial reduction in force; to save money, it furloughed employees. To add to the chaos, OPM reorganized three times during this period. At the same time, much of the agency's attention was focused on managing the RIFs in other agencies, working out the RIF rules, educating the agencies in their use, and working on outplacement and rehiring programs for those who were RIFed out of their agencies.

The Reagan era reduction in force at OPM resulted primarily from a huge budget cut. The first Reagan round of cuts for 1982 was 4 percent, followed by a second cut of 12 percent for the same budget year. Such a large budget cut in an agency that consisted primarily of personnel necessitated staffing reductions. However, many employees believed that the full 12 percent cut could have been resisted and was successfully resisted by many other agencies; they also believed that attrition reductions would have been more cost-effective and would have involved many fewer people. The insistence on the more disruptive RIF is one of the factors that made employees believe that they were guinea pigs, being used to try out RIF regulations.[13] This image of the agency cutting itself was reinforced by Director Don Devine's testimony on the Hill that OPM was taking the lead in economizing and had taken cuts substantially in excess of agency averages.[14]

In the early Reagan years, OPM experienced not only RIFs and a furlough, but also three reorganizations. The purpose was initially to drop or deemphasize the function of teaching the agencies how to comply with civil service regulations (as these functions were decentralized, presumably the agencies needed less instruction). The later reorganizations were for the purpose of concentrating policymaking power in the hands of the director and a few chosen subordinates.[15] Communication with those below this policymaking level became problematic as a result.

Budget and staffing cuts as well as the reorganizations had negative impacts on OPM's ability to accomplish its mission. As a Merit Systems Protection Board (MSPB) evaluation of OPM in 1989 noted, "Hampering OPM in its ability to meet those expectations, however, was a steady decrease in actual staff resources at the same time the demands for OPM leadership, innovation, and expertise were increasing."[16] These decreases took place in oversight, and also in research capability.

OPM was supposed to delegate a variety of personnel powers to the agencies and tended to do so agency-by-agency and personnel power–by–personnel power. Over the Reagan years, the frequency of delegation of personnel management authority was reduced. At the same time, oversight of the agencies that had received delegated authority was also reduced, as OPM substituted a less expensive survey-based reporting system for on-site evaluations. OPM increasingly depended on agency self-evaluations at a time when the agencies were curtailing their evaluation efforts. Also, due to budget reductions, the agency seriously reduced its research capacity and demonstration projects, precisely the role that it was supposed to enhance as it carried out the decentralization.[17] For the Reagan period, OPM nearly froze in place, only slowly delegating personnel authority and not adopting the research role necessary to be a policy leader in the personnel field.

Director Donald Devine emphasized what to him were the critical areas of personnel, including testing and recruitment and benefits management. Testing and recruitment became less important, however, as RIFs and freezes took place all over the federal government and as testing powers were decentralized. Testing was not a function that OPM could maintain over the long haul. Managing benefits proved a more durable role.

After the Reagan administration, with a change in director, delegation of authority to the agencies increased and more attention was paid to oversight. Staffing after the Reagan administration improved somewhat. However, it is not clear that OPM ever fully recovered from the Reagan era. One observer writing in 1992 noted that the two units in OPM doing research on the entire civilian labor force together had only seventy staff, while the Army Research Institute, which focused only on uniformed Army personnel, was much larger and had ten times the budget.[18]

Writing in 1994, during a preliminary evaluation of OPM's redesign to meet its new mission requirements, Scott Fosler of the National Academy of Public Administration (NAPA) noted that the redesign was oriented almost exclusively to making OPM a model agency and on retailing administrative processes and services to customers; it was not oriented to getting OPM prepared for a policy leadership role: "As Mr. Cushing [OPM chief of staff] notes, and we agree, you will need to broaden the skill base of OPM's staff as OPM changes to a more strategically oriented operation."[19] Given the intense downsizing that followed this advice, OPM was not able to broaden its skill base and recover its policy-making and research capacity.

THE NATIONAL PERFORMANCE REVIEW: PHASES 1 AND 2

NPR reports claimed that OPM had remained too rule-bound to fulfill its mission of facilitating decentralization of the personnel function to the agencies. NPR recommendations included the jettisoning of the federal personnel manual and a change in OPM's role and culture from rule enforcement to serving customers and leading the government by proposing new personnel systems.[20] The NPR also indicated the need for further downsizing and reorganizing, and for making examining potential job candidates a reimbursable activity. NPR phase 1, in 1993, reported that OPM had not succeeded in delegating responsibility for personnel decisions to the agencies, but that some progress had been made in the early 1990s.

At the end of December 1994 Vice-President Gore announced phase 2 of the NPR, which emphasized further cuts, reductions in regulations, program termination, and privatization. Both Congress and the NPR had emphasized the desire to cut back staffing levels, passing the Federal Workforce Restructuring Act in

March 1994, reducing government by 272,900 full-time-equivalent (FTE) employees through 1999. The new Congress, which took its seat in 1995, was more conservative than its predecessor, and many members enthusiastically embraced the idea of more federal privatization.

OPM was thus affected both by the broader mandate to cut employees, especially its budgeters, accountants, and human resource personnel (who presumably curtailed the authority and eagerness of other managers), and by the specific mandates to cut OPM's staff when it was impinging on the management prerogatives of other agencies.

OPM took the mandate to reduce staff seriously. While the average NPR cuts were about 12 percent, intended to be taken over a number of years primarily by attrition, OPM cut itself by nearly 49 percent, using a series of reductions in force and privatization efforts. In January 1993 OPM reported a total of 6,861 employees; by March 1997 it reported 3,507, a decline of 48.9 percent.[21] From 1993 to 1999 full-time-equivalent staffing dropped about 51 percent (table 9.1). Beginning from 7,285 FTE in 1981 and declining to 2,984 in 1999, OPM dropped 59 percent over the entire period.[22]

Where did OPM take these personnel cuts? A GAO study offered a breakdown by major unit (table 9.2, p. 260). The GAO study came at a moment just before the final reduction in the investigations unit, which was privatized, leaving only a few staff members to oversee contracted services. Because the GAO study reports in the middle of that privatization, it understates the effect of the reduction in the investigations unit. Even so, the largest losses in staff, both in absolute numbers and in terms of the percentage of total OPM losses, were in investigations, training, and administrative services, in that order. Employment services (attracting and testing candidates for agencies) were deeply cut, in part due to automation, while personnel systems and oversight were initially zeroed out but later merged into a new and expanded unit.

Table 9.1 OPM, FTE Employment, 1993–99

Year	OPM, FTE Employment
1993	6,208
1994	5,931
1995	5,472
1996	3,934
1997	3,363
1998	3,005
1999	2,984

Source: OPM 1999, 2000 budget requests.

Table 9.2   OPM Components, FTE Reductions, FY 1993–96

Component	FTE Reduction	Percentage of FY 1993 FTEs Reduced	Percentage of Total OPM FTE Reduction
Investigations Service	898	60.6	36.1
Human Resources Development	520	100	20.9
Administrative Services	518	76.3	20.8
Employment Services	469	40.7	18.8
Personnel Systems and Oversight	380	100	15.3
Other Components[a]	+296	+17.8	+11.9
Total	2,489	42.3	100

Source: GAO calculations based on agency-provided data. Table from GAO, *Federal Downsizing: Agency Officials' Views on Maintaining Performance During Downsizing at Selected Agencies,* GAO/GGD-98-46, 24 March 1998.

[a]Includes three components that lost FTEs and three components that gained FTEs, resulting in a combined FTE increase.

Note: OPM's reported staffing levels do not match GAO's exactly, but the two series are generally close and consistent.

Fifty-six percent of the reduction reported by GAO from 1993 to 1996 was the result of privatization of training functions and investigations. The actual numbers cut grew as investigations completed its transition to an ESOP. But even these larger numbers underestimate the impact of this decision to privatize, because the fee-based activities in OPM were required to share in overhead costs in proportion to their revenue (not in proportion to overhead costs generated), and so they contributed generously to the administrative costs of running OPM. When training and investigations were privatized, their contribution to administrative costs was lost. The result was cuts in overhead and in central administrative staffing.

OPM officials argued that they had to downsize the administrative staff as the agency shrank; despite all the downsizing up to that point, administrative overhead had not been pared down. That explanation for reductions in administrative staff makes sense on the face of it, but not when looked at in detail. Training and investigations, the largest component of the reductions, did not use much in the way of overhead service, so their loss would not reduce by very much the need to perform overhead functions. More likely, OPM administrators agreed to privatize training and investigations to please the vice-president and the White House and then wrestled with the consequences later, including a secondary effect on administration, because the revolving funds had been contributing generously to overhead functions.

Privatizing Training and Investigations

Partly due to the requirement to shrink staffing and partly due to pressure from NPR phase 2, OPM agreed to be a leader in privatization. The two functions sorted out for privatization were training (Human Resources Development, or HRD) and investigations. The choice of these services to privatize was problematic and contentious. According to observers, the purpose was not to increase efficiency, but to reduce federal staffing levels. Inside the agency, however, the argument was made that these two functions were running deficits and privatization would solve that problem and save money:

> The second piece was NPR and reinvention 2; I think it was January 1995. REGO II [Reinventing Government Phase 2]. The decision was announced by NPR [that] training and investigations would be privatized. Was it privatized? The goal was, get bodies off the payroll. I was talking to the fellow responsible for the [investigations] ESOP the other day. People were asking him about efficiency, but that wasn't relevant. What was relevant was getting people off the payroll. Investigations may have begun to turn around by then [in terms of generating deficits].[23]

Privatizing training made a kind of sense, given the overall rule that anything that the private sector could do as well, it should do, provided that there was no essentially governmental aspect to the work. Training had long been a shared function, with some OPM training and some private-sector training. There was good evidence that the private sector could perform this function with no ill effects.

Looked at more closely, however, not selecting training as a core function of OPM seems odd. Training was not part of the regulatory function of OPM, no agency was required to accept OPM training, and it was a reimbursable function. It represented precisely the market orientation, the customer orientation, that OPM was trying so hard to achieve. Teacher, helper, those were the roles OPM was working at; voluntary training represented those values. If agencies did not consider this service useful, they did not have to use it. Revenues to the training function were actually increasing, suggesting that its products were in considerable demand. But its costs were going up even faster, partly because OPM shifted costs to the revolving fund when the appropriated budget was cut.

Though the training function was experiencing real financial problems, observers described the decision to privatize as a political one. When Vice-President Gore announced the REGO II in December 1994, he invited OPM director Jim King to the microphone to announce efforts to privatize training at OPM. King did so and then went back to OPM to figure out how to do it. OPM discovered at that point that the training program was not a saleable commodity, because anyone could get OPM's training modules for free and imitate them.

Despite its inability to sell the operation, OPM proceeded to privatize the training function by laying off some staff and transferring others to the USDA Graduate School, a mostly private operation loosely affiliated with the Agriculture Department and open to the public.

Privatization of the training function was not a financial decision—studies had not been made of options and costs and savings before the announcement of privatization. Nearly up until the decision was announced, efforts were being made to improve financial systems, set the price of products to cover expenses, reduce overhead, and improve marketing. All the key observers, including GAO and the inspector general's office, seemed to agree that the major causes of financial problems were being addressed. Then the privatization decision was announced.

After the decision to privatize was made, OPM, with the help of OMB, made cost estimates of savings. Even to make the political argument work, OPM had to argue that privatization would save money. OPM argued that the revolving funds, which included both training and investigations, were in financial trouble; they had been losing money, and the agency had to get rid of them to stem the red tide. Of course, that avoided the question of why OPM did not fix the problems instead. There is evidence that OPM had in fact already fixed the major financial problems by the time that privatization took place.

Before the privatization took place, OPM had taken a number of steps to close the spending revenue gap in the training division. By the end of 1993 the following steps had been taken: standardized courses were instituted to make products more uniform, reducing unnecessary course development costs; a nationwide marketing strategy was implemented to make course offerings better known and more accessible; a standard approach to pricing was developed that captured all costs, including overhead and system and development costs for all training products; an automated management information system was installed to help managers monitor the status of TMA projects (training provided through contractors); and the billing reconciliation process was improved. With new planning assumptions of constant income, a cost-cutting program was put in place, with new pricing guidelines to assure that income would recover costs while services remained competitive; cost-reduction targets were set for each training delivery center; and overhead costs were to be reduced through downsizing and delayering initiatives already begun. A reduction in force was planned for 1994 to reduce compensation costs. The plan was to break even in 1994 and reduce the deficit by $3 million a year through fiscal 1997.[24]

By August 1994 the Office of the Inspector General for OPM reported that the surcharge that the training unit put on its assistance in getting private contractors for the agencies was increased from 15 to 18 percent in April, that Human Resources Development Group (HRDG) internal overhead had been reduced, including executive, managerial, and support staff and space rentals. The IG approved of the overall plan, making suggestions only to help assure successful implementation.[25] The General Accounting Office looked at the revised plan to calculate total costs for each course and set fees to recover those costs, and it agreed that the plan should solve the financial problems of the training program.[26]

All this activity would not have been necessary if a decision had been made that training was not a core function and should be privatized. OPM was acting as if it had a managerial problem that was gradually coming to light and needed to be fixed. By the end of 1993, however, a considerable deficit had accumulated from year to year, about $9 million for the training section. An additional deficit was projected for the whole revolving fund for 1994, and that deficit was considered a reason for immediate action to privatize. What was not discussed, however, was how the accumulated deficit would be paid off when these two programs were privatized. Nor was it clear how much of the predicted additional deficit in 1994 was attributed to the training group as opposed to investigations.

Not only did it look as if the major underlying issues of financial management had been addressed before the privatization, but the size of the deficit in the revolving funds was also questionable, especially because OPM had put more costs into the revolving funds when its appropriated budget was cut. This strategy was begun in the Reagan administration and was continued during Gramm-Rudman-Hollings and the Clinton administration cuts. While there may not have been many staff at OPM who remained throughout all the years from Reagan to Clinton to pass on any learning, once an expense had been shifted to the trust fund, it remained there and became a lesson to others of what could be done. The budget, in essence, provided institutional memory, locking in particular solutions and inviting more of the same. (One could argue for a parallel mechanism in HUD, when HUD reduced the duration of the Section 8 contracts.)

The Inspector General's Report on the underlying issues behind the revolving fund deficits offers a fascinating chronology of shifting general agency expenses into the revolving fund. The passage of Gramm-Rudman-Hollings in 1985 had the effect of cutting the basic appropriation of the agency, leading to "greater reliance on the revolving fund to take up some of the slack."[27] In 1986 the revolving fund reported a negative fund balance, or deficit. After that, new expenses were often placed in the revolving fund, whether they were appropriate there or not. In 1988 the Washington Area Service Center was opened, which added substantial overhead costs to the revolving fund programs; in 1989 the policy staff in the training component of the Career Entry Group was expanded by twenty to thirty FTE, to expand OPM's ability to provide policy direction to the federal government. This function was then incorporated in the training group. The result is that a function that was clearly a general OPM function that could not have charged a fee for service was placed not only in the revolving fund, but also in the training unit.[28] If the number of staff so placed was thirty and the average salary with benefits was around $70,000, the cost to training would have been more than $2 million for this one item.

The training function also had to cope with assignment of staff with no experience in training and for whom there were no jobs. Individuals returning from long-term temporary assignments elsewhere in the federal sector and individuals losing their positions during reorganizations in OPM were sometimes assigned to revolving fund programs until better placements could be found.[29] According to one estimate, the training group was paying more than $1 million in excess annual salaries at the beginning of FY 1994.

One of the other ways that OPM put regular operating costs into the revolving fund was to put into overhead charges some services that the functions in the revolving fund did not use, general costs for running the agency that should have been picked up by appropriations, such as the Office of International Programming and a portion of the director's office. Putting these items into overhead for training forced the training function either to raise the costs of its training to the agencies (possibly pricing itself out of the market) or to run deficits. OPM administrators, when confronted with this argument by the inspector general's office, responded that the inclusion of these items in training's overhead would not increase the course costs by much. They expressed no intention of putting these items back into general appropriations. What they did not say was that doing so would have forced cuts elsewhere in the appropriated budget and they preferred to have training increase its fees.

It was not only that some inappropriate items were charged in the overhead to the revolving funds; it was also that the charges became heavier over time as the appropriated budget was cut. OPM required the revolving funds to pay a share of overhead based not on use of services but on its proportion of total revenues. When the appropriated budget was cut, the revolving funds became a larger share of the total budget and hence were taxed more heavily for overhead functions such as public relations, legal services, and the library. Many were services that were never or seldom used. Not only did OPM's declining appropriation translate into a higher tax on training; if training brought in more revenues through successful programs, it had to pay more for overhead. However, when training began to suffer declines in demand (when some of the other governmental agencies that used OPM training suffered budget cuts and froze or cut their training budgets), the assessment for overhead did not decline.[30] A more reasonable and flexible assessment for overhead and a better accounting system would have gone a long way to balancing the training unit's budget.

When OPM tried to justify its privatization decision for training, it claimed savings based on the size of deficits the training function and investigations were experiencing. While annual reports made it appear that training in particular had been running deficits for several years, part of that deficit, if not all of it, was based on the overhead charge that OPM put on the training function. Getting rid of training would not solve the problem of the deficit.

In fact, deficits persisted in the revolving funds after privatization, and the funds remained unauditable, due in part to incomplete agency record keeping, according to the Inspector General's Office in its 1999 report. OPM's FY 1999 performance report claimed that in 1999 the agency reversed a ten-year trend in the revolving fund of an increasing deficit condition in retained earnings. According to this summary of accomplishment, privatization of training and investigations took place in 1995 and 1996, but through FY 1998 the revolving funds had continued to run deficits. The annual performance report claimed that in 1999 current revenues would cover current costs, but it suggested that accomplishment might not show up in the reports because of an extraordinary event adjustment to prior years based on cash reconciliation to Treasury's balance. OPM expected continuing offsetting adjustments based on continuing research in 2000. Not only did prior years seem to swamp the current achievement of balance, but OPM announced in this annual report that substantial price decreases to agency customers had been issued. The reasons for and the implications of this set of price decreases were not made clear in the annual performance report.

If the decision to privatize training was controversial, the decision to privatize investigations was even more so. There was general agreement that the private sector could provide training, that it was not an inherently governmental function. In investigations, there were questions about whether it was an inherently governmental function, whether local police would cooperate with a private investigations company, and whether a contracted service would be effective. Prior efforts to supplement the workforce through the use of private companies had failed badly in quality of the investigations and had resulted in overbillings and other accounting problems.

Investigations and the Employee Stock Ownership Plan (ESOP)

Investigations' deficits were much larger than training's deficits. They were created by fluctuating demand for services triggered by the major staffing reductions mandated by NPR and Congress (fewer background investigations were needed) and by the heavy overhead burden placed by OPM on investigations. In order to successfully privatize this function, which is to say, get the employees off the government payroll, OPM had to come up with a formula that would use prior investigations staff to ensure security and competence. What the agency came up with was a proposal for an ESOP, a company that would be owned primarily by the employees currently being RIFed from OPM. OPM would draw up an exclusive contract with the ESOP for several years and then, presumably, open the contract up for bid. Given the requirement of providing experienced staff and prior unhappy experience with private sector contractors, it seemed unlikely that the contract would be shifted to other companies after a few years. The result was less than the open competition that those in favor of privatization insisted on, but it accomplished the administration's goal of reducing the number of staff on the federal payroll. OPM expected that contract costs would be cheaper than providing services in-house.

The idea for the ESOP came from a proposal developed in the mid-1980s. President Reagan had made privatization a key objective of his second term. OPM, in an effort to encourage privatization in the federal government, tried to work out a plan that would bypass some of the traditional obstacles. Adapting a model of privatization that had been successful in Britain, OPM came up with an employee-owned company that would work for the federal government. Ownership of the new company would presumably give government workers an incentive to get out of federal employment and move into the new privatized company.

To handle at least some of the problems that would result from such an arrangement, including the blocking out of current potential private-sector bidders, OPM proposed a joint arrangement, in which the highest private-sector bidder would get 51 percent of the business and the current employees 49 percent. An agency or neutral oversight organization would determine the current cost of a particular in-house commercial activity and set necessary performance standards. A newly established firm would be given a sole source contract to perform the activity for a fixed term at current costs, with normal performance requirements. At the end of the fixed term, the contract would be rebid, with no preference for the joint venture firm: "Based on experience, however, incumbents have a high probability of retaining the contract."[31] This Fed Co-op plan was available for use, with modifications, when OPM needed to figure out how to privatize investigations.

Privatizing investigations was fought every step of the way by employees, despite the stock ownership plan. Director King had to defend the decision to privatize. He argued that the investigations unit had been running deficits and therefore had to be cut back. Privatization was an alternative to reductions in force. That argument was true to an extent, though the reality was not as bleak as King suggested. For example, King reported that over a period of nearly a decade, investigations was never out of debt, but in the four years prior to the privatization decision, from 1990 to 1993, investigations made a substantial profit in 1990 and 1991, ending 1991 with a positive fund balance. Demand for the services of the investigations unit dropped precipitously with budgetary cutbacks in the agencies over the next two years, causing the financial troubles King noted.[32] As he pointed out, staffing had to be reduced to meet the shrunken demand. But as King also pointed out, this downsizing was accomplished in May 1994, before privatization occurred. With these reductions in staffing and other planned measures to reduce costs, investigations was scheduled to break even in 1995. Privatization was announced in December 1994, seven months after the RIFs to reduce costs had been implemented and before the RIFs had a chance to reduce costs.

The implementation of the ESOP was sufficiently contested to warrant a delay and more study of feasibility. The General Accounting Office got the job. It concluded that the ESOP might not save any money. Privatization proceeded despite this conclusion. Timothy Bowling, associate director of Federal Human Resource Management Issues, testified:

> Although OMB estimated a $30 million savings by privatizing OPM's investigative and training functions, it is uncertain whether the proposed ESOP would achieve greater financial stability and cost savings for the government than OPM's current method of providing investigative services. Also, based on OPM Inspector General (IG) reports and our analysis, the deficit that has been attributed to the Investigations Service revolving fund—about $30 million—is questionable.
>
> Previous IG reports have noted several deficiencies in the management of OPM's investigative activities. For instance, the IG reported that OPM has not been able to accurately forecast its investigative workload and adjust staffing levels accordingly. Also, the IG noted that OPM's investigative services had been burdened with an excessive share of OPM's overhead charges.
>
> Our work confirmed the IG's finding that OPM appeared to be charging an excessive share of overhead to investigative services. Although this activity requires a low level of oversight and is intended to be self-supporting, we found that the cost of common OPM services such as staff support were charged to investigative services based on a flat rate rather than on the actual cost of the services provided. To illustrate, under OPM's current methodology, the overhead allocation rate is determined based on the Investigation Service's total expenses as a percent of OPM's total budgetary obligations. During fiscal year 1994, this calculation yielded a rate of 19 percent for total overhead charges— a percentage that we consider to be high in view of the low level of common services and oversight attention required for this activity.
>
> The amount of overhead allocated to the investigations function has a considerable effect on the fund's financial position and, in all likelihood, has contributed to the fact that with the exception of fiscal year 1991, OPM has consistently reported a deficit for investigative services every year since fiscal year 1986. During fiscal year 1994, for example, the fund reportedly incurred an $11.8 million deficit. However, before overhead charges of $18.3 million were applied, the fund's revenues exceeded expenses by $6.5 million.

Because of issues such as the above, it is difficult to determine whether greater cost savings could result from privatizing this activity than would result from improved management or the application of a more realistic overhead charge. Also, care needs to be taken to be sure that OMB's savings estimate is clearly understood. OMB's estimate is not based on an analysis of how costs could be reduced or revenues could be increased by privatizing the investigative function. Rather, the $30 million figure was derived by estimating the savings from privatizing both OPM's investigative and training functions. According to OMB, this figure was arrived at by assuming that annual savings would be 4 percent of OPM's investigations and training expenses, including overhead, over a four-year period. OMB said the 4 percent figure was based on rates of savings found in earlier studies on the results of contracting out other federal functions.[33]

In GAO's testimony in June 1995, well after the decision to privatize had been announced and OPM had decided on an ESOP, Timothy Bowling observed that work plans had not been drawn up for the ESOP, so it was impossible to know whether there would be savings, let alone whether the ESOP would work. That the decision to privatize using the ESOP had been arrived at without such prior analysis is striking. One observer argued that from OPM's perspective, failure to estimate the number of investigations and tailor staff accordingly resulted in embarrassing numbers in the revolving funds, and to get rid of the whole problem, the agency suggested privatization rather than fixing the problems. In any case, one has to wonder about privatization that seems to take place for its own sake, rather than after a careful study of costs and savings.

While it was never clear how much, if any, savings would be achieved by contracting with the new worker-owned Investigative Services, preliminary reports suggest that the privatized service is functioning well. Clients report high satisfaction levels.

REORGANIZATION

Cutback was the major effort of OPM, as it struggled to comply with NPR mandates. But it was also trying to implement the required decentralization of personnel functions to the agencies and the necessary oversight of those decentralized functions. To accomplish this oversight function better than in the past, it had to devote more resources to the function, despite the downsizing. As a result, in 1995 OPM reorganized, merging two units that had had some oversight function into one, now larger unit, swelled by the ranks of those displaced by reductions in force. The new office was called Merit Systems Oversight and Effectiveness. The Merit Systems Protection Board, OPM's sister agency with oversight of OPM, watched the reorganization closely, issuing an evaluation report in 1998.

The MSBP evaluation noted that the reorganization gave more resources to the new unit and better access to upper levels of administration. The reorganization made another very important change: oversight had been funded by fees, with employees encouraged to spend part of each year on reimbursable contracts to pay their salaries. The older function had little credibility and dwindling resources. In the reorganized unit, services were covered by appropriations, not fees. OPM had redefined its core activities, and oversight of the merit system was now defined as part of the core.

Staff who were bumped into the new unit tended to be expensive senior people who had little experience with oversight. The new unit was thus more expensive but did not necessarily acquire new expertise. Observers were asked about whether the new oversight office had the necessary expertise to help the agencies. The answer was, in some substantive areas, yes, and in others, no.

The new unit did redesign the work process in some important ways. OPM has improved its databases and does more preliminary work from them to figure out the focus of studies in particular agencies. These studies concentrate on three areas, government-wide questions, agency-specific questions, and questions posed by the agencies themselves. Presumably including the latter will help pique the interest of the agency managers and help get their support for the process. Before reorganization, agency oversight focused nearly exclusively on governmentwide, across-the-board rules.

Not all the agencies had been reviewed under the new system between 1995 and the beginning of the MSPB study, but those that had been reviewed under the new system were more positive about the process than those that had not. Even so, the rate of approval of OPM's oversight was moderate at best. Fifty-two percent of twenty-three department and large independent agencies surveyed rated OPM's effectiveness as very great or considerable in protecting merit-based civil service; only 26 percent identified OPM positively in making suggestions and finding opportunity for improvement, and similarly, only 22 percent gave a positive rating to OPM's ability to help them achieve their own mission and goals. Part of the reason for not seeing OPM as very helpful in achieving their missions was that they did not see HRM in general as central to achieving their missions.

According to the MSPB study, OPM has had trouble linking the policy formulation part of the substantive offices with the oversight function of turning up problems in other agencies. OPM is supposed to propose solutions to problems as they are discovered and get those solutions implemented. From the agencies' perspective, until OPM can forge this link, it is not likely to be very helpful.

OPM was trying to implement the decentralization mandated by its legislation in 1978 and reinforced by the NPR. OPM was supposed to change from the role of supervisor to helper of the agencies. It was, finally, changing its role, but only with moderate success, still strongest in its most traditional area, ensuring merit-based civil service. Even there, OPM was still struggling with the new flexibility that was antagonistic to simple implementation of rules. Finding a new balance was a difficult task that resulted in some absurdities as OPM struggled to link all personnel issues to basic ones of protecting merit hiring, retention, and evaluation.

ASSESSMENT

Did budget cuts improve efficiency and effectiveness in OPM? Much of what happened at OPM was driven by staffing cuts rather than a plan to increase efficiency—or any kind of plan. OPM seemed to be in a perpetual state of reaction. One interviewee, when responding to a question about why there were so many separate RIFs at OPM, responded, "I think there was no planning. No long-term planning. They told people that there would be one RIF. Then they did another. One RIF occurred because they didn't anticipate the effects of cutting training."[34]

For many years OPM experienced a rolling, roiling process of adaptation to cuts. Describing the years from 1992 to 1996, one informant noted,

> Change was cumulative rather than in phases. It began with the Clinton administration cuts, which were to everyone. I remember we had to do exercises of 5 percent and 10 percent cuts. It all happened during the planning stage. It wasn't 12 percent cut and those people go, and then another 12 percent. We were planning for 12 percent, and before it was done, it got bigger. It was 12 percent cut or bumped, deficits in the revolving funds, REGO II, the redesign task force, that looked neater in retrospect, all influenced each other at different times.[35]

The confusing mix of RIFs, reorganization, and privatization meant that the actual losses in staff morale and expertise were greater than the staffing reductions themselves. RIFs meant that some people were moved to positions they had little experience with, because they had bumping rights through seniority; reorganization meant that some people moved from one unit to another and switched functions; the continuing uncertainty and threats of agency as well as program termination caused professionals to leave when they could. One OPM staffer who was RIFed went back after the RIF to see what the agency had become:

> I went back later and talked to people. Some were going to the USDA and some were going out the door. We used to be a group of people with a common goal. Literally everyone was displaced. A year prior we were an organization doing work; now there was no longer an entity. There were no two people who had worked together who were still together. Parts were completely disbanded. Programs were renamed, but no one remained who knew how the work had been done even a year

prior. OPM had dismembered the organization so that not even two people could have a conversation about how it was done. No two people were in the same place. Institutional capacity? There was not even a conversation there.[36]

Despite this chaos, much was accomplished after 1995. OPM had been unable to deliver on decentralization and reconceptualization of its mission in the years after its formation in 1978, despite its mandate in the CSRA. But by 1998 OPM had begun to deliver, not only on decentralization, but also on oversight of that decentralization. Changes in OPM were driven by decentralization, not by budget cuts, but the budget cuts forced the issue and made decentralization happen:

> What has been driving these changes over time? Not the budget. The agencies want to be free of control. The budget dollars help; the pressures continue. Centralization was a priority through the 1960s; in the 1970s decentralization began, with Scotty Campbell and Carter. There was a blip under Devine, recentralization on that point, not huge, but enough to stop and reverse the decentralization where possible, and then the decentralization continued. We stayed on that track. None of that was budget driven.
>
> Budget cuts get used in a way that interrupts people's arguments for the status quo. Any change from the center was as much a result of the fact that it was logical to delegate more as it was to budget pressures increasing. And Congress allowed it to happen.
>
> Budget pressures exaggerated—no, they finally made the decentralization happen. I don't like central agency management. It [the budget cuts] helped to get it [decentralized]; it turned policy decisions into practical discussion that had to be resolved.[37]

But while budget pressures accelerated decentralization of functions to the agencies, they made it more difficult for OPM to supervise that decentralization. Staff that had been RIFed from other sections of OPM were bumped into the new oversight unit. Thus the new unit, though larger than its predecessor, was composed in part of people without training or background in oversight. Staffing reductions stripped the agency of young people who might have had new ideas and made it nearly impossible to create a substantial research focus to come up with suggestions for the agencies: "OPM didn't have the expertise to be bold. It had more expertise in terms of following rules than innovative personnel practices."[38] Evaluation was not feeding into new legislative proposals. To gear up for this new function it would probably have been necessary to recruit new staff, which OPM was not able to do.

Was OPM's survival strategy successful? Was OPM more focused on surviving than on managing better with less? The relative balance is difficult to measure, but it is clear that OPM had virtually no support anywhere. OMB had been able to temper NPR's antiregulatory spirit, but OPM could not; it felt the full brunt of that spirit. That pressure included massive cutbacks and the termination of the federal personnel manual and ultimately privatization of two major functions. Rather than a plan of its own, OPM seemed to be following an NPR plan of the administration. Whatever was asked of it, OPM wanted to do more and be a model. OPM was in the odd position of needing to survive by complying with a policy to cut itself. It has survived, in considerably shrunken form, but implementing new thrusts with such limited staff has been difficult. After shrinking so dramatically, OPM needed some new blood and some new expertise, but its staffing levels were frozen at the new lower level. Whatever skills gaps it had developed had to be dealt with through training of existing employees.

Was OPM able to learn from its experiences? In some ways, yes, and in other ways, no. While the agency experienced reductions in force in the early 1980s, it did not seem able to learn from that experience, as other agencies did, to avoid RIFs or to make them more targeted and limited in effect. Nor was it able to plan and consolidate the RIFs it did have into one episode and begin recovery. OPM experienced multiple RIFs as its problems and solutions evolved. Some individual staff members were RIFed more than once. The RIFs, reorganizations, and self-cutting caused low morale. Many experienced staff either retired or quit while those in place fewer years were RIFed. The result was that almost no one who was around in the early 1980s was still there in the 1990s to convey what had been learned:

> There was a large exodus of senior people at the passage of CSRA. Then a lot have left. . . . I don't know how neat you can make it, but a lot of people who were around in the late 1980s, most of them are gone. I am one of the last ones. In 1985–86 there were three people, one retired, one went to HHS . . . there were a lot of retirements and people taking other jobs. The personnel director in the early 1980s is gone, at MSPB. There isn't a core of old-timers. There are still people with a lot of OPM experience, but lots of new people too.[39]

Others agreed that those who could get out did so: "If people could duck for cover, they did; if they could get out, they did. They moved every SESer. No one had any knowledge of their job; 92 percent of SESers changed."[40]

The traditional expectation has been that the career officials remain in an agency and keep the organizational learning and pass it on when and how they can. But in a cutback environment, this assumption is sometimes violated, not only because of extensive staff turnover, but also because of poor or nonexistent communication between senior career staff and politically appointed officials. Learning, to the extent that it takes place, has to occur in a different way. For OPM, there were two other kinds of learning that came to light in the case study. In one, budgetary adaptations left their own imprint and remained available for future use. Thus pushing additional expenditures into the revolving fund was done in a limited way in the early Reagan administration and again during Gramm-Rudman-Hollings, and from then on, more general agency functions were shifted to the revolving funds. A second method was to write a memo that was stored in a library, available for future searching by new staff who had no memory of the prior events, or access to anyone who might have been involved in the earlier proposals. Thus the proposal for the ESOP was a revamped version of a 1986 proposal for worker-owned enterprises. The idea had not been implemented at that time, so there was no possibility of observing it in practice and modifying it based on that practice, but at least the idea itself remained available for later use.

CONCLUSIONS

As at HUD, budgetary strategies had limits that played themselves out during the span of the study. Just as HUD reached the limit of shortening of its Section 8 contracts, when it had reduced them from fifteen or twenty years down to one-year renewals, OPM reached the limit of putting operating costs into the revolving funds, because such burdens exaggerated other management problems in the training and investigations units and caused visible deficits, threatening at one point to violate the antideficiency act.

OPM's budgetary strategies also resembled Congress's efforts to support the Patent and Trademark Office (PTO) exclusively by fees. By encouraging fees, regular appropriations could be freed up for other unrelated purposes. Similarly, OPM used the fee-generating power of the training and investigations units for other, unrelated expenses. Fiscal stress tends to erode earmarks on fee revenue and threatens second-level reactions, as when supporters of the PTO voted to eliminate fees entirely, and the even more extreme privatization of training and investigations in OPM. In OPM's case, since the revolving funds were required to cover their costs, if OPM put more costs in its fund, the revolving fund functions would eventually have had to raise their prices to cover these costs, gradually becoming less competitive. If allowed to continue, demand would have dropped and staffing levels would have had to continue to shrink, because the product was overpriced. It is not possible to compete commercially and subsidize other operations at the same time.

Considering Commerce and OPM together, despite their different sizes and functions, raises the issue of financial and substantive interdependence. Both Commerce and OPM were threatened with termination. Commerce was threatened with dismemberment, which seemed reasonable because there was so little connection between the functions its programs performed and because there was so little financial interdependence among programs. Parts of Commerce could come and go, taking their administrative superstructure with them. There were some overhead charges, but the central administration was thin, the charges not extensive. OPM had more central structure, more overhead, including the OPM director's office, and the charges to the internal units were more extensive to support this infrastructure. As appropriations shrank, dependence on fee income to cover this central structure increased. Without a history of getting and losing agencies, as Commerce had, OPM was unprepared for the results when it privatized training and investigations. It had to cut back on administration, not just because it had fewer staff, but because the money it had used to support that administration was gone. The result was not just a longer period of roiling confusion, but also loss of the limited policy function the agency had, which was funded out of the revolving fund.

OPM was praised for cutting specific units, defining its core activities, and getting rid of the rest in response to pressures to cut itself, and OPM did in fact drop functions. But it is not clear that this was a deliberative process rather than a series of responses to NPR demands and then responses to the unanticipated consequences. OPM did not do much planning, and what planning it did seemed to be quickly overwhelmed by events. The USDA tried to learn from its earlier mistakes and incorporate what it learned into a plan; as long as USDA was able to implement that plan, it minimized managerial and programmatic damage. By contrast, OPM seemed to lack a plan, despite claims that it was protecting its core activities.

One of the themes that emerges from an examination of OPM's history over this period is that there is no meaningful definition of its core. The core is not a reality that needs to be discovered by analysis, but a shifting political definition of what remains after cuts. The term is likely to be used as the opposite of being nibbled to death by ducks; that is, any effort to cut specific functions rather than cut across the board is likely to be defined as protecting core functions and shrinking in a logical way. But cuts that are targeted are not necessarily logical in terms of their relationship to the rest of the organization. Don Devine was not particularly supportive of the benefits functions of OPM; he thought that the benefits were too generous and should be cut back. Director Jim King believed that the benefits management function should be protected as part of the core of the agency. Devine thought testing was a core function of OPM; by King's time, testing had devolved to the agencies, with some OPM help, but was no longer a core function of the agency. What is core is defined by the priorities of the director, by the exigencies of decentralization (what functions the agencies want to provide for themselves), by changing technology, and by the skills remaining in the organization after prior reductions in force.

Without new hiring, it is difficult to go in new directions, or even in old directions for which the staff are no longer available. With emphasis on broader position descriptions and forced marches into functions that still have needs, the requirements for additional training increased during cutback, but training tends to be the most deeply cut, creating rigidities and inabilities to adapt in particular directions. OPM still gets higher marks in enforcement of personnel rules than it does in helping agencies come up with new solutions or taking the policy lead in personnel for the federal government.

The issue of interdependence comes up in a different way in the OPM case. That is, through the revolving funds, OPM was providing services to other agencies for a fee. It was therefore vulnerable to changing demands from those other agencies. The ideology suggests that if you are engaged in competitive activities, you will have to watch your costs and prices, will be less wasteful, and will be rewarded with high demand for a good product at moderate prices. But that view neglects the idea that a provider agency is also vulnerable to budget cuts in the agencies it does business with. Since training is one of the items budgeters tend to cut first during financial cutbacks, even the very best of trainers can be idled during such a period; investigation of new job candidates also drops precipitously during budget cutbacks, regardless of the quality and cost of services. The need is to become flexible in terms of staffing size, going up and down with demand over which you have no control. That need for flexibility has suggested that the private sector can do it better, because it can hire and fire temporary and part-time employees. But going to the private sector has not always produced good results, as prior experiences with investigations demonstrated. The profit motive and tendency to hire the cheapest possible labor made the quality of the product decline. The Census Bureau learned how to cope with fluctuating workloads; investigations had not learned how before it was privatized.

CHAPTER 10

Eating the Seed Corn
and Trimming the Herds

OVER THE YEARS from 1981 to 1998, to what extent did the federal government eat its seed corn or trim its herds? To what extent did it create a government that "works better and costs less" as the National Performance Review mandated? Rejecting the either-or framing of the question, informants throughout the study replied that they had devoured some of their seed corn and done some herd trimming.

In this study, eating the corn was operationalized in several ways. In some cases, it referred to senior staff with years of program knowledge retiring and not being replaced, and the hiring freezes that made it difficult to fill skills gaps. In some cases, such as GAO, it also referred to the reduced ability to initiate studies and carry them on in the background while responding to congressional requests. As the years went by, agencies were drawing down their reserves of knowledge. Eating the seed corn also referred to taking actions that may have saved the programs or even the agency in the short run, but that caused more problems in the out-years.

Trimming the herds was defined in terms of the agencies' ability to pare back its staffing and its expenditures in such a way that the quality of its services was maintained. Such efforts included increases in productivity, resulting from increased computerization and job reinvention, and from program simplification, including revision of grant and loan applications and shifting away from complicated agricultural support programs to simpler market-based strategies. Trimming the herds included efforts to define core functions and drop, privatize, or contract for the remaining services and functions. Dropping less important functions entailed a kind of prioritization that enabled remaining units to maintain their quality. Trimming the herds also included efforts to plan and an ability to implement those downsizing plans, rather than taking an ad hoc approach to whatever current threat was facing the agency. When agencies were not allowed to carry out plans, drop the less important or more labor-intense functions, or simplify their operations enough to match the new lower levels of staffing, the result was consumption of seed corn.

In the information agencies, examples of eating the seed corn included cutting back on research in the Bureau of Labor Statistics, reducing sample sizes in the Census surveys, and reducing the level of data checking of self-reported information. Even the BLS, which had the best record among the agencies studied of being able to drop product lines and maintain quality, was not able to maintain the necessary amount of underlying research required to improve measures of the economy. The erosion of the quality in the statistical agencies is a good example of eating the seed corn. As former CBO director Rudy Penner described,

> A significant portion of [estimating] errors are made because the data with which we work is of very low quality, does not exactly fit the concepts that we require, or is outdated because it is made available with a very long time lag. Sometimes data on important concepts is not available at all. As we continue to cut the budgets of our statistical agencies, this problem can only get worse.[1]

Penner warned the budget committees,

> The Congress should be careful about further cuts in the budgets of the main statistical agencies. They provide information needed for much of the estimating process. They have been under severe budget duress for years. They are not able to adjust statistical concepts as rapidly as the economy is evolving or to develop new products that would be useful to the budget estimating process and to other economic analysts.[2]

With respect to trimming the herd, informants reported greatly improved use of computers within agencies and between agencies and their customers, some program simplification, and clarification of the criteria for grants and awards. The National Partnership for Reinventing Government (the newer name of the National Performance Review) reported the results of an employee survey in 1998 and 1999, in which questions were asked about productivity. In 1998, 43 percent agreed and in 1999, 40 percent agreed that productivity had improved in their agency over the prior two years. Similar proportions of employees reported that they had been given more flexibility in how to carry out their work assignments. In addition to productivity improvements, some agencies worked hard at improving their financial management tools and reports.

BUDGET PROCESS AND TRADEOFFS

Central to the evaluation of the extent to which government can continue to provide or improve the quality of services at lower costs is the ability to prioritize. All informants noted that the spending caps and pay-go requirements generally worked during the period of the study; that is, until the budget reached balance in 1998, the budget process helped hold down the rate of growth in outlays. However, the budget process shifted from stressing priorities to stressing enforcement, a shift that became apparent in the mid-1980s with Gramm-Rudman-Hollings and its emphasis on across-the-board rather than programmatic cuts.[3] The Budget Enforcement Act (BEA) of 1990 continued that enforcement orientation. Rather than a policy focus, the BEA concentrated on ceilings for discretionary spending and offset requirements for tax reductions and legislatively approved increases in entitlement spending. Spending caps and hard distinctions between mandatory and discretionary categories affected the way budgeting was carried out, sometimes in odd and seemingly irrational ways, ratcheting down discretionary spending disproportionately.

Observers argued that an overemphasis on rules made it more difficult to make good policy decisions about how to cut back spending: "If they started somewhere else, such as, we have these six public policy objectives, how should we get there, they would end up in a different place. [Instead] they have a $20 billion target and need to write legislation to meet that goal. It is a wildly different orientation."[4]

Rudy Penner described the result of this rule-bound budgeting:

> Given the extraordinary number of arbitrary elements in the way that the Congressional budget process is administered, it is difficult to love. In an ideal world, it would not be necessary to have all these rules. The Congress would take a disciplined approach to budget matters because it is the right thing to do and not because it is required by some arbitrary rules. However, the Congress has lost faith in its ability to discipline itself without rules and we live with the arbitrary results of that decision. Given their arbitrary nature, the rules have worked remarkably well in preventing the fiscal situation from getting worse in the aggregate, although they have done little to force it to become better and some strange micro decisions are being made along the way.[5]

Ironically, then, the effort to rebalance the budget shifted the process away from prioritization and policy goals toward seemingly arbitrary rules and ceilings. The emphasis on controlling the totals pushed the question of what would be cut down to the level of the appropriations subcommittees, forcing comparisons of spending alternatives within smaller chunks of the budget. The budget process intensified competition within appropriations subcommittees, within departments, and within agencies.

On the face of it, such explicit tradeoffs seem like an improvement that has long been sought in budgeting. Which is more important, *a* or *b*, and why? But those kinds of questions can be answered meaningfully only within a budget process that logically groups items together for consideration. The actual framing of the tradeoffs in the budget process sometimes did not compare similar or even related items.

The Budget Enforcement Act of 1990 set up spending caps on the discretionary side of the budget. The sum of spending by the appropriations subcommittees was not to exceed the total caps. Each subcommittee was given its own target. Within those targets, if a subcommittee wished to give one agency or program in its jurisdiction more money, it had to take that money from elsewhere in that department, or from elsewhere in the subcommittee's jurisdiction. How a program fared depended on which other departments or programs shared the jurisdiction of the appropriations subcommittee.

The Department of Housing and Urban Development (HUD) competed with the Veterans Administration (VA) and independent agencies such as the Federal Emergency Management Administration (FEMA). Department of Commerce programs such as the Census Bureau and the National Weather Service had to compete with programs in the Department of State and the Department of Justice. If one of these departments or programs grew, because it was more popular or its needs seemed more urgent at the moment, the others were sometimes forced to take a hit or grow more slowly. Agencies were not necessarily cut because they were poorly managed or accomplished less than growing programs, but because if one program was increased, another had to be cut to compensate.

Judy England-Joseph of GAO argued that some of HUD's budget stress occurred because HUD was in the same appropriations subcommittee jurisdiction as FEMA. HUD's mission was broad and vague, but

> lumped in with HUD on the subcommittee are agencies with clear missions and lots of support—and EPA, it took a hit to support HUD, but now it's getting the attention. That may cost HUD. The big one is FEMA. Where is HUD if there is a big snowfall on the East Coast? Disaster funding used to be part of the supplemental process, but not anymore. They use good estimates based on history; they budget for FEMA up front.
>
> The last 10 years, FEMA's history included three of the most expensive disasters, Northridge [earthquake], [Hurricane] Andrews, and the floods. That is hitting HUD. People won't spend less on disasters. Most of the money that is spent is in future years. Budgeters don't know the total costs until 3 or 4 or 10 years later. FEMA comes back and says [that] structural damage from the quake will cost more than we estimated. If the bill increases, they just pay for it. You have more proof of damage later. So HUD is in a tough bind in its jurisdiction. Its ability to compete is weak. I can understand why the last couple of years has been so tough.[6]

NOAA's Weather Service had to compete with clean water and runoff protection in the Commerce, State, and Justice appropriation. One representative proposed an amendment to take $15 million from the Weather Service to provide an additional $8 million for cleaning up waterways. Legislators anguished over having to deny one good program to provide funding for another one. After already deep cuts, the Weather Service was able to beat back this further intrusion. What was especially interesting about the proposal was that the members of Congress proposing the shift of funds thought there were carryover funds that could be taken in this manner, but supporters of NOAA argued that those funds had already been taken for some other purpose. Carryover funds and other unspent monies, even if needed within a year, became valuable sources of flexibility, to be spent, even if temporarily, on other highly valued projects.

The intense competition for dollars within each appropriations subcommittee led to increased emphasis on fees to cover costs wherever feasible, so that the appropriation that would otherwise be consumed by an agency would be freed up for reallocation. In the extreme, in the Patent and Trademark Office (PTO), fee revenue was levied not only to pay for services formerly paid from appropriations, but also was increased to create additional revenue that could be allocated by the committee, setting off a fight over the ownership of the fees and their appropriate size. Similarly, at about the same time, a 4.3-cents-a-gallon tax on gasoline (also a user tax) was passed for the purpose of reducing the deficit, instead of its more traditional use to support highway construction. By 1997 highway supporters managed to put the 4.3-cents tax into the highway trust fund. The use of fees for general rather than earmarked purposes led to competition for those fees and ultimately the restoration of their initial purposes.

Competition also led to intensified fencing of revenues. Fear that windfalls would be used for something else led supporters of particular programs not only to argue for bigger portions of the pie, but to earmark those portions so others could not successfully compete for them. When highways got an increase in funding in 1998, that funding was fenced. The fencing was called a "firewall." The allocations could have gone to the subcommittee dealing with transportation, but instead, the ceiling was raised only for the firewall programs. Without the firewall, all the programs in the committee jurisdiction would have had access to the funds; with the firewall, highways and mass transit were protected but other transportation agencies were not.

Amtrak was funded, but some of the requests of the Coast Guard were not. The following excerpt from the *Congressional Record* makes clear how the committee expected the Coast Guard to respond when Congress forced its priority program into the Coast Guard budget:

Returning to the Coast Guard, the bill provides $2.7 billion, essentially a hard freeze. Within these funds, the Committee has increased funds allocated to fight the war on drugs to $446 million, an increase of 11 percent. The previous commandant and many members of the House advocated this increase. Unfortunately, given the tight budgetary caps this year and the firewalls imposed on the Committee, the Committee was unable to provide resources above the overall Coast Guard budget request without unacceptably harming critical safety programs of other DOT agencies. Clearly, the funding levels contained in this bill will require the Coast Guard to prioritize its activities and missions.[7]

When overall constraints were tight and one unit or program required or was forced to accept an increase, the result was often to force a secretary or an agency head to propose offsetting cuts.

Deficit reduction targets in general and committee spending caps in particular were not adaptive to bumpy outlays. Thus the Census Bureau's rise and decline in spending over a decade were problematic for the Commerce Department; spending for FEMA, which varied from year to year, also caused problems for others sharing the same appropriations subcommittee. Capital construction in the highway program, and renewing Section 8 highway contracts, lumpy by nature, caused tumult because of the possibility that others would have to pay for their increases.

Efforts to cope with lumpy expenditures fell into two categories. One was to take money from other necessary expenses elsewhere in the same department; a second was to gather up loose funds, that is, money that was not yet spent but that was earmarked for a specific purpose, and spend it for the lumpy cost, with the idea that the money would be paid back later. A too-short blanket was being pulled this way and that, to cover the most urgent expenditures at the moment. It was never clear whether the money that was earmarked would be there for its initial purpose when it was needed; for example, renewals of Section 8 housing contracts were in doubt each year for several years. And the agencies that had set money aside for capital purchases or for contingency funds found themselves donors for other urgent needs, setting in motion an effort to either commit funds earlier so they would not be available for this blanket grabbing or to hide the totals and make them available only when agency heads or secretaries could collect considerable political payoff for them. As opposed to prioritization of needs, so that lower priorities could fund higher priorities, lumpy spending tended to drive out regular spending and savings. The sources of funding were not necessarily lower priority, but often delayable.

The requirement for secretaries to make tradeoffs within their own departments was reinforced in the budget request process, because OMB could no longer hold back funds for special requests from the departments. OMB's estimates shifted to close estimates of statutory maximums, with no play or give. If the secretaries needed to add something to the budget request, they needed to be prepared to subtract something else.

The second pattern, taking loose or uncommitted funding to cover lumpy expenditures, showed up most clearly in the nonemergency supplemental appropriations. Emergency supplementals did not have to be offset, but nonemergency supplementals required specific reductions elsewhere in the budget. A norm gradually developed to gather as yet unspent funds, even if they were only temporarily unspent, to fund supplemental needs. Thus unspent funds became highly precious sources of revenue, leading to some uneven trades, where some agencies gave more heavily than others because they were more likely to have or be able to create unspent funds or scoring changes that could provide flexibility within the caps.

In 1997 and again in 1998 supplementals drew on HUD Section 8 reserves for funding. Estimates of the size of these reserves grew during the period, in part because more effort was made to find out the real size of the balances and in part through a redefinition of need as the length of time for contracts decreased, lowering risk. Some members of Congress were suspicious about the sudden increase in the estimated size of the reserves; HUD was suddenly able to find money to support an administration initiative, when it could not find such balances when members of Congress asked for them. As Congress became more assiduous in searching out and using carryover funds of various sorts, some agencies became more cautious about leaving those funds uncommitted. NOAA at one point committed funds for a major purchase well in advance of need, thereby preventing Congress from using the funds, much to the aggravation of its appropriations subcommittee.

One of the major tradeoffs was from low-income housing to FEMA. One member of Congress estimated, "In the past two years, including this [supplemental] legislation before us today, we have cut almost $12 billion from other VA-HUD programs—principally low-income housing—to pay for FEMA disaster relief."[8]

The need to come up with money from low-income housing for FEMA resulted in part from prior years' efforts to take money from FEMA for presidential initiatives. Costs for FEMA vary from year to year, not only because disasters vary in number and intensity each year, but also because it is difficult to predict how long it will take before all the bills come in for any given disaster. Thus in one year actual costs might be lower than budgeted and in another year higher. Budgeting for FEMA in advance (based on averages from prior years) helped reduce its impact on the deficit but created shortfalls and surpluses because the prior years' averages were sometimes too high and sometimes too low. The surpluses could have been kept to pay for the eventual shortfalls, but with budget needs elsewhere so acute, the surpluses tended to be snapped up, creating difficulties of finding the funds when there were shortfalls.

Taking the money from HUD Section 8 funds had the same effect that taking the money from FEMA did, because the money was going to have to be spent a year or two later. The savings from the unobligated contract reserves was intended to go toward renewing the Section 8 contracts when those costs began to increase due to shorter contracts and more rolling over each year. For 1998, however, Congress did not abide by its own policy. The unobligated reserves for Section 8 were set aside to fund the contract renewals, but when it came time for supplemental appropriations, temptation to spend the balances on something else proved too great.

In short, when the caps were tight, they contributed to more importance being placed on supplementals (committee chairs sometimes argued that they could not accommodate this under the caps, but would try to find money during the supplemental), and also put a premium on finding money during the year to fund them. Until 1998 the emergency clause in the budget was not abused as a way out of the caps; offsets had to be found for supplemental spending. Congress began to emphasize and insist on finding every loose cent, every contingency fund, every dollar set aside for purchases not yet made, every dollar of carryover. It pushed the agencies to find such dollars and free them up for reallocation during the year. The result was that agencies that planned major capital purchases or that had contingency funds that could be redefined were disproportionate losers, not because they were badly administered or low priority, but because they had the kind of money that could be available for reallocation during the year. The result was a form of *rebudgeting*, storing and finding surpluses and then giving them up for higher political priorities during the year.

In fact, any program that was complex enough to be redefined for scoring savings was a possible source of money to reallocate. The fight for resources then revolved around whether those funds should go to the department that freed them up or to other committee priorities. There was no programmatic or policy analysis that said this program should yield these resources and that one should gain them.

These efforts to find or create loose money were not all congressionally based. The redefinition of Section 8 contingency funds was suggested by the administration first. Congress decided to put a surcharge on the Patent and Trademark Office fees and make the fees large enough to help reduce the deficit; the administration did not initially go along with diversion of the funds from the PTO office but did so later.

Though Congress and the president included their policy preferences in the budget, they often left the decision of what to cut to the secretaries; the secretaries sometimes left those decisions to the agencies. While policy trade-offs could have been made at the department and program levels, Congress and the president sometimes made it difficult to make cuts based on policy, especially when the choices dealt with refocusing missions and dropping programs.

DEFINING CORE FUNCTIONS

In order for agencies to downsize with the maximum of efficiency and effectiveness, they have to simplify their programs to meet reduced staffing levels and eliminate programs no longer considered part of the core, or major focus of the agency.[9] The result would be fewer services, or simplified services, provided at continuing high quality. Program simplification and paring back to core functions proved difficult, however. Some agencies in this study were able to achieve some program simplification and elimination of less-core functions, but many were not, or were able to do so only partially.

Why has this part of downsizing been so difficult? One reason is that there is no logical best way to group functions. Many functions could be placed in one department or agency or another. Over time, a particular group of functions may have ended up in one place. Some departments and agencies are loose associations of semirelated functions. As a result, it may be difficult to define what the core mission of a department or bureau really is. Another reason that it sometimes proves difficult to define core functions is that there is little political agreement on what those core functions should be or what functions should be shed. As a result, the department or agency may not be granted enough autonomy to reorganize itself.

To some extent, the disparity of functions that ends up in one agency or department reflects coalition building, an intentional accumulation of different clienteles. The more a department or agency is under threat of termination, the more likely its officials will try to expand its support by addition of missions, programs, and clientele groups. Whether these groups are compatible or not seems irrelevant to survival. But once evoked, interest groups lock onto their programs, making these programs difficult to eliminate. Program beneficiaries often speak through their legislators who refuse to allow a program to be cut out or simplified.

If a department or agency is composed of subunits that are highly interdependent, either programmatically or financially, the ability to reduce or eliminate whole functions may be compromised. Sometimes programs have little to do with each other programmatically but are financially interdependent, as when one of them generates revenue that others share, possibly through financing overhead costs. When such units are cut or transferred or made independent financially, there may be repercussions on other unrelated agencies in the same department or agency. The dropping of functions or trading them or privatizing them may occur, but the expected benefits may not.

Finally, program administrators and departmental managers may be reluctant to propose termination of programs because it is much more difficult to get initial approval for a new program than to rejuvenate one that has become moribund or that has not been funded for years.

In the study, several agencies tried to redefine their core activities and cut the rest. Some were successful, others much less so.

General Accounting Office

The General Accounting Office was able to reorganize, dropping some of its divisions and merging others. The GAO was able to accomplish this goal in part because it had one major customer, Congress, and it tried hard to keep abreast of congressional needs and demands and organize itself around those demands. If Congress was no longer interested in a topic or area of research, the GAO could eliminate it organizationally, without any constituents to complain about the change. The GAO had been adapting in this manner for many years, well before the recent staffing reductions.

Bureau of Labor Statistics

The BLS had an accounting and decision-making system in place before the cuts that allowed decision making by product line. In addition, BLS was a highly professional statistical agency, the value of whose product lay in its precision and integrity. If the agency allowed budget and personnel cuts to erode all product lines across the board, none would have sufficient quality to be useful. Not only could the agency staff perceive quality changes, so could the agency's clientele. In many other agencies, quality is more difficult to perceive, a slight erosion of quality may be acceptable, and even a considerable erosion of quality and timeliness usually leaves a product that is still useful.

The BLS's failures are as illuminating as its successes. Some of the bureau's proposed targeted cuts were rejected by the White House and Congress, as program advocates argued for continued funding for their programs. Administrators at BLS pointed out that the interdependence that results from contracting with other agencies further reduced discretion in terms of defining core activities and programs. The bureau found that it was especially difficult to fund the research necessary to update its products and improve the underlying statistics.

While the BLS was not able to pare back exactly as agency officials planned, they were able to get approval for many of their proposals. As time passed, however, the agency's ability to plan cuts programmatically declined. The excellence of programs had little to do with the funds they were allocated. Attention shifted to stretching dollars and budget implementation and away from budget justifications. It became nearly impossible to make and justify proposals based on what the agency believed it needed with any hope that those proposals would be funded.

The Census Bureau

The Census Bureau had a harder time than the Bureau of Labor Statistics defining its core and preserving quality in its core activities while dropping other less-important programs. For one thing, some members of Congress decided as a matter of policy what portion of the Census they thought should be dropped, pushing particularly for the elimination of the long forms that were sent to a sample of the population and for simplification of the short form. A second problem was that the bureau was often unable to fully fund its studies done with sample surveys but was allowed to drop only a few of them. Until 1996 the Census did not have an accounting system that would allow it to make the kinds of adjustments that the BLS routinely made, making it more difficult to cut product lines. The result was a continuing erosion of the existing programs and particularly a reduction in sample size and delayed products. Smaller sample size resulted in less reliable data; delayed surveys resulted in less timely products.

Office of Personnel Management

In order to survive as it changed its mission to overseeing a highly decentralized federal personnel system, OPM had to downsize and reorganize. According to agency officials, as OPM downsized, it considered its core functions and shed the noncore functions. But it is unclear which OPM functions were not core to a central personnel agency. In an effort to cut personnel deeply, possibly to win support for its continued existence, OPM privatized its training and investigations units, both of which could easily be defined as core activities of a personnel office in a decentralized system, especially because both services were offered on a reimbursable basis, and therefore reflected the desires of the agencies rather than central direction. But both of these activities, because they were fee based, could be privatized more easily than the remaining activities, such as oversight of the merit system and management of insurance benefits. Core functions were defined as those that remained after whatever could be privatized or contracted out was offloaded. Rather than defining and reemphasizing the core activities in an agency that had grown too far afield, OPM responded to a series of pressures to decentralize, to downsize, to privatize, to deregulate. When programs that were supposed to not only cover their own costs but subsidize other activities began to run deficits, they were privatized. The reconceptualization of the agency was done by the NPR, by listening to the complaints of federal officials who resented the inflexibility of OPM rules.

HUD

HUD had experienced a loss of support due to prior financial scandals and the proliferation of economic development programs in other departments. Like OPM, HUD tried to win support from the executive branch by cutting its staff far more than the minimum required for each agency. But unlike OPM, and more like Census and the Bureau of Labor Statistics, HUD's programs were oriented externally, and interest groups and supporters of those programs, in the White House and in Congress, made it impossible for HUD to simplify its programs to deal with its downsized staff.

HUD represents an extreme of the inability to downsize by redefining the core. On the one hand, HUD made proposals (which were rejected by Congress) to reorganize and simplify programs; on the other hand, HUD continued to add new programs and divide existing programs into more earmarked components. These new programs, often referred to as boutique programs for their quality and small size, put increasing demands on a shrinking pool of managers. Because of its political vulnerability, HUD was not able to say to supporters: no, we cannot do that; we do not have the staff.

Department of Agriculture

The USDA was a mixed case. In the initial round of cuts, USDA did not make any effort to reorganize and combine or drop programs, because Congress had so hamstrung it with constraints, it was clear that no such reorganization or refocusing would pass. In the second round of cuts, it was much clearer that failure to reorganize to cope with reduced budget and spending was wreaking havoc with program management. Department administrators were able to design and pass a reorganization that merged several major programs, provided colocated services, and closed a number of field offices. This reorganization did not actually drop functions, however, and its main goal was to save money. A major component of the Agriculture Department, the Forest Service, was not permitted to reorganize, having been caught up in a policy dispute about its proper functions and core activities.

In sum, some agencies were better able than others to cut product lines. In this regard, the agencies with only internal constituencies had an easier time than those with external constituencies. A second problem that some agencies faced as they tried to simplify their programs and downsize was that there was little agreement between Congress and the president about what the focus of an agency was supposed to be and hence which programs should be preserved and which ones decommissioned. Members of Congress or the executive branch would sometimes tell the agencies what to cut and what to preserve or even add, based on political priorities rather than on the importance or effectiveness of programs or their centrality to the mission of the agency.

Another obstacle to redefining the core activities had to do with threats to survival. Some of the agencies in this study found that they were fighting not only cuts, but agency termination or dismemberment. When an agency's survival is threatened, its ability to say no to new, boutique programs may be minimal.

Its ability to cut programs that have political support may be minimal as well. Ironically, then, agencies most seriously threatened are often least able to use the strategy of refocusing the core and concentrating on carrying out a smaller number of activities well. Agencies that have never had a focused core and were never granted legitimacy in their domain are more likely to have grown by adding new constituencies and are the ones most likely to be politicized, least able to resist political pressures, most likely to be threatened with termination, and least able to cut back in a rational way without further risking their support base.

RESPONDING TO STAFFING REDUCTIONS: INCREASED EFFICIENCY AND CONTRACTING OUT

The NPR, with its focus on staffing reductions in the supervisory positions, and the Workforce Restructuring Act of 1994 targeted a reduction of more than 270,000 positions. It was never clear to anyone where that target came from or how it would be allocated out to agencies and programs, some of which were overstaffed and others of which were understaffed. The staffing levels were often unhitched from the budget and from the complexity of work tasks.

An unstated assumption seemed to underlie this radical separation of budget, mission, and staffing, namely, that if staffing were reduced, efficiencies would be introduced to compensate for reduced staffing and consequently government would cost less and work better. This process of matching managerial improvements to reduced staffing levels proved difficult in a number of agencies, especially because many of these improvements were dependent on the reinvention and computerization of work tasks and took place at the same time that agencies were being pressed to come up with performance measures and plans and to create their first auditable annual financial reports. With these multiple new tasks, constrained budgets, and emerging skills gaps because of the inability to hire new staff, getting new computers and new software up and running was much slower than anticipated. Start-up dates were often pushed back several times, or, as in several agencies, new systems were implemented too quickly without enough pretesting and consequently collapsed dramatically. The difficulty of funding the computer modernization efforts resulted in several agencies having to cut staff even further to come up with the resources to spend on computers.

While agencies had difficulty adapting to lower staffing levels, by and large they succeeded. GAO reinvented its work process, making it more focused and efficient, allowing it to produce the same number of reports and testimony with fewer staff and field offices. The USDA reinvented its work processes and was struggling to achieve one-stop shopping through computerization, to make farmers' contacts with agricultural agencies simpler. The USDA and HUD made grant and loan applications simpler, and HUD, like the USDA, made its computer access to its customers much more attractive and easier to use. The

Department of Commerce reinvented its purchasing processes for large capital items, considerably shortening the period of time from decision to purchase to receipt of these items.

The adaptations agencies made to cope with lower staffing levels sometimes had secondary consequences. As GAO reinvented its work processes, the agency made it clear that Congress was its only client and that congressional needs and demands would be met. GAO's role as watchdog for the public at large was accordingly deemphasized. The USDA farm programs had been nearly invincible politically for many years because the farm service met with and helped farmers; the new computerized interfaces and reduced regulations meant that farmers needed and got much less personal help—weakening the political links that had supported the agency. Moreover, the computerization of applications for support left out the poorest farmers who were most in need of additional help, raising again equity concerns that dogged the agency in recent years. The simplification of loan processes also brought with it concern for minimums: How little information could an agency require and still run a responsible loan program? The possibility existed that oversimplification would make an agency vulnerable to financial abuses and scandals of the sort that had plagued HUD.

When mission was not reduced proportionately to staffing, in addition to improving their efficiency, agencies often increased their contracting out. Such contracting allowed agencies to reduce the number of government employees while continuing to perform key functions. To the extent that it was less expensive to provide services through the private sector, money would be saved. Both Congress and OMB pushed the contracting option, arguing that competition would lower costs.

The agencies in this study increased their contracting out, but often not as much as some members of Congress would have liked. Staff at HUD reported that contracting was a blessing, that they never could have done their work without it, and that the private sector's superiority in using modern computer technology had been essential to them. NOAA, with the support of the National Performance Review, was able to come up with a middle option between contracting out for nearly all research and mapping and maintaining the status quo, increasing its contracting, but maintaining and renewing its fleet of research vessels. OPM privatized its training function and contracted with its former employees for its investigations function.

Contracting raised a number of questions. First, was there sufficient in-house expertise to supervise the contract? Second, did contractors take with them all the experience of a contract when contractors changed, so that learning in the agency was reduced to nearly zero? Third, were there any inherently governmental functions that should not be contracted out, and if so, what might those functions be?

The OPM investigations case raised the issue of inherently governmental functions. The solution was a strange compromise. OPM contracted with a company formed of its own former employees. The expertise, access, and reputation for integrity of the agency's former employees assured a smooth transition for the agency's clientele—they could hardly feel the difference. Shortcomings in service level that the agency had experienced in earlier efforts to contract with the private sector were thus bypassed. But this solution did not really allow for other companies to compete for the business; investigations had to be provided by former OPM employees. Thus the advantages of competition in keeping costs down could not be claimed.

At OPM, it was not clear whether contracting out would save money. OMB averages of savings from prior cases of contracting were used in lieu of predictions based on the specific circumstances. In the event, however, saving money was probably not the determining factor in contracting out. What pressed agencies to contract out was the need to seriously reduce staffing levels without dropping functions and with limited ability to increase efficiency to offset the staffing losses. While much of the contracting that went on was probably beneficial, some of it cost the government more than public-sector provision would have cost.

DURATION

The model of cutback and adaptation suggests that there are limits, that the cutback will be a one-time permanent downsizing, which can be adapted to through dropping product lines and reorganizing and redeploying staff and increasing their training. In reality, as opposed to the model, the downsizing was not of short duration. The determination to use attrition rather than RIFs spread out the process in time, freezing new hiring for years and providing incentives for early retirements.

The long duration of the downsizing had a number of consequences. One was that staffing imbalances and skills shortages gradually emerged. Over time the cessation of recruitment resulted in an aging workforce, with no new blood, fewer new ideas, and little in the way of recruitment for current statistical or technical skills. In some agencies, organizational memory became a problem because there were so few people left who had been in the agency more than a few years. Loss of skills was difficult to remedy without new hiring. Additional training, which should have been in demand because of the downsizing, cost money the agencies did not have and often resulted in cutting even more staff to create the funds to retrain.

A second problem resulting from the long duration of the rebalancing period was that many strategies were played to their logical end and used up. Once agencies had pared down to their core activities, they could not readily pare back a second or third time. Some agencies did the paring slowly, dropping one function at a time, but eventually they reached a point at which that tactic could not be used again. Unfortunately, no bells went off to signal that enough cutting had been done. Some agencies were able to negotiate limits to cuts, with varying success (the first time GAO tried to negotiate limits, the limits did not hold; the second time, they did). But other agencies were unable to negotiate any consensus on how long cuts should go on or how deep they should be.

Agencies experiencing continuing erosion of resources ran the risk of eroding service levels. It was very difficult for them to fight back. Most agency administrators believed they had to demonstrate that they were continuing to do a good job, no matter how much their budgets were cut. If they appeared to be failing, they risked further cuts. They argued that they were coping, they were reinventing, their programs were working, their customers were happy, happier than before. They argued that further cuts *would* hurt them, but not that prior cuts *did* hurt them. Administrators risked teaching Congress that they could be cut without any negative effects.

Because the reductions in staffing and budget took place over a number of years, the agencies often reused strategies they had used before, only more extremely, until they provoked some kind of reaction or created a new set of problems. One example of developing a strategy early and then using it again and again occurred in HUD. Initially, HUD shortened the period for the renewal of the Section 8 contracts moderately, but as the budget pressures continued, HUD repeatedly shortened the period of contract renewals, until they were only annual. Not only could that source of "savings" not be used any more, but the cost of annual renewals began to go up, causing a crisis in funding, and threatening the possibility that other HUD programs would be cut to fund the Section 8 renewals. In the event, that outcome did not occur and the contracts were renewed, but there were some very difficult budget years resulting from the repetition of this budget strategy.

A second example of a strategy that was used repeatedly and more extremely each time occurred in OPM, as the agency charged the revolving funds for a proportion of overhead. As the financial situation worsened, the agency increased the expenditures that were distributed to the programs that brought in fee revenue, pushing up its costs and eventually causing or increasing deficits in those funds. Those deficits were used as a reason or excuse for privatizing those functions or contracting them out. Because they had supported other functions in the agency, when training and investigations were spun off, there were secondary consequences in the units that had depended on revenue from these functions. OPM experienced RIF after RIF, keeping the agency in turmoil for much longer than would otherwise have been the case.

The development of a strategy and its reuse at increasingly extreme levels until it caused a reaction also occurred in Congress. Congress tried to substitute fee income for tax revenues where possible, to free up revenue under the spending caps. In the Patent and Trademark Office, this strategy evolved into a fee so large that it not only covered the operating costs of the patent fees but also became a source of revenue for deficit reduction. Ultimately, revenue was diverted from the Patent and Trademark Office to provide this alternative source of revenue under the caps. Inventors were thus required to help pay for the deficits. This strategy was in place long enough to mobilize supporters of the Patent and Trademark Office and inventors, who eliminated the fee entirely and ultimately created a new fee structure. The Patent and Trademark Office was made a performance-based organization, giving it considerable financial autonomy from the Commerce Department. Its income could no longer be spent for other purposes.

Many of the agency strategies might have been successful in preventing severe and irrecoverable damage if they had been done for a short time or if they had not become extreme, but because the crisis lasted so long, the strategies were played out to their limits, sometimes causing new problems.

STRATEGIES

Agency strategies were varied. Some tried to delay the severe staffing reductions and programmatic cuts as long as they could, hoping that the budget situation would improve in later years and that the political environment would become more favorable as they worked to comply with critics' complaints. What they needed was time. Others tried to take the cuts as quickly as they could, to get over them, and get past them, possibly trading depth of cuts for speed of recovery. What they needed was to get back to normal as quickly as they could. Some agencies seemed to aggressively cut themselves, possibly to create some financial resources they could trade for political support in the administration. What these agencies needed most was political support for their continued existence. Most agencies combined elements of different strategies, sometimes trying one first, and then another. HUD, for example, began with a strategy of delay, to protect programs and staffing, pushing for programmatic simplification and reorganization; but when it found itself unable to get such legislation passed, it shifted to what it could control, its staffing levels, reducing staffing in a dramatic effort to gain some political credit.

Delaying tactics included HUD's efforts at budget gaming or scoring of its programs, to achieve savings that could be used for gaining political credit, by changing program structures and timing of revenue flows. HUD also initially used a tactic of "nickel and diming" internally, cutting postage and telephone costs, to gain time to plan cuts and staffing reductions. OPM's practice of putting general expenses in the revolving funds was also a kind of delaying tactic. Quicker cuts occurred in GAO, which traded its agreement to deep cuts for autonomy in deciding how those cuts would occur and an agreement that its funding would not continue to erode. The Commerce Department tried initially, during the 1980s, to protect programs, but found fairly quickly that it could not do so and then developed a kind of triage, sorting out those programs that could not be protected from those that would be defended. In the later round of cuts and threats of departmental dismemberment, the secretary spiritedly defended the whole department. When the threat is to eliminate a whole department, there may be less fear of loss of support by fighting back. A substantial threat was met with compliance; a total threat was met with resistance.

The strategy of aggressive self-cutting to win political support was a dangerous one. If programs were cut too far, reductions would offend customers and alienate political supporters. Loss of senior staff due to early outs made productivity improvements more difficult, and lack of funding for computer modernization further slowed down agencies' ability to provide quality services. HUD discovered that it was unable to perform its tasks with staffing as low as it had promised, especially in light of additional boutique programs and their start-up needs. OPM had a difficult time reinventing itself as an energetic and creative agency after a severe drop in staffing and repeated reductions in force. The USDA acknowledged that it had cut staffing too deeply.

Another class of strategies revolved around trying to answer critics. Many of the agencies in this study were criticized for some perceived failure or set of failures. For example, the Agriculture Department had had performance problems as a result of earlier rounds of budget cuts; the General Accounting Office was criticized for its appearance of partisanship and blindsiding members of Congress with its report results; HUD was criticized for financial scandals, which had probably been exaggerated by a deregulatory atmosphere and shrinking programs and lack of sophisticated staff to run complex programs. The Economic Development Administration (EDA) was criticized for slow response to emergencies and potentially politically motivated responses.

The General Accounting Office responded by making it clearer that it served primarily the committee chairs of whichever party was in the majority, and published a set of decision rules for how projects were decided that made it abundantly clear that partisanship did not enter into the calculus. GAO also made clearer the rules for announcing study results, so that members of Congress would not think that the GAO would embarrass them with publicized results of reports. HUD struggled for improved financial controls and set up its program implementation in a more bottom-up manner, in response to critics who had found the agency too bossy and Washington-oriented. The EDA clarified its criteria for providing assistance and worked hard to demonstrate its speed and effectiveness.

Responses to critics, like agency adjustments to downsizing, had the potential for unintended consequences. For example, the EDA had been supported over the years precisely because it had provided an old-fashioned pork-type distributive program; to the extent that the agency provided aid more neutrally based on need, it might have fewer funds available to distribute for political credit and hence erode its own political base. HUD's decentralization included the hiring and training of new community-based workers, inviting future efforts to cut that visible new program, and opening the agency up to future criticism for inability to control its programs.

A third kind of strategy was to come up with a plan for downsizing that linked budget, staffing, reorganization, and program simplification and substitute this agency plan for less managerially rational cuts dealt out by Congress and the administration. At least in the milder stages of the cuts, the Agriculture Department found careful planning that linked reorganization with budget cuts helpful at managing the cutback process and assured continuing performance of its responsibilities. Over the longer term, however, spending ceilings overwhelmed the plans. Program simplification and attendant cost savings were washed out by agricultural crises and ad hoc rescues. It seemed likely that program simplification as seen in the Freedom to Farm bill would be replaced when it came up for renewal. Agency management was sometimes held hostage to policy disputes between the administration and Congress, as occurred in the Forest Service, where the administration and Congress fought over the goals of preserving forests and using them for industrial purposes. While this conflict was raging, the Forest Service was not allowed to reorganize. A major policy dispute between Congress and the administration over how the census would be carried out resulted in budget freezes for the Census Bureau, ultimately requiring the bureau to drop years of planning and return to an older, more expensive (and error-prone) technique of counting.

Downsizing and money-saving plans can be seen as efforts to trim the herds, as opposed to eating the seed corn, but they were generally ineffective in the face of the duration of financial problems and lack of policy agreement. Events often seemed to overrun plans when agencies made them, and some agencies never seemed to make a plan, but just responded to a rolling set of events.

LEARNING

Despite considerable skepticism about how much learning could take place in the federal government, this book provides ample evidence of learning, both at the macro and the micro levels. Sometimes actors did not learn what one might hope they would learn, but past history was carried by individuals, by organizations, and by networks and brought out for reuse when appropriate. The reason that so many public officials claimed there was no learning in government is because the same issues cropped up again and again. Agency staff had to educate their appointees, congressional staff had to educate their members, and both had to educate the general public. They often found those tasks frustrating. As Gene Brewer, of the Farm Service Administration, observed,

> [Aaron] Wildavsky constantly reminded us that public policy is dynamic and evolutionary. From time to time, a policy's life support system weakens and must be discarded or strengthened if the policy is to survive. This support system includes diverse elements such as the policy's intellectual undergirding, the bonds between the implementing agency and its clientele, overhead political support, etc. . . . To me, one of the most frustrating things about working in a democracy is the necessity of this cycle. We periodically repeat old mistakes in order to convince naysayers and prove the worth of what we do. Much is said about the importance of "learning organizations," but very little has been said about the importance of having a "learning democracy."[10]

For many of the agencies that were most severely cut or threatened, efforts to balance the budget were not just across-the-board cuts in inflated bureaucracies, signifying nothing. Many agencies found their legitimacy questioned and their continued existence doubtful. They struggled not only to improve their financial management, but to prove their worth, to demonstrate their achievements, and to redefine their domain. Some agencies welcomed the Government Performance and Results Act for the opportunity it provided to measure and demonstrate their effectiveness and responsiveness. The agencies in this study also paid much more explicit attention to their clients, surveying them, and disseminating the happy results. This process of defending and defining themselves was traumatic for agency personnel, but it may be necessary in a democracy.

The seventeen-year effort to balance the budget was not only about learning, at the macro and micro levels, but also about teaching. The agencies were taught, again, that they answer to Congress, the president, the inspectors general, and the public, and that they have to demonstrate, not assume, their worth. Sometimes the agencies became so responsive they made themselves more vulnerable, ensuring their present survival but making future survival more questionable. Administrators were taught that the bureaucracy can be cut back too far, that senior civil servants maintain the culture and history of public organizations and their ability to learn, and that neutral competence can be a viable defense when an information agency is being pressured to come up with results favoring one or another policy.

The repetition of old mistakes, precisely what made some skeptics question if there was or could be any learning, was the rather inefficient means of learning, at intervals. One would like to think there is a better way to learn these lessons, but if there is, we have not yet discovered it.

Notes

CHAPTER 1   1981–98: BALANCING THE BUDGET: WHAT HAVE WE LEARNED?

1. Allen Schick, *The Federal Budget: Politics, Policy, and Process* (Washington, D.C.: Brookings Institution, 1995), 2, 3.
2. George Strauss, former OMB staffer, interview by author, 10 January 1996.
3. Al Kliman, phone interview by author, 10 April 1996.
4. Robert Reischauer, former director of the Congressional Budget Office, interview by author, 16 July 1996.
5. "Politicians Perform a Bad Balancing Act with Nation's Budget," *Chicago Tribune,* 7 May 1997.
6. Aaron Wildavsky and Naomi Caiden, *The New Politics of the Budgetary Process.* 3d ed. (New York: Longman, 1997), 288.
7. Joseph Minarik, OMB, interview by author, 25 September 1996.
8. Ibid.
9. Ron Boster, CED, interview by author, 26 September 1996.
10. Martha Phillips, Concord Coalition, interview by author, 22 July 1996.
11. Reischauer interview, 16 July 1996.
12. Dynamic scoring means assuming positive effects of current policies on the economy and, as a result, increasing estimates of revenues. Some feedback effects are routinely included in budget projections; the pressure was to increase estimates of those effects.
13. Barry Anderson, OMB, interview by author, 18 July 1996.
14. Tom Cuny, interview by author, 13 August 1996.
15. Kliman interview, 16 July 1996.
16. Reischauer interview, 16 July 1996.
17. Bill Dauster, interview by author, 7 August 1996.
18. Reischauer interview, 16 July 1996.
19. Ibid.
20. Ibid.
21. Bob Kramer, BLS, e-mail correspondence with author, 29 January 1997.
22. Dauster interview, 7 August 1996.
23. Ibid.
24. Allen Schick, interview by author, 29 October 1996.
25. The caps held as long as the budget was not balanced. After balance was declared and surpluses began to build, the caps were exceeded and evaded.
26. Allen Schick, Brookings Institution, testimony at the hearing on the proposed balanced budget amendment to the Constitution, House Committee on the Budget, U.S. House of Representatives, 5 February 1997.
27. Dauster interview, 7 August 1996.
28. Ibid.
29. Ibid.
30. Jim Blum, CBO, interview by author, 8 August 1996.

31. Ibid.
32. Justine Rodriguez, OMB, interview by author, 4 September 1996.
33. Ibid.
34. Blum interview, 8 August 1996.
35. Boster interview, 26 September 1996.
36. Ibid.
37. Ibid.
38. Irene S. Rubin, *Shrinking the Federal Government* (New York: Longman, 1985).

CHAPTER 2   WHAT HAPPENED AND WHAT WAS LEARNED

1. According to a former staff member of the Senate Budget Committee, Sen. Pete Dominici tried to convince the president that the tax cuts were too large, but President Reagan would not listen. Rick Brandon, interview by author, 9 October 1996.
2. Richard Darman, *Who's in Control? Polar Politics and the Sensible Center* (New York: Simon & Schuster, 1996), 73.
3. Alison Mitchell, "As Deficit Shrinks Parties Rethink Their Core Goals," *New York Times*, 28 December 1997.
4. Sen. Byron Dorgan, *Congressional Record*, Senate, 16 February 1995, S2181.
5. Congressman Martin Sabo, statement on Congressional Budget Cost Estimating, Joint House-Senate Budget Committee Hearing, 10 January 1995.
6. The actual number of people who were forced to leave their agencies because of reduction-in-force procedures was relatively small in 1981 and 1982. The Merit Systems Protection Board estimated that 12,594 people were directly affected by the RIF actions in 1981; that is, they were either separated or forced to retreat to earlier positions, or bumped someone else with less seniority. About half of those were separations (Merit System Protection Board, *Reduction in Force in the Federal Government, 1981: What Happened and Opportunities for Improvement*, Government Printing Office, June 1983). The GAO used the figure of 10,000 as the predicted number of separations through RIF for 1982, which would mean approximately 20,000 people were directly affected by RIF that year (General Accounting Office, *Federal Civilian Personnel: A Workforce Undergoing Change*, 14 October 1982). These numbers underestimate the impact, however, because some agencies had relatively large reductions in force, such as the Census Bureau and the Department of Energy, and even in agencies with small RIFs, no one knew whose job would be affected, so many more people feared the RIFs than were actually affected by them. For more on the effects of RIFs on individual agencies in 1981 and 1982, see Irene Rubin, *Shrinking the Federal Government* (New York: Longman, 1986).
7. A Merit System Protection Board study found that 32 percent of surveyed personnel in RIF-affected agencies did not think their agencies would carry out a RIF in good faith. About the same proportion were confident the agency would conduct a RIF in good faith. The others did not know or had no strong opinion (Merit System Protection Board, *Reduction in Force*).
8. Ibid.
9. Merit System Protection Board, *Reduction in Force,* and General Accounting Office, *Reductions in Force Can Sometimes Be More Costly Than Attrition and Furloughs* (Washington, D.C.: Government Printing Office, 1985).
10. Rep. Steny Hoyer, Reductions in Force at the Census Bureau, joint hearings, Subcommittee on Human Resources and the Subcommittee on Census and Population of the Committee on Post Office and Civil Service, House of Representatives, 97th Congress, 2d session, 10 June 1982.
11. General Accounting Office, *Reductions in Force;* General Accounting Office, *Workforce Reductions: Downsizing Strategies Used in Federal Organizations* (Washington, D.C.: Government Printing Office, 1995); General Accounting Office, *Federal Downsizing: The Costs and*

Savings of Buyouts Versus Reductions in Force (Washington, D.C.: Government Printing Office, 1996); U.S. Office of Personnel Management, *Downsizing in the Federal Government*. Karen Bandera and Sherman Chin. Office of Merit Systems Oversight and Effectiveness (Washington, D.C.: Government Printing Office, 1998).

12. Rick Brandon, Democratic Chief of Staff for the Senate Budget Committee, 1975–1985, interview by author, 9 October 1996.
13. Interview by author, name withheld by request, 11 July 1996.
14. PL 99-177.
15. Brandon interview, 9 October 1996.
16. Interview by author, name withheld by request, 9 October 1996.
17. Richard Kogan, Center for Budget and Policy Priorities, interview by author, 11 July 1996.
18. The sequestrations were across the board only for programs that were not exempted. But major entitlements were exempted and Medicare had special sequester rules.
19. Under the BEA, spending was divided into two categories, one for discretionary accounts, one for mandatory spending. Discretionary spending included the routine annual appropriations, while mandatory spending included the entitlements and debt service.
20. Longtime staffer on the Hill, interview by author, name withheld by request, 17 October 1996.
21. Ibid. This was less true several years later, as the budget came into balance. Rather than lift the caps, Congress and the president used the emergency provisions to add some spending that did not require offsets. It was true, however, as long as reducing the deficit was perceived as an urgent problem.
22. U.S. Budget, 1991, 229.
23. The Credit Reform part of the BEA in 1990 did not actually include insurance, though the inclusion of insurance remains on the policy agenda a decade later.
24. Justine Rodriguez, OMB, interview by author, 4 September 1996.
25. Office of Management and Budget, *Report of the President's Commission on Budget Concepts* (Washington, D.C.: Government Printing Office, 1967), 47.
26. Thomas Cuny. 1991. "Federal Credit Reform." *Public Budgeting and Finance* 11 (2 September): 23.
27. Ibid., 26.
28. Congressional Budget Office, *Credit Reform: Comparable Costs for Cash and Credit* (Washington, D.C.: Government Printing Office, 1989).
29. Tom Cuny, interview by author, 13 August 1996.
30. Richard Darman, *Who's in Control? Polar Politics and the Sensible Center* (New York: Simon & Schuster, 1996), 235.
31. Congressional Budget Office, *Credit Reform*, preface.
32. Ibid., 22.
33. Roy Meyers, "Federal Budgeting and Finance: The Future Is Now." *Public Budgeting and Finance* 12, 2 (1992): 8.
34. E-mail correspondence with author, name withheld by request, 1 March 1998.
35. The expected costs of loan guarantees also reflects the performance of the economy; when the economy is booming there are likely to be fewer loan defaults.
36. Marvin Phaup, "Credit Reform, Negative Subsidies, and the FHA." *Public Budgeting and Finance* 16, 1 (1996): 23–36.
37. Phil Joyce, former CBO staffer, interview by author, 9 July 1996.
38. Clay Chandler, "Budget Bonus Presents Clinton with Choices; Hill Analysts' New Projections May Allow Softer Spending Cuts, Bigger Tax Breaks, Easier Route to Zero Deficit," *Washington Post*, 25 December 1996, D1.
39. Cuny interview, 13 August 1996.
40. PoliticsNow Web site, run by the *Washington Post*, 11 January 1997.
41. Herb Percil, former budget director at HUD, interview by author, 31 July 1996.
42. Phil Joyce, interview by author, 9 July 1996.
43. Peter Passell, "The Tax Credit for Research and Development: Free Lunch," *New York Times*, 5 February 1998.
44. Roy Meyers, former CBO staffer, interview by author, 10 July 1996.

45. Joyce interview, 9 July 1996.
46. Ibid.
47. Susan Tanaka, former OMB staffer, interview by author, 26 July 1996.
48. Ibid.
49. Joyce interview, 9 July 1996.
50. Ibid.
51. Tanaka interview, 26 July 1996.
52. Sen. Robert Byrd, *Congressional Record,* Senate, 5 February 1997, S994.
53. Clay Chandler, "Experts See No Long-Term Fix," *Washington Post,* 3 May 1997.
54. Sen. Edward M. Kennedy, "Seven Questions About the Budget Agreement," http://www.ombwatch.org/ombwatch.html, 7 May 1997.
55. Ibid.
56. Ibid.
57. Jim Blum, interview by author, 8 August 1996.
58. Al Kliman, former budget director, HUD, interview by author, 1 July 1996.
59. Richard Moose, interview by author, 2 October 1996.
60. Kliman interview, 1 July 1996.
61. Interviewed by author, name withheld by request.
62. Dona Wolf, former OPM official, interview by author, 12 December 1996.
63. Bryant Benton, Bureau of the Census, interview by author, 6 November 1996.

CHAPTER 3   INFORMATION AGENCIES: BUREAU OF LABOR STATISTICS AND BUREAU OF THE CENSUS

1. Sen. Daniel Patrick Moynihan, *Congressional Record,* Senate, 9 November 1995, S16932–3.
2. Janet Norwood, interview by author, 26 September 1996.
3. Dan Lacey, interview by author, 25 July 1996.
4. Joseph P. Goldberg and William T. Moye, *The First Hundred Years of the Bureau of Labor Statistics* (Washington, D.C.: Government Printing Office, 1985).
5. Lacey interview, 25 July 1996.
6. Norwood interview, 26 September 1996.
7. Ibid.
8. Katharine Abraham, testimony before the House of Representatives, Committee on the Budget, Washington, D.C., 12 March 1997.
9. Norwood interview, 26 September 1996.
10. Lacey interview, 25 July 1996.
11. Norwood interview, 26 September 1996.
12. Lacey interview, 25 July 1996.
13. Most federal agencies' staff are organized into grade levels, differentiated by amount of responsibility, experience, and expertise, as well as salary. Part of the NPR reform proposals was to reduce the number of people at higher grade levels. Pressures to control the numbers of higher-graded positions had occurred before, however.
14. Norwood interview, 26 September 1996.
15. Ibid.
16. Ibid.
17. Bob Kramer, BLS, e-mail correspondence with author, 29 January 1997.
18. Rep. Newt Gingrich, *Congressional Record,* Senate, 18 January 1995, S1125.
19. Sen. Ted Kennedy, *Congressional Record,* Senate, 4 January 1996, S47.
20. Katharine G. Abraham, "Statistics in the Spotlight: Improving the Consumer Price Index: Statement," Bureau of Labor Statistics, paper presented at meeting of the American Statistical Association, Chicago, 6 August 1996.
21. Louis Uchitelle, "Survey Supports the Theory That Inflation Is Overstated," *New York Times,* 13 February 1997.

22. Kennedy, *Congressional Record*, S47.
23. Katharine Abraham, testimony before the Senate Finance Committee, 11 February 1997.
24. Clay Chandler, "CPI Proposal Gets Mixed Reaction," *Washington Post*, 26 February 1997, C13.
25. Eric Pianin, "Lott Urged to Tone Down Call for Inflation Panel," *Washington Post*, 7 March 1997, A11.
26. David Espo, "Cost of Living Adjustment Eyed," *Washington Post*, 28 February 1997; on-line at http://www.washingtonpost.com.
27. John M. Berry, "Inflation Index Puts Abraham in Thick of Budget Battle," *Washington Post*, 9 March 1997, H1.
28. Alan Greenspan, testimony before the Committee on the Budget, U.S. House of Representatives, 4 March 1997.
29. Clay Chandler and Eric Pianin, "President Won't Back CPI Panel; GOP Says Decision Threatens Budget Deal," *Washington Post*, 13 March 1997, A1.
30. Posted on the BLS Web site at http://stats.bls.gov/cpigmo2.htm.
31. John M. Berry, "Inflation Index Puts Abraham in Thick of Budget Battle," *Washington Post*, 9 March 1997, H1.
32. Bryant Benton, interview by author, 6 November 1996.
33. From notes taken at an advisory commission meeting by a bureau staff member, posted on the Census Bureau's Web site.
34. See, for example, House Report 104-821.
35. Ibid.
36. Departments of Commerce, Justice, and State, the Judiciary, and Related Agencies appropriations for 1996, hearings before a subcommittee of the Committee on Appropriations, House of Representatives, 104th Congress, 1st session, 16 March 1995, 329.
37. Ibid.
38. House Report 104-821.
39. Committee on Government Reform and Oversight, Subcommittee on Government Management, Information, and Technology, on H.R. 1756, the Department of Commerce Dismantling Act, statement of Ronald H. Brown, Secretary of Commerce, 6 September 1995.
40. Departments of Commerce, Justice, and State, hearings before a subcommittee of the Committee on Appropriations, 911.
41. "Weary of Political Sniping, Census Bureau Chief Quits," *New York Times*, 13 January 1998.
42. D'Vera Cohn, "GOP, Democrats Spar Over Census Funding, Sampling Issues, *Washington Post*, 9 July 1998, A17.
43. Ibid.
44. Mark Wegner, "Dems: GOP Bills 'Micromanage' Census," *Government Executive*, 18 March 1999; http://www.govexec.com/dailyfed/0399/03199t3.htm.
45. Ibid.
46. Census Monitoring Board, "The Myth: Statistical Adjustment Will Correct Severe Undercounts in Predominantly Minority Neighborhoods," 30 September 1999; http://207.54.174.87/reports.asp?FormMode=Summary&ID=4475671649.
47. *Congressional Record*, Opposition to Frameworks Language in Conference Report to H.R. 2670, Senate, 26 October 1999, S13158.
48. PL 106-113.
49. Benton interview, 6 November 1996.
50. Ibid.
51. Martha Riche, hearing of the Commerce, Justice, State, and Judiciary Subcommittee of the House Appropriations Committee, on FY 1997 appropriations, 2 May 1996, 878.
52. Benton interview, 6 November 1996.
53. Hearing of the Commerce, Justice, State, and Judiciary Subcommittee of the House Appropriations Committee, on FY 1998 appropriations for Census and the Statistical Agencies, 10 April 1997.
54. Ibid.
55. Benton interview, 6 November 1996.

CHAPTER 4 BUDGET OFFICES

1. Philip Joyce, "Congressional Budget Reform: The Unanticipated Consequences for Federal Policy Making," *Public Administration Review* 56, 4 (1996): 317–26.
2. Phil Joyce, interview by author, 9 July 1996.
3. Ibid.
4. Date of House amendment, 10 July 1996.
5. Eric Pianin, "Gingrich Presses for Another Cut in the Top Capital Gains Tax Rate: Action Would 'Supercharge' the Economy, Speaker Predicts," *Washington Post,* 25 June 1998, A4.
6. Ibid.
7. Jim Blum, interview by author, 8 August 1996.
8. June O'Neill, letter to Senate Budget Committee chair, Pete Dominici, printed in the *Congressional Record,* 18 October 1995.
9. Sen. Dale Bumpers, *Congressional Record,* 18 December 1995.
10. Sen. Byron Dorgan, *Congressional Record,* Senate, 14 February 1995, S2595–2596.
11. Excerpts from author's field notes, lunch in the GAO cafeteria, 20 November 1996.
12. Ken Bentsen, *Congressional Record,* CBO's Independence Threatened by Partisan Politics, House of Representatives, 16 June 1998.
13. David Baumann, "Congress Seeks More Oversight of Budget Office," *Government Executive,* 12 August 1998; http://www.govexec.com/archive.
14. Robert Pear, "Ex-Aide to Reagan Will Head Budget Office," *New York Times,* 14 January 1999.
15. Ibid.
16. Stan Collender, "Budget Battles: CBO in the Crippen Era," *Government Executive,* 15 December 1999; http://www.govexec.com/archive.
17. Blum interview, 8 August 1996.
18. Hugh Heclo, "OMB and the Presidency: The Problem of 'Neutral Competence,'" *Public Interest* 38 (1975): 80–98.
19. Tom Cuny, interview by author, 13 August 1996.
20. Joseph Minarik, interview by author, 25 September 1996.
21. Richard Kogan, interview by author, 11 July 1996.
22. Allen Schick, *The Federal Budget: Politics, Policy, and Process* (Washington, D.C.: Brookings Institution, 1995), 22–24.
23. Ron Boster, interview by author, 26 September 1996.
24. Rick Hale, interview by author, 1996.
25. Cuny interview, 13 August 1996.
26. Rusty Moran, OMB, interview by author, 13 September 1996.
27. "Who Pays for a Balanced Budget?" *Washington Post,* 13 December 1996, A22.
28. Clay Chandler, "Budget Bonus Presents Clinton with Choices: Hill Analysts' New Projections May Allow Softer Spending Cuts, Bigger Tax Breaks, Easier Route to Zero Deficit," *Washington Post,* 25 December 1996, D1.
29. John F. Harris, "As Clinton's Deal Maker, Bowles Means Business," *Washington Post,* 12 May 1997, A1.
30. Minarik interview, 25 September 1996.
31. Interview by author, name withheld by request, 14 October 1996.
32. Shelley Tomkin, *Inside OMB* (New York: M. E. Sharpe, 1998), 63, 106.
33. Ibid., 153.
34. Ibid., 104–5.
35. Ibid., 104.
36. Ibid., 105.
37. Ibid.
38. Franklin Raines, testimony before the Subcommittee on Treasury, Postal Service, and General Government, Committee on Appropriations, U.S. House of Representatives, 11 March 1997; http://www.whitehouse.gov/WH/EOP/OMB/Testimony/19970311-22242.html.
39. Cuny interview, 13 August 1996.

40. Rodriguez interview, 4 September 1996.
41. Interview by author, name withheld by request, 14 October 1996.
42. Moran interview, 13 September 1996.
43. Tomkin, *Inside OMB,* 185.
44. Ibid.
45. General Accounting Office, "Changes Resulting from OMB2000 Reorganization" (Washington, D.C.: Government Printing Office, 1995), 29 December, hearings before the Government Reform and Oversight Subcommittee on Management Information and Technology on splitting OMB into two sections, 4 February 1999.
46. Ibid.
47. Ibid.

CHAPTER 5   GENERAL ACCOUNTING OFFICE

1. Dexter Peach, assistant comptroller general for Planning and Reporting, interview by author, 26 August 1996.
2. Harry Reid, *Congressional Record,* Legislative Branch Appropriations Act, 23 July 1993, S9341.
3. The National Academy of Public Administration, *The Roles, Mission, and Operation of the U.S. General Accounting Office* (Washington, D.C.: Government Printing Office, 1994).
4. Phil Joyce, interview by author, 9 July 1996.
5. Joan Dodaro, ACG for Administration, interview by author, 29 July 1996.
6. See, for example, GAO, Training Institute Participant Manual, The New Job Process, 7 February 1996, Release 3.
7. David Walker, comptroller general GAO, testimony before the House Appropriations Subcommittee on Legislative Appropriations, 29 February 2000.
8. Comptroller General's 1996 Annual Report (Washington D.C.: Government Printing Office, 1997), 71.
9. Comptroller General's 1995 Annual Report (Washington D.C.: Government Printing Office, 1996), 60–61.
10. GAO notes that letters and correspondence are now posted on the agency's Web site and are not private. Briefings, however, still remain out of the public view.
11. Dodaro interview, 29 July 1996.
12. Comptroller General's 1995 Annual Report, 59.
13. Dodaro interview, 29 July 1996.
14. "GAO Realignment: Major Elements," memo, 3 February 2000.
15. GAO Management News, "The New GAO: CG Outlines New Headquarters Structure, Names New Leadership Team," vol. 27, no. 31 (2 May 2000). This article was posted on the GAO Intranet and made available by a staff member.
16. From the transcript of the comptroller general's video on internal reorganization, 28 April 2000.
17. Dodaro interview, 15 August 1996.
18. GAO, "GAO's Congressional Protocols," January 2000.
19. David Walker, comptroller general, testimony before the Subcommittee on Government Management, Information and Technology, Committee on Government Reform, House of Representatives, 18 July 2000, 44.
20. Dodaro interview, 15 August 1996.
21. Ibid.
22. Data provided by GAO, "Historical Trends of Basic Legislative Responsibility Work vs. Congressional Work," 4 June 1996; 1997 and 1999 annual reports; and David Walker, GAO, testimony before the Subcommittee on Government Management, Information and Technology, Committee on Government Reform, House of Representatives, 18 July 2000.
23. David Walker, FY 2000 budget request testimony before the House Appropriations Committee, 29 February 2000.

24. Dodaro interview, 29 July 1996.
25. Ibid.
26. Interview by author, name withheld by request.
27. Interview by author, name withheld by request.
28. Dexter Peach, interview by author, 26 August 1996.
29. Walker testimony, 18 July 2000, 16.
30. Susan Irving, interview by author, 29 July 1996.
31. Comptroller General's 1995 Annual Report, 2.
32. Comptroller General's 1997 Annual Report.
33. Comptroller General David Walker's testimony, House Appropriations Subcommittee on the Legislative Branch, 29 February 2000.
34. Peach interview, 26 August 1996.

CHAPTER 6 DEPARTMENT OF AGRICULTURE

1. Stephen B. Dewhurst, "Downsizing: A View from Inside," *Public Budgeting and Finance* 16, 1 (1996): 49–59.
2. U.S. Budget, FY 2001, Historical Tables, Table 17.3, Total Executive Branch Civilian Full-Time Equivalent Employees, 1981–2001.
3. Ibid.
4. Ibid.
5. USDA, FY 1999 budget request.
6. Effects of Balanced Budget and Emergency Deficit Control Act of 1985 on U.S. Department of Agriculture Programs, hearings before the Committee on Agriculture, House of Representatives, 99th Congress, 2d session, 29 January 1986, 156.
7. Dewhurst, "Downsizing," 51.
8. Douglas Ihrke, "Job Burnout in an Evolving Federal Agency: A Model Based on Environmental Change and Performance Strategies." Ph.D. diss. (Dekalb, Ill.: Northern Illinois University, 1996), 53–64 and appendix.
9. Dewhurst, "Downsizing," 51.
10. General Accounting Office, *U.S. Department of Agriculture: Farm Agencies' Field Structure Needs Major Overhaul.* RCED-91-9 (Washington, D.C.: Government Printing Office, 1991a).
11. *U.S. Farm Policy: Proposals for Budget Savings,* hearing before the Task Force on Urgent Fiscal Issues, of the Committee on the Budget, House of Representatives, 101st Congress, 2d session, 28 June 1990, 14.
12. Charles Schumer, *U.S. Farm Policy,* 25.
13. Ibid., 26.
14. Ibid., 49–50.
15. General Accounting Office, *U.S. Department of Agriculture: Interim Report on Ways to Enhance Management.* RCED-90-19 (Washington, D.C.: Government Printing Office, 1989).
16. General Accounting Office, *U.S. Department of Agriculture: Strengthening Management Systems to Support Secretarial Goals.* RCED-91-49 (Washington, D.C.: Government Printing Office, 1991b).
17. General Accounting Office, *Agricultural Trade, Improvements Needed in Management of Targeted Export Assistance Program.* Nsiad-90-225 (Washington, D.C.: Government Printing Office, 1990).
18. Allan Mendelowitz, GAO, statement to Budget Committee Task Force, U.S. Farm Programs, Proposals for Budget Savings, 28 June 1990, 71–72.
19. Rep. Dan Glickman, *Congressional Record,* extension of remarks, 11 March 1993, S602.
20. Stephen Dewhurst, testimony before the Subcommittee on Department Operations, Nutrition, and Foreign Agriculture, Committee on Agriculture, House of Representatives, 14 May 1997, 19.
21. Sen. John McCain, *Congressional Record,* on FY 1998 Agriculture Appropriations Bill, 23 July 1997, S7931.
22. Stephen Dewhurst, budget director, USDA, interview by author, 24 July 1996.

23. Sen. Patrick Leahy, *Congressional Record*, Interior Appropriations Bill, FY 1995, Forest Service reorganization, 26 July 1994, S9717–9718.
24. Sen. Robert Byrd, *Congressional Record*, Interior Appropriations Bill, FY 1995, Forest Service reorganization, 26 July 1994, S9717–9718.
25. Sen. Don Nickles, *Congressional Record*, Interior Appropriations Bill, FY 1995, Forest Service reorganization, 26 July 1994, S9717–9718.
26. Sen. Richard Lugar, *Congressional Record*, Interior Appropriations Bill, FY 1995, Forest Service reorganization, 26 July 1994, S9717.
27. Dewhurst interview, 24 July 1996.
28. Rep. Bob Goodlatte, "Forest Service's Fiscal Year 2000 Budget," hearing before the House Agriculture Subcommittee on Department Operations, Oversight, Nutrition, and Forestry, 11 March 1999.
29. General Accounting Office, *Farm Programs: Administrative Requirements Reduced and Further Program Delivery Changes Possible*. Letter rept. (Washington, D.C.: Government Printing Office, 1998a).
30. General Accounting Office, *USDA Service Center IT Modernization* (Washington, D.C.: Government Printing Office, 1998b).
31. Keith Kelly, USDA, Farm Service Agency, statement before the Subcommittee on National Economic Growth, Natural Resources, and Regulatory Affairs, Committee on Government Reform, U.S. House of Representatives, 15 April 1999.
32. Joshua Dean. 1999. "USDA Gets by Y2K, Money Problems with Stopgap Measure," *Government Executive*, 7 December.
33. Richard Rominger, Deputy Secretary, statement before the Senate Committee on Agriculture, Nutrition, and Forestry, 29 July 1998.
34. Bryan Friel, "Downsized USDA Forced to Call in Temps," *Government Executive*, 26 (1999).
35. Kelley Lunney, "House Directs USDA to Beef up Online Services," *Government Executive*, 12 (2000).
36. Jerry Hagstrom, "Gathering Storm," *Government Executive* (1998); General Accounting Office, *USDA Reorganization: Progress Mixed in Modernizing the Delivery of Services*. GAO/RCED-00-43 (Washington, D.C.: Government Printing Office, 2000).
37. Hagstrom, "Gathering Storm."
38. Rep. Charles Stenholm, Information Technology Procurement Practices, hearing, House Committee on Agriculture, Subcommittee on Departmental Operations, Nutrition, and Foreign Agriculture, 14 May 1997, 35.
39. Gene Brewer, e-mail correspondence with author, fall 1998.
40. Ibid.
41. General Accounting Office, *USDA Reorganization*.
42. Dewhurst interview, 24 July 1996.
43. Ibid.
44. General Accounting Office, *USDA Reorganization*.
45. Roger C. Viadero, Inspector General, Office of Inspector General, U.S. Department of Agriculture, statement before the House Appropriations Subcommittee on Agriculture, Rural Development, Food and Drug Administration, and Related Agencies, 17 February 2000.
46. Dewhurst interview, 24 July 1996.
47. General Accounting Office, *Farm Programs: Impact of the 1996 Farm Act on County Office Workload*. GAO/RCED-97-214 (Washington, D.C.: Government Printing Office, 1997a).
48. General Accounting Office, *Forest Service Decision Making: A Framework for Improving Performance*. GAO/RCED-97-71 (Washington, D.C.: Government Printing Office, 1997c).
49. Anne Reed, Information Technology Procurement Practices, hearing, House Committee on Agriculture, Subcommittee on Departmental Operations, Nutrition, and Foreign Agriculture, 14 May 1997.
50. General Accounting Office, *Federal Downsizing: Buyouts at the Farm Service Agency*. GAO/GGD-97-133 (Washington, D.C.: Government Printing Office, 1997b).

51. Kenneth Ackerman, administrator for the Risk Management Agency, United States Department of Agriculture, statement before the Subcommittee on Risk Management and Specialty Crops, U.S. House of Representatives, 10 March 1999.
52. General Accounting Office, *USDA Reorganization.*

CHAPTER 7   DEPARTMENT OF COMMERCE

1. GAO, "Statistical Agencies: Consolidation and Quality Issues," testimony, 9 April 1997, GAO/T-GGD-97-78.
2. Ibid.
3. Historical Tables of the U.S. Budget, 2001; outlays for 2000 are estimates.
4. Mark Brown, budget director, interview by author, 17 July 1996.
5. Paul Blustein, "Cloud Over Commerce: Politics May Have Tainted Choices, Policy," *Washington Post,* 22 December 1996.
6. Raymond G. Kammer Jr., acting chief financial officer and assistant secretary for administration, U.S. Department of Commerce, prepared statement before the Senate Committee on Commerce, Science, and Transportation, 14 May 1997. Provided on the Internet by Federal Information Systems Corporation, Federal News Service.
7. Ron Brown, secretary of commerce, statement to Committee on Government Reform and Oversight, Subcommittee on Government Management, Information, and Technology, on H.R. 1756, the Department of Commerce Dismantling Act, 6 September 1995.
8. Alan Balutis, chief information officer, Department of Commerce, interview by author, 25 October 1996.
9. Brown, interview by author, 17 July 1996.
10. Brown statement, 6 September 1995.
11. Alan Balutis, interview by author, 25 October 1996.
12. Andy Moxam, deputy CFO and chief administrative officer, NOAA, interview by author, 5 November 1996.
13. Kammer statement, 14 May 1997.
14. U.S. Department of Commerce, Office of the Secretary, *From Lighthouses to Laser Beams; A History of the U.S. Department of Commerce* (Washington, D.C.: Government Printing Office, 1988).
15. Ibid., 25, 41.
16. Balutis interview, 17 July 1996.
17. Stuart Eizenstat, hearings, House Appropriations Subcommittee on Commerce, Justice, State, FY 1998, Internet version, 14 March 1997.
18. Phillip Singerman, testimony before the Appropriations Subcommittee on Commerce, Justice, and State, 16 April 1997.
19. Balutis interview, 25 October 1996.
20. Frank DeGeorge, inspector general, U.S. Department of Commerce, prepared statement before the Senate Commerce, Science, and Transportation Committee, 14 May 1997.
21. Agency Reports, Commerce, National Performance Review, Internet version, at www.npr.gov.
22. Wilbur Hawkins, interview by author, 19 November 1996.
23. Ibid.
24. Ibid.
25. Ibid.
26. Ibid.
27. Department of Commerce, accompanying report of the National Performance Review, Office of the Vice President, September 1993, 5. On the Internet, http://www.npr.gov. . ./agnrpt93/doc.html.
28. Hawkins interview, 19 November 1996.
29. Ibid.

30. Senate Report to accompany S2364, the 1998 reauthorization of the EDA programs, 105th Congress, 2d session, 14 September 1998.
31. Howard Coble, Extension of Remarks, *Congressional Record,* 23 April 1998, E671.
32. Press Release: PTO 95-29, PTO Responds to Senate Appropriations Budget Allocations for Fiscal Year 1996.
33. Howard Coble, Extension of Remarks, *Congressional Record,* 11 February 1997, E201.
34. "Reducing Pendency and Maintaining Quality Top List of PTO Millennium Budget Priorities," *The PTO Pulse,* February 1999.
35. Moxam interview, 6 November 1996.
36. Ibid.
37. Ibid.
38. Ibid.
39. Ibid.
40. Ibid.
41. Ibid.
42. Dr. D. James Baker, undersecretary for Oceans and Atmosphere and administrator of National Oceanic and Atmospheric Administration, U.S. Department of Commerce, before the Subcommittee on Science, Technology, and Space, Senate Committee on Commerce, Science, and Transportation, 15 May 1997.
43. Ibid.
44. Ibid.
45. Kammer statement, 14 May 1997.
46. Dr. D. James Baker, undersecretary for Oceans and Atmosphere, National Oceanic and Atmospheric Administration, U.S. Department of Commerce, testimony before the Subcommittee on Commerce, Justice, State, the Judiciary, and Related Agencies, Committee on Appropriations, U.S. House of Representatives, 19 March 1998.
47. Joel C. Willemssen, director, Civil Agencies Information Systems, Accounting and Information Management Division, and L. Nye Stevens, director, Federal Management and Workforce Issues, General Government Division, U.S. General Accounting Office, prepared statement before the House Committee on Science, Subcommittee on Energy and Environment, 24 February 1999.
48. Moxam interview, 6 November 1996.
49. Baker testimony, 15 May 1997.
50. Moxam interview, 6 November 1996.
51. National Performance Review, Streamlining and Reinvention, FY 1999 Budget Request of the National Oceanic and Atmospheric Administration, on-line at http://www.noaa.gov.
52. William Stelle Jr., regional administrator, National Marine Fisheries Service, Northwest Region, testimony before the Committee on Resources, U.S. House of Representatives, Boise, Idaho, 3 September 1998.

CHAPTER 8 DEPARTMENT OF HOUSING AND URBAN DEVELOPMENT

1. Susan Gaffney, HUD inspector general, statement before the Subcommittee on VA, HUD, and Independent Agencies, Committee on Appropriations, U.S. House of Representatives, 27 March 1996; Audit-related Memorandum Number 98-HQ-179-0801, for Dwight P. Robinson, deputy secretary, from Kathryn M. Kuhl-Inclan, assistant inspector general for Audit, Subject, Interim Review of HUD 2020 Management Reform Plan, 25 November 1997.
2. Irene S. Rubin, *Shrinking the Federal Government* (New York: Longman, 1985), 105–6.
3. Al Kliman, interview by author, 1 July 1996.
4. Rubin, *Shrinking the Federal Government,* 112–13.

5. Irving Welfeld, *HUD Scandals: Howling Headlines and Silent Fiascoes* (New Brunswick, N.J.: Transaction Press, 1992).

6. House Government Operations report on the Abuses and Mismanagement at HUD, 1990, quoted in Welfeld, *HUD Scandals,* 116.

7. Welfeld, *HUD Scandals,* 47.

8. Ibid.

9. National Academy of Public Administration, *Renewing HUD* (Washington, D.C.: National Academy of Public Administration, 1994).

10. Ibid., 23, 29–30.

11. Ibid., 34–35.

12. Ibid., 33.

13. Gaffney statement, 27 March 1996.

14. Henry G. Cisneros, testimony before the Senate Banking, Housing, and Urban Affairs Subcommittees on Housing Opportunity and Community Development and HUD Oversight and Structure, 29 March 1995.

15. Andrew Cuomo, statement before the House Appropriations Committee, VA, HUD, and Independent Agencies, FY 1999 Appropriations Hearing, 26 March 1998.

16. Ibid.

17. Ibid.

18. Ibid.

19. Ibid.

20. Rick Hale, General Accounting Office, interview by author, 15 October 1996.

21. Ibid.

22. Kliman interview, 16 July 1996.

23. Ibid.

24. Ibid.

25. Hale interview, 15 October 1996.

26. Helen Dunlap, "Point of View," National Low Income Housing Coalition Newsletter, vol. 3, 12 (27 March 1998).

27. "Understanding the Project-based Section 8 Renewal and Restructuring ('Mark to Market') Program," National Low Income Housing Coalition, http://www.nlhic.org/marktomarket/whydoes.htm.

28. Judy England-Joseph, GAO, interview by author, 24 September 1996.

29. Ibid.

30. Interview by author, name withheld by request.

31. Interview by author with HUD employee, name withheld by request, 25 September 1996.

32. *Renewing HUD,* 143.

33. Judy England-Joseph, testimony before the Senate Banking, Housing, and Urban Affairs Committee, Subcommittee on Housing and Opportunity and Community Development, hearing on issues relating to the implementation of the Department of Housing and Urban Development's "HUD 2020" Management Reform Plan, 7 May 1998.

34. Ibid.

35. Ibid.

36. HUD had to absorb mandated salary increases without additional funds and separation leave pay, a cost of downsizing, and pay for additional training, all from the salaries and expenses budgets.

37. Kliman interview, 16 July 1996.

38. Interview by author with HUD official, name withheld by request.

39. England-Joseph interview, 24 September 1996.

40. Sen. John McCain, talking points on FY 1998 VA, HUD Appropriations Bill, 22 July 1997.

41. Mark Gordon, interview by author, 14 November 1996.

42. England-Joseph interview, 24 September 1996.

43. Interview by author with HUD official, name withheld by request, 25 September 1996.

44. Ibid.

45. National Low Income Housing Coalition,
http://www.nlhic.org/marktomarket/whydoes.htm.
46. England-Joseph interview, 24 September 1996.
47. Passback occurs after an agency has prepared its budget proposal and it has been examined
by the Office of Management and Budget. OMB may reduce some items or alter others and
then pass back the request in altered form. The agencies may then try to negotiate with
OMB about the most important items of difference.
48. National Low Income Housing Coalition, Memo to Members #39: Weekly Housing
Update, 20 December 1996.
49. Gordon interview, 14 November 1996.

CHAPTER 9 OFFICE OF PERSONNEL MANAGEMENT

1. Dona Wolf, interview by author, 28 August 1996.
2. Curtis Smith, interview by author, 29 August 1996.
3. CFO Annual Report, FY 1992, OPM.
4. Merit Systems Protection Board (MSPB), *U.S. Office of Personnel Management and the Merit
System: A Retrospective Assessment* (Washington, D.C.: Government Printing Office, 1989).
5. U.S. Office of Personnel Management, *Deregulation and Delegation of Human Resources
Management Authority in the Federal Government* (Washington, D.C.: Government Printing
Office, 1998).
6. Janice R. LaChance, statement before the House Appropriations Subcommittee on Treasury,
Postal Service, and General Government, FY 1999 Appropriations Hearings, 105th Congress,
2nd session, 13 March 1998.
7. National Performance Review, *Office of Personnel Management: Accompanying Report of the
NPR* (Washington, D.C.: Government Printing Office, 1993).
8. General Accounting Office, *Managing Human Resources: Greater Leadership Needed to
Address Critical Challenges.* GAO/GGD-90-19 (Washington, D.C.: Government Printing
Office, 1989).
9. Larry Lane and Gary Marshall, "Reinventing OPM: Adventures, Issues and Implications,"
paper presented at the American Society for Public Administration, San Antonio, 3 July,
1995.
10. Jim King, "The Privatization of OPM's Investigative Services," House Committee on
Government Reform and Oversight, Subcommittee on Civil Service, 17 October 1996;
posted on OPM's Web site in testimony archives:
http://www.opm.gov/news/testify/1996/101796.htm.
11. Gary Marshall, former OPM employee, telephone interview by author, 19 November 1996.
12. MSPB, *Office of Personnel Management*, 23.
13. Irene S. Rubin, *Shrinking the Federal Government* (New York: Longman, 1985), 170–71.
14. Ibid., 172.
15. Ibid., 177.
16. MSPB, *Office of Personnel Management*, 4.
17. Ibid., 5.
18. Terry Newell. 1992. "Our Endangered Human Resources Investment," *Government Executive*
24, 1 (January): 42–43.
19. Scott Fosler, letter to James King, OPM director, 16 September 1994.
20. National Performance Review, *Office of Personnel Management.*
21. OPM Monthly Report of Federal Civilian Employment, 22 May 1997.
22. FTE for 1981 is from GAO; data for 1993 to 1999 is from the OPM 1999 and 2000 budget
requests.
23. Smith interview, 29 August 1996.
24. OPM Financial Statement, FY 1993, 35–36.

25. Office of the Inspector General, OPM, *Evaluation Report: Systemic Issues Contributing to the Financial Difficulties of the OPM Revolving Fund* (Washington, D.C.: Government Printing Office, 1994).
26. General Accounting Office, *OPM Revolving Fund: OPM Sets New Tuition Pricing Policy.* GAO/GGD-94-120 (Washington, D.C.: Government Printing Office, 1994).
27. Office of the Inspector General, *Evaluation Report,* 15.
28. Ibid., 44.
29. CFO Annual Report, 1992, OPM, 45.
30. Wolf interview, 28 August 1996.
31. OPM, "Federal Employee Direct Corporate Ownership Opportunity Plan (Fed Co-op): An Alternative Contracting-Out Approach, July 1986.
32. Financial Statements, U.S. Office of Personnel Management, 1993, 33.
33. Timothy P. Bowling, associate director, Federal Human Resource Management Issues, General Government Division, GAO testimony before the Committee on Government Reform and Oversight, House of Representatives Subcommittee on Civil Service, Privatizing OPM Investigations, 15 June 1995.
34. Wolf interview, 28 August 1996.
35. Smith interview, 29 August 1996.
36. Gary Marshall, e-mail interview by author, 10 November 1996.
37. Smith interview, 29 August 1996.
38. Marshall e-mail interview, 10 November 1996.
39. Smith interview, 29 August 1996.
40. Wolf interview, 28 August 1996.

CHAPTER 10   EATING THE SEED CORN *AND* TRIMMING THE HERDS

1. Rudy Penner, testimony before a joint hearing of the House and Senate Budget Committees, 10 January 1995.
2. Ibid.
3. Gramm-Rudman-Hollings applied across-the-board cuts to the programs that remained after a number of major programs had been removed from consideration. So it was not completely without programmatic focus, but the cuts that were to be implemented were supposed to be across the board.
4. Phil Joyce, interview by author, 9 July 1996.
5. Penner testimony, 10 January 1995.
6. Judy England-Joseph, interview by author, 24 September 1996.
7. *Congressional Record,* Department of Transportation and Related Agencies Appropriations Act, 1999, House of Representatives, 29 July 1998.
8. Sen. Christopher Bond, *Congressional Record,* Supplemental Appropriations and Rescissions Act of 1997, Senate, 6 May 1997, S3986.
9. This material is taken from Irene Rubin, "Downsizing: Managing the Muddles," *M@n@gement* (spring 2000), on the Web at http://www.dmsp.dauphine.fr/Management/
10. Gene Brewer, e-mail correspondence with author, 28 September 1998.

Index